Presidents and the Press

Presidents and the Press

The Nixon Legacy

Joseph C. Spear

The MIT Press
Cambridge, Massachusetts
London, England

This book was set in Baskerville by The MIT Press Computergraphics Department and printed and bound by Halliday Lithograph in the United States of America.

Permission to use an excerpt from *RN, The Memoirs of Richard Nixon,* is gratefully acknowledged. Copyright 1978 by Richard Nixon. Used by permission of Grosset & Dunlap, Inc., and Warner Books, Inc.

Library of Congress Cataloging in Publication Data

Spear, Joseph C.
    Presidents and the press.

    Bibliography: p.
    Includes index.
    1. Nixon, Richard M. (Richard Milhous), 1913–
2. Government and the press—United States—History—20th century.
3. United States—Politics and government—1945–
4. Presidents—United States—History—20th century. I. Title.
E856.S63   1984   973.924'092'4   83–26304
ISBN 0-262-19228-4

For my father Joseph Ward Spear

Contents

6
Intimidation

7
Watergate

8
Review

Preface

Since June 1979, when I contracted to write this book, I have been asked 3,285 questions about it. My answers, I think, pretty well summed up my professional philosophy and, in extract, amount to what I would like to say by way of prologue. Herewith, a distillation:

Q: Why would you want to devote a large chunk of your life to a book on such an esoteric subject as presidents and the press?

A: I know it sounds naive, probably even mawkish, but I love the First Amendment and all that it stands for. I have a congenital compulsion to resist any effort to restrict what I can read, hear, say, or write—and this is especially true of information that concerns government and politics. Ours is a government of the people. We are the sovereigns; those who work in government are our servants. We have a right to know what they are doing; they have no right—except in instances where the collective security is genuinely in jeopardy—to restrict or withhold information. It is this principle that the First Amendment embodies and protects, and I consider it the bedrock upon which our participative system rests. Richard Nixon and his associates, I think, cared very little for this love of mine—indeed, I believe they deliberately attempted to smother it. And I think that most presidents have priorities that tend to relegate freedom of speech and press to the wings. I would like the public at least to be aware of this, and it is toward this end that I have labored.

Q: Most Americans probably appreciate their basic freedoms, but many of them also believe the press does a miserable job of informing them. They view journalists as elitist, arrogant, liberal, rapacious, and unpatriotic. One recent Harris poll showed that the public regards the press as less "believable" than the White House. So shouldn't you be writing about how the press kicks the presidents around, rather than the reverse?

A: It has been said many times but, according to *Bartlett's*, Sophocles said it first: "Nobody likes the man who brings bad news." So it was four centuries before the birth of Christ, so it is now, so it shall forever be. Journalists worry too much about their popularity; it is inherently a lost cause. They should simply report the news and raise hell—as fairly, accurately, and responsibly as they can. That is their duty. It is nice but not necessary to be liked—only to be read. As for the specific charges, they are largely irrelevant. Of course there are some journalists who are elitist, arrogant, liberal, and rapacious. Most are not, but in any case, what does this have to do with the way they perform their basic function of informing the public? Are there good lawyers who are liberal or rapacious? Would elitism and arrogance make a doctor a quack? And a lack of patriotism? Does commentary, interpretation, and criticism constitute treason? A quintessential American named Mark Twain had an answer to that question. Said the protagonist in *A Connecticut Yankee in King Arthur's Court*:

My kind of loyalty was loyalty to one's country, not to its institutions or its office-holders. The country is the real thing, the substantial thing, the eternal thing; it is the thing to watch over and care for and be loyal to; institutions are extraneous, they are its mere clothing, and clothing can wear out, become ragged, cease to be comfortable, cease to protect the boy from winter, disease, and death. To be loyal to rags, to worship rags, to die for rags—that is the loyalty of unreason, it is pure animal; it belongs to monarchy, was invented by monarchy; let monarchy keep it. I was from Connecticut, whose Constitution declares that "all political power is inherent in the people, and all free governments are founded on their authority and instituted for their benefit. . . ." Under that gospel, the citizen who thinks he sees that the commonwealth's political clothes are worn out, and yet holds his peace and does not agitate for a new suit, is disloyal; he is a traitor."

It is a fact that we are going through a period of government-knows-best, and the press is not very popular. But it is also a fact that the press protects the public interest and forces the politicians and the bureaucrats to be accountable. The press surely has its faults, but if we are to remain a free people, there are no alternatives.

Q: What about the casual manner in which the press deals with classified information? Journalists don't seem to care about the national security.

A: Of all the vile canards that politicians and government officials have used to provoke the public's wrath against the press, none is more invidious and fallacious than that. It is a sham; it is humbuggery; it is charlatanism of the highest order. In the first place, most classified information has little to do with the national security and a lot to do with covering up malfeasance, political motives, and embarrassing events. The secrecy stamp is the equivalent of the censor's scissors. Second, the record shows that journalists deal with national security matters in a far more responsible manner than the politicians and government officials whose activities they cover. And nobody—but nobody—is more adept at manipulating the national security concept for their own gain than the presidents of the United States and their minions.

When FBI agents traced money found in the accounts of Watergate burglars to a Mexican bank, Richard Nixon invoked "national security" to call the investigators off the trail. When Jimmy Carter was accused of being soft on defense matters, he declassified the details of research on "stealth" technology that would make American aircraft "invisible" to enemy radar. When the Nixon administration dragged the *New York Times* and the *Washington Post* into court in an attempt to stop them from publishing the Pentagon Papers, the judge asked the government's attorneys to pinpoint the most sensitive secret that might be revealed. The lawyers selected "Operation Marigold," a 1966 U.S. attempt to negotiate with North Vietnam through Polish diplomats. In fact, the details of Operation Marigold had already been disclosed in several publications—including *Vantage Point*, the memoirs of Lyndon Johnson. Indeed, the incident was indexed in Johnson's book, and several hundred words were devoted to an explanation of what it was all about. And Johnson had based his account of Operation Marigold on classified documents that he had carted off to Texas for enshrinement in his presidential library.

Q: What are you so worried about? We have had freedom of speech and press in this country for 200 years. It is guaranteed by the Constitution and will always exist. So what's the big deal?

A: I am convinced that freedom of speech and press would dissipate without constant vigil. It frightens me to think what might have happened, for example, had the Watergate scandal not forced Richard Nixon from office. After the 1972 election, he was flying high and his opponents (his "enemies," to use his word) were in hiding. After four years of relentless pounding, journalists were debilitated by battle fatigue and the First Amendment was in need of a wheelchair. Had Nixon remained in office, it is entirely possible that freedom of the press would exist mainly on paper and Americans would be reading and watching nothing more controversial than reports on presidential pronouncements, the weather, and pork belly futures.

Richard Nixon was unique only by virtue of his chutzpah and his excess. Day after day in Washington, D.C., politicians and government officials chip away at the First Amendment with chisels that are sometimes blunt, sometimes sharp. Journalistic access is denied here, a Freedom of Information Act request is turned down there. Cost overruns are stamped secret, suspected sources are hooked up to polygraph machines. Consider a few of the events that have transpired just since this manuscript was completed:

• On September 11, 1983, the National Security Council met at the White House to discuss, among other things, what could be done to protect U.S. Marines stationed in Lebanon. The following evening NBC News reported that "top administration officials have asked the president to seriously consider ordering U.S. air strikes on Syrian positions in Lebanon." Later the same evening CBS and ABC aired the story, and the following morning the *Washington Post* published a similar report. In each case the story was confirmed by White House officials. Said the *Post*'s White House correspondent Lou Cannon: "Short of dropping leaflets over Washington announcing the new policy, it is difficult to know what more the administration could have done to advance the story." But national security adviser William Clark was incensed over the leaks and urged President Reagan to find and punish the sources of the stories. The president dispatched a letter to Attorney General William French Smith instructing him to use "all legal means" to find the leakers. FBI agents interviewed several cabinet officials and most of the White House staff and closed the investigation in mid-December without identifying anyone who had provided the information to reporters. "There is no evidence that reporters were told anything we didn't want them to know," one administration official said.

• Beginning on October 25, some 6,000 U.S. paratroopers, soldiers, and Marines invaded the Caribbean island of Grenada, ostensibly to rescue an estimated 1,100 Americans who, it was believed, might be held hostage by the nation's restive Marxist rulers. American servicemen were ordered to put their lives on the line, and the taxpayers' dollars funded the operation—but the American press was completely shut out. White House spokesmen were not told of the invasion and thus fed false information to inquiring reporters. Four journalists who made it to the island during the initial hours of the invasion were flown to a helicopter carrier and held incommunicado. Two days after the operation began, the Pentagon released to the networks film that had been shot by military photographers and cleared by Defense Department censors. Meanwhile, administration officials and spokesmen used every forum they could find to defend the action. Defense Secretary Caspar Weinberger said the officers in charge of the operation had decided they didn't want to have to cope with the press, and he "wouldn't ever dream of overriding a commander's decision." Secretary of State George Shultz said it seemed to him that "reporters are always against us. . . . They're always seeking to report something that's going to screw things up." White House deputy press secretary Larry Speakes claimed the presence of journalists might "distract" military commanders.

• In early December, White House communications director David R. Gergen informed his superiors of his intention to resign and accept a teaching position at Harvard University. His job was abolished and his duties were assumed by deputy chief of staff Michael Deaver and presidential assistant Richard Darman. The scholarly Gergen, who had also worked in the Nixon and Ford administrations, was one of the few officials in the Reagan White House who consistently urged the president and his top aides to moderate the methods they used in dealing with the press. According to published reports, Gergen was disturbed by the efforts to identify and discipline reporters' sources, upset by the decision to restrict news coverage of the Grenadan invasion, and perturbed over his colleagues' efforts to impede the flow of information to the press in general. He was "concerned about this administration falling into the trap of seeing the press as the enemy," said one White House official.

• As this book went to press, the administration was persisting in its efforts to implement President Reagan's March 1983 directive (chapter 8) that would possibly subject to lie detector tests some two-and-a-half million government employees who hold security clearances. The same edict would compel in excess of 125,000 government employees and former employees who dealt with certain types of classified information to submit all their written works to the federal government for "prepublication review." Put another way, Reagan proposed to have the government censor all books, speeches, novels, and newspaper articles prepared by officials or former officials who handled the nation's secrets. At a hearing held by the House Government Operations Committee in October, former under secretary of state George Ball lambasted the Reagan directive as "an appalling document" and "an absurdity." Said Ball, "This would require the establishment of a censorship bureaucracy far larger than anything known in our national experience." Both the House and the Senate passed legislation to put the executive order on temporary hold. The furor, however, did not deter deputy assistant attorney general Richard K. Willard, the pleasant, reasonable-sounding, thirty-five-year-old official who headed the task force that authored the directive. He just wanted to intimidate federal employees, Willard once said, "change the attitudes of government officials" so they would "come to believe that it is wrong" to leak. "I think if we can reduce the volume of leaks by 50 percent," Willard said, "that would make a very serious contribution to improving our country's ability to carry out foreign policy, defense policy, and improving the effectiveness of our intelligence agencies."

In other words, you should know only what the government deems you should know. Makes things easier, you see.

Acknowledgments

This book began in 1970 as a magazine article that was never published because the editors thought the thesis incredible: No president, they said, would knowingly trample on the First Amendment for political gain. The discredited opusculum evolved into a Master's thesis and then into a mountainous manuscript which was sculpted into the product you hold in your hands. I was assisted and supported on ths arduous journey by many valued friends and associates. Among them were these:

Jack Anderson: My employer and friend, whose compassion and joyous spirit belie his image as a hard-bitten muckraker. He tolerated my absences of mind and body.

Opal Ginn: Professional associate and boon companion. She advised, edited, and typed.

Charles Bermant, Keith Sinzinger, Matt Speiser, Scott Bernard, and Bill Bartman: Research assistants. They are young and talented journalists who labored hard for small recompense.

Bob Blanchard, Ed Bliss, Kate Cissel, and Bill Crockett: Teachers. They inspired and motivated me.

Stephen Paley and Less Whitten: Spiritual advisers. They helped me handle the highs and the lows.

Will and Margie Deane Gray; Jack Maser and Susan Lutz; Al and Sheila Pires; Peter and Connie Robinson; Joe and Ann Schantz: Friends of the highest calibre. Their unflagging support and constant encouragement kept me going.

Linda Mahaffey Spear: My wife and best friend. She endured.

Presidents and the Press

The Tudor-Stuart theory of the function of the press which justified its control was that the safety, stability, and welfare of the state depended on the efforts of the crown and therefore anything which interfered with or undermined those efforts was to be suppressed or at least controlled.

Fredrick Seaton Siebert, *Freedom of the Press in England 1476–1776*

The Pentagon Papers leak came at a particularly sensitive time. We were just three and a half weeks away from Kissinger's secret trip to China, and the SALT talks were under way. . . . We had lost our court battle against the newspaper that published the documents, but I was determined that we would at least win our public case against the man I believed had stolen them, Daniel Ellsberg. . . . Whatever others may have thought, I considered what Ellsberg had done to be despicable and contemptible. . . . I believed that national security was involved. I still believe it today, and in the same circumstances I would act now as I did then.

Richard M. Nixon, *RN: The Memoirs of Richard Nixon*

1

Preview: "You Don't Tell Us How to Stage the News, and We Don't Tell You How to Cover It"

Future historians of the presidential-press relationship will surely regard the decade of the 1970s as epochal. During this period the chief executives virtually mastered the media.

It is arguable, of course, that in a free society no one can best the press. The institution is too large, too diverse, too pervasive. And it always has the last word. But observe closely the nose of a Washington reporter—particularly a White House reporter—who says he or she is never manipulated; it will grow a bit each time the utterance is repeated.

The fact is that over the past ten to fifteen years the presidents and their aides have been fine-tuning a press manipulation strategy that rarely fails in any momentous way. It is executed by teams of sophisticated media specialists who swarm through the White House and its overflow corral next door, the old Executive Office Building. There are spokesmen who give the impression of saying a lot while actually saying little; pollsters whose fingers are constantly on the public pulse; image merchants who strive to design impressions that will convince the public it is getting what it wants; television experts who stage news events and turn popes and monarchs into presidential props; media monitors who maintain a continuous watch on the press, spot trends, and provide early warnings of trouble; "enforcers" who use a variety of techniques to cow recalcitrant reporters and their sources. Taken together this cadre of specialists constitutes an awesome apparatus whose sole function is to mold the news to reflect favorably on the president. They attempt to manage the news. They are extraordinarily successful.

This is not to say that the First Amendment is in imminent danger of collapse. A president cannot be faulted for exploiting every legal means at his disposal to communicate with the public and, indeed, most journalists who cover his activities largely depend on his use of them for their livelihood. Lyn Nofziger, a former political aide to President Ronald Reagan, described the symbiotic relationship this way: "There is a mutual use of each other. The press uses the president for their news, and to get what they want. It would be ridiculous to expect then that the president or the White House or the administration would not use the press for its purposes whenever it can. That's the way the system works."[1]

In short presidential manipulation of the press is not a sinister practice, but it is an insidious one, for when the press is being used, the public is being used. The best way to avoid becoming a victim of the media maestros is to know their tactics and strategies.

What then is the press manipulation strategy that White House communications experts have honed and polished to virtual perfection in recent years? Basically it breaks down into three parts, all of which function simultaneously: the president is isolated and the press is appeased with positive or harmless news; television and propaganda tactics are used to evade the press and address the people directly; and the flow of negative news is stemmed through the intimidation of reporters and their sources and through the use of censorship techniques, such as the classification of information.

Appeasement

Most modern presidents have operated on the theory that limited exposure to the press reduces the risk of error and negative coverage. But since the public is unlikely to rally behind a hermit, the trick has been to appear accessible without actually being so. It is accomplished by appearing before news people only under the most tightly controlled of circumstances.

Jimmy Carter practiced the technique with flair. He endeavored to portray himself as a man of the people, carrying his own luggage, eschewing a limousine and walking the inaugural route down Pennsylvania Avenue from Capital Hill to the White House, speaking often during his prolonged and relentless campaign for the presidency of the "open" style of administration he would establish. "I would do everything that I could to open up the government to the people," he vowed. He would conduct open meetings with the Congress and open cabinet sessions.[2] At his second meeting with the cabinet, on January 31, 1977, the new president announced his tentative decision to honor his campaign commitment; permitting the press to witness their conclaves, he said, would "let the American public know their government is in good hands."[3] Seventeen days later Carter had done an about-face. His cabinet secretaries were almost unanimously opposed to the idea of open meetings, and he had had "second thoughts," the president said. He was, however, toying with the idea of releasing the minutes of cabinet meetings to the press.[4]

This capricious behavior became a pattern in Carter's dealings with the press. The president regularly blew hot and cold, alternating periods of intense contacts with journalists and long weeks of relative isolation. It was as if his head wanted to get along with the press, but his heart kept rebelling.

The public was largely unaware that Carter was an intensely private man. "I'm not going to relinquish my right to go to the zoo with my daughter, to the opera with my wife or to pick up arrowheads on my farm without prior notice to the press," he told a group of reporters shortly after his inauguration. He could, he continued, "get away from you when I want to."[5] Even as he uttered that boast, Carter had already proved his ability to elude newsmen almost at will. As a presidential candidate and as president elect, he had often managed to deceive reporters by ordering his Secret Service driver to turn off the headlights and depart in darkness. His Secret Service protectors had also occasionally led the press on wild goose chases in Carter's car while Carter sped off in the opposite direction in a different vehicle.[6] Shortly after he was sworn in, the president, his wife, Rosalynn, and his daughter, Amy, slipped away from the White House to view a performance of *Madame Butterfly* at the Kennedy Center. Several furious reporters complained that members of the president's staff had lied to them by claiming that Carter was in the executive mansion when in fact he was at the opera. The president's assistants, said press secretary Jody Powell, had "overzealously" interpreted Carter's orders not to announce the excursion. Powell continued: "The President does wish to reserve his right to go places for strictly family or personal reasons without prior announcement. . . . The President has a right to go to the opera without prior public knowledge."[7]

By June 1979 Carter had secretly evaded the press corps that normally followed him on at least ten occasions. He had gone fishing and skiing and had dined at public restaurants in Washington. The evasion route to one restaurant was so complicated that the president's dinner companions got their instructions mixed up; Carter arrived and sat at the table alone for fifteen minutes until the others showed up.[8]

Gerald Ford liked reporters and appreciated their role. He had been a congressman for twenty-five years, considered himself a professional, and considered his critics in the Fourth Estate as professionals also. During the first year in the White House, he was among the most accessible of presidents. As the 1976 campaign year rolled around, however, his advisers decided to exert more control over the presidential image and began to draw a curtain around him. He ignored the national press, preferring instead to answer only the more uninformed questions posed by local reporters wherever he traveled. Newsmen on the White House beat, said Associated Press correspondent Frank Cormier, began to grow frustrated: "During the early stages of the '76 campaign [Ford] would go out on the road and would take questions only from the local press. He would ignore questions shouted . . . by those traveling with him, which led to a great scene in the Rose Garden. Walt Rogers of AP radio shouted at him: 'Would you take a few questions from the local press?' As I recall, Ford declined."[9]

As the election drew nearer, Ford became even more inaccessible. "The polls showed him losing popularity every time he campaigned heavily," his press secretary, Ron Nessen, later wrote.[10] The president was thus advised to remain in the Rose Garden until the final weeks of the campaign, handing out awards, signing bills, and looking presidential for the television cameras. When Ford did go on the road, the White House press went along but rarely got close to him. At a fund-raising dinner in Los Angeles, for example, reporters were met at the ballroom door by an usher in a tuxedo who led them to a roped-off section on one side of the room.[11] Reporters also had to view political rallies from roped-off areas or remain on the press bus and listen to a pool reporter's piped-in version of an event. "We're trapped in a steel cocoon," complained *Philadelphia Bulletin* correspondent Larry O'Rourke. "We're fed what they want us to know."[12]

Ronald Reagan, however, makes Ford and Carter look like tyros in the game of appearing accessible without being so. Reagan guards his privacy assiduously and his staff exposes him to reporters with great care; there is rarely more than one tightly controlled appearance per day. This not only reduces the risk that Reagan may utter a wrong word—he is extremely prone to making gaffes—but it also forces the reporters who are covering him to chew on the one bone of news they have been tossed that day. Thus the nightly news often features film of the president, but it is usually coverage of a set speech or of Reagan tossing off some quick remark as he exits or enters his limousine. The president's media advisers do not like it when he is confronted with questions that demand spontaneous answers. They invented the "engine drown-out" technique, for instance, to discourage reporters from asking questions when Reagan is ready to board the presidential helicopter. As soon as Reagan appears in the White House doorway, the helicopter engines are started. The television cameras capture his smile and his waving hand, but he does not answer any questions because he cannot hear them.[13]

Much of the news footage of Reagan is shot during photo opportunities, occasions when photographers, camera crews, and reporters are briefly allowed into the Oval Office to take pictures of Reagan and his official visitors and guests. In the first weeks of his tenure the president would answer two or three questions from reporters during such sessions, but his aides began to fear he would say the wrong thing and instructed newsmen to hold their tongues. As Reagan's assistant for communications, David Gergen, put it, the president "has the right to conduct the office with some dignity, to have opportunities when he's meeting with a visitor to have photos taken. I don't think he necessarily ought to be subjected to questions every time he does that."[14]

Many reporters resisted the White House edict. While Reagan was meeting with Egyptian president Hosni Mubarak in February 1982, ABC correspondent Sam Donaldson popped a question about Cuba. Deputy press secretary Larry Speakes leaped forward. "Lights!" he screamed, giving the signal that the photo opportunity was over and the press was to leave. He angrily lectured Donaldson for asking a question that could cause an "international incident" and later decreed that reporters would be barred from photo opportunities.[15] A compromise was eventually struck, and reporters are still asking occasional questions at picture-taking sessions, but they rarely fail to elicit rebukes from the White House media team. Said United Press International's veteran White House correspondent Helen Thomas, "Whenever I can get two words in, I fire questions at [Reagan]. His aides become absolutely apoplectic. You can see them thinking. 'My God, they're at it again.' They overprotect him, even to the point of forming a human shield around him when they don't want questions."[16]

All presidents who served during the 1970s and since have kept track of how well their news managers were doing their jobs through the perusal of news digests, daily and weekly summaries of stories that appear on television news shows and in newspapers and magazines around the country, prepared by staff assigned to that task. Purportedly the news digests are prepared for informational uses only, but in fact they are used to monitor the press. Carter's news summary staff, for example, was instructed to give priority to adverse stories and commentary when there were space restrictions. This undoubtedly gave readers of the digest a skewed view of what was being reported.[17] The Reagan news summary, according to David Gergen, is "not a management tool. . . . It is used more for information purposes."[18] Just a few months before Gergen made that statement, syndicated columnist Jack Anderson put together a story alleging that Secretary of State Alexander Haig might be dismissed. A copy of the column was received in the White House news summary room before it was published and was passed on to Gergen. He called Anderson to deny the story, then alerted Haig of the upcoming column. Haig called Anderson to deny it. Finally Ronald Reagan called the columnist from the presidential retreat at Camp David to express his confidence in Haig. Anderson then pulled the Haig story and substituted one describing the frantic efforts to scuttle it.[19]

The person charged with keeping the press as contented and occupied as possible, while the man they are at the White House to cover remains out of sight, is the presidential press secretary. Because his job is to entertain as much as it is to inform, he should be intelligent and humorous. Because he must convey an impression of authority, he should have direct and frequent access to the president. And because he has to keep the press out of the way, he should be very attentive to their needs. He should keep the news releases coming and answer reporters' telephone calls. When the president is on the road, the press secretary must keep the bar and refrigerator on the press plane well stocked and must see that reporters' luggage is delivered intact and on time.

The rule of thumb, in short, is to keep reporters happy and make them think they are getting real news. It is not an easy task.

Among the least qualified in recent years, judging from his bad reviews, was President Ford's second press secretary, former NBC correspondent Ron Nessen. He was a hard-driving and hard-working spokesman but he was not temperamentally suited for the job. He was combative, sensitive to criticism, and given to sarcastic putdowns of his interrogators, traits he later acknowledged were not compatible with the position: "I think that, had I had the same kind of even temperament that Ford had, I wouldn't have been so prickly. He was always kind to reporters, never showed his irritation. . . . I'm relatively thin-skinned; I don't respond very well to criticism."[20]

One of the very best was Jimmy Carter's press secretary, Jody Powell. In spite of Powell's frequently expressed contempt for news people, his tart tongue, and temper tantrums, he was often compared to Steve Early, James Hagerty, and Pierre Salinger, the well-liked press secretaries who served Presidents Franklin Roosevelt, Dwight Eisenhower, and John Kennedy, respectively.[21] Veteran correspondent John Osborne of the *New Republic* was an unabashed admirer: "Jody Powell . . . is one of the best White House press secretaries I've dealt with, off and on, over the past forty-five years. In some respects he is *the* best."[22]

Three personal assets rescued Powell from perdition: He was extremely close to the president and thus spoke with authority, he was undeniably intelligent, and he had an unfailing, if sometimes acerbic, sense of humor. Whatever their reservations about Powell, most reporters found themselves guffawing as he broke up tense situations and turned aside harsh questions with witticisms, one-liners, and pointed barbs. In 1977, for example, the Russians booted an AP correspondent out of the Soviet Union, and a reporter asked Powell if President Carter would respond in kind. Retorted the press secretary: "We did discuss something along those lines. It was our feeling that if the Russians got to kick an AP correspondent out of Moscow, we ought to get to kick an AP correspondent out of here."[23]

"What saves Jody much of the time from just being totally hostile is that he does have a sense of humor," said NBC's Judy Woodruff. "He kids hard and is kidded hard back."[24] Jack McWethy of *U.S. News & World Report* summed up the Georgia-born press secretary's personality this way: "Powell is an amazing combination of country bumpkin and a very, very slick PR man. He is not dumb by any means. And he's an extremely good deflector of serious questions with humorous replies. On his bad days, those replies are very barbed. On his good days, he's as funny as a stand-up comic. For the reporters who depend on that daily briefing, it can be very frustrating."[25]

The Reagan White House suffered an enormous setback on March 30, 1981, when a would-be assassin attempted to take the president's life. Not only was Reagan hospitalized with a bullet to the chest, but his press secretary, James Brady, suffered severe brain injury. Had he not been debilitated, Brady probably would have been ranked with the best White House spokesmen. He had access to Reagan and his top aides and spoke with authority. He is intelligent, irreverent, articulate, affable, and possessed of a quick, wry wit. Reporters liked "the Bear," as the six-foot, 235-pound Brady was affectionately nicknamed. He was ideally suited for the task of keeping the White House press corps occupied and entertained.[26]

In the wake of Brady's injury, the job of briefing reporters every day fell to deputy secretary Larry Speakes, a forty-four-year-old former newspaperman from Mississippi. Reagan's top advisers were displeased with his performance, however, and arranged for the briefing duties to be shared with the assistant for communications, David Gergen, a gangly, forty-one-year-old, Yale- and Harvard-educated lawyer. But he proved vague and guarded in his responses to reporters, so the daily briefing once again became Speakes's exclusive province.[27]

Speakes has matured into a competent handler of the White House press corps. He is not perceived as a member of Reagan's inner circle but is regarded as pleasant, unflappable, hard working, responsive, and at times even humorous. He has become the "cowboy" of the Reagan press operation; through a combination of cajolery and threats and an occasional push, he has managed to keep reporters assembled into a reasonably intact herd. On March 24, 1983, for example, Speakes stated that no "internal investigation" of White House contacts with officials of the scandal-ridden Environmental Protection Agency was underway. The following day he acknowledged that an internal review was being conducted. NBC correspondent Chris Wallace characterized Speakes's earlier response as a "lie," and the press secretary took umbrage. "That's the most serious charge that you can level at me," he snapped. Following the briefing, Speakes said to Wallace: "I'm not having anything to do with you Chris. You're out of business as far as I'm concerned."[28] When reporters complained about how one news event was being handled, Speakes admonished them, "You don't tell us how to stage the news, and we don't tell you how to cover it."[29]

How effective are Reagan's media specialists at shaping the news by dangling him in front of the press a few minutes at a time and by handing out nuggets of information one at a time? UPI's Helen Thomas commented: "We're pretty tightly managed and controlled. . . . They plan the day's story and try to keep our eye on that ball. We have only limited access to the president. We can go for days without seeing him. They seem to think that it is bad manners to ask him questions except under certain controlled conditions. Every day, they calculate what we do and how we jump."[30]

The least controllable confrontation between president and press is the news conference, and few things are more indicative of the modern president's casual concern for the approbation of the national press than their indifferent approach to such meetings. In the age of television there are many easier, less perilous ways of delivering a message and projecting a desired image.

It is undeniably true that the presence of television cameras at news conferences has turned them into theater. The president usually comes across as a heroic castellan holding off a mob that has laid siege to the gates. Shouting reporters strive to get the attention of the president and of the electronic eye that will show family, friends and supervisors how involved and important they are. But in our system of government, news conferences are the only opportunities the public has, through its press surrogates, to demand that a president defend his decisions and policies. Press conferences ought to be regarded by presidents as integral to the democratic process, but they are usually endured only when other television formats have been used to excess or when the clamor for a conference becomes embarrassing.

Gerald Ford was a refreshing exception. He seemed to thrive on press conferences. He made an effort to respond fully to questions, gracefully evaded queries he did not want to answer, and rarely showed anger over a hostile question. By the end of February 1975, however, White House reporters were complaining of too many press conferences. Not enough good questions were being asked, and the president was acting as if he was on a soapbox. "He has devalued the press conference," one newsman griped.[31]

As president elect, Jimmy Carter announced that he would hold regular press conferences once every two weeks, events permitting, and a minimum of twenty per year. He actually convened fifty-nine formal press conferences during his four years in office, twenty-one short of his goal.[32] Carter should have met the press more often, for when he did he was usually a boffo performer. At a press conference on June 30, 1977, to cite just one example, the president began with the announcement that he was terminating the Defense Department program to build the B-1 manned bomber. His was a "lonely" task, he said, and this in particular was "one of the most difficult decisions that I have made." He then discussed U.S. relations with the Soviet Union, Israel, Taiwan, and mainland China, as well as domestic issues. The final question was asked by Lester Kinsolving, an Episcopal priest-journalist and right-wing gadfly. Given Carter's rigid views on monogamy, Kinsolving wanted to know, why didn't he do something about those people working for him who "were promiscuously with other women"? Carter smiled and said, "If there are some who have slipped from grace, then I can only say that I will do the best I can to forgive them and pray for them." The attending newsmen erupted in laughter and applauded as Carter departed. The following day *Washington Post* correspondent Haynes Johnson praised the president as being "alternately serious and deft, solemn and humorous. And he was always in command." The *Post*'s editorial writers, however, wondered about the competence of the Washington press corps: "Over the years, presidents have occasionally complained that Washington reporters seem to live on a different planet than the rest of the country does. Any citizen watching the press conference . . . might have come to the same conclusion."[33]

In the Reagan White House press conferences seem to rank with cancer and airplane crashes as things to be avoided. During his first year in office the president called six formal meetings with the press. His seventeenth press conference was held in the twenty-eighth month of his tenure.[34]

Reagan is not the most energetic of presidents; he does not like to deal with detail, prefers instead to delegate it, and spends his limited hours in the office making big decisions. When a press conference can no longer be avoided, therefore, he must work hard to master the minutiae he has previously shirked. Even after studying his briefing books and partaking in practice sessions, however, his press conference performances have often been sloppy. His answers frequently have been too sweeping and simplistic; he has braced his opinions with facts and figures pulled from the air; he has attempted to support his conclusions with evidence that is distorted or does not exist.

The president's media advisers have thus been compelled to search for ways to control press conferences as tightly as possible. Reagan is urged to study and rehearse. Reporters are instructed to keep their seats and quietly raise their hands when they have a question. A lottery was once used to determine the order of questioners, but network officials complained when their correspondents did not get picked so the idea was dropped. The president is provided with seating charts and photographs and first names of reporters so he can call on the journalist of his choice and make it appear that he is on intimate terms with the person asking the question. Prior to March 31, 1982, Reagan's press conferences were held in the afternoon; thereafter they were moved to the prime-time evening hours to deny reporters and producers for the evening news shows the opportunity to prepare film clips of, and commentary on, his bloopers. Seating arrangements for reporters are carefully calculated. There is some concern, for example, that Reagan may be asked questions as he makes his exit and utter an ill-considered, off-the-cuff answer. "We keep the nuts and dodos off the first row on the right so they can't grab him on the way out," said a senior White House aide. The front section on the right is stacked with what are called "known friendlies," reporters thought to be sympathetic to Reagan and not inclined to ask difficult questions. The president is then told by his media team that when he is confronted with an uncomfortable line of questioning, he should "go to the right."[35] At a press conference on July 28, 1982, Reagan tried what might be called the "McClendon bailout." He called on Sarah McClendon, a feisty, dogged veteran correspondent for a group of small newspapers who has a penchant for asking tough but offbeat questions. This time the McClendon bailout backfired: she demanded to know why Reagan was suppressing a Justice Department investigation on discrimination against women. As he fumbled for answers, she peppered him eleven times with questions and caustic comments.[36]

Evasion

While the Washington press corps is kept occupied and content with appeasement tactics, the president seeks to go over their heads and address the public directly, primarily through the use of television. The leader of the nation can thus chat with the people without having his remarks filtered through the press. He can make announcements, allow himself to be interviewed, even arrange events to demonstrate to the public what a decent, honest, strong, compassionate, presidential person he is. Whatever he chooses to do, the cameras will be there; the networks need him as much as he needs them.

Take Jimmy Carter, for example. Sometimes it seemed that every move he made was designed to impress the television audience with his credentials as a leader. "No administration in the television age has studied the methods of the medium more religiously than this one," wrote *Boston Globe* reporter Curtis Wilkie in November 1980. "And none has designed its actions more accordingly." The Carter White House lacked a theme, Wilkie continued, but it had a scheme:

Carter went into office with the idea of using television to his own advantage, and from his walk down Pennsylvania Avenue on his Inauguration Day to his first "fireside chat" in a cardigan sweater to his more recent appearances in the White House press room to deliver personal statements, it has all been orchestrated with TV in mind. . . .

The scheme was to maintain an endless campaign. . . . The goal of Jimmy Carter and his coterie of advisers has always been simple and singular: To promote and perpetuate Jimmy Carter as president. Carter's photogenic grin and glib speaking qualities are their political platform and television is their political machine.[37]

Carter's public relations specialists did seem obsessed with television. "The presidency has become an ongoing series for television," communications director Gerald Rafshoon once said.[38] Tony Schwartz, a media consultant who helped produce Carter's campaign commercials, offered this candid remark: "Whether it's Coca-Cola or Jimmy Carter, what we appeal to in the consumer or voter is an attitude. We don't try to convey a point of view, but a montage of images and sounds that leaves the viewer with a positive attitude toward the product regardless of his perspective."[39]

Carter's image team was particularly adept at staging media events that resulted in favorable coverage for the White House and simultaneously satisfied the networks' appetite for visual drama. One of the preferred varieties of this genre was the road show; the most telegenic one was a 660-mile, 47-stop trip down the Mississippi River from St. Paul to St. Louis aboard an old-fashioned steamboat, the *Delta Queen*, in August 1979. It was billed as a "working vacation," during which Carter would push his energy program. It was, in fact, a political campaign swing—as *Time* magazine put it, "a waterborne version of the whistle-stop tour."[40]

Although a presidential road show has many public relations advantages, it has one inherent shortcoming: Newsmen cannot be controlled as tightly as when they are confined to the White House press room. Photographers and television crews sometimes catch the president in an embarrassing situation or making an unbecoming gesture.

As the *Delta Queen* excursion was being planned, Jody Powell drew up some stern rules to control press coverage: photographers and television camera crews would be allowed to film the president only in designated areas and during stipulated periods; news agencies and magazines would not be permitted to purchase photographs taken by tourists; pictures published by local newspapers could not be distributed nationally; no photographs could be used without White House approval. The restrictions were promulgated on the grounds that Carter desired some privacy. "We can't have a situation in which the president is followed by a pack," grumbled Powell.[41] Said another White House aide: "If the press has its way, you'd have a goddam bazaar all over the boat."[42] The *Washington Star*, however, had a different viewpoint: "Now, if Mr. Carter were a rock-and-roll star or a business tycoon or a sports celebrity, he probably could get away with those guidelines. But he isn't. He's the president of the United States, and his constituents are picking up a fair piece of the tab for the trip and its presidential trappings. If they want a look at his grin as he sails past Hannibal and St. Louis, they're entitled."[43]

The news agencies and magazines agreed and informed Powell they would boycott the trip. Staff photographers would not be assigned to cover it. Hugo Wessels of UPI notified Powell by letter that his news agency would "pursue such other avenues as may be open to us" to guarantee that subscribers received "adequate and unrestricted picture coverage."[44]

That was hitting the White House media manipulators where it hurt the most: what good was a presidential trip if you could not stage photo opportunities? Powell relaxed the rules.[45]

Carter, Rosalynn, and daughter Amy bounded up the red-carpeted gangplank of the stately sternwheeler in St. Paul as a crowd of several hundred watched and a Dixieland band played "When the Saints Go Marching In." As the vessel crept down the river at three miles per hour, boats full of sightseers circled it. At night people camped by the river. Smiling and waving Carter repeatedly yelled at almost everyone he spotted. "Hi, I love you," he said. At scheduled stops and at virtually every lock and dam, he plowed into the crowds, shaking hands and kissing babies. While the ship's calliope bleated out "God Bless America," the president urged onlookers to help "make the greatest nation on earth even greater." In rain and fog and at all hours of the day and night, he preached his energy ethic: turn your thermostats down, insulate your homes, drive less, drive slower, use car pools. He fished, danced, drank gin-and-tonics, gazed through binoculars at the shoreline. He also insisted on jogging every day. The first morning, he was up at 6:30 a.m., doing twenty-two laps around the deck. But the passengers sleeping below complained about his clomping feet, so for the next six days, he obligingly jogged ashore. He hosted a radio talk show for forty-five minutes in Davenport, Iowa. He presided over a town meeting on a gentle bluff overlooking the river in Burlington, Iowa, and gushed when a citizen named Gertrude Gerdom asked him if he had caught any fish. "Gertrude, that is the kind of question I never get from the Washington press corps," Carter said. "I love you, Gertrude."[46]

As the *Delta Queen* pulled into St. Louis, Carter was greeted with a spectacular finale carefully arranged by his media men. A flotilla of tugboats and other vessels surrounded the steamboat; fireworks shot into the sky; fire hoses spouted water high into the air; a multicolored hot-air balloon carried aloft the words, "Hello, Jimmy." After a reception with local politicians, the president flew back to the White House, and then went on to Camp David for a rest from his "vacation."[47]

With the election of Ronald Reagan the age of the television presidency burst into full flower. As journalist David Halberstam wrote about the 1980 campaign, "Politics is television, television is entertainment, and entertainment is politics."[48] When the campaign ended, a professional actor became the president of the United States.

The fact that most of the fifty-four films that Ronald Reagan appeared in were of the grade-B variety is deceiving: the man is an excellent actor. His every gesture, every bob of the head, every smile, chuckle, and wave of the hand is practiced. He is comfortable in front of the camera and knows it is his friend.[49]

His closest aides, some of them trained public relations specialists, know it too. The world is their "telestage," to use Halberstam's word, and Ronald Reagan is their star performer.[50] Events are plumbed weeks in advance to determine how they can be exploited for television. Reagan is told only what scene he will be playing; he needs no direction. As former Reagan aide Lou Gerig put it, presuming to advise the president on the use of television "would be like attempting to advise the Pope on the subject of Catholicism."[51]

No example better illustrates the attitude and expertise of Reagan's television team than the July 1980 GOP convention in Detroit. The entire four-day event was scripted as a television show that would be played to an audience of 40 million viewers. "The whole idea," said the convention's program director, Ken Reitz, "is to make the event into a TV production instead of a convention. The most important thing we can get out of our convention is TV coverage."[52]

As the network cameras looked on, the first-night festivities began with the pledge of allegiance led by crooner Pat Boone. Country-western singers Glen Campbell and Tanya Tucker sang the national anthem, and evangelist Billy Graham delivered the invocation. Then followed an hour of patriotic performances by singers and entertainers Susan Anton, Vicki Carr, Buddy Ebsen, Chad Everett, Dorothy Hamill, Michael Landon, Vicki Lawrence, Wayne Newton, Donny and Marie Osmond, Ginger Rogers, Jimmy Stewart, Lyle Waggoner, and Efrem Zimbalist, Jr. The balloting came on the third night, and when Montana's twenty votes gave Reagan his victory, the crowd leaped to its feet. Precisely on cue twelve thousand red, white, and blue balloons fell from the ceiling, and the band struck up a series of Sousa marches. On the fourth and final evening Reagan moved to center stage. He delivered his acceptance speech artfully, as if he were speaking extemporaneously; in fact he was using a teleprompter that displayed the words on transparent glass. At the end Reagan asked the conventioneers to join him in a few moments of silent prayer. The hall fell quiet until the candidate dramatically broke the silence with the words, "God Bless America." The crowd erupted into a twenty-minute ovation and sang along as the band played "God Bless America" and "This Land Is Your Land." Republican Governor Robert Ray of Iowa pronounced Reagan's performance "dynamite." Exulted Ray, "He touched the soul of America. He's off to a flying start."[53]

Presidential advisers are keenly aware that the successful exploitation of television requires that the viewing public have a positive image of the man in the White House. They spend hours conjuring up ways to project such an image as well as protect the president from anything that may cause the public to perceive him negatively. The offensive (as opposed to defensive) techniques are generally designed to show that the president is a nice guy, is certainly head and shoulders above anybody the opposition could put forth, and is above all a leader—strong, forceful, above politics, presidential.

When the nation's medical experts recommended in 1976 that a massive inoculation program be undertaken to protect citizens against an expected epidemic of swine flu, Gerald Ford stepped forward and took his shot—in front of the television cameras. With his Whip Inflation Now (WIN) campaign, Ford tried to demonstrate that he was capable of leading the nation out of its economic doldrums. But his simplistic approach—"take all you want but eat all you take," ride bicycles, search the trash for waste—was heartily jeered by cartoonists, columnists, and commentators. In May 1975 a U.S. merchant ship, the *Mayaguez*, and its thirty-nine crewmen were seized by a Cambodian patrol boat. Ford called in the Marines and ordered air strikes against targets on the Cambodian mainland, and the ship and its crew were released within two days. Much to the dismay of the White House media team, however, Pentagon spokesman Joe Laitin leaked the news of the rescue and stole the president's thunder. But Ron Nessen came up with a scheme to remind everyone it was Jerry Ford who led the nation through the crisis: "I had an idea how Ford still could get press attention at his moment of success. 'Look, we have one thing that Laitin doesn't have,' I suggested. 'We have the president. Why doesn't the president go out and announce the recovery of the *Mayaguez* and the crew on live television, in the middle of the Johnny Carson show?' " 'That's a good idea,' Ford agreed."[54]

Because Jimmy Carter put so much emphasis on presenting himself as a humble man of the people, looking like a leader was sometimes a difficult task. But his media specialists tried to portray him as a populist who could also play the provost.

Most important was physical appearance. Prior to the first Ford-Carter debate in 1976 Carter's television adviser, Barry Jagoda, demanded that the taller Ford stand in a depression in the stage. Barring that, said Jagoda, Carter should be permitted to stand on a riser. Jagoda also argued that Ford should be addressed by questioners as "Mr. Ford" instead of "Mr. President." The demands were rejected by Ford's image experts.[55] In 1978 Carter started jogging and was soon running up to six miles a day. His weight fell, and aides informed him he was no longer telegenic. He promptly cut back his running to three miles per day.[56]

Carter also made a conscious effort to act presidential. Among other things this meant he had to appear deeply concerned and hard working. An NBC crew filming a day in the life of the president "caught" Carter complaining because he had to take an hour away from his paperwork to talk to anchorman John Chancellor. While preparing a speech on energy in July 1979, Carter sent for a network camera crew so they could film him working in rolled-up shirtsleeves.[57]

Acting presidential also called for an occasional display of toughness. When Carter purged his cabinet in July 1979, it was generally seen as a deliberate effort to demonstrate that the ship of state was being guided with an iron hand.[58] At a White House buffet for eighty congressmen in June 1979, Carter was asked what he thought of Senator Edward Kennedy's hints that he would challenge the president in the 1980 primaries. "If Kennedy runs in '80," Carter responded, "I'll whip his ass." "Excuse me, Mr. President," said Congressman William Brodhead of Michigan from across the table, "what did you say?" "I don't think the president wants to repeat what he said," interjected Connecticut congressman Toby Moffett. "No, I'll repeat it," said the born-again Baptist president. "If Kennedy runs in '80, I'll whip his ass."[59]

Given Ronald Reagan's fundamental disinterest in all but the pageantry of the presidency, he presents a stiff challenge to the image merchants who seek to sell him as a forceful, involved leader. They try, though, and for the most part are successful. In an effort to portray him as a leader of all the people, for example, they arranged to kick off his 1980 campaign in the shadow of the Statue of Liberty. One thousand people representing various ethnic groups were bused in to hear Reagan condemn Jimmy Carter's treatment of the common folk. "The Lady standing there in the harbor has never betrayed us once," he said. "But this administration in Washington has betrayed the working men and women of this country." News photographers and camera crews worked to capture the candidate as he closed his performance with a dramatic embrace of Stanley Walesa, father of Polish strike leader Lech Walesa.[60]

The "flood gimmick" has occasionally proved a useful device to divert the public's attention from Reagan's lengthy vacations and his troubles with Congress. When he was under fire in March 1982 for his conservative economic program, his advisers arranged a quick stop at a flood site in Fort Wayne, Indiana, where he was photographed as he helped a flood-control crew pass sandbags.[61] In January 1983, following a week-long stay at the Palm Springs estate of millionaire

Walter Annenberg, Reagan landed in the flood-ravaged community of Monroe, Louisiana, and helped fill sandbags for eleven minutes as the television cameras looked on. He then hopped aboard a Salvation Army jeep and made his way through two feet of water to a radio station where he was to deliver a short address. At one point Reagan stopped and waited for the camera crews to get ahead so they could film him as he arrived in the jeep.[62]

A leader must have followers, of course, and the Reagan media team endeavors to assemble photogenic crowds for the president. When Reagan returned from a ten-day trip to Europe in June 1982, he was greeted at Andrews Air Force Base by 15,000 cheering, flag-waving diplomats and government workers, most of whom had been assembled by the White House and hauled to the arrival gate in rented buses. A smiling president professed his "complete surprise" at the festive welcome and then delivered his prepared remarks.[63]

Few occasions afford a better opportunity for a leader to show his mettle than an international summit, so when the heads of state of seven industrialized democracies gathered in Williamsburg in late May 1983 for a U.S.-hosted discussion of the world economy, the White House media maestros geared up for a major effort. On April 25 National Security Council director William Clark circulated a memorandum, stamped "Confidential," to key advisers outlining a "Framework for Public Affairs Strategy." The "primary perception" that would be sought, wrote Clark, was this: "The President as *leader of vision*, whose policies spearheaded U.S. recovery and help strengthen the West as a whole (Reaffirmation of U.S. Leadership Role)." Clark also listed "Some Desired Headlines," among them these: "President's Domestic Policies Highlight Summit Deliberations," "Reagan: Jobs a Central Subject at Williamsburg," and "Summit Partners Praise Williamsburg Organization."[64] During the conference the only journalists allowed near the president, with rare exception, were photographers and camera crews. Reporters were largely confined to press tents. Hot food was available around the clock, but hot news was available only when official spokesmen spooned it out.[65] As the image team planned, Reagan dominated the headlines and news shows, avoided major gaffes, and came across as an intelligent and strong chief executive well versed in international economics. Noted *Washington Post* columnist Richard Cohen:

This president is treated by both the press and foreign leaders as if he were a child. He earns praise for the ordinary, for what used to be the expected. His occasional ability to retain facts is cited as a triumph when it should, in fact, be a routine occurrence. . . .

The press, joined by foreign leaders and led by the pompon boys on the White House staff, wind up celebrating the mundane, and we all get the feeling we are watching home movies—look at Ronnie walk. . . .

How smart is Reagan? It's obvious.

A lot smarter than we are.[66]

The past few presidents have maintained what is generally known as an office of communications, ostensibly fashioned to service the non-Washington press. It has, in fact, functioned as a public relations agency for the executive branch and is little more than another device designed to evade the press that directly covers the president. It would be more accurate to call it the office of propaganda. The presidential assistant who manages the office supervises the preparation of so-called fact kits—collections of statements, speeches, press releases, editorials, and newspaper clippings—which are routinely dispatched to the hinterlands press, special interest groups, and ethnic organizations. Nothing of a partisan nature is ever sent out with public funds, of course—just the facts that the White House press corps ignore. If it is deemed necessary to educate the editors around the nation in matters that are manifestly political, the Democratic and Republican National committees usually foot the bill.

In most administrations the head of the communications office also coordinates the activities of the public affairs offices of the various agencies of the executive branch; arranges for administration officials to hold regional briefings for reporters in various parts of the country; schedules speaking dates and television appearances for White House and cabinet officials; and brings out-of-town journalists—usually publishers, broadcast executives, editors, and columnists—to Washington to chat with the president or other top-level officials.

During most of Gerald Ford's twenty-nine months in the White House, the office of communications was supervised by deputy press secretary Gerald Warren and five assistants.[67] According to Ron Nessen the operation was conducted quietly to avoid undue publicity.[68] The fact kits, however, were a staple product. When Ford put forth a series of economy and energy proposals in January 1975, for example, Warren organized a mailing to hundreds of editors. He also arranged for administration officials to publish bylined newspaper editorials.[69]

In the Carter administration the functions of the communications office were initially supervised by Jody Powell. But Powell lacked administrative skills and eventually surrendered many of his ancillary duties. Had he possessed any talent as an executive, he might well have created a communications empire. In November 1976, before

Carter was sworn in, the press secretary designate paid a visit to the White House to see how Ron Nessen organized his office. Nessen later told a reporter: "He [Powell] was curious about other parts of the White House that he thought might fall under his jurisdiction logically, such as speechwriting, advance and the photo office. They're not currently under us, but, you know, I think he's probably on the right track with that kind of view of organization, given the fact that he has a close relationship with Carter. It makes sense to put all the elements of White House communications under one man."[70]

That is precisely how Powell proceeded to set up his office and organize his staff of forty-plus. Five divisions reported to him: the news and information staff, the news summary team, the speechwriters, the arrangers of television and radio appearances, and the office of media liaison (the bureau that administered to the needs of the hinterlands press). A deputy press secretary, Patricia Bario, was appointed to run this shop on a day-to-day basis.[71]

In July 1978, with Carter's popularity on the wane and his image as an inept leader gaining credence, Gerald Rafshoon, a professional public relations man who had been tinkering with Carter's image off and on since 1966, joined the White House staff as an assistant for communications and immediately began packaging and selling the president in a coherent fashion. He also began supervising the speechwriters and the press advance team and arranging photo opportunities and interviews for Carter and his aides. Powell, his kingdom now substantially reduced, readily admitted he had not been up to the task: "It was a fact. I never really got depressed about it. It was obvious to me I had bitten off more than I could chew. And I had two ways of looking at it. Either the problem was that there was more to do than anybody could handle, or anybody could have done it except for me." He chose to accept the first option, he said.[72]

When Bario took charge of the office of media liaison, she promised to provide out-of-town reporters with the "same loving care" that Jody Powell lavished on their Washington colleagues. The media liaison staff thus became a font of knowledge about Jimmy Carter. A journalist could call and find out what tie Jimmy wore to his inauguration (the same "good luck tie" he had worn on primary election nights); his dimensions (five-foot-nine, 155 pounds; 33-inch waist, 39-inch chest); his favorite poet (Dylan Thomas); his favorite books (*Let Us Now Praise Famous Men* by James Agee and *War and Peace* by Leo Tolstoy); his favorite spectator sport (stock car racing); his favorite automobile (a Studebaker Commander that he owned in 1948); his age when he first began to date (thirteen).[73]

Bario also prepared and dispatched fact kits, regularly mailing packets of material—photographs, briefing transcripts, backgrounders on such issues as inflation, energy and foreign policy—to editors, columnists, special interest groups, and assorted individuals. Every few months a booklet entitled "President Carter Speaks on the Record" was sent to editors and broadcast news directors; a reporter in search of a presidential quote to round out a story had only to check the alphabetized list of issues to see what Carter had said on the subject at hand.[74] One survey revealed that the office of media liaison mailed an average of 35,551 items per month from June through September 1978.[75]

With the March 1981 assassination attempt on Ronald Reagan and the disabling brain injury suffered by press secretary James Brady, it took about a year for the White House to organize an office of communications. Once it was done, however, the Reagan administration had put together what is probably the most efficient White House propaganda office ever assembled. David R. Gergen supervised the construction of the organization and now runs it. His official title is assistant to the president for communications, but it would not be inaccurate to describe him as a communications czar. His job, as he casually describes it, is to "hold an umbrella" over the press office, the speechwriting staff, the public affairs office (which coordinates the activities of other executive branch public information offices), and the media liaison office (which, as in the Carter administration, caters to the out-of-town press). In addition Gergen does long-range planning, which means that he keeps track of coming events and devises schemes to extract positive publicity from them.[76]

Gergen has proved particularly adept at farming out purely partisan public relations projects to outside groups. When Reagan went before Congress in February 1981 to urge passage of his economic proposals, Gergen launched a campaign to enlist public support. Editors and columnists were brought to the White House for briefings by the administration's economic experts, and television appearances were arranged for Reagan's spokesmen. A volunteer committee was organized to sell the president's economic package to the country; a public relations firm, Wagner & Baroody, was hired to handle the details and prepare fact sheets for newspaper editors, broadcast executives, trade associations, labor unions, and other special interest groups.[77] The effort to push through Reagan's budget proposals was given an additional boost three months later when the White House, the Republican National Committee, and congressional Republicans launched a three-prong attack. Two dozen speakers were dispatched to the home districts of conservative Democrats whose votes the administration needed; the national committee sent letters to 200,000 Republican contributors urging them to fill out enclosed postcards and mail them to House Speaker Thomas "Tip" O'Neill (D-Mass.); House Republicans, reacting to O'Neill's warning to Reagan that he would have to "play hardball" to get his proposals passed, stood on the Capitol lawn and waved baseball bats for the television cameras.[78]

Intimidation

There comes a time in every administration when the presidential-press relationship starts to turn sour. Usually it begins when the polls show the president's popularity is dipping, or when a major effort to push a program through Congress falls flat, or when a high-level aide becomes embroiled in scandal. The press, which the public generally dislikes anyway, becomes an ideal scapegoat. Suddenly all those journalists who had heretofore demonstrated outstanding wisdom in carrying White House–fed stories about the president's strength, intelligence, and endearing human qualities find their credibility challenged. They find themselves being chided for their obsession with "bad" news and find that government gumshoes are on the prowl for their sources. It is an extremely dangerous game because the more the president and his surrogate enforcers attack the press, the more the press tends to counterattack. Unless it is kept under careful control, it can get out of hand.

Gerald Ford and Jimmy Carter were acutely aware that engaging personally in pitched battle with the press does not pay. By and large they kept whatever negative feelings they harbored about reporters carefully hidden and let their subordinates berate the press when it was deemed necessary. Ronald Reagan, who has an inherent distaste for confrontation anyway, has followed a similar pattern.

President Ford complained in private, sometimes bitterly, when he felt he had been mistreated by the media, but rarely voiced such feelings in public. Said one top official in the Ford White House, "My theory is that it bugs him nearly as much as it bugs me and others when he gets an unfair rap, but I can't imagine him saying it out loud. It's part of his political personality. Down deep he has this private rule: 'Don't attack the press.' "[79] Ford was upset, for example, when news stories and photographs depicted him as clumsy, and he griped to friends. After all he had been a college football player and was an active skier. But when asked by two *Washington Post* reporters how he felt about his doltish image, this was the president's "complaint": "Most of the critics . . . have never played in a ball game, never skied.

I don't know whether it is a self-defense mechanism in themselves or what, but I'm kind of amused at that. It doesn't bother me at all."[80]

The Ford administration's chief enforcer was press secretary Ron Nessen. Some of his quarrels with reporters were premeditated, but most were the product of his hair-trigger temper. He did not appreciate, for example, a question posed by UPI's Helen Thomas at a Ford press conference and, at the next day's regular briefing, the press secretary rebuked the reporter by name. "We can take a break here for the filing of corrections," sneered Nessen, "if anyone wishes to do so."[81]

On occasion Nessen attempted to intimidate reporters with calculated tantrums, the most notable of which was a late June 1975 exhortation to reporters to cease their "blind, mindless, irrational suspicion and cynicism and distrust." Another premeditated outburst occurred while the Ford family was on vacation in Vail, Colorado, during the 1975 Christmas season. Ford took a spill on the ski slopes, and pictures of the presidential pratfall were prominently displayed on front pages across the nation. Nessen asked White House chief of staff Richard Cheney for advice on how to put an end to the stories about Ford's clumsiness, and Cheney suggested that the press secretary show some anger in background sessions with the press. The following day Nessen strolled into the press room and delivered a diatribe to a half-dozen reporters. The stories they had been writing, he fumed, were "the most unconscionable misrepresentation of the president. . . . He is healthy, graceful, and he is by far the most athletic president in memory."[82]

Almost from the moment Ford took the oath of office, he and his key aides were engaged in a struggle to stop leaks of sensitive information. In October 1974, for instance, the White House ordered that no one receive economic statistics in advance save the administration's chief economist, Alan Greenspan, in order to plug premature leaks to the press.[83] In early January 1976 President Ford let it be known he was angry over published reports that the United States was secretly involved in the war in Angola and had attempted to manipulate the domestic situation in Italy.[84] A few weeks later CBS newsman Daniel Schorr obtained the secret report of a House Select Committee on Intelligence investigation of Central Intelligence Agency activities and passed it on to the *Village Voice*. A furious Gerald Ford offered House Speaker Carl Albert (D-Okla.) the full "resources and services of the Executive Branch" to probe the leak.[85] At about the same time the president dispatched to Congress a proposal that would, among other things, impose a fine of up to $5,000 and a five-year prison term on any government official who disclosed intelligence secrets, even if the disclosure were made after the official left public employ.[86]

The press was not held in high esteem in the Jimmy Carter camp. Carter "thinks he's ninety-nine percent smarter than anybody who's around him," said *New York Times* reporter James Wooten, who covered the Carter campaign and the first year of his administration. "He has no respect for scribes; he hates the press."[87] This observation by an outsider was later confirmed by an erstwhile insider, Assistant Secretary of State for Public Affairs Hodding Carter. The president and his associates viewed "the press as the enemy," said Hodding Carter in an interview with the *Boston Globe*. "They think that reporters are clods and animals and that you simply feed them."[88]

This was a curious attitude given the fact that throughout his political career, Carter was the beneficiary of generally favorable treatment by the press. He was "discovered" as the governor of Georgia and catapulted onto the national stage in 1971 when *Time* magazine featured him on a cover. The artist who painted Carter's portrait for the magazine was instructed to make him look like John F. Kennedy.[89]. In early 1976 *Time* ran a full-page ad in about two dozen magazines, ostensibly to tout its election coverage. The ad depicted Carter sitting in a rocking chair, as John Kennedy had, and served to promote his fortunes as much as those of *Time*.[90] After Carter had been in office almost two years, *National Journal* correspondent Dom Bonafede concluded that "few modern presidents have enjoyed more favorable treatment at the hands of the news media."[91]

But Carter saw it differently. As a candidate in 1976 he complained that the press concentrated on his mistakes while treating Ford with deference.[92] Four years later it was Reagan who got the free ride from the news media.[93] *Boston Globe* correspondent Martin Nolan once described Carter's attitude toward the press as one of "bemused contempt."[94] Journalist Sanford Ungar noted during the 1976 campaign that Carter "has his own list of 'enemies' in the press, believes that some of the negative articles about him are motivated by pure maliciousness, and forgives very slowly, if ever, for any coverage that he considers unfair."[95]

But Carter managed, for the most part, to restrain whatever vindictive urges he may have felt. The intimidation tactic he used most often was the simple tongue lashing. During an appearance on NBC's "Meet the Press" shortly before the 1976 Democratic convention, for example, Carter was asked a question about his coverage. "That assumes the press is unbiased, which I have a hard time doing," he said.[96] In August 1979 ABC news reported that U.S. intelligence agencies had planted an electronic eavesdropping device in the New York apartment of UN ambassador Andrew Young and thus knew in advance of a secret and controversial meeting between Young and an official of the Palestine Liberation Organization. Later Carter spotted ABC's White House correspondent, Sam Donaldson, and snapped, "You were wrong." Replied the newsman, "We're concerned with accuracy." As he stalked off, Carter growled, "I wish you would demonstrate it."[97]

Among individual jounalists no one raised Carter's choler with more consistency and intensity than syndicated columnist Jack Anderson, who fixed the president in his sights shortly after Carter settled in the White House. Anderson broke numerous significant stories about budget director and presidential friend Bert Lance, presidential brother Billy Carter, and presidential friend and adviser Dr. Peter Bourne. But the day that Carter became an implacable Anderson hater was August 18, 1980, when the columnist published the first of a five-part series charging that the president was planning to rescue the American hostages then being held in Iran by ordering a major invasion of that nation. Moreover, wrote Anderson, Carter intended to schedule the operation during the final weeks before the presidential election. The story, Anderson later said, came from disgruntled Democratic appointees and sources with access to classified documents prepared for the Joint Chiefs of Staff.

The White House responded with a furious denial: "The suggestion that this or any other administration would start a war for political benefit is grotesque and totally irresponsible. The allegation made by Jack Anderson is absolutely false." Several of Anderson's clients, including the *Washington Post*, refused to publish the series. The *Post* claimed it "could find no substantiation for the assertions in Anderson's column."[98] Other news organizations published stories that tended to support the columnist's charges. On August 16, 1980, for example, UPI cited the upcoming Anderson columns and reported that "Congressional sources say the administration has fashioned a new plan to rescue the fifty-two American hostages in Iran."[99] Eight months later journalist Richard T. Sale reported in the *Atlanta Journal and Constitution* that following the unsuccessful hostage rescue attempt in April 1980, Carter had instructed "the Joint Chiefs of Staff to develop an even larger, more powerful military operation against Iran."[100]

Jimmy Carter, however, remained defiant. When a television reporter asked him on October 21, 1980, to respond to the Anderson columns, Carter snapped, "Jack Anderson is the one columnist in this nation who habitually lies."[101]

Although Carter usually managed to avoid direct confrontation with reporters, he had in his inner circle a press kicker who seldom hesitated to make use of his considerable talent. And White House reporters were well aware that when Jody Powell jumped on them, he was acting as Carter's surrogate. "Jody pretty well reflects the mood of the president," said the *Washington Star*'s Phil Gailey. "When Jody is pissed off at the press, you can bet the president is pissed off."[102]

Many times, of course, Powell's temper tantrums were merely spontaneous bursts of anger. White House correspondents believed, however, that he often had an ulterior motive when he snarled at them. "Jody practices winning through intimidation," said one veteran reporter. "He can bully reporters and hopes you'll be a little less aggressive next time."[103] Chris Ogden of *Time* magazine agreed: "There was a certain bit of the bully to him. You had to yell back at him or he'd spot it as a weakness."[104]

Shortly after Carter took office Powell took umbrage at an AP story on the administration's arms limitations proposals. He rousted reporter Rick Meyer out of bed at 6:15 A.M. and bawled him out. When the *Washington Post* reported in early 1978 that White House chief of staff Hamilton Jordan had spit a drink down the blouse of a female customer at a Washington singles bar, Powell went into a rage. He labeled the story "sleazy crap," issued a thirty-three page denial and, in the words of John Osborne, "rebuked and harangued the assembled White House press corps for days afterward and expanded the lectures and protests in prolonged telephone calls—one lasting forty-five minutes—to individual reporters"[105]

Jimmy Carter and his top aides were obsessed by leaks of sensitive and embarrassing information and engaged in an unceasing campaign to contain them. During one search for reporters' sources in the spring of 1979, investigators in two government departments told *New York Times* correspondents that they were looking for "an example—a case that would really slam an employee and possibly embarrass the news organization that dealt with him."[106]

Carter's concern over leaks became evident in February 1977, a month after he was sworn in, when he ordered that the number of officials who enjoyed total access to intelligence information be cut from forty to five.[107] When the details of a National Security Council meeting were reported in the press in August 1977, a gag order quickly made its way down through the White House hierarchy.[108] Two months later the White House launched what one official called a "witch hunt supreme" in search of the individual who had whispered to reporters the details of tax reform proposals then under consideration.[109]

Early in 1978 Jack Anderson began publishing excerpts of the minutes of cabinet meetings. The documents were dry—Carter and his colleagues seemed to spend much of their time reviewing their press notices and carping about negative and "inaccurate" news accounts of their activities—but that apprently mattered little to the president. A leak was a challenge, and it had to be plugged. The president who entered office vowing to hold open cabinet meetings ordered his cabinet secretary, Jack Watson, to investigate the leak of the minutes and submit a memorandum on his progress. Instructed the president, "We've got to stop Jack Anderson putting in his column what's going on at cabinet meetings."[110] Time and again, the subject came up. Item 6 in the minutes of August 7, 1978, for example, stated, "The president asked that cabinet members treat the minutes of the cabinet meetings with the care that should be given confidential documents. He said that for the last several cabinet meetings, Mr. Watson has been distributing the minutes to cabinet members marked 'for their eyes only.' "[111]

Carter's concern about leaks seemed particularly intense in the spring and summer of 1978. In April he summoned senior White House staff members and cabinet officials to Camp David to discuss how they might iron out their differences. One of their biggest problems, said the president, was leaks. They had to stop cutting each other up in the press. They should begin practicing the art of taciturnity, he instructed, by remaining silent about what went on at that very conference. "Only Jody Powell is to do the talking on this meeting," Carter said.[112] According to Health, Education and Welfare Secretary Joseph Califano, who was present at the meeting, the president also said: "The problems [news leaks] that we do have I attribute primarily to the White House. Some leaks from the White House are inexcusable—derogatory remarks about [certain cabinet officials]. If I could find out who did it, I would kick his ass out of the White House."[113]

When it comes to the needs of the poor and deprived, Ronald Reagan's political opponents have said, the president has a warm smile and a cold heart. Journalists could say the same thing about his attitude toward them: he is probably the best-liked menace to a free press since Theodore Roosevelt, who fulminated about muckrakers and filed libel suits against publishers and editors.[114]

The amiable, avuncular Reagan is popular with the reporters who cover him, and this kindly sentiment has spilled over into their news stories. The president's campaign press secretary and former political aide, Lyn Nofziger, is one of the most irascible and acerbic press critics on the national scene. But in March 1982 he had this to say about the way reporters have treated Reagan: "Overall, I don't have any real complaints about the way the press has covered this administration."[115] Wrote C. T. Hanson, one of the *Columbia Journalism Review*'s Washington editors, "The White House press served with unusual frequency during Reagan's first two years as a kind of *Pravda* of the Potomac, a conduit for White House utterances and official image-mongering intended to sell Reagonomics."[116]

Reagan knows that one of his most valuable assets is his good press, and he has taken care to safeguard it. Like all other presidents he has privately bristled over things written and said about him; on occasion he has let his feelings get the better of him and voiced his complaints publicly. During the 1980 campaign he accused the press of giving too much credence to Jimmy Carter's criticisms of him. "I think they [the news media] have gone off half-cocked," Reagan fumed.[117] In an interview with *TV Guide* published in March 1982, Reagan asserted that television newsmen were putting "a kind of editorial slant" on their stories about the U.S. effort to help the government of El Salvador defend itself against lef-wing guerrillas. He expressed a wish that reporters would "trust us, and put themselves in our hands, and call and say, 'I have this story' when dealing with sensitive information."[118] The day that news accounts of the interview appeared, Reagan sat down with reporters from the *Daily Oklahoman* and censured television journalists for their "constant downbeat" stories on the economy: "You can't turn on evening news without seeing that they're going to interview someone else who has lost his job or they're outside the factory that has laid off workers or so forth—the constant downbeat—that can contribute to slowing down a new recovery that is in the offing. . . . Is it news that some fellow out in South Succostash someplace has just been laid off that he should be interviewed nationwide?"[119]

Within twenty-four hours Reagan apparently realized he had escalated the presidential-press cold war to a dangerous level, and he digressed from a speech before the National Association of Manufacturers to offer a truce. "I hope I didn't touch a nerve with any of the press a few days ago," he said, "because I think that most of the time the overwhelming majority of them are doing a fine job."[120]

With these and a few other exceptions President Reagan, like Ford and Carter, has depended on subordinates to keep the press in line. The person who most often reads the riot act to reporters is press secretary Larry Speakes. He has summoned White House correspondents to his office for lectures on their raucous behavior during press conferences. A reporter for the Independent Television News Association once interjected at a news conference with a pointed question, and Speakes theatened to ban him from future sessions. The sentence was eventually commuted to exile in the back row of the cavernous East Room.[121]

In an offhand remark to a group of Massachusetts business executives in January 1983, President Reagan allowed that it was "hard to justify" the federal income tax on corporations. When the story was reported, Speakes chastised reporters for putting too much emphasis on it and accused them of "jumping up and down, licking their chops, clapping their hands and doing back flips." In a speech to the National Association of Government Communicators a few days later, Speakes reproved the press for what he said was a twenty-year crusade against presidents: "My question to you is, can the modern presidency survive the modern media? Can any man in public office stand up to the daily drumbeat of morning newspapers and the flashing symbols of evening television shows? The steady denigration of the president has gone on for two decades. It has been directed not only at the president but at his use of presidential powers." It was a chicken-and-egg situation, Speakes said: "Does the public perception that things are bad come first or does the public say things are bad after they've seen the bad news night after night?" What was needed, said Speakes, was a "good news" segment on the nightly news shows.[122]

Communications director David Gergen is not as quick to challenge the press, but he occasionally wields a big stick. CBS news, for example, aired a documentary, "People Like Us," on April 21, 1982. Anchored by reporter Bill Moyers, the show featured the stories of four poor or disabled people who were enduring hardships brought on by President Reagan's budget cuts. "There's no question but that federal programs are riddled with waste and fraud," said Moyers in his concluding remarks. But in making his budget decisions, Reagan had "chosen not to offend the rich, the powerful and the organized," opting instead to "take on the weak" by advocating budget cuts that fell "most heavily on the poor."[123]

The gripping report had thrown the spotlight on what one White House official called a "goddam touchy" issue: the public's perception that Ronald Reagan is a rich man's president who is heedless of the needs of the disadvantaged. Several times before the show was aired, Gergen demanded that the network include a response from the administration, but the requests were rejected on the grounds that the film had already been distributed to affiliates and that the network had given the administration's point of view intensive coverage during regular news broadcasts.[124]

After the documentary was shown, Gergen called in reporters for a series of briefings to rebut CBS's facts. "Frankly, this one was below the belt, and we're going to respond," Gergen himself said during one forty-minute session with newsmen. The individuals whom CBS had featured "clearly had difficulties in their lives," he said. "What we clearly have problems dealing with is a story that lays all the problems of that sort on Ronald Reagan's doorstep." He called on CBS to give the White House a half-hour in prime time "to present our side of the story." Once again the network refused. Although the White House counterattack failed, Gergen professed satisfaction. He had "put the media on notice," he said, "that when there is something unfair we're going to respond to it, so people will be more careful next time."[125]

Verbal intimidation of journalists is but one of the tools presidents and their aides use to keep the lid on negative news. A far more pernicious tactic is the use of the government's vast resources to intimidate and locate reporters' sources and to restrict the transmission of information through the use of the secrecy stamp and other censorship devices. It is in this area that Ronald Reagan's cold heart threatens to freeze the flow of news.

The president, like his predecessors, does not like leaks—by which he does not mean acclamatory leaks but unauthorized leaks of bad news or of news that preempts his own announcements or actions. At times, according to one White House official, Reagan's concern over leaks amounts to "an obsession."[126] In February 1981 he returned from a weekend at Camp David in high dudgeon over a series of news stories about proposed foreign aid cuts. "He was ticked off and said so," said one of the president's aides. "He let it be known in no uncertain terms that fights over policy are not to be waged through the press."[127] A spate of stories in January 1983 about White House budget deliberations sent Reagan into what one presidential assistant called "a towering rage."[128] Declaring he had "had it up to my keister" with leaks, he ordered subordinates to issue "guidelines" to regulate contacts with the press by White House officials. David Gergen formulated the rules, which designated a small number of officials who would be permitted to speak about various subjects and required that all other staff members clear journalists' requests for information with the office of communications. "I would not call it a gag order," Gergen told reporters. "We are going to try and serve you to insure that we get a full and free flow of information."[129]

Reagan and his top aides have occasionally launched investigations to find out who talked to newsmen. A *Wall Street Journal* article about the 1982 congressional elections, for example, carried several quotes from anonymous White House officials, and the telephone logs were scrutinized in search of those who had spoken out of turn.[130] In March 1983 Reagan and his top aides discussed several options for nuclear arms limitation proposals that could be raised in negotiations with the Soviet Union. Details of the discussions appeared in the *Washington Post*, and the president's minions attempted to find the transgressor.[131] On April 7, 1983, the *New York Times* printed part of the text of a National Security Council document outlining the administration's plans for containing the spread of Soviet and Cuban influence in Central America. National Security Adviser William Clark called in the FBI and instructed the agency to locate the person who had leaked the document.[132]

President Reagan, in stark contrast to the six chief executives who preceded him, has also taken extraordinary steps to tighten government secrecy. He signed an executive order on April 2, 1982, that greatly extends the authority of government officials to classify national security information. The order, nineteen pages long, supersedes regulations promulgated by Jimmy Carter in 1978 and eliminates a requirement that government officials consider "the public's interest in access to government information" before stamping a document "Top Secret," "Secret," or "Confidential." The Reagan rules also do away with the requirement that information can be classified only if its disclosure would result in identifiable damage to the national security; the classified stamp may now be used only if unspecified damage "reasonably could be expected." In addition Reagan's executive order instructs government officials that when they are in doubt about which category of classification to use, they should always give the benefit of doubt to the higher level of secrecy.[133] That is merely the most outstanding instance of Reagan's efforts to stifle the flow of government information to the public. There have been many similar efforts, which, taken together, have weaved a noose that threatens to choke the First Amendment.

In December 1982 the Defense Department announced that polygraph tests would be given to military and civilian personnel selected randomly. One official told the *New York Times* that as many as 15,000 to 20,000 people could be examined. Pentagon spokesman Henry Catto, Jr., said the program was designed to reduce a "hemorrhage of information" to the press.[134] On March 12, 1983, the White House released without fanfare an executive order compelling all federal employees with access to classified information to submit to polygraph tests on request. Officials with security clearances, stated the order, "may be required to submit to polygraph examinations, when appropriate, in the course of investigations of unauthorized disclosures of classified information."[135]

The same executive order imposed yet another, even more odious system of censorship on every government employee with access to classified information: whether actively employed in the government or not, they must now obtain written approval for everything they plan to say or write about their activities as a government official. The rules apply to books, book reviews, speeches, even works of fiction. Everything will be submitted to government censors, who will then determine what the public will be permitted to see, hear, and read. Such regulations had previously applied only to employees of the intelligence services.[136]

The White House has proposed legislation and supported other efforts to restrict severely the types and amount of information obtainable under the provisions of the Freedom of Information Act. Outrageously high search fees have been routinely charged to persons who have asked for documents. Attorney General William French Smith decreed in May 1981 that information requested under the FOIA could be denied on purely technical grounds.[137] And in April 1983 an interagency task force set up by national security adviser William Clark recommended that the administration request legislation that would make it a federal crime for government employees to disclose classified information. Malfeasors could be punished by as many as three years in prison and a fine of $10,000. The task force also suggested that unauthorized recipients of classified information, including journalists, by subjected to civil penalties.[138]

These instances illustrate how the press manipulation strategy adopted by modern presidents—appeasement, evasion, and intimidation—is used to mold public perception and opinion. How did it all come about? Who taught the presidents how to appear accessible to the press without actually being so? Who showed them how to rope reporters off, how to restrict them to the press bus, and force them to listen to piped-in speeches and other events? Who formalized the daily press briefing and the photo opportunity? Who invented the daily news summary as a device to monitor the press? Who wrote the press secretary job description, which stipulates that the main task is to coddle the Washington press and convince reporters the president's schedule is hot news? Who taught presidents how to exploit television by staging events, scripting political conventions, timing the descent of the balloons? Who perfected the techniques for taking the show

2

Perspective: "I Don't Think There Ever Was a Time When Newspaper Lying Was So General and So Mean as at Present"

On the principle that a free people cannot long enjoy such a condition without a free flow of information, the founding fathers adopted the First Amendment to the Constitution, which strictly forbids Congress from making any law "abridging the freedom of speech, or of the press." But government officials, and especially presidents, have not been so willing to concede the founders' wisdom. For in adopting the First Amendment, they created an independent press that, with certain exceptions that have evolved in case law, is answerable to no one but its customers and its conscience. Presidents have positions and programs to push, and they want the people to agree with them. They also do and say things they do not wish the public to know about.

Therein lies the rub: the press does not have to agree with presidents, and it has no obligation to hide any foibles. Skeptical reporters and editors can write what they wish, and the product frequently differs from what presidents want, which is precisely what the founders intended.

This was not a conclusion idly come by. The founding fathers feared despotism, and they were aware that one of the tools that the British monarchy had used to manipulate the people was a controlled press. In England men and women had died in the struggle for a free press; they had been imprisoned, whipped, pilloried, put on the rack, had their hands and ears cut off, their noses slit, their faces branded—all for the crime of expressing their opinions in print.[1] So the founders created a free press in America. It was frequently strident, often shrill, sometimes pugnacious.

George Washington stepped into the presidency just as the press was becoming flagrantly partisan. Not long after he won the nation's first presidential election without opposition, Republican papers began pelting him. Most of the criticism centered around his aristocratic inclinations, which led detractors to believe he had designs on becoming America's first monarch. When all present stood at one of his receptions, for example, he was accused of wanting to be a king.[2]

A cold, reserved man, Washington rarely dealt with the press personally or aired his displeasure publicly. Instead he vented his spleen in conversations and correspondence. At a cabinet meeting one of his officers mentioned a satirical article he had recently read, and Washington let loose a furious tirade. Secretary of State Thomas Jefferson captured the moment with this description:

The President was much inflamed, got into one of those passions when he cannot command himself, ran on much on the personal abuse which had been bestowed on him, defied any man on earth to produce one single act of his since he had been in the government which was not done on the purest motives, that he had never repented but once the having slipped the moment of resigning his office, & that was every moment since, that *by God* he had rather be in his grave than in his present situation. That he had rather be on his farm than to be made *emperor of the world* and yet they were charging him with wanting to be king. That that *rascal Freneau* sent him 3 of his papers every day, as if he thought he would become the distributor of his papers, that he could see in this nothing but an impudent design to insult him. He ended in this high tone.[3]

Flash forward to the twentieth century and to President Lyndon Johnson. As he became entangled in the Vietnam war and the criticism mounted, he tended to take it personally. At one point CBS correspondent Morley Safer reported that U.S. Marines had deliberately destroyed a Vietnamese village for no discernible reason. A livid Johnson telephoned the network president, Frank Stanton. Journalist David Halberstam described the scene:

"Frank," said the early-morning wake-up call, "are you trying to fuck me?"

"Who is this?" said the still sleepy Stanton.

"Frank, this is your president, and yesterday your boys shat on the American flag," Lyndon Johnson said, and then administered a tongue-lashing: How could CBS employ a Communist like Safer, how could they be so unpatriotic as to put on enemy film like this?

Johnson was furious, he was sure that Safer was a Communist and he sent out a search party to check his past, and the Royal Canadian Mounted Police checked out everything about Safer, including his sister, finding that he was indeed totally above suspicion and law-abiding. (Johnson was not very happy about the result and went on insisting that Safer was a Communist, and when aides said no, he was simply a Canadian, the president said, "Well, I knew he wasn't an American.")[4]

In 1798 a Federalist Congress passed four laws designed to curtail the criticisms of those who were not "Americans." They were called the Alien and Sedition Acts, and they gave the government extraordinary authority to imprison aliens and citizens who opposed its actions. President John Adams, who occasionally lamented the censurious comments about him that appeared in public print, signed the measures into law with no overt sign of regret. Adams and his subordinates used the laws to prosecute detractors, including publishers.[5]

"Freedom of the press in America owes as much, if not more, to Thomas Jefferson than to any other public man," wrote historian James Pollard. This judgment is remarkable in light of the fact that Jefferson was frequently the target of intense, bitter, and scurrilous newspaper attacks. He was accused of being an atheist, of cowardice, of keeping a mulatto house servant as his mistress, of selling his children born of slaves, of attempting to seduce the wife of a friend, of not having been the real author of the Declaration of Independence.[6] Such harsh attacks sometimes compelled even this most vaunted champion of a free press to deplore the liberties taken by journalists. "Nothing can now be believed which is seen in a newspaper," he once wrote. "Truth itself becomes suspicious by being put into that polluted vehicle." In another letter he decried "the putrid state into which our newspapers have passed, and the malignity, and vulgarity, and mendacious spirit of those who write for them."[7]

Despite their love-hate attitudes toward the press, presidents gradually began to realize they could use it to further their own policies and political interests. The first to appreciate the public relations value of a friendly press was Andrew Jackson, who rewarded his journalistic friends with the fruits of the spoils system. He appointed so many editors to posts in his administration that the *Richmond Enquirer*, a Jackson supporter, complained: "We wish the Executive would let the Press alone. We cannot . . . approve of the appointment of so many of its conductors to office. . . . We know that General Jackson solemnly disclaims all intentions to *reward* his supporters or to bribe the Press to support his measures. And we believe him—we know also, the reasons by which he justifies these appointments. . . . But we are better satisfied with his *motives* than his reasons—with the integrity than with the expediency of the appointments."[8]

As American newspapers slowly evolved from political sheets into independent journals, the art of manipulating them became more demanding. For all his reputed simplicity Abraham Lincoln had a natural talent for the task: he knew how to cultivate newsmen and how to manipulate them for his purposes. In an interview with a *New York Herald* reporter, Lincoln displayed his soft touch:

The press has no better friend than I am—no one who is more ready to acknowledge its great power—its tremendous power for both good and evil. I would like to have it always on my side, if it could be so; so much, so very much depends upon sound public opinion. . . . Do you gentlemen who control so largely public opinion, do you ever think how much you might lighten the burdens of men in power—those poor unfortunates weighed down by care, anxieties, and responsibilities? If you would only give them a consistent and hearty support, bearing patiently with them when they seem to be making mistakes and giving them credit at least for good intentions, when these seem not to be clear, what comfort you would bestow![9]

When Lincoln was succeeded by Andrew Johnson, presidential-press relations took a severe turn for the worse and remained strained for decades. As he stepped forward to take on the impossible task of filling Lincoln's shoes, Johnson's critics condemned him as a drunk, a Catholic, an atheist, and an illegitimate child. The *New York World* berated him as "an insolent drunken brute in comparison with whom Caligula's horse was respectable."[10] Ulysses Grant, Rutherford B. Hayes, James Garfield, and Chester Arthur continued to suffer the slings and arrows of the press.[11]

Then came Grover Cleveland, the first president to trade insults openly and publicly with a press that was lurching into a sensationalist phase. In an address on the occasion of the 250th anniversary of Harvard College, Cleveland declared that "American love of fair play and decency . . . would not encourage, if their extent were fully appreciated, the silly, mean and cowardly lies that every day are found in the columns of certain newspapers, which violate every instinct of American manliness, and in ghoulish glee desecrate every sacred relation of private life."[12] To a friend Cleveland wrote: "I don't think there ever was a time when newspaper lying was so general and so mean as at present, and there never was a country under the sun where it flourished as it does in this."[13]

Decade after decade the battle raged. Theodore Roosevelt filed libel suits against editors and publishers. Woodrow Wilson upbraided reporters and threatened to thrash them for their persistent stories about his daughter. Harry Truman publicly labeled columnist Drew Pearson an "SOB."[14]

As the years passed, however, newspaper empires emerged, communication technology grew more sophisticated, and it became even more important for the presidents to master the beast that baited them. Among the best manipulators were Theodore Roosevelt, Woodrow Wilson, and Franklin Delano Roosevelt.

In one of his first acts as president Theodore Roosevelt called some reporters together to establish the ground rules by which he would deal with the press. He would cooperate by providing stories, he said, but he was not to be quoted directly, and reporters were not to publish news he did not approve. Offenders would be ostracized. "All right, gentlemen," he said, closing the meeting, "now we understand each other."[15] Roosevelt actively cultivated reporters and gave them their first press room in the White House. Occasionally he held group sessions with newsmen in the form of audiences that were granted when he sat down for his late afternoon shave. He formalized the official leak and the trial balloon.[16]

Woodrow Wilson is credited with initiating regular press conferences as they are known today. He held his first just eleven days after his inauguration and said:

I feel that a large part of the success of public affairs depends on the newspaper men—not so much on the editorial writers, because we can live down what they say, as upon the news writers, because the news is the atmosphere of public affairs. Unless you get the right setting to affairs—disperse the right impression—things go wrong. . . .

If you play up every morning differences of opinion and predict difficulties . . . you are not so much doing an injury to an individual or to any one of the groups of individuals you are talking about, as impeding the public business. Our present business is to get together, not to get divided. . . .

I sent for you, therefore, to ask that you go into partnership with me, that you lend me your assistance as nobody else can, and then after you have brought this precious freight of opinion into Washington, let us try and make true gold here that will go out from Washington.[17]

Franklin D. Roosevelt used the press as no other president before him had. With some exceptions he liked reporters, enjoyed parrying with them, and went out of his way to satisfy their thirst for news. He held 998 press conferences in his four terms, an all-time record.[18] FDR also established strict rules for reporters covering the White House. He banned direct quotation of his remarks except when authorized. He established background sessions in which everything said was totally off the record and could be cited only on the reporter's own authority. White House regulars who violated his rules or wrote unfavorable stories were attacked and ridiculed.[19]

Radio provided Roosevelt with direct access to the people, and he used the medium masterfully. Whenever he wanted to say something without filtering it through the Washington press corps, he went on the air with the fireside chats that have become legendary. He polished his radio speeches assiduously and practiced them for several days in advance of a broadcast in order to perfect his rhythm and cadence. He strove to make his radio appearances sound informal and to personalize them. If broadcasting on a hot day, for example, he might pause in midsentence and ask an aide for a glass of water.[20] And he knew how to manipulate the medium. During the campaign of 1944 he purchased fifteen minutes of air time and then learned that his opponent, Thomas E. Dewey, had reserved the next quarter-hour for a response. Roosevelt spoke for fourteen minutes and stopped. Perplexed by the silence, millions of listeners fiddled with their dials, found other sounds to listen to, and were not there when it was Dewey's turn to speak.[21]

A new development highlighted Dwight D. Eisenhower's relationship with the press: he was the first president to have his news conferences filmed and broadcast on television. The president, blessed with the famous, infectious Eisenhower smile, went over well in the new medium, and his press secretary, James Hagerty, guarded the image by reserving the right to edit the films of Ike's news conference performances.[22] John F. Kennedy—handsome, articulate, witty, always ready with a quip—was the first president to comprehend fully that television could be an extremely valuable tool. He was the first chief executive to permit live telecasts of his news conferences. The broadcast press loved the innovation, but print reporters soon came forth with charges that televised conferences made them feel like props in a staged show.[23]

Indeed the press conferences were as staged as Kennedy and his aides could make them. At least one day in advance of his appearances press secretary Pierre Salinger called in public information specialists from each executive department and went over with them answers to questions likely to be asked. Then, said Salinger, "I would give the material to the president early in the evening and he would study it before going to bed. The next morning, with his top advisers, we would go through a dry run at breakfast. . . . I would sit directly across the table from JFK and fire the questions at him (between forkfuls of ham and eggs) in the language I thought the press would use." As a result Kennedy usually managed to outmaneuver his questioners. "He either overwhelmed you with decimal points or disarmed you with a smile and a wisecrack," said *New York Times* newsman James Reston.[24]

An ardent student of the press and a former reporter himself, Kennedy was liked and respected by the White House press corps. But charges soon arose that the administration was managing the news. The witty, cigar-smoking Salinger, it was learned, coordinated the news policies of other executive departments. There was evidence also that the Kennedy administration leaked selected information to favored reporters. The controversy concerning manipulation boiled over when Pentagon spokesman Arthur Sylvester defended the government's "inherent right to lie" in certain situations.[25]

The record thus shows that all presidents had differences with the press and wanted to manipulate, intimidate, and muzzle it. Some tried and a few succeeded. Others cursed and threatened it. Some simply seethed. But Richard Nixon was different. His efforts to cow his critics in the Fourth Estate were more deliberate, systematic, and exhaustive. And he was peerless in his hatred.

It was early November 1969, and the president of the United States was angry. Beleaguered by anti-Vietnam war demonstrators, he had taken to the airways on November 3 and exhorted "the great silent majority of my fellow Americans" to support his "plan for peace." The nationally televised "silent majority" speech, in Richard Nixon's judgment, had been an unqualified success. "Very few speeches actually influence the course of history," he later wrote. "The November 3 speech was one of them."[26]

Commentators for the three major television networks were not so rhapsodic. Following the president's appearance they had analyzed, criticized, and rebutted his remarks. This was the source of Nixon's anger. Their comments, he felt, were "biased and distorted" and interfered with the president's privilege "to appeal directly to the people," a right he considered to be "of the essence of democracy."[27]

Now one of his aides, Patrick Buchanan, had come before him with a scheme to strike back at the networks. The proposal called for Vice-President Spiro Agnew to attack the network news organizations in a speech scheduled for November 13 in Des Moines, Iowa. Buchanan, a no-holds-barred press critic himself, had written a strident, harsh, and threatening draft. It blatantly pointed out to television officials that they were licensed by the federal government and implied that what the government had granted, the government could take away. Nixon liked the speech. He went over it line by line, toughening the language. "This really flicks the scab off, doesn't it?" he chortled.[28]

It was an adroit analogy. In twenty-three years of public life up to that moment, Richard Nixon's relations with the national press had been vitriolic most of the time, tempestuous at best. He considered journalists to be liberal, biased, elitist, arrogant. He tried to ignore them and found he could not, so he accused them, cursed them, tried to intimidate them. "I must have heard Richard Nixon say 'the press is the enemy' a dozen times," wrote William Safire, a speechwriter during Nixon's first term.[29]

There was no discussion in the Nixon White House of the First Amendment as a fundamental freedom. No majestic rumination about the free press's organic role in a government of the people, by the people, for the people. No pondering of such subtle but momentous concepts as the public's right to know or the press's right to be wrong.

"One hell of a lot of people don't give one damn about this issue of the suppression of the press," the president fumed to his counsel John Dean in the privacy of the Oval Office.[30] "Let's just not have all this sanctimonious business about the poor repressed press," he growled to television personality David Frost during a series of interviews in May 1977. "I went through it all the years I've been in public life and I have . . . they have never been repressed as far as I am concerned."[31] Frost wondered about Nixon's intellectual grasp of the free press concept:

I cited for him the well-known opinion of Chief Justice Charles Evans Hughes: "The greater the importance of safeguarding the community from incitements to the overthrow of our institutions by force and violence, the more imperative is the need to preserve inviolate the constitutional rights of free speech, free press and free assembly in order to maintain the opportunity for free political discussion to the end that government may be responsive to the will of the people."
Bewilderingly, Nixon replied that the period during which Hughes was writing—the 1930s—was one of little domestic violence and scant concern about rebellion "because Communist subversion hadn't reached a very significant level till long after Hughes left the bench."
I thought that a startlingly tranquil description of the Depression years at home and the growth of Hitler's Nazi Germany abroad, but I let it pass.[32]

How could the founding fathers have foreseen the depths to which modern journalists would plunge? "Nowadays," the president once told author Allen Drury, reporters "don't care about fairness, it's the in thing to forget objectivity, and let your prejudices show."[33] How could Charles Evans Hughes foretell that the journalistic community would come to be dominated by liberals and leftists who would have few qualms about not hiding their biases? The 1968 election was a good example: "I had no idea that the favoritism toward Humphrey was so strong until Edith Efron's carefully researched book, *The News Twisters*, was released in 1971. In it she documented the number of words spoken 'for' and 'against' me by reporters on the three networks. She found that the ratios were 11 to 1, 67 to 1, and 65 to 1—all 'against.' "[34]

Nixon managed to overcome it all in 1968, however, and as he prepared to be sworn in, he contemplated how he would handle his relations with the media. In his particular case, he believed, "the problems were more than institutional. The majority of New York and Washington newspaper reporters, news executives, columnists, and opinion-makers are liberals. I am not, and for many years we had looked at each other across an ideological chasm. . . . I considered the influential majority of the news media to be part of my political opposition."[35]

Nixon was convinced that journalists, in addition to their political differences with him, found him personally distasteful. He "personalized press criticism," said William Safire, "He took everything critical as a personal blast at him; when he read a by-line, the writer came to life in his mind, grinning evilly at him."[36] From outside the White House, Arthur Schlesinger, Jr., noticed the same reaction. Nixon, he wrote, "incredibly manages to conceive himself as the pitiful and helpless victim of a media conspiracy. He seems by cast of mind and temperament to be a man to whom the most trivial criticism is intolerable."[37]

Until the Watergate scandal broke and insiders began talking, such observations were primarily conjecture, for Nixon strove to project the image that he was personally above the battle. He insisted to journalist Jules Witcover that he did not let reporters intrude on his solitude: "I'm not one of those guys who reads his press clippings. I believe in never being affected by reports about me. I may read some selected clippings a week or so later, when somebody sends them to me, but never the next morning. I never look at myself on TV, either. I don't want to develop those phony, self-conscious, contrived things. One thing I have to be is always be myself."[38]

Nixon did, in fact, read newspapers and occasionally watch a news show on television. " 'I pay no attention to them,' Nixon insisted, but he paid a great deal of attention to them," said William Safire.[39] Reporters such as Theodore White could see it in 1972: "The president feigned indifference to the press and New York-based television networks. And, indeed, he behaved as he insisted he must—he must act by his own instincts and judgments, not heeding what the nets and liberals said. Yet a reporter could never rid himself of the realization that the hostility of the Liberal Press obsessed Nixon."[40]

Behind the scenes, he read the news summary prepared by his staff and fretted. In a span of one month in 1969—between September 16 and October 17—Nixon personally sent out no fewer than twenty-one requests to aides, instructing them to challenge various news reports. Assistant Peter Flanigan was ordered to "take action to counter" a CBS story by Dan Rather; communications director Herb Klein was told to send letters to *Newsweek* and to "take appropriate action to counter biased TV coverage of the Adm. over the summer"; Pat Buchanan was asked to inform "appropriate columnists . . . of the extemporaneous character of presidential press conferences."[41]

In public Nixon often attempted to disguise his antipathy for reporters with humor, but the bitterness usually showed through. On a 1969 around-the-world trip he first set down on an aircraft carrier in the Pacific to greet the Apollo 11 astronauts who had just returned from the moon. Two weeks later, in England, he told Prime Minister Harold Wilson that he was going to send moon rocks to all heads of state; he was also going to search for some "contaminated" pieces to give to the press.[42]

When the defensive tactics failed, he lapsed into fits of billingsgate. He raged against journalists; he confounded them, damned them, called down curses upon their heads. In his best moments, Nixon made routine references to "the soft-heads in the press" and the "clowns who write for the media."[43] When his nerves were frayed, he expressed his feelings with the flair of a longshoreman. Columnist Jack Anderson was "contemptible"; CBS correspondent Daniel Schorr was a "son of a bitch."[44] Sometimes he gave them a sailor's blessing in one fell swoop: "They're all sons of bitches."[45]

Shortly after Nixon was reelected in 1972, the Watergate scandal began to unfold, and his fuse grew shorter in direct proportion to the exposure it received. News correspondents, he fumed, "talked in apocalyptic terms" and reported "almost hysterical," "tasteless," and "inflammatory" stories.[46] In one memorable press conference he exploded at television reporters with the charge that he had "never heard or seen such outrageous, vicious, distorted reporting in 27 years of public life."[47]

There is considerable and conclusive evidence to demonstrate in hindsight what was only suspected in the earliest days of Richard Nixon's tenure: that Nixon and his associates entered the White House with a scheme in mind to manipulate, intimidate, control, and evade the press. Forged in the fires of bitter experience, the plan was based on the premise that the national press was not essential to Nixon's success. He did not want to incur its wrath unnecessarily. The press was to be serviced by being supplied with innocuous material to write about. With the press thus occupied, Nixon could evade it—"end run" it, to use a football metaphor. This part of the grand strategy would be carried out primarily through the use of television and secondarily through the use of propaganda techniques. He would, in short, go above and around the press and address the people directly. If reporters became obstreperous, steps could be taken to intimidate them and dilute their credibility and effectiveness with the public.

The plan worked. It functioned masterfully until a brisk day in March 1973 when federal judge John J. Sirica read in open court a letter from Watergate burglar James McCord charging that he and his six codefendents had been subjected to political pressure and that perjury had been committed during their trial. It was then that reporters fully realized they had been bamboozled for months by White House denials, dissimilations, and lies.

But for four years the strategy had succeeded. Press secretary Ron Ziegler practiced his keep-them-comfortable-but-keep-them-ignorant techniques with panache. A propaganda operation under the direction of Herbert Klein, the director of communications for the executive branch, was used to manipulate editors and publishers across the country. Those who reported stories Nixon did not like were denied access to him and his subordinates; they were investigated, wiretapped, and surveilled by the FBI and CIA. And Richard Nixon took to television like a born talk-show host. Just a year into the first Nixon administration, *Wall Street Journal* columnist Alan L. Otten commented:

The Democrats have just begun awakening to a crucial fact of political life. In Richard Nixon they face a president who, thus far at least, have proven remarkably adroit and effective in using the mighty medium of televison. . . .

Might not a president use the medium to manipulate the nation in dark and devious ways.?

There's really been no president yet with the chance or talent. Television hadn't arrived under Truman. Ike was a television natural, but rarely tried to use it as a political weapon. Kennedy wasn't around long enough, and Johnson came across as a television heavy.[48]

The president's effective use of the electronic media was made possible because of the continued improvement of the technology of communication. When he traveled to Europe and Asia in 1969, the trip was beamed live into the nation's living rooms by satellite, the first such transmission from Eastern Europe.[49] The heralded 1972 trip to China became a prime-time spectacle because of dramatic, live satellite transmission.

Nixon's television performances were also enhanced by the expertise of his own associates, many of whom were trained in the advertising and public relations professions. Most important was chief of staff H. R. Haldeman, whose talents were grudgingly acknowledged by Dan Rather: "[He] thinks he knows more about my business than I do, and I'm inclined to think he's correct. . . . He came out of an advertising agency in Los Angeles. He's made a lifetime study of the techniques of manipulating my business." President Kennedy, continued Rather, had the knowledge but not the will to manipulate the press. Lyndon Johnson had the will but not the knowledge. But the Nixon men, Rather said, "have both the will and the determination to try to manipulate the media, and the know-how. . . . All politicians in my experience want to do in one degree or another what Mr. Nixon and his people are doing."[50]

A fundamental question is thus raised: Was Richard Nixon all that different?

3

Evolution: "Gentlemen, This Is My Last Press Conference"

Throughout his career Richard Nixon pointed to his early years as a congressman, in the late 1940s, as the period when his problems with the press began. There is some evidence, however, that his basic attitudes toward the Fourth Estate developed many years earlier. At the age of sixteen he wrote and delivered a prize-winning speech, "Our Privileges under the Constitution," in which he said:

During the struggle for freedom, our forefathers were in constant danger of punishment for exercising the rights of freedom of speech and freedom of the press. Again the cause of their danger was the intolerance of men in power toward others with different views. The framers of the Constitution provided that we, their descendants, need not fear to express our sentiments as they did.

Yet the question arises: How much ground do these privileges cover? There are some who use them as a cloak for covering libelous, indecent, and injurious statements against their fellow men. Should the morals of this nation be offended and polluted in the name of freedom of speech or freedom of the press?

In the words of Lincoln, the individual can have no rights against the best interests of society. Furthermore, there are those who, under the pretense of freedom of speech and freedom of the press, have incited riots, assailed our patriotism, and denounced the Constitution itself. They have used constitutional privileges to protect the very act by which they wished to destroy the Constitution. Consequently laws have justly been provided for punishing those who abuse their constitutional privileges—laws which do not limit these privileges, but which provide that they may not be instrumental in destroying the Constitution which insures them. We must obey these laws, for they have been passed for our own welfare.[1]

Here, enunciated by a very young Richard Nixon, is the first principle in his philosophy of the press: there is nothing sacrosanct about the First Amendment.

Nixon, a native of Whittier, California, went on to Whittier College and Duke University Law School. He then returned home to work for a local law firm and married Thelma Catherine Patricia Ryan. In 1942 Nixon went to work for the Office of Price Administration in Washington, D.C., and eight months later applied for a navy commission. Three months before his military career ended in January 1946, he received a telegram from a group of local Republican leaders in Whittier inquiring whether he would be interested in running for Congress. He replied in the affirmative, and the group crowned him as its candidate.[2]

Realizing the neophyte politician would need help, the group's chairman contacted Murray A. Chotiner, a Beverly Hills lawyer and public relations specialist who had managed California Governor Earl Warren's successful campaign and was then involved in publisher William Knowland's race for the U.S. Senate. Chotiner agreed to help Nixon as a part-time consultant.

It was an augural event. In the years to come Chotiner would exercise a powerful influence on Nixon's career. Chotiner was a short, stocky, shrewd, preeminently pragmatic political gut-fighter who seemed to have but one interest in life: winning elections. His methods remained secret until 1955 when a reporter obtained the transcript of a fourteen thousand-word Chotiner lecture and published it. Among his precepts were:

• "Never let the public know all your opinions."

• "Advance to the attack but side-step the smear. It is not a smear, if you please, when you point out the record of your opponent. Of course, it is always a smear, naturally, when it is directed to your candidate."

• "Organize a Democratic or Independent 'front.' At the very beginning of a campaign, Republicans should make sure they have a separate organization of Democrats or Independents or whatever you want to call them."

• "Create a favorable image with the press."[3]

The Nixon-Chotiner strategies worked, and Richard Nixon was sent to Congress with a victory margin of 15,592 votes.[4]

In his first few months as a lawmaker Nixon labored to understand the idiosyncrasies and learn the customs observed in the unfamiliar world of Capitol Hill. He was but one of 531 faces in the Eightieth

Congress. "I had the same lost feeling in those early days that I had when I first went into the military service," he later said.[5] But he was young and ambitious. And he had the good fortune to be assigned a position on the House Un-American Activities Committee (HUAC), whose function was to ferret subversives from American government and society.

The vehicle that launched the obscure freshman congressman into the national spotlight was Alger Hiss, a well-born intellectual and important former State Department official accused of being a member of an underground Communist group. In a sensational investigation Nixon relentlessly pursued Hiss, who eventually was convicted of perjury and sentenced to five years in prison.

Many newsmen who covered the Hiss affair and several who subsequently investigated it recall a Nixon who was comfortable with the press. Nixon was "one of the most useful 'leaks' that friendly correspondents could seek out." wrote Theodore H. White. "With the nation then at a hysteria pitch in the great Red hunt . . . there were many friendly correspondents, and their stories of the young California patriot on the train of a conspiracy made Nixon a national figure."[6] Julian Goodman, later chairman of the board of the National Broadcasting Company, recalled that Nixon was extremely helpful to radio reporters seeking access to the HUAC hearings.[7] "Most of the working press had been far from hostile during the Hiss case," wrote David Halberstam, "and Nixon was regarded by the main working reporters as the prime and most reliable source on the committee." Nixon formed a close alliance with Bert Andrews of the *New York Herald Tribune*, who "proved to be an invaluable connection and friend. He not only helped brief the younger, rawer Nixon on strategy, he helped legitimize him with other reporters." There was some editorial support for Hiss in the beginning, concluded Halberstam, but in the end, "it was Hiss who finally suffered from bad press relations. Nor was Hiss very much of a symbol to working reporters. Most of them thought he was guilty of perjury."[8]

In Nixon's mind, however, it was different. It had been his first great "crisis," he later said, and he had triumphed. But he had paid a stiff price: "As an aftermath of the case, I was subjected to an utterly unprincipled and vicious smear campaign. Bigamy, forgery, drunkenness, insanity, thievery, anti-Semitism, perjury—the whole gamut of misconduct in public office, ranging from unethical to downright criminal activities—all these were among the charges that were hurled against me, some publicly and others through whispering campaigns which were even more difficult to counteract."[9] His pursuit of Hiss, he repeated in his book *Six Crises,* "left a residue of hatred and hostility toward me . . . among substantial segments of the press and the intellectual community."[10] He was still brooding over it on November 7, 1962, when, in what he called his "last press conference," he gave vent to his innermost feelings: "And as I leave the press, all I can say is this: For sixteen years, ever since the Hiss case, you've had a lot of fun—a lot of fun—that you've had an opportunity to attack me and I think I've given as good as I've taken."[11]

From the Hiss experience evolved the second principle in Richard Nixon's philosophy of the press: reporters are liberal, favor leftist causes, and dislike Richard Nixon.

Nixon ran for Congress again in 1948, easily retained his seat, and shortly after announced his candidacy for the U.S. Senate. His 1950 race, once again guided by Murray Chotiner, is often recalled as a classic example of the smear campaign. Nixon painted his opponent, former actress Helen Gahagan Douglas, as a Communist sympathizer. Chotiner printed a half-million copies of her liberal-to-moderate voting record on pink paper and had them distributed across the state. So no one would miss the message, Nixon repeated the calumny: "Helen Gahagan Douglas is pink right down to her underwear." He won by a resounding 680,000 votes.[12]

In July 1952 General Dwight D. Eisenhower selected Richard Nixon as his vice-presidential running mate, and a short time later *Time* magazine featured the young senator on its cover. Nixon, exulted *Time*'s scribes, was "a good-looking, dark-haired young man with a manner both aggressive and modest, and a personality to delight any political barker. He seemed to have everything—a fine TV manner, an attractive family, a good war record, deep sincerity and religious faith, a Horatio Alger-like career."[13]

Nixon's bubble burst in September when several reporters heard about a secret fund collected for him by a group of wealthy Californians. Columnists Drew Pearson and Jack Anderson asked the Nixon camp about the rumor and received a call from William P. Rogers, who was then with the campaign train in Montana. Rogers, who would become secretary of state in 1969, had represented Pearson in several libel cases and knew him well. But Rogers was not friendly this time. He told Anderson that if he and Pearson ran the story, "Nixon would have no recourse but to retaliate by discrediting Drew as a Communist operative."[14] A short time later columnist Peter Edson caught Nixon following an appearance on "Meet the Press" and asked about the fund. The vice-presidential candidate denied the fund was secret and claimed the money was used to offset legitimate expenses incurred in his official role as a senator. In fact, he told Edson, the details could be obtained by calling Dana Smith, the fund's treasurer. Nixon then gave Edson Smith's telephone number. Four reporters called Smith on the same day to ask about the fund.[15]

Despite Nixon's claim that he was innocently accepting money only to help out with legitimate expenses, there was considerable evidence of a quid pro quo. According to Jack Anderson:

He had intervened with the Justice Department in behalf of a $100,000 tax refund for the lawyer who set up the fund, Dana Smith; Nixon had again interceded for Smith, this time with the American ambassador in Cuba, to help Smith out of a jam occasioned by his failure to pay a $4,200 gambling debt at Havana's Club Sans Souci; again two oilmen contributors, Tyler Woodward and William O. Anderson, who had been refused government permission to explore for oil on a military reservation, were now the beneficiaries of a Nixon bill to open up that reservation for exploration.[16]

On September 18, 1952, Nixon was whistle-stopping on the West Coast when the story broke in the *New York Post*. His first thought, he later wrote, was that "the *Post* story did not worry me. It was to be expected. The *Post* was and still is the most partisan Democratic paper in the country. It had done an unusually neat smear job."[17] That was the Chotineresque message he began preaching to the crowds as he traveled about, but it proved an inadequate defense. The *New York Herald Tribune*, a Republican paper and traditional Nixon supporter, called on him to withdraw from the ticket.[18] Eisenhower's closest associates gave him the same advice, but Nixon refused to make any move until he had talked to Ike himself. Eisenhower finally called and told Nixon, in essence, that it was up to him. Nixon replied that he wanted a chance to tell his side of the story.

Nixon then turned to Murray Chotiner, who provided another lesson in how to deal with the press: "Every time you get before an audience, you win them. What we have to do is get you before the biggest possible audience so that you can talk over the heads of the press to the people. The people, I am convinced, are for you but the press is killing you." Nixon conferred with his other advisers; they all told him the same thing: "Everyone agreed that somehow I had to get an opportunity to tell my story to millions rather than to the thousands who were coming out to hear me at the whistle-stops. There was only one way to do this—through a national television broadcast."[19]

Principle 3 in the Nixon philosophy of the press: a skillful politician can use television to end run reporters.

The possibility of going on a network public affairs panel show such as "Meet the Press" was considered, but Chotiner advised against the idea. Such a show said Chotiner, according to Nixon, "would be a bad format because the program should give me an opportunity to state my side alone, without interruption by possibly unfriendly press questioners." When he announced his intentions, reporters clamored for some hint of what Nixon would say, but he was adamant: "This time I was determined to tell my story directly to the people rather than to funnel it to them through a press account. Consequently, [a press aide] made arrangements for the reporters to see my speech at television monitors in a separate room, with no advance text and with no notice of what I would say."[20]

Principle 4: When you take your message directly to the people, control it as tightly as possible; keep the press comfortable, but do not give it any news.

The famous Checkers speech has come to be regarded as a classic. In the words of David Wise, Nixon "invoked Pat's Republican cloth coat, his little girl Tricia, and his little black and white cocker spaniel dog ('regardless of what they say about it, we are going to keep it')."[21] It was an evasive, folksy, blatant appeal to the emotions, as well as a masterful display of practical politics. In the end Nixon threw the ball back to Eisenhower by calling on other candidates in the race to join him in disclosing their finances. Because of some questionable financial arrangements of his own, Eisenhower would never do this and Nixon knew it.[22]

Nixon left the studio with mixed feelings about his performance, but press aide Jim Bassett reassured him: "What the reporters think about the content of the speech is not important now. That's an old story anyway. The big story now is not the speech itself but the public reaction to it and on that one we can't help but win."[23] Bassett had gauged the situation expertly. A group of young supporters—a youthful H. R. Haldeman among them—gathered at the studio to cheer Nixon.[24] Millions of telephone calls, telegrams, and letters poured into the Republican National Committee headquarters and other GOP offices around the country. After some hesitation, Ike met Nixon in Wheeling, West Virginia, and told him, "Dick, you're my boy." Nixon wept on Senator William Knowland's shoulders.[25]

In later years Nixon often spoke of his battle over the fund and of how he faced "the overwhelming hostile reaction of the press."[26] But in fact the affair was handled cautiously by many of the nation's largest and most respected newspapers, the vast majority of which had endorsed Eisenhower. The *New Republic* polled seventy daily newspapers in forty-eight states and found that only seven published the story the first day they had it. A number of the papers that did carry it buried it in the back pages. The AP waited seven hours after getting the story before putting it on the wires. Other papers mentioned the story only in connection with Nixon's subsequent charge that it was a Communist plot. But to Richard Nixon the Checkers affair was a turning point in his relations with the press.[27]

Nixon learned two more lessons about television in 1959 and 1960, the first to his delight and the second to his chagrin. In 1959 Nixon visited Moscow, and his host, Nikita Khrushchev, took him to the Moscow Fair. At the U.S. exhibition Khrushchev began taunting the vice-president, and the two leaders launched into what came to be known as the kitchen debates. William Safire, later a speechwriter in the Nixon White House, was the public relations specialist representing the home builder in whose "kitchen" one of the debates took place. He watched as Nixon appeared to lose an actual debate but seemed to win when television tapes of the event were played. And Nixon seemed to comprehend and appreciate the phenomenon. "What's on the tube is what counts," he would tell Safire. "I've never been able to get anybody in my speech operation who understood the power of television."[28]

The following year Nixon moved out of Eisenhower's shadow and prepared to run for the presidency. The 1960 race proved to be one of the closest in the nation's history, and Kennedy's victory has often been attributed to his superior performance in the nationally televised debates. There has been much speculation over why Nixon agreed to debate his opponent. As the vice-president he was well known and had much to lose, little to gain. Earlier in the campaign the proposal was rejected outright. "In 1946," Nixon told aides, "a damn fool incumbent named Jerry Voorhis debated a young unknown lawyer and it cost him the election." But suddenly, without consulting anyone, he changed his mind.[29]

The debates were supposed to end the old-fashioned way of politicking—the hand shaking, back slapping, and arm twisting; the dodging and ducking; the seamy business of saying one thing in one part of the country and something else in another, depending on the audience. From this point on, the pundits reasoned, candidates would have to deal with issues. Whatever they said would be heard by the entire electorate. Just the opposite proved to be true.[30]

The Kennedy style was worrying Nixon as the debates approached. The urbane Harvard graduate, scion of a wealthy and socially prominent family, was everything that Nixon imagined himself not to be.

on the road? Who demonstrated for them the importance of image, the necessity for a good public relations program, and PR experts to implement it? Where did they learn the flood gimmick and the Statue of Liberty trick? Who invented the office of communications? Most important, who taught modern presidents that it does not pay to provoke the press personally, that it is better to let subordinates administer the spankings?

The answer: Richard Nixon. The post-Nixon presidents do not admit it and do not hang their diplomas on their walls. But they are all graduates of the Richard Nixon School of Media Manipulation.

The vice-president sensed that the Kennedy image would be an advantage. With only a few minutes to state their positions on extremely complex issues, the content of their answers would mean little. What would matter was how they looked to the 70 million Americans watching.

Nixon paid too little attention to his own instincts. He campaigned hard right up until the first debate in Chicago on September 26, 1960, grabbing his free moments to study for the occasion. His television advisers were excommunicated and had to make arrangements with little consultation with their candidate. They did what they could, jockeying lights and tables. They asked that Nixon's left profile not be photographed. When the candidate finally arrived at the studio, he made only one request: that the cameramen not focus on him when he was wiping sweat from his face. He refused makeup, permitting only a light coating of facial powder to hide his heavy beard.

When the red light went on, Nixon appeared nervous, taut, and hollow eyed. The heavy campaign schedule and an eleven-day stay in the hospital with a bad knee some weeks before had combined to cause a weight loss. His suit looked baggy and tended to blend with the background. His shirt collar hung loose. As the panel began asking questions, Nixon tended to go on the defensive, answering Kennedy point by point and ignoring his huge audience beyond the camera. Kennedy, by contrast, appeared rested, calm, informed, cocksure. Whatever the question, he aimed his answer at the millions of Americans viewing the program in their living rooms.[31]

It was an unmitigated disaster for Nixon, In the second, third, and fourth debates, he managed to recover somewhat from his initial poor performance, but it was too late. Surveys showed than an overwhelming percentage of the television audience had judged Kennedy the victor.[32]

Nixon later admitted the folly of his concentration on the issues. In a remarkably frank self-appraisal in his book, *Six Crises*, he reached this conclusion:

I spent too much time on substance and too little time on appearance: I paid too much attention to what I was going to say and too little time on how I would look. Again, what must be recognized is that television has increasingly become the medium through which the great majority of the voters get their news and develop their impressions of the candidates. There are, of course, millions of people who still rely primarily on newspapers and magazines in making up their minds on how they will vote. But the fact remains, one bad camera angle on television can have far more effect on the election outcome than a major mistake in writing a speech which is then picked up and criticized by columnists and editorial writers. I do not mean to suggest that what a candidate says is not important; in a presidential election, in particular, it should be all-important. What I do mean to say is that where votes are concerned, a paraphrase of what Mr. Khrushchev claims is an "ancient Russian proverb" could not be more controlling: "One TV picture is worth ten thousand words."[33]

Principle 5: when addressing the electorate directly by television, image is more important than substance.

Despite his own mistakes in the 1960 campaign, Nixon still felt the press had much to do with the outcome. "I have always felt," he later said, "that a reporter has a right to any political bias whatever provided that he keeps it out of what are supposed to be straight news stories." This, he felt, they did not do in 1960: "During the campaign they quite naturally—and often as not, perhaps, quite unconsciously—favored the candidate of the party of their choice."[34]

If Nixon's coverage lacked zest, there may have been reasons other than political bias. David Halberstam covered the 1960 campaign and noted later:

I was twenty-six years old and working for the Nashville *Tennessean* that fall and, like every other reporter who covered that campaign, no matter how briefly, I will never forget the difference between the two camps: the ease and camaraderie of the Kennedy plane and camp, the capacity of the Kennedy people to imply that this was one big happy family and to suggest that the Kennedys were for the good, civilized things that civilized mankind wanted; the Nixon camp, by contrast, filled with the shadows of mutual suspicion and distrust and barely concealed anger, a coldness and distance which somehow implied darker things covered up and hidden. Nixon held the press at bay, even the pool press; Kennedy, as Teddy White wrote, would as soon have flown off without his copilot as leave his pool reporters behind.[35]

But Nixon did not see it that way. He doubted, he said, "if any official in Washington had greater, more sincere respect for the press corps than I, or had tried to be more fair in his treatment of them." His opponent, he claimed, had done just the opposite and had gotten away with it: "Kennedy, Salinger, and several top members of the Kennedy staff followed the practice during the campaign of complaining to individual reporters about the fairness of their stories. In several instances, Kennedy himself and members of his staff went over the heads of the reporters to their publishers and to the top officials of the radio and television networks, when they felt they were getting less than fair treatment in news stories or on TV and radio reports.

Never once during the course of the campaign did I resort to such tactics, regardless of what opinion I had of the coverage of my activities."[36]

Principle 6: it pays to complain about press coverage.

In 1962 Nixon decided to run for the office of governor of California against the Democratic incumbent, Edmund G. "Pat" Brown. Many of Nixon's key advisers recommended against the race, but he was adamant, and a campaign team was assembled. Among them were names that later became well known: H. R. Haldeman, campaign manager; Maurice Stans, financial chairman; Herbert Kalmbach, campaign chairman for southern California; Caspar Weinberger, state GOP chairman; John Ehrlichman, chief advance man for southern California; Herbert Klein, press spokesman; Ronald Ziegler, advertising adviser; and Dwight Chapin, stenographer-clerk.[37]

Seventy percent of the California papers endorsed the former vice-president. Their coverage of the campaign, moreover, was a model of objectivity—perhaps too much so. They simply permitted the candidates to speak and then faithfully recorded their comments. Much was said that needed interpretation and background, but this was not provided. "The effect on the reader," wrote San Francisco State College professor Walter Gieber, "was apparently the effect gained from watching two wrestlers work out in the mud." If the press helped to defeat Nixon, it did so only by quoting his own words. As one reporter remarked to Gieber, "If there's anything dirtier than libel, it's telling the facts."[38]

Nixon lost.[39] With the election returns in, his top press aide, Herb Klein, approached the candidate in his room in the Beverly Hilton Hotel in Los Angeles to urge his concession. Klein had just come from the Cadoro Room below, where reporters were waiting for Nixon's appearance. "They're all waiting," Klein told Nixon. "You've got to go down." "Screw them," Nixon said.

His aides and advisers discussed the situation for a few minutes. "Screw them," the former vice-president kept repeating. Klein finally went down to give a statement on Nixon's behalf.[40] While he was bantering with reporters, Nixon suddenly appeared, took the microphone, and launched into what has become known as his last press conference:

Good morning, gentlemen. Now that Mr. Klein has made his statement, and now that all the members of the press are so delighted that I have lost, I'd like to make a statement of my own. . . .

I appreciate the press coverage of this campaign. I think each of you covered it the way you saw it. You had to write it in the way according to your belief on how it would go. I don't believe publishers should tell reporters to write one way or another. I want them all to be free. . . .

I am proud of the fact that I defended my opponent's patriotism. You gentlemen didn't report it, but I am proud I did that. I am proud also that I defended the fact that he was a man of good motives, a man that I disagreed with very strongly, but a man of good motives. I want that—for once, gentlemen—I would appreciate it if you would write what I say, in that respect. I think it's very important that you write it. *In the lead. In the lead.* . . .

I say these things about the press because I understand that that was one of the things you were particularly interested in. There'll be no question at this point on that score. I'll be glad to answer other questions. . . .

One last thing . . . I said a couple of things with regard to the press that I noticed some of you looked a little irritated about. And my philosophy with regard to the press had never really gotten through. And I want it to get through. This cannot be said for any other American political figure today, I guess. Never in my sixteen years of campaigning have I complained to a publisher, to an editor, about the coverage of a reporter. I believe a reporter has got a right to write it as he feels it. I believe if a reporter believes that one man ought to win rather than the other, whether it's on television or radio or the like, he ought to say so. I will say to that reporter sometimes that I think, "Well, look, I wish you'd give my opponent the same going over that you give me."

And as I leave the press, all I can say is this: for sixteen years, ever since the Hiss case, you've had a lot of fun—a lot of fun—that you've had an opportunity to attack me and I think I've given as good as I've taken. . . . I think that it's time that our great newspapers have at least the same objectivity, the same fullness of coverage, that television has. And I can only say thank God for television and radio for keeping the newspapers a little more honest. . . .

I leave you gentlemen, now, and you will now write it. You will interpret it. That's your right. But as I leave you I want you to know—just think how much you're going to be missing. You won't have Nixon to kick around anymore, because, gentlemen, this is my last press conference, and it will be one in which I have welcomed the opportunity to test wits with you.

I have always respected you. I have sometimes disagreed with you. But unlike some people, I've never canceled a subscription to a paper, and also I never will.

I believe in reading what my opponents say, and I hope that what I have said today will at least make television, radio and the press, first, recognize the great responsibility they have to report all the news and, second, recognize that they have a right and a responsibility, if they're against a candidate, give him the shaft, but also recognize if they give him the shaft, put one lonely reporter on the campaign who will report what the candidate says now and then. Thank you gentlemen, and good day.[41]

As he finished, Nixon turned and strode from the room. Behind him stood a disconsolate Herb Klein, normally a statue of placidity, his eyes now focused dolefully on the floor. "I know you don't agree," Nixon said to Klein as he passed by. "I gave it to them right in the behind. It had to be said, goddamit. It had to be said."[42] To H. R. Haldeman, he declared, "I finally told those bastards off, and every goddamned thing I said was true."[43]

Principle 7: if you feel so strongly about your press coverage that you cannot complain about it with eloquence and dignity, then let someone else do your complaining for you.

Principle 8 came hard on the heels of principle 7. On the Sunday after the election ABC's Howard K. Smith hosted a half-hour documentary, "The Political Obituary of Richard M. Nixon." Four guests appeared—two pro-Nixon, two critical of him. One of the latter was Alger Hiss, who said of Nixon's investigation of him: "He was less interested in developing the facts objectively than in seeking ways of making a preconceived plan appear plausible. I regard his actions as motivated by ambition, by personal self-serving." Smith and ABC were inundated with telephone calls. Eighty thousand letters and telegrams poured in from irate citizens, including some, curiously, who admittedly had not seen the show. Walter Annenberg, later to become Nixon's ambassador to the United Kingdom, ordered two stations that he owned to cancel the show. The *Chicago Tribune* decried the incident on its front page. The Pacific Hawaiian Company of California dropped some of its plans for advertising. The Kemper Insurance Company attempted to cancel half a million dollars in advertising. And the Schick Safety Razor Company threatened to break a million-dollar contract with the network.[44]

Principle 8: countless Americans deeply resent the press, and they will express their anger if sufficiently stimulated.

After his disastrous defeat in California, most political experts thought Nixon was finished politically. He had other ideas. He moved east, accepted a well-paying partnership in a New York law firm, and began a concentrated program of foreign travel. Ostensibly he was globe-trotting for business purposes, but he spent much of his time with world leaders. During the 1964 campaign he made 150 appearances in thirty-six states for presidential contender Barry Goldwater and other Republican candidates. At a cocktail party in St. Louis in late 1965 he was cornered by a young, aggressive editorial writer named

Patrick Buchanan. If Nixon was going to run in 1968, Buchanan said, he wanted to be there. A few months later Buchanan joined Nixon's staff as a researcher and speechwriter. It was the first overt sign of a plan he had been nurturing for many months: Richard Nixon was going to attempt another run at the White House. "I did not reveal to my family or anyone else that this was what I had in mind," he later wrote. "I knew that Pat and the girls would again be disappointed. But I had finally come to the realization that there was no other life for me but politics and public service."[45]

In dealing with the press in his 1968 campaign, Nixon put to use all the lessons he had learned over the years. He hired expert public relations help and, for most of the race, left his campaign in their competent hands. As for reporters he pampered them and showered them with materials, but he cut them off almost completely from his other activities.

Jules Witcover, then with the Newhouse newspaper chain, followed Nixon on the hustings and observed that his campaign seemed to be conducted on two tracks. One was the standard campaign of hoopla — rallies and speeches complemented by bands, parades, and cheer-leaders. In contrast to his frenetic 1960 effort, however, Nixon in 1968 carefully paced himself, making only one or two major stops a day. Most of the candidate's energy was conserved for the second track. This was his media campaign — the low-keyed, tightly controlled television and radio commercials and shows in which he attempted to convey his ease and expertise in dealing with weighty issues.[46]

Planning for the media blitz began in June 1967 shortly after Nixon received a lengthy memorandum from his old campaign manager, H. R. Haldeman, advising the extensive use of television in the upcoming race. "The time has come for political campaigning — its techniques and strategies — to move out of the dark ages and into the brave new world of the omnipresent eye," wrote Haldeman, who would not join Nixon's organization on a full-time basis for almost a year. The advertising man's advice called for the elimination of barn-storming and frenzied rallies and the packaging of Richard Nixon. He would sell Nixon like a new soap or soda pop. Within days after the receipt of the Haldeman memo Nixon's campaign advisers were at work devising a television strategy. They decided, said Nixon, "that I would use the question-and-answer technique extensively, not only in press conferences and public question sessions with student audiences, but also in my paid political programming."[47]

One of Nixon's law partners, Leonard Garment, began hiring advertising and television experts. One was Harry Treleaven, a former vice-president of the J. Walter Thompson advertising agency. While with the Thompson firm Treleaven had produced commercials for Lark cigarettes, Ford, Pan American airlines, RCA, and others. He had also worked on the political campaign that put Congressman George Bush, Republican of Texas, in office. One of the lessons he learned from the Bush campaign, Treleaven once wrote, was that "most national issues today are so complicated, so difficult to understand, and have opinions on that they either intimidate or, more often, bore the average voter."[48] The second expert Garment hired was Frank Shakespeare, a former CBS official and ardent political conservative. It was this trio—Garment, Treleaven, and Shakespeare—who put together the media campaign.[49]

As the Nixon team began preparing for the first primary in New Hampshire, they consulted with and passed memoranda to each other. Harry Treleaven advised that Nixon had actually gained in popularity during his long layoff, and this, the media expert wrote, was not due to any change in Nixon but to a change in the voters. "Add a little warmth," suggested Treleaven, "a touch of humor, an aura of confidence—then publicize poll results, favorable articles, friendly quotes, and anything else that says 'winner.' "[50] William Gavin, a former high school teacher who had impressed the Nixon team with his knowledge of the media, counseled avoidance of issues: "Reason pushes the view back, it assaults him, it demands that he agree or disagree; impression can envelop him, invite him in, without making an intellectual demand, or a demand on his intellectual energies. He can receive the impression without having to think about it in a linear, structured way. When we argue with him we demand that he make the effort of replying. We seek to engage his intellect, and for most people this is the most difficult work of all. The emotions are more easily roused, closer to the surface, more malleable."[51]

Raymond Price, the former editorial writer for the *New York Herald Tribune*, agreed with Treleaven that Nixon the man was in fine shape, but his image needed restructuring: *"We have to be very clear on this point: that the response is to the image, not to the man*, since 99 percent of the voters have no contact with the man. It's not what's *there* that counts, it's what's projected—and, carrying it one step further, it's not what *he* projects but rather what the voter receives. It's not the man we have to change, but rather the *received impression*. And this impression often depends more on the medium and its use than it does on the candidate himself."[52]

On his first day of campaigning in New Hampshire Nixon slipped out of his hotel unnoticed and traveled to the town of Hillsboro, where he met with a panel of ten citizens and ten college students, all hand-picked, for an 'entirely unrehearsed" discussion. It was filmed, and selected excerpts subsequently were used in television commercials throughout the state. Reporters covering Nixon were disturbed over being left out. Patrick Buchanan, then acting as a press spokesman, explained that they might "inhibit those people" on the panel. Reporters were not invited along, he said, "so that people would feel at ease."[53]

Nixon's face and his commercials became standard fare for television viewers. To the traveling press, however, he was a virtual stranger, but not, surprisingly, a hostile stranger. The early team that guided Nixon through the 1968 primaries—Buchanan, Garment, Safire, Price, and old friend Bob Finch—were generally held in high regard by reporters. There was some bickering, but it was considered little more than the normal give-and-take between a campaign organization and the press that covered it. Nixon himself appeared to have softened his strident approach to newsmen, occasionally mingling and bantering with them. Stories began to appear describing the "new Nixon." Then shortly after the last primary battle in Oregon, a new person joined the team, and things changed. As Nixon's personal secretary of eighteen years, Rose Mary Woods, put it, "It was all so warm and friendly and cozy until suddenly, in May, Bob Haldeman arrived."[54]

Overnight, Nixon the stranger became Nixon the solitary as far as the press was concerned. "The curtain was drawn between Mr. Nixon's forward cabin and the press seats aft on his campaign plane," reported *Newsweek* magazine. "Staffers who drank, socialized with the press or mixed in the normal ribbing about the candidate were bumped from the entourage."[55] A protective cocoon was thrown around Nixon; the television end run strategy would prevail the rest of the way. Haldeman later offered his explanation of why Nixon suddenly called off his already limited contacts with the press: "They [had] responded with much kinder treatment than in the old days. But this never fooled Nixon. He knew they were still the enemy and they could not be trusted. This was only a temporary aberration. Things would revert to normal before long."[56]

Was Haldeman accurately describing Nixon's feelings, or was he really reflecting his own prejudices? Or was it a bit of both—Haldeman reinforcing Nixon's own worst instincts? Whatever the answer the candidate had stormed through the primaries, and he arrived at the Republican convention in Miami Beach with the nomination wrapped up. His plane landed at the Miami International Airport, where a crowd of 2,000 awaited him at 6:25 P.M. At precisely 6:38 P.M. he stepped from the aircraft for a prearranged live appearance on the network news shows.[57]

Nixon's well-oiled machine maneuvered him through the convention in fine style. He gave a punchy acceptance speech and basked afterward in the remembrance of it: "The press won't like it at all, they'll climb the wall. None of them could write a speech like that, one that reaches the folks, and they hate me for it. . . . They call me 'intelligent, cool, with no sincerity'—and then it kills them when I show 'em I know how people feel. I'd like to see Rocky or Romney or Lindsay do a moving thing like that 'impossible dream' part, where I changed my voice. Reagan's an actor, but I'd like to see him do that."[58]

Shortly after his nomination Nixon appeared at a press conference and proclaimed, "I am not going to barricade myself into a television studio and make this an antiseptic campaign."[59] But it was—except that it was even more efficiently antiseptic than his primary races. Anyone searching for reasons to vote for the candidate could find them, for there was a Nixon that catered to any fancy. On the hustings he was aggressive; in the television studio he was confident and knowledgeable; in radio speeches he was pensive; in campaign literature he was the man most world leaders knew and trusted.[60] He leaped at every oportunity to get before the public, going so far as to appear on NBC's comedy show, "Laugh In," where he cooperated in a slapstick routine.[61]

In the wake of his success in the primaries, Nixon's distrust of television seemed to evaporate. He began to pay acute attention to technique. "Hubert just doesn't know how to talk to that tube," he said after watching Humphrey's acceptance speech at the Democratic convention. He worried that the opposition was devoting more attention to television than was his team. "Be sure we outspend them on television, especially in the last three weeks," he repeatedly urged Haldeman. "Remember '60—I never want to be outspent again."[62]

A staple of the television campaign was the one-hour panel show in which Nixon appeared before groups of local citizens in various cities to answer questions. The queries were a snap for the experienced Nixon, and he invariably handled them with ease. In the staged shows panelists were always carefully chosen to get balance—a black, a Jew, a housewife, and ethnic or two. Studios were packed with Republican spectators whose enthusiastic and cued applause gave the impression that Nixon would be joyously mobbed if the crowd could but get to him.[63]

While the panel shows were convincing the voters that Nixon had an encyclopedic grasp of the issues, other television advertising campaigns were buttressing his image in other ways. The candidate himself made different commercials for different parts of the country to demonstrate that he understood local problems. While filming these he was careful to keep people out of his line of vision "so I don't go shifting my eyes." To demonstrate he was well thought of by the famous, Nixon also used television spots containing the endorsements of such celebrities as Art Linkletter, Connie Francis, Pat Boone, and John Wayne.[64]

Image was never far from H. R. Haldeman's mind. He ordered thousands of copies of a new paperback edition of a Nixon biography scrapped because the cover depicted Nixon in an unpresidential frown. The campaign chief instructed his team to develop themes in their speeches and discussions with the press. The comeback theme emphasized Nixon's tenacity "despite the overwhelming opposition of the financial establishment and the press establishment and without huge financial resources, PR gimmicks, etc." Another theme stressed the "calibre of the Nixon team" and another the "youth of the RN organization." His purpose, said Haldeman, was to "take a leaf out of the Kennedy book and recognize that at least 50% of the credit for his win in 1960 and also for his immensely good press after the 1960 election was due to the fact that his staff and friends were constantly running their own campaigns in his behalf, and not just waiting for him to carry the ball."[65]

The campaign finished with an election-eve telethon in which Nixon answered questions called in from all over the country. Actually the queries were written in advance to conform with the answers Nixon had been rehearsing for nearly two years. When a question was called in that fit a general area, the prepared question was passed on to Nixon.[66] The tremendous effort to blanket the country with Nixon's smiling image had one overriding purpose, which Frank Shakespeare summed up:

Without television, Richard Nixon would not have a chance. He would not have a prayer of getting elected because the press would not let him get through to the people. But because he is so good on television, he will get through despite the press. The press doesn't matter anymore. . . . Television reaches so many more people. You can see it in our attitude toward print advertising. It's used only as a supplement. TV is carrying our campaign. And Nixon loves it. He's overjoyed that he no longer has to depend upon the press. . . . He has a great hostility toward the press and as President he should be shielded.[67]

Reporters covering the Nixon campaign did not need Frank Shake-speare to tell them the Nixon camp viewed them as excess baggage. They knew it because they just could not get any real news.

Before the New Hampshire primary Patrick Buchanan wrote that "rather than political reporters walking through the office, I would like to see an AP feature writer maybe and some (friendly only) mag-azine writers." He called for "controlled ads, RN smiling when cam-paigning, RN the statesman when speaking." Buchanan continued, "We don't need any press conference type stuff where RN is being baited by reporters and saying why he would oppose the rat control bill or something. We just don't need that; and it should be considered a necessary evil when we have to have it."[68]

There were press conferences, or press availabilities, as Nixon's Madison Avenue team preferred to call them, but they were usually short sessions, held as the candidate stepped off his plane to give his stock answers to local newsmen who crowded around and thrust microphones in his face. When a reporter of the regular entourage wanted answers, he had to deal with Ron Ziegler, a twenty-nine-year-old advertising expert and Haldeman protégé. Nixon was rarely avail-able. When it became impossible to ignore a reporter representing a large-circulation publication, the journalist was hustled forward to Nixon's cabin a few minutes before the plane landed so Nixon would not have to talk too long. "Three-bump interviews," some called them. Hugh Sidey termed it "fuselage journalism."[69]

Reporters were smothered, on the other hand, with a steady flow of position papers and handouts. There was always something for both morning and afternoon papers. Nor were the Sunday feature writers ignored. "We must keep control of the news," Nixon preached to his aides. "I want two or more statements a week dealing with order, two dealing with our credentials in the foreign field—play to our strength—two that have to do with the money side." But it all had to be cleverly worded, he added. "Never mention programs spe-cifically. Work up some sharp rhetoric to be included in the basic speech. If you argue specifics, you are against the old ladies and kids."[70] But when Nixon taped a television show or submitted to a local interview or gave a speech, the transcripts were never available until the next day, when reporters were safely out of the area and in a different city that called for a fresh dateline.[71] "Sure made the press work hard, writing those stories on the long speeches at the last minute," Haldeman later gloated. "Kept 'em out of mischief."[72]

After refusing interviews through most of the campaign, Nixon, with his poll ratings dropping, agreed to appear on "Face the Nation" ten days before the election. In this, the first occasion as a candidate that he faced a professional team of national reporters before the entire nation, his performance was far from perfect. The newsmen bore in relentlessly; Nixon appeared harassed, nervous, and a little irritable toward the end. One of his advisers attributed the candidate's poor showing to technical factors. "The camera height was wrong," he said, "I didn't like the chair, and there was a bad shot of the back of his head which made it look like he had a point there."[73] Even Nixon regarded these assessments as ridiculous. The experts told him, for example, that he should have smiled more. "Can you imagine? 'The war in Vietnam is terrible,' " he said to aides, and he flashed a fake, incongruous smile.[74]

His strategy worked. Richard Nixon reached his goal in 1968, and a good portion of his success undoubtedly could be attributed to the manner in which he applied the lessons he had learned about how to cope with the press. His end run had been successful; he had taken his tightly controlled message directly to the people. The reporters who had bothered him in the past had been courteously dealt with, but as far as hard news was concerned, they had been kept in the dark.

Would the grand strategy work once Nixon was in office? Would he still be able to control the flow of information to the public? In his memoirs he described what was going through his mind during the interregnum, and his words revealed that he had learned something about manipulation, intimidation, and evasion of the press:

Since the advent of television as our primary means of communication and source of information modern Presidents must have specialized talents at once more superficial and more complicated than those of their predecessors. They must try to master the art of manipulating the media not only to win in politics but in order to further the programs and causes they believe in; at the same time they must avoid at all costs the charge of trying to manipulate the media. In the modern presidency, concern for image must rank with concern for substance. . . .

I knew that as President my relations with the media would be at best an uneasy truce. Some of the problems were simply institutional. . . . But in my case the problems were more than just institutional. The majority of New York and Washington newspaper and television reporters, news executives, columnists, and opinion-makers are liberals. I am not, and for many years we had looked at each other across an ideological chasm that Vietnam only deepened further. After the press treatment I received during the Hiss case and the fund episode, and later after the flagrant media favoritism for Kennedy in 1960, I considered the influential majority of the news media to be part of my political opposition. . . .

I was prepared to have to do combat with the media in order to get my views and my programs to the people, and despite all the power and public visibility I would enjoy as President, I did not believe that this combat would be between equals. The media are far more powerful than the President in creating public awareness and shaping public opinion, for the simple reason that the media always have the last word. . . .

Within the White House I created the post of Director of Communications for the executive branch. Herb Klein, who had served as my press spokesman in 1960 and 1962, headed this new office. One of his tasks was to stay in touch with the media in the rest of the country, bring their reports to me, and get my ideas out to them."[75]

A more graphic hint of what lay in store for the press came in the aftermath of Nixon's victory speech. The Nixon team of advance men gathered around to congratulate each other. Roy Goodearle, a tall, stocky Agnew aide, turned to his comrades and said, "Why don't we all get a member of the press and beat him up? I'm tired of being nice to them."[76]

Appeasement: "Give the Press a Lot of Copy, Then They Won't Have Too Much to Squeal About"

As they prepared to enter the White House, Richard Nixon and his aides promised that the new administration would be an open one. They would strive, they said, for "a spirit of openness, honesty, and mutual respect."[1] By "open" Nixon meant he would go before the public more often than any president before him. The problem for reporters was that he would do it by television. The press that would find the administration accessible was the hinterlands press, the smaller dailies and weeklies across the country that were not represented in Washington by their own correspondents. The national press, in short, was nonessential.

But Nixon realized that some means had to be devised to keep the Washington press diverted while he executed his end runs. The answer to this problem evolved out of his 1968 campaign. "Give the press a lot of copy," he had lectured his aides in September, "then they won't have too much to squeal about."[2] There would be little to gain by deliberately antagonizing the press, so he would not do that unless it became necessary. As he had done in the campaign, he would be as amenable to reporters as his prejudices and desire for privacy permitted. He would see that they always had something to write about. It would be nothing controversial or unfavorable, but it would be something.

The plan worked so well that two years after Nixon was sworn in, H. R. Haldeman bragged to some colleagues: "Considering the opposition of the newspapers like the *Times*, and magazines like *Life* and *Look*, it's something of a miracle that [Nixon] survived so well. The secret is, he has not made an effort to cater to the press, he ignored them and talked directly to the country without using the press as a filter. Meanwhile, we have kept the press serviced, not using him, which is the way we want it."[3]

The keep-them-comfortable-but-keep-them-ignorant phase of Nixon's grand strategy began on election day 1968 when the candidate flew from Los Angeles to New York with but one pool reporter, Anthony Day of the *Philadelphia Evening* and *Sunday Bulletin*, aboard his plane. The meagre representation was not the choice of the journalists who had been following Nixon since the New Hampshire primary. Day repeatedly sought permission to speak with the president elect but was refused even a three-bump interview. Once Nixon strolled past the reporter but said nothing to him.[4]

A few months after taking the oath, Nixon refurbished Air Force One, the presidential Boeing 707 jet, and had it divided into four compartments. The president's new quarters were now the farthest forward in the plane; the press was all the way to the rear. Nixon did not appreciate Lyndon Johnson's arrangement in which the press was berthed next to the president.[5]

Putting distance between the president and the meddlesome press became an obsession in the Nixon White House. Like one of his boyhood heroes, Woodrow Wilson, Nixon zealously guarded his privacy. He seemed to thrive on isolation and frequently spent long periods without contact with others.[6] Even telephone contact with the president was limited. Lyndon Johnson once visited Nixon and was amazed to find that he had only one telephone on his desk, and it was equipped with only three buttons.[7] Nixon disliked the "laying on of the tongues," as his aides put it, much preferring to have his information put in memorandum form rather than receiving it orally.[8] Sometimes his assistants segregated all of the paperwork dealing with a particular issue and bound it in large black notebooks. Nixon then took these home in the evening or with him to the presidential retreat at Camp David, Maryland, or to Key Biscayne, Florida, for study. The president's men always left an "order blank" in the back of the book for Nixon's thoughts and instructions.[9]

The president even isolated himself from his cabinet. When he called a meeting of the cabinet secretaries, it was usually only for the purpose of telling them about his plans.[10] Senators, congressmen, reporters, prominent citizens, special interest groups—all were regularly turned away from the White House. The situation became so bad at one point, reported *Time* magazine, that senators found themselves "ludicrously blurting ideas to Nixon during 15-second encounters in White House reception lines."[11] Others tried to grab a few moments of the president's time during Sunday religious services at the White House. Once Transportation Secretary John Volpe, after being denied an audience with Nixon for months, finally managed to slip into the Oval Office as an escort for a visiting archbishop.[12]

President Nixon's isolation was so perfect that even newspapers and television news shows did not penetrate it. He received almost all of his news from the summary that was prepared daily under the direction of speechwriter and in-house media watchdog Patrick Buchanan. Following a practice that had begun during the 1968 campaign, Buchanan's assistants assembled summaries of newspaper and magazine articles, editorials, columns, and news broadcasts and inserted an average of twenty-five pages per day into a blue, looseleaf notebook. The front of the binder was emblazoned with the title, "The President's Daily News Briefing," embossed in gold.

Lyndon (Mort) Allin, a former high school teacher from Wisconsin, and a staff of four culled the news in the digest from some fifty newspapers, forty magazines, network news shows, and other public affairs programs. The digest of television news was usually prepared daily by Buchanan personally. Originally items in the summary were classified according to the type of publication they were drawn from. Later they were arranged according to subject. News stories were reduced to a few paragraphs, written in a breezy, clipped style. Names were reduced to initials; acronyms abounded. The emphasis was almost always on how the administration was being viewed by reporters, sometimes characterized with snide remarks.[13] A typical item, drawn from a daily digest in the spring of 1971, stated, "NRA turns down EMK bid to address its convention." This meant that the National Rifle Association would not permit Senator Edward Kennedy of Massachusetts to speak at its convention.[14]

A longer item, which appeared in the digest on November 28, 1972, concerned a story written by John Osborne in the *New Republic*: "New Republic's Osborne w/another critical piece on RN's 'charade' and the CD [Camp David] meeting—only for public effect. Osborne says reorg. plans are the only way RN could find to create impression that 2nd term is going to be, on the domestic front, more than a mere and sterile extension. But the reporter acknowledges that restructuring is serious business in RN's view. Still he wonders why and how RN let [White House] become biggest in history."[15]

The president's aides insisted that the daily news summary was consistently written in an objective fashion. It was difficult to imagine, however, how Nixon could grasp the subtleties of prevailing public attitudes from a news digest.[16] Moreover, as press critic Ben Bagdikian pointed out in 1973, the digest was filled with mistakes "for which major news organizations would fire a reporter. Yet it is precisely the practitioners of this slovenly and misleading reporting who for five years have been lecturing the American press on accuracy, fairness and balance."[17] Author Frank Mankiewicz drew an invidious analogy. The spectre of a president who read no newspapers and viewed no television news programs and relied instead on summaries prepared by his staff, said Mankiewicz, reminded him of a letter written by Albert Speer, architect and adviser to Adolf Hitler. In "Hitler's Germany there was no free press," Speer had written, and "in the evaluation of domestic conditions Hitler was forced to rely on reports of his colleagues, which went through [chief of staff Martin] Bormann's hands and were filtered by him."[18]

Nevertheless Nixon apparently felt the news digest was sufficient to keep him current with events and referred to it as his after-breakfast "mint." He was "constantly amazed at the brilliant work done in the news summary" he once wrote to Buchanan in a marginal note. "It is invaluable to all of us."[19] On many occasions, the president scribbled notes in the margin to other assistants or dictated instructions and comments to aide Alexander Butterfield.[20]

While a boy in Whittier, California, Richard Nixon used to climb up to the bell tower of an old church his father had converted into a grocery store, and there he would sit for hours, reading and thinking in solitude. It turned into a habit that remained with him.[21] Even before he was sworn in as the thirty-seventh president, he began setting up hideaways. His most immediate escape hatch was a comfortably decorated office in the Old Executive Office Building. He retired there frequently to ponder the affairs of state and routinely used it on Wednesdays when no meetings, visitors, or picture-taking sessions were scheduled.[22]

Nowhere was the president's desire for seclusion more evident than in his frequent trips to Camp David, the one-hundred-acre presidential retreat in the forests of Maryland's Catoctin Mountains, a thirty-minute helicopter ride from the White House. Far more frequently than his predecessors—forty-two trips in his first eighteen months in office alone—Nixon retired here to swim in a heated pool, bowl, watch motion pictures, read memoranda, and write speeches. "I find that up here on top of a mountain," he once said, "it is easier for me to get on top of the job." Some irreverent staff members subsequently began referring to Camp David as "Mount Sinai."[23]

It was also easier for him to get away from reporters. The White House staff did not appreciate it when reporters followed Nixon to his mountain. Press secretary Ronald Ziegler consistently refused to permit the press to tour the facility. Originally an area was walled off with saplings for reporters to stand behind and observe the helicopter landings. But even this was declared off limits, and reporters were confined to a ten-foot by fifty-foot trailer dubbed "Poison Ivy," which contained ten telephones. Ten additional telephones were installed outside; in inclement weather newsmen had to cover themselves with plastic sheeting. The facilities were hardly sufficient for the seventy-plus reporters who regularly followed the president. Briefings were held in the helicopter hangar, but most reporters took the hint and began staying behind at the White House. The president's men encouraged this practice by piping the daily briefings from Camp David into the White House press room.[24]

Similar constraints restricted coverage of the president's activities at his winter home and office compound in Key Biscayne, Florida, and at the Western White House in San Clemente, California. Reporters who accompanied Nixon were usually quartered in hotels as far as six miles away in Key Biscayne and fifteen miles away in San Clemente. They were bused in to hear statements or briefings, then carted back to their lodgings. At Key Biscayne Nixon's neighbors were instructed to affix special stickers to their cars and had to identify themselves to guards who barricaded the street entrance. Even when Nixon was not there, the Coast Guard patroled Biscayne Bay to keep boats at least a half-mile from the presidential compound. Members of the Key Biscayne Yacht Club were warned not to bring photographers or reporters to the club. The president's close friend Bebe Rebozo docked his houseboat there and apparently feared that someone would snap a picture while Nixon was aboard. One club member allowed photographers on his vessel and "heard from Bebe" so fast it made his "head swim." Neighbors were also cautioned to avoid the press. One man who let photographers in his backyard to take pictures of the Nixon homestead also heard from Rebozo.[25]

The person charged with the job of juggling people, paper, and press in a manner that protected Nixon's privacy was his chief of staff, H. R. "Bob" Haldeman. A graduate of the University of California at Los Angeles, where he had agitated against communists and admired from afar the native son who was making life difficult for them in Washington, Haldeman took a job with the J. Walter Thompson advertising company and eventually became a vice-president and manager of the agency's Los Angeles office. He joined Nixon's 1956 campaign as an advance man and continued to help him in that capacity in the 1958 congressional campaign and the 1960 presidential race. Haldeman managed Nixon's disastrous 1962 campaign against

California Governor Pat Brown and the victorious 1968 presidential campaign.[26]

A rigid man with a stern crewcut that matched his personality, Haldeman hated anyone who challenged his authority, the counterculture, and anything associated with it.[27] Ever conscious of image, he maintained a deep tan, wore conservative suits, white shirts, narrow ties, and dictated that his assistants report for duty every day in similar uniform.[28] His memos to aides were signed with an imperial "H" because "HRH" might cause recipients to ridicule him as "His Royal Highness."[29]

Haldeman played many roles in Nixon's White House. One of them was as captain of the president's image and press policy team. Nixon himself set the policy; Haldeman reinforced it and saw that it was carried out on a day-to-day basis. "The chain of command" in the administration's "communications effort," wrote former speechwriter James Keogh, "ran directly to Haldeman and ultimately to the President himself."[30] Haldeman personally chose the White House spokespersons, whose main function was *not* to speak of anything significant. He hired Mrs. Nixon's first press secretary, Constance Stuart, and he selected Ronald Ziegler, from the Los Angeles office of J. Walter Thompson, to be the president's press representative. Herb Klein, Nixon's friend and press emissary for two decades, was given a new post, director of communications for the executive branch. A Haldeman protégé, Jeb Stuart Magruder, was installed in Klein's shop to give the chief of staff effective control of it.[31]

On occasion Haldeman personally took command of the press control operation. At White House parties, said UPI reporter Helen Thomas, Haldeman "always seemed to fear that we reporters would commit some grievous social faux pas. He stood, arms crossed like a bouncer, and glared at us as if we were potential rowdies. Once he suggested that we cover a State Dinner while standing behind velvet stanchions in the foyer of the first floor."[32]

Organizing and guarding the presidential castle, however, were the major roles assigned to Haldeman by Nixon. The president had "strong opinions," he said, about "the way a President should work" and felt that "matters brought before a President for decisions should be only those that cannot or should not be made at a lower level on the White House staff." He also regarded cabinet meetings, by and large, as "unnecessary and boring." These problems called for a "funnel" and a "gatekeeper."[33]

Haldeman pursued his gatekeeping role with a vengeance. In December 1968 he assembled staff members who had been hired to serve in the new administration and read the rules to them:

On procedure: there has always got to be a written agenda. Nobody goes in without a piece of paper on what he's going to talk about, because maybe somebody else should be there.

He will also have meetings without staff members present. We'll develop a procedure to follow up these meetings by the right staff people.

No request for Presidential time goes direct to the President. If you go to him and say, "I need an hour," he will say, "Sure, come in tomorrow at five," and seventeen people will be there tomorrow at five.

If you bring a visitor in, and he wants to ask RN to go to the Boy Scout Jamboree, turn that off beforehand. Don't let them take paperwork in to him. It goes right to the bottom of his briefcase and never gets seen again, or it gets signed and becomes an order. All paper has to go into my office, and it will get to him after it has been staffed.[34]

And that is the way the system worked. Virtually every document that Richard Nixon saw, Haldeman saw first. If Haldeman did not approve of what he read, Nixon did not see it.[35] The chief of staff also screened Nixon's telephone calls, and sometimes his rejections were harsh. A staff member once recommended that the president call a Republican senator who was mortally ill. But Nixon would eventually have to call the widow anyway, and Haldeman was not one to let the president make two calls where one would do. Thus the suggestion was turned down with the imperious command: "Wait until he dies."[36]

Haldeman scheduled Nixon's time and determined whom he would see and for how long. Congressmen were rarely welcome because, according to one who was there, Haldeman regarded them as "venal, vulnerable politicians willing, in most cases, to barter away their corrupt souls for a project in their state, a social invitation to the White House, a few words of praise from the President, or, in a few instances, to avoid investigation by the Internal Revenue Service or the Justice Department."[37] Staff members and presidential advisers were subjected to strict rules. Fed chairman Arthur Burns once left Nixon's office, remembered something he had forgotten to mention, and turned around to go back. Haldeman blocked his path: "Your appointment is over, Dr. Burns." Burns said it was an important matter and he would need but a moment. "Submit a memorandum," replied Haldeman coldly.[38]

The chief of staff's campaign to isolate Nixon reached its nadir when even the president's wife began to be shunted out of his activities. On August 11, 1970, Mrs. Nixon's press secretary, Constance Stuart, dispatched a memo to Haldeman to complain that she and her staff were being kept in the dark about the first family's travel plans.[39]

John Ehrlichman was the president's second line of defense. A graduate of UCLA, where he became a close friend of H. R. Haldeman, Ehrlichman went on to Stanford Law School and returned to his native state of Washington. He set up a law practice in Seattle, specialized in real estate and land use, and by the 1960s was reputed to be the best zoning lawyer in the city. At the urging of his old friend Haldeman, Ehrlichman joined Nixon's 1960 campaign as an advance man; he performed the same task in he 1962 California campaign and rejoined the Nixon team in June 1968 at about the same time that Haldeman arrived.[40]

In the White House Ehrlichman served as the president's chief domestic affairs adviser. He was generally thought of as less rigid and ideological than Haldeman and more gregarious and expansive. Ehrlichman's purview ran the gamut of domestic policy from general questions of health, education, and welfare to such specific chores as inquiring of the Internal Revenue Service whether Nixon could pay daughter Julie to act as a White House guide and deduct it as a business expense.[41]

Haldeman and Ehrlichman were frequently referred to as the "Berlin Wall" or "the Germans." Insiders, stung by their dictums, referred to Haldeman as "Hans" and to Ehrlichman as "Fritz."[42] A classic example of the manner in which they operated occurred when Walter Hickel, Nixon's first Secretary of the Interior, incurred their wrath and was dismissed for the transgression. In his work with the Interior Department Ehrlichman had often been irritated by the independence of Hickel and his top associates. In early 1970 he attempted to see Nixon on several occasions but was repelled by the Berlin Wall. Thoroughly frustrated the feisty Hickel finally sent Nixon a lengthy and critical letter, which found its way into reporters' hands almost immediately. A few days later Haldeman again called Hickel, this time to tell him not to come to the Sunday religious services at the White House, an exquisite form of excommunication in the eyes of those who guarded Nixon's gate. The decision was made not to fire Hickel right away but to wait until after the November elections. On Thanksgiving eve 1970, Hickel was summoned to the Oval Office where Nixon, with Ehrlichman at his side, fired his interior secretary.[43]

By his second year in office Nixon was walled off from the outside so efficiently that he apparently became concerned he was neglecting his friends. He hired an old friend, Roger E. Johnson, as a special assistant and charged him with keeping the president's "friends of the president he would like to see but doesn't have time to." But even Johnson was not going to be bothered with just casual acquaintances of the president. Any correspondents or callers, he said, would "have to be fairly close friends or they're not referred to me."[44]

The criticism over Nixon's isolation occasionally moved White House spokesmen to deny that any such situation existed. Press secretary Ziegler once carefully cited several instances when Nixon had met with outsiders. In the first sixteen months of the president's first term, he said, there had been eighteen cabinet meetings and many other meetings with subcabinet groups, including the National Security Council. White House reporters pointed out that such affairs were hardly an effective means of keeping Nixon's fingers on the public pulse.[45]

Nixon's staff was almost as isolated. Reporters were considered people to steer clear of. When contact was unavoidable, the aides and advisers were about as communicative as CIA agents.[46] Although Haldeman and Ehrlichman were the president's two most powerful assistants, they remained virtually unknown to the public throughout Nixon's first term. Even journalists who covered the administration sometimes got the two confused. It was only when the Watergate scandal began to unfold that the public began to recognize them and became aware of their tremendous power and influence.

Even when they talked publicly, Nixon's aides were unusually cautious. *Washington Post* reporter Sally Quinn once attempted to write a story on Haldeman, but he would not talk to her at all, nor would most of his friends and associates. "Several of Haldeman's friends," wrote Quinn, "first assured a reporter they would be happy to talk about him but they were busy just then and would call back. An hour later they somehow found they 'really don't know much about the guy at all.' "[47]

In the wake of the ITT affair—the furor that erupted when columnist Jack Anderson published a confidential memorandum written by International Telephone and Telegraph lobbyist Dita Beard suggesting the firm was planning to underwrite the 1972 Republican convention— the president's staff was instructed to avoid writing memos when a telephone call would suffice. The concern was that reporters would obtain the documents and publish them. In a discussion with a junior aide, reported *Time*, a Nixon assistant "produced a presidential directive cautioning against treating mere memo writing as a sign of productivity." The orders, said *Time*, "were, of course, delivered orally."[48]

The responsibility for executing the president's policy of keeping the press comfortable but ignorant fell to his press secretary, Ron Ziegler. He was admirably suited for the task, went about it with controlled enthusiasm, and accomplished it exceedingly well. While in college at the University of Southern California, Ziegler worked part-time at Disneyland, where he was a tour guide on a boat cruise through a papier-mâché jungle teeming with plastic reptiles. There he learned a litany that he sometimes recited, and in which White House correspondents claimed they found deep meaning: "My name is Ron and I'll be your guide down the rivers of adventure. As we pull away from the dock, please turn around and take a good look. You may never see it again. . . . Note the alligators. Please keep your hands inside the boat. They're always looking for a handout. . . . On your left, the natives on the bank. Please be quiet. The natives have only one aim in life—and that is to get ahead."[49]

While he was at USC Ziegler began doing volunteer work for the Republican party and made the press arrangements for a campus visit by Richard Nixon in 1960. He continued working for the party after graduation and joined the Nixon-for-governor team in 1962. His basic task during the campaign was handling the physical arrangements for the press entourage that accompanied Nixon. After his candidate's defeat Ziegler accepted a job offer from Nixon's campaign manager, H. R. Haldeman, and went to work for the J. Walter Thompson advertising agency in Los Angeles.[50] He left to join Nixon's 1968 campaign team as a press spokesman.[51]

White House correspondents began to get an idea of their place and Ziegler's when the Nixon staff was taking shape and it was announced that the president would have no press secretary; Ziegler, it was said, would be a press assistant. Haldeman, realizing that his young protégé was embarrassed by the lowly title, finally relented and Ziegler was annointed a full-fledged press secretary.[52] He turned out to be an affable, usually friendly emissary, and his handsome, innocent-looking face frequently broke into a puckish grin when he bantered with reporters. "To bait him," wrote one columnist, "would be like kicking a puppy."[53] He wore the requisite dark suit, but he occasionally defied Haldeman's white-shirt dictum by showing up in a blue one. He drank Chivas scotch, chewed two sticks of gum at once, and bridled at his Secret Service code name of "Whaleboat," a cognomen that became increasingly appropriate as his all-work, no-exercise regimen pushed his weight from a normal 180 pounds to over 200.[54]

The presidential press secretary could be arrogant, demanding, and imperious. His secretaries were compelled to carry his dirty laundry to the cleaners and shop for his clothes, bringing in items for his perusal and lugging the rejects back to the store. Other staff took his shoes to a hotel barbershop to be shined. He insisted that his coffee be served in a china cup just like the president's and his Chivas only in a cocktail glass adorned with the presidential seal. Each morning a secretary arranged his desk top with cigarettes, a presidential match pad, and breath mints.[55] Ziegler's office, just a few steps from the Oval Office, was lavishly decorated with a blue rug, sofa, arm chairs, bookshelves, a telephone with a silver receiver, and two television sets with remote control. The door that opened to the hallway leading to the press room was kept locked. Above another door, the working entrance, were two lights—one red, one white. By flipping a switch on his desk, he could flash the red light to show that visitors were not welcome.[56]

Although reporters generally found Ziegler amiable, his approach to his job frequently gave them the impression that he still believed he was fending off plastic alligators. He refused to be pinned down to specifics; his information often was erroneous and incomplete; he regularly refused to answer the most innocuous questions except in general terms.[57] He was a master of Madison Avenue prattle, speaking an impenetrable language peculiar to the advertising trade. He leaned to such terms as *time frame*, *input*, and *program*. Many questions met with such responses as, "I am completed on what I had to say," or, "This is getting to a point which I am not going to discuss beyond what I have said." He once accused a reporter of "trying to complexify the situation" and firmly disallowed one query with, "I won't be responsive to your follow-up question on the original question to which I told you I wouldn't be responsive." He declared that he could "only be as factual as the facts permit." Once he was asked whether Henry Kissinger used an interpreter during peace talks with the North Vietnamese. Ziegler responded, "I can't provide you that information, but Dr. Kissinger does not speak North Vietnamese." White House reporters eventually began referring to such evasions and circum-locutions as "zieglerisms."[58]

The Washington press corps appeared to be about evenly divided on the question of whether Zielger and his staff were exceedingly clever or exceedingly ignorant. My own survey of a number of White House reporters on the subject of Ronald Ziegler elicited similar re-sponses about his syntax and helpfulness. Some journalists said they liked Ziegler, but most had mixed feelings. One summed it up in a manner that seemed typical: "Ziegler is charming, but he's arrogant and cocky. At times I want to punch him."[59]

If Ziegler seemed unawed by the reporters he matched wits with, the same could not be said for the men for whom he worked. He seemed insecure about his role in Nixon's White House, the result of

disdainful treatment by Haldeman, and he habitually reminded outsiders of his importance. "I can walk into the President's office any
time I like without going through any secretary or any other individual,"
he said, as if he could not really believe it.[60] As the Watergate scandal
forced the resignations of other aides, Ziegler's influence increased
and so did his ego-reinforcing affirmations of authority. "Things aren't
like they were when you were here," he told Clark Mollenhoff who
worked in the White House in 1968 and 1970. "I have a lot of input
and a lot to do with policy."[61]

An average day in Ron Ziegler's life began at 6:40 A.M. when he
left his white brick home in Alexandria, Virginia, and climbed into a
chauffeur-driven Chrysler New Yorker dispatched from the White
House motor pool. As he was being driven to work, he read four
newspapers and whisked through Patrick Buchanan's news digest, all
of which were waiting for him in the car. In the office he pored through
stacks of intelligence reports. He noted on a yellow legal pad the
various subjects he expected would be brought up in his press briefings
at 11 A.M. and 4 P.M. He researched sensitive subjects himself by calling
cabinet officials or White House aides; other potential questions were
researched by his staff. At 8:15 each morning he met with senior
aides, including Haldeman and Ehrlichman, who outlined for him
precisely what information he could give the press on important subjects. If especially sensitive information was discussed, he wrote down
exactly what he expected to say, and frequently he held in reserve a
few bits of information that he would allow to be drawn from him
as the questioning proceeded. No matter how many times a question
was asked or in how many different forms, he would never go beyond
what he had already prepared as an answer.[62] If a news briefing
promised to be troublesome, Ziegler would invoke what White House
reporters called the "squeeze play": he would delay his appearance
until well after eleven o'clock, knowing that wire service and broadcast
journalists had to file their reports by 11:45 in order to meet their
clients' deadlines. Showing up late ensured that the reporters would
not press for a lot of detail about events and the statements that
Ziegler issued.[63]

Ziegler's main chore was performed twice a day (once a day after
the Watergate affair broke open) when he mounted a podium in the
White House press briefing room and parried questions. Briefings
usually began with a prepared statement and announcement of the
president's schedule. Then Ziegler began taking questions, usually with
a cup of coffee in one hand and a cigarette in the other. On a typical
day in January 1973 Ziegler began his morning briefing by outlining

the president's schedule. Then he went over a list of resignations the president was accepting with "deep regret." Next he discussed a fishing rights treaty being negotiated with Colombia. The reporters who were present shortly became restless with such trivia, and their complaints elicited an admonition from Ziegler: "In all due respect gentlemen, these announcements must be made somewhere!" The tittering reporters were brought up short with a Ziegler command: "Write it down! These are government actions!" The press secretary noted that Nixon would be celebrating his birthday with a dinner "at the appropriate time." Then followed a discussion of the president's neckties.[64]

Ziegler's press aides were even less informative than their leader. Most were young and inexperienced when they were hired. In 1970 only one of Ziegler's assistants was a veteran reporter; three of the remaining four were in their mid-twenties. Wherever the president went, the press aides preceded him, primarily to protect Nixon from unfavorable publicity.[65] When the president did not want an event photographed or filmed, for example, his wishes were enforced. While on a summer stay at San Clemente in 1973, the Nixons visited some of Pat Nixon's relatives near Los Angeles. A no-picture order was issued, but as the Nixon helicopter landed in a schoolyard, ABC cameraman Robert Hemmig began rolling his film. Two Nixon aides frantically instructed him to stop, and he complied. One of Ziegler's press officers, Jack D'Arcy, asked Hemmig for the film, and after some discussion, the footage of a safe helicopter landing was surrendered. Throughout the rest of the Nixon visit, news photographers had to keep their cameras by their sides as bystanders and sightseers snapped away.[66]

Although reporters were aware of Ziegler's proficiency in keeping them ignorant of the real news, many seemed to be oblivious to his second, far more subtle task of diverting them with creature comforts. He gained his reputation as a superb technician while working on the president's 1968 campaign. As he kept reporters from the candidate's door, he swamped them with innocuous statements, position papers, and similar handouts on such matters as the national defense, the economy, and foreign affairs.

Ziegler's experience as the presidential press secretary further honed his skills. When traveling by plane, he strictly enforced a rule that forbade the press pool from wandering forward of their section in the rear of the aircraft, which was equipped with a galley and a well-stocked bar. Members of the White House staff, however, were free to stroll through the press section to distribute handouts, issue statements, talk, or grab a drink at the bar.[67] While traveling in motorcades a small pool of about a dozen reporters and sound and camera crews were permitted to ride along two or three cars behind the president. The rest of the press trolled along in buses well to the rear and listened to their pool colleagues as they gave a running commentary over a special radio communications system. Reporters wrote their stories by piecing together the pool's remarks, their own observations of the crowds, and the information listed in White House press office handouts. But they did not have to worry about tickets, luggage, chartering buses, or leasing automobiles. The White House Transportation Office handled all these chores, as well as the arrangements for hotel rooms. On many trips reporters' families were induced to go along with cut-rate fares and inexpensive lodgings.[68]

For years before the Nixon presidency, reporters worked in a room off the West Lobby of the White House. It was congested and uncomfortable but the lobby was also the official entrance to the executive mansion, and visitors could be observed and interviewed as they came and went. But about a year after the new president arrived, Nixon himself strolled into the press room, looked around at the cluttered mess, and said, "This is a disgrace." Shortly after, under Ziegler's supervision, construction began on new press quarters.[69] At a cost of over a half-million dollars, the Nixon men boarded over the old White House swimming pool and topped it with what was dubbed the "West Terrace Press Center." In one room were the working quarters complete with forty desks, some enclosed in glass booths, twelve broadcast booths, telephones, typewriters, and piped-in music. Just off this area was the briefing room. A built-in stage could be swathed in spotlights at the flip of a switch; the floor was covered with cinnamon-colored pile carpeting; Elizabethan chairs and tufted suede Chesterfield sofas were scattered about. There was also a snack area with vending machines filled with sandwiches, cakes, sweets, and soft drinks. Several glass coffee pots were always hot and full.

The maneuver worked its charm on some White House reporters, who were accustomed to inadequate space. "If the history books record that the press in time came to no longer want to 'kick Richard Nixon around' (in his phrase)," wrote one reporter, the new press room "may be one small, unworthy reason."[70] But the president had ulterior motives. White House reporters were now confined to the new press center, which was out of sight of the official entrance and the visitors who used it. "We began to see the renovation of our offices as a subtle part of the Nixon war against the press," said Helen Thomas.[71]

As the Watergate affair unraveled, slowly at first and then more rapidly, the White House press corps became exasperated with Ziegler, and the daily briefings grew acrimonious. Day after day the press secretary mounted the podium, excoriated the press, and issued blanket denials of White House involvement in the burglary at Democratic headquarters, the cover-up, and in political espionage. On April 17, 1973, he suddenly backed off and acknowledged that all of his previous statements were now "inoperative." The normal din of give-and-take turned into a roar of insults and angry exchanges. It became increasingly apparent to Nixon and his top aides that Ziegler could no longer appease White House reporters and was, in fact, exacerbating them. In June he was relieved of the responsibility of conducting the daily briefings and was promoted to presidential assistant. He subsequently became one of Nixon's closest advisers, and the daily task of meeting journalists was taken over by deputy press secretary Gerald Warren.[72]

President Nixon's policy of deliberately shunning the press was most obvious in the manner in which he virtually abandoned the institution of the formal press conference. In his five and one-half years in office, Nixon held thirty-nine such affairs, an average of far less than one per month. This figure includes nontelevised press conferences, which were usually held in the Oval Office or the press briefing room. Franklin Roosevelt, by contrast, averaged almost two press conferences a week.[73] Presidents Truman, Eisenhower, Kennedy, and Johnson met the press on the average of twenty-four to thirty-six times a year—as many news conferences, in most cases, as Nixon held during his entire first term in office. The situation had deteriorated so badly by 1972 that the Washington News Committee of the Associated Press Managing Editors Association reported, "President Nixon has come close to killing off the presidential press conference as a public institution during his term in office." The report continued:

As of Jan. 31 [1972], the most recent presidential press conference was on Nov. 12.
    In the interim, full-scale fighting broke out between India and Pakistan; James Hoffa was sprung free from federal prison by presidential order; the President held pre-summit meetings with Canada, Great Britain, France, West Germany and Japan; Congress adjourned and then reconvened; the Anderson papers exploded on the Washington scene; the President issued his State of the Union and budget pronouncements; the President said he had been conducting secret negotiations with the North Vietnamese, just to name a few controversial happenings.[74]

Most reporters and most of Nixon's staff felt that when he did face the press in a formal situation, he performed well. He was always fully prepared; he was a master debater who organized his points with great facility; he routinely foiled reporters by couching responses in cleverly constructed generalities that resisted follow-up questions. Why, then, did he not meet the press more often?

The easiest answer was that he did not relish the thought of accounting for his decisions, errors, and broken promises, especially not before millions of television viewers. Also he probably could not help but dwell on the painful memory of his "last press conference" in 1962. While traveling with Nixon in 1966 reporter Jules Witcover noticed that he seemed to think of the press conference as the ultimate battlefield, the supreme test of the public figure. "Intellectuals have a double standard," Nixon told Witcover. "If you happen to support their point of view, you can be a drunk, a stupe, *fall on your face in a press conference*, and they will still back you."[75]

But the most likely reason Nixon shunned press conferences was that they did not fit into his media manipulation plan. He wanted to end run the press, not face it. He wanted to address the people on his own terms and in situations he could control. He wanted to convey the message he wanted to convey, and he wanted it delivered undiluted and unsullied by the persistent critics of the press. His communications director, Herb Klein, said as much. Referring to the writing press as "the Gutenberg set," he wrote, "Let's face it: A Presidential news conference with 300 reporters clamoring for their moment on camera and with 50 million viewers watching—is not the ideal format to reveal policy to world powers or to explain it in depth to the nation."[76]

Lest there by any question from whom the president's men were taking their cues, this is how Nixon put it in December 1970: "My job is, among other things, to inform the American people. One of the ways to inform them is through a press conference. . . . Another way is through making reports to the nation, as I did on several occasions about the war in Southeast Asia. Another is an interview, an hour's interview with the three anchormen of the three networks, which mainly dealt [with] Southeast Asia."[77]

Even when he agreed to meet the press formally, he refused to call it a press conference. Instead it was termed a news conference as a way of reminding correspondents that it was the president's conference and not the press's.[78] All of the vast resources of the federal bureaucracy were cranked up to make the confrontation as controllable as possible. The president and the bureaucrats did their job well; the final performance was usually as well staged as a Broadway show.

As much as a week before a press conference was scheduled, the White House staff was organized to gather information. A domestic affairs team under Buchanan's direction collected data from every executive department and agency, including any policy statements the bureaucrats wanted publicized. Another team, supervised by national security adviser Henry Kissinger, gathered information on foreign affairs. Ziegler and Klein put together scores of questions they thought might be asked. The material was then arranged in question-and-answer form, placed in two looseleaf notebooks, and forwarded to the president. Updated information was constantly provided to Nixon. The system worked so well, said White House insiders, that they pinpointed as many as 90 percent of reporters' questions in advance.

The president then secluded himself and crammed. He underlined key words and catchy phrases, memorizing some of them. He rewrote a few of the answers. Usually he tried to arrange two or three study sessions before going on stage.[79] The night before his press conference, the president tried to get at least seven hours sleep. Before facing the reporters, he shaved with a safety razor, submitted to a light application of makeup, and often ran in place two hundred times to bring color to his cheeks.[80]

Meanwhile, Ziegler arranged for the White House regulars to be seated in the first three or four rows of the center section directly in front of the president. Nixon knew which of these reporters would treat him with deference, and it was to them he would turn if he felt the need for a safe question. A seating chart was made available to Nixon before he began.[81]

As he moved into the East Room of the White House, where most of his formal press conferences were held, he mounted a spare, square stage and faced a single microphone. He never used notes and usually avoided lecterns. The purpose of the bare setting was to create an impression of direct contact with the television audience. When he answered a question, he would be talking to the viewer, not to the correspondent who asked it.[82]

In contrast to the extensive preparations the president had made, many of the reporters sitting out front had more than likely composed their questions on the way to the White House. Others had put more thought into what they would ask if called on, but only in rare cases had they the time or the resources to prepare for the task ahead of them as had the president. When they assembled, moreover, they faced almost insurmountable problems.

The East Room was usually crowded with journalists, rendering it almost impossible to string together a series of challenging follow-up questions. Relatively few reporters were called on in the half-hour allotted, and if they did ask a tough question, the president had the option of filibustering or moving on quickly to someone else, perhaps a reporter he believed would ask an easy question.

More often, however, the questions in a televised press conference were not tough. This was due, in large part, to the extended lapses between Nixon's press conferences; issues, events, and frustrations piled up and questions tended to be too general. Also reporters, as much as the president, wanted to appear professional before the vast audience of employers, peers, and viewers, so many would read questions they had prepared in advance; in many instances the queries had little to do with what had gone on before. Other reporters, disdaining written questions, would drone on endlessly, often taking more time to pose the query than the president would take to answer it. The result, in too many cases, was a series of soft questions. Would he comment on this or relate his feelings about that? The hard questions that used to be posed to presidents before press conferences were televised live went unasked.

On May 8, 1970, President Nixon held a press conference in a time of unusual turmoil. Since he had last faced the press, there had been an invasion of Cambodia by American forces; students had been shot down on the campus of Kent State University; demonstrators were on their way to Washington; the stock market was plummeting; Interior Secretary Walter Hickel's letter critical of Nixon had been leaked. The president strode into the East Room and, in the words of *New York Times* reporter Hedrick Smith, "held the assembled reporters at bay as easily as Cassius Clay dabbling with a clutch of welterweights":

One reporter noted that some young people were saying the United States was headed for revolution or repression and asked the President's view: true or false? Another invited Mr. Nixon to tell the public about the isolation of the presidency. A third inquired whether the President thought the Vietnam War worthwhile. A fourth wanted to know if the President was prepared to pursue a political settlement in Paris with fervor. A fifth asked for "comment" on the Hickel letter.[83]

In sum television robbed the press of their own conference and gave it to the president. It gave him, in the words of John Kennedy's press secretary Pierre Salinger, a "chance to dominate the news once a week."[84] Now it was Nixon's show, and it is surprising that he did not use the format more frequently. Even during the worst days of Watergate, when he badly needed to influence public opinion, he called press conferences infrequently. When he did, it was usually for the purpose of condemning press coverage of the scandal and the various investigations of it. He often called on reporters who were certain to act and speak outrageously as a way of informing the millions of viewers that he was being unfairly assaulted by an unprincipled enemy.[85]

Nixon's reluctance to hold press conferences was due to one overriding concern: despite all of his preparation, he could not exert absolute control over reporters and the questions they asked. The one occasion on which a handful of reporters attempted to improve their performance by meeting and organizing questions prior to a 1970 press conference so infuriated Nixon and his aides that they considered asking Sigma Delta Chi, the professional society for journalists, to denounce the offenders.[86]

What Nixon most feared about press conferences, apparently, was that he would lose command of the event, that reporters would get tough, that the message he wanted to get across to the public would be distorted. His fears were realized on one occasion, June 1, 1971, when several reporters set aside their prepared questions and bored in on the president with a series of follow-up queries. The experience proved extremely unnerving for Richard Nixon.

It began when Herbert Kaplow, then the White House correspondent for NBC news, asked Nixon for his thoughts on how the Washington, D.C., police force had handled May Day antiwar demonstrators. The police had swept thousands of people off the streets, making wholesale arrests with little regard for civil liberties. Did the president think, asked Kaplow, that "the police handled it properly"? Had he thought about "the broader constitutional question involved of protecting individual rights in a difficult situation to control"? Nixon, in debater's style, separated the answer into two parts. First, there were such things as demonstrators who had the legal right to protest peacefully. Then there were "vandals and hoodlums and lawbreakers" who "should be treated as lawbreakers." These were the types the police had arrested, he said, and he approved. He had not, however, addressed the question of whether the civil liberties of innocent bystanders had been violated. Indeed the cases of some two thousand of those arrested had already been dropped by the courts.

Two questions on different subjects were answered. Then Forrest J. Boyd of the Mutual Broadcasting System asked if preventing the "closing down [of] the government . . . was so important that some methods, such as suspending constitutional rights was justified." Nixon replied briefly that Boyd was exaggerating the situation. J. F. terHorst of the *Detroit News* rose to ask if that were so, then why were the courts releasing so many of the arrested? Arrest, said Nixon tensely, "does not mean that an individual is guilty." Again the response evaded the point that numerous illegal arrests had been made. James Deakin, veteran reporter for the *St. Louis Post-Dispatch*, was recognized. To Nixon's obvious chagrin the reporter wanted to know if people were "being released on the grounds that they weren't properly arrested." Nixon's answer was a curt defense of police tactics, delivered while he looked around desperately for a safe face. He found it in Sarah McClendon, who came through in characteristic style: "Mr. President, sir, I wonder what you are going to do about the oversupply of goods in Vietnam. I understand we have enough telephone poles over there for 125 years and acres of trucks and other communications equipment. Will that be brought back, and where will it be put?"[87]

Nixon was off the hook. But it had been a magnificent display of how a press conference was supposed to work. It was also Richard Nixon's last live, televised press conference for one year and twenty-eight days.[88]

In the interim John Ehrlichman visited Los Angeles and was asked, in a television interview, why the president did not meet the press more frequently. He responded, "Well, he doesn't get very good questions at press conferences, frankly. He goes in there for half an hour; he gets a lot of flabby and fairly dumb questions, and it doesn't really elucidate very much. I've seen him many times come off one of those things and go back in and say, 'Isn't it extraordinary how poor the quality of the questions are?' "[89]

Evasion: "Without Television It Might Have Been Difficult for Me to Get People to Understand a Thing"

As he was isolating himself from Washington journalists and attempting to keep them appeased with positive news and creature comforts, Richard Nixon set about to end run them and deliver his message directly to the people. He accomplished this by manipulating the medium of television and by concurrently promoting and protecting a presidential image. As a complement to his use of the electronic media to evade Washington reporters, he attempted to manipulate the hinterlands press through the employment of sophisticated propaganda techniques.

In the use of television Nixon was a pioneer; his ascendancy marked the dawn of the age of the electronic presidency. He took to the airways like no chief executive before him, and in retrospect it appears that it was inevitable. In 1952 his nationally televised Checkers speech had saved his political career; in 1962 in his farewell to the press, he had declared, "Thank God for television and radio for keeping the newspapers a little more honest"; in 1968 television took him to the White House. Given Nixon's distaste for the press—his conviction that reporters hated him, his reluctance to face them, his deep-rooted belief that they would never treat him fairly—it is not surprising that he decided to devise an arrangment so that he would never have to deal with reporters again except on his own terms. Television was the answer—television and the expertise to take advantage of it. And Richard Nixon knew how to use it. Modern presidents, he wrote, "must try to master the art of manipulating the media" and at the same time "avoid at all costs the charge of trying to manipulate the media."[1]

If, during the 1968 campaign, many newsmen did not realize that Nixon had tamed the electronic beast to serve him, they received another lesson during the transition period before Nixon took office. On December 11, 1968, the first Nixon television extravaganza was aired when the president elect went before the cameras to announce all twelve of his cabinet appointments. This in itself was a slap in the face to reporters. Traditionally, cabinet officers were named one or two at a time to permit reporters time to criticize, analyze, and, in effect, pick the appointees apart. The process was beneficial to the president as well as to the press; if any of his appointees had shortcomings, he would discover them before it was too late.

But Richard Nixon remembered that John Kennedy had announced his cabinet appointments out of doors in sunny Palm Beach and windy Hyannisport, Massachusetts, and he wanted to top that performance.[2] He also wanted the public to make up its mind about his new cabinet without help from the press. Nixon achieved what he sought: television viewers got a look at the new team, and the press analysis came later. It was, in the words of one-time Nixon speechwriter James Keogh, a "striking indication of how he preferred to communicate with the people."[3]

On his first day in office, Nixon ordered the cabinet secretaries to report to the Oval Office at 8:00 A.M. to be sworn in. He wanted the nation to know he believed in the work ethic, and to make sure the message was not missed, NBC's "Today" show cameras were there to record the event.[4]

In the next five and one-half years, the viewing public was treated to "the Richard Nixon show" as often, in some periods, as every three days. Both the president and the vice-president made guest appearance on entertainment shows. Nixon accepted an invitation to appear with Art Linkletter and later when on the NBC "Today" show; Spiro Agnew starred in the Bob Hope Palm Springs golf classic, twice went on the Johnny Carson show, and spent ninety minutes as the sole guest of talk-show host David Frost.[5] In his first seventeen months Nixon also starred in a dozen of his own productions and ten additional televised news conferences.[6] At midterm an awestruck broadcasting executive, CBS president Frank Stanton, remarked that the president had "appeard on network prime-time television as many times as Presidents Eisenhower, Kennedy and Johnson combined."[7] Within a nine-day period in 1970 Nixon preempted the networks three times: on January 22 for his State of the Union message, on January 26 to veto an HEW appropriation bill, and on January 30 for a press conference.[8] By May 1972 the president had commandeered television time twenty-nine times for his own "major announcements," ten of which were devoted to a defense of his plans to end the Vietnam war.[9] "My object was to go over the heads of the columnists," he said after one such speech in 1969. "We have been getting the reaction from across the country, and it's been pretty good. We've got to hold American opinion with us for three or four months and then we can work this Vietnam thing out."[10] While discussing the Vietnam conflict on another occasion, Nixon remarked that "without television it might have been difficult for me to get people to understand a thing."[11]

In most appearances Nixon maintained tight control of the format and enjoyed immediate access to a nationwide audience whenever he asked for it. "Our attitude," said NBC president Julian Goodman in late 1971, "is the same as our attitude toward previous presidents: He can have any goddamn thing he wants."[12] Only in mid-1974, after it became obvious that Nixon would be impeached, did the networks become sufficiently emboldened to deny White House demands for television time. "We like to maintain control of our own product," avowed CBS officials at the time.[13]

Although he appeared on television frequently, Nixon took great care not to try the patience of viewers. He believed the audience would rather be watching reruns anyway, and he constantly beseeched writers to hold his speeches to ten minutes so he would not interfere with regular programming.[14] On May 8, 1970, he delayed a live press conference for an hour—from 9:00 P.M. to 10:00 P.M.—so his show wouldn't conflict with a basketball game on ABC. The network volunteered to squeeze the President in at half-time, but he refused.[15] Nixon violated his don't-vex-the-viewers rule only to plead his case during the Watergate affair.[16]

The White House did not neglect radio. It had been a favorite of Nixon since the 1962 debates, which some polls showed he won with the radio audience at the same time he lost with television viewers. Nixon made heavy use of radio in his campaigns of 1968 and 1972; it proved to be an ideal method for discussing issues without having to submit to the troublesome questions of well-informed reporters. Nixon also used radio for some of his first-term speeches. Both he and his media men believed he had a good radio voice and came across the airwaves as concerned and cerebral. The myriad problems associated with television, moreover, did not hamper radio productions. There was no need for makeup. There were no hot lights to make Nixon's lip sweat, and nobody could see him if it did. There was no need to worry about his heavy beard. He could read from his text and use his reading glasses, which he never wore on television. The average audience of several million, furthermore, was often enhanced with a new twist: Nixon's media advisers sometimes permitted television cameras to record selected portions of the president's presentations. In addition to the radio audience, therefore, he received exposure on nationwide television news shows.[17]

But television was the medium that commanded most of the president's attention; he used it imaginatively and sometimes diabolically. Perhaps the low point of his "media governing" during the first term came on January 26, 1970, when he requested time and went on the air at 9:00 P.M. For ten minutes he discoursed about the inflationary aspects of a $19.7 million appropriations bill, which Congress had passed for the Labor and Health, Education and Welfare departments. The president objected to provisions for increased aid to college students and to public health service grants. As he finished his defense of what he was about to do, the president picked up his pen and with a tight smile vetoed the bill before millions of viewers.[18] Prior to his broadcast the mail on Capitol Hill had been running ten to one in favor of the HEW appropriation and against the president's viewpoint. The day after he vetoed the legislation in front of the entire nation, Congress was inundated with 55,000 telegrams supporting Nixon's action. The mail in the days that followed ran five to one in favor of the president.[19]

As time passed, Nixon varied the format for communicating directly with the public. In January 1971 he sat beside the fireplace in the White House library and engaged in a conversation with four television correspondents—Eric Sevareid of CBS, John Chancellor of NBC, Howard K. Smith of ABC, and Nancy Dickerson of the Public Broadcasting System. It was another public relations triumph for Nixon. He was serene, presidential. When answering questions, he addressed the audience rather than his interviewers. The interrogators avoided discomfiting questions and, apparently not wanting to dominate the show, failed to ask searching follow-up queries. It was a polite, chatty hour that revealed little new information but a lot of warm Richard Nixon.[20]

A few weeks later Howard K. Smith spent an hour on the air with the president. The respectful Smith drew little more from Nixon than a defense of his actions in Southeast Asia. Only weeks before South Vietnamese units, with U.S. help, had executed an incursion into Laos. Many of the Vietnamese soldiers had retreated in a panic, some of them hanging onto the skids of helicopters. Press coverage of the withdrawal, Nixon complained to Smith, was a good example of how the news media distort the facts; photographers and reporters, the president said, had paid too much attention to isolated incidents. He neglected to mention that most of the press had been barred from covering the invasion and could hardly be held accountable if they did not cover the entire campaign.[21]

One of the classic examples of how Nixon preferred to use television to evade the press and sell his programs came with the announcement of a turnabout on economic policy in August 1971. Until the day he went on nationwide television to announce wage and price controls, among other changes, he gave little hint that any such abrupt move would take place. Indeed he had adamantly and publicly resisted any suggestion of economic controls. Thus when he went on the air on August 15, most reporters were caught off guard. *National Journal* reporters surveyed their colleagues and found that "only one of the three economic writers in *The New York Times* Washington bureau was in the city; Murray A. Seegar, economics writer for the *Los Angeles Times*, was on vacation, as were Joseph R. Slevin of the Knight newspapers and Norman Kempster, Treasury Department correspondent for United Press International."[22]

Radio and television reporters were given a one and one-half hour headstart to prepare for the analysis that would follow immediately after the broadcast. An hour before the president went on the air, the "pencil press" was called in, some in blue jeans and golfing slacks, for a briefing. Since many eastern newspapers have a 9:00 P.M. deadline, they had only a few minutes to write a complicated, major story. *Time* and *Newsweek*, both of which went to press Sunday evening, were not alerted.[23]

Nixon was aware that if his campaign to end run the press with television was to succeed, he had to cultivate and project the proper image and protect it from anything that would cause the public to view him negatively. But he was sensitive to charges that he allowed public relations experts to tinker with his image, and he pretended indifference to their profession. In March 1971, for example, Nixon accepted an invitation proffered by Barbara Walters to appear on NBC's early morning "Today" show. It turned out to be a conversational two hours, with Nixon devoting much comment to his alleged lack of concern with image. "The president, with the enormous responsibilities that he has," Nixon said to Walters, "must not be constantly preening in front of a mirror, wondering whether or not he is getting across as this kind of individual or that." The image makers, he went on, were struggling in vain when they tried to work their humbuggery on him: "These public-relations experts always come in and are constantly riding me, or they used to in the campaign, and they do now. 'You have got to do this, that, and the other thing to change your image.' I am not going to change my image, I am just going to do a good job for this country."[24]

In fact the record shows that Nixon pursued a presidential image with gusto. He was very conscious of his physical appearance. He ate cautiously in order to hold his weight to 170 pounds. For exercise he ran in place every morning and bowled occasionally. However tense the situation, he attempted to get to bed by 11:30 or midnight and arose around 7:00. He shaved as often as three times a day and maintained a tan with frequent trips to Key Biscayne and San Clemente.

In 1970 Nixon changed barbers and his hair style. Nixon's hair "used to stick out in back," said stylist Milton Pitts; the old cut was "too thin on the sides and . . . too full just above the ear. Now with a balanced sculpture cut, he has a more oval look." At least one reporter, John Osborne, claimed that Nixon colored his hair.[25]

A president, Nixon apparently felt, should project an image of being cool, detached, immune to physical impairment, unfettered by emotion. Although he clearly enjoyed dancing with his wife, for example, he refused to do it publicly until Tricia's wedding in June 1971. He was sometimes moved to tears by such events as awards ceremonies but never wanted his emotion to be known. "I just can't stand to see anybody else with tears in his eyes," he finally admitted in 1977.[26] He instructed his aides to put out the word "that the president never misses any of the things he's scheduled to do because of illness." He refused to tell his doctor about his hay fever, resisted treatment for a cracked toe, insisted on traveling to Egypt in 1974 despite a bout of phlebitis, which could have proved fatal.[27]

Nixon also made an extraordinary effort to project himself as a wholesome, moral person. He bolstered this image by maintaining close friendships with men of the cloth and counted evangelist Billy Graham and Norman Vincent Peale among his closest associates. Shortly after moving into the White House, Nixon began holding Sunday services in the East Room. They soon became official events; attendance was virtually mandatory for cabinet secretaries and high-level White House aides.[28]

The president also let it be known that only family-type movies were shown in the White House. John Wayne films were said to be popular with the First Family. The president himself became en-amoured with George C. Scott's portrayal of General George Patton and watched the movie several times.[29] The image of the asexual man who eschewed all but the most salubrious movies, however, was tainted somewhat in August 1972 when director Peter Bogdanovich was invited to a party at the Western White House and took actress Cybill Shepherd with him. Shepherd had starred in the Bogdanovich-directed movie, *The Last Picture Show*. In one scene she had stripped atop a diving board. Although the movie had been rated "R" (restricted) because of the nude scenes, Nixon told Bogdanovich he had seen the "remarkable" film at Camp David. Bogdanovich described the conversation:

To my amazement, he launched into a very flattering paragraph about the movie. Then he turned to Cybill, putting a hand on her arm, "And what part did *you* play?"
    "Jacy," she said.
    I said, "She was the one who stripped on the diving board."
    The President paused. He looked at me, but kept his hand on Cybill's arm. "Well, everyone gave a remarkable performance in that film," he said, and then, still not looking at Cybill, but patting her arm as he spoke and with the barest flicker of a smile, "And, of course, I remember *you* very well now, my dear."[30]

Such an admission of libidinous thoughts was rare with Nixon, who customarily went out of his way to preserve the image of a straitlaced moralist. When the Commission on Obscenity and Pornography concluded in its 1970 report that there was little correlation between bawdy films and sexual depravity, Nixon instructed his aides to let the country know he felt otherwise.[31] Nixon also rejected outright the report of the Commission on Population Growth and the American Future because it recommended such population controls as abortion, family planning services, and distribution of birth control devices to minors. "Such measures," the president said, "would do nothing to preserve and strengthen close family relationships."[32]

There was political support and votes to be had by being perceived as an armchair athlete, so Nixon carefully cultivated this image as well. If he had not gotten into politics, he used to tell his associates, he would have liked to have been a sports writer or broadcaster.[33] He had been a little-used benchwarmer on the Whittier College football team and had a genuine fondness for sports. He frequently called coaches and players after a big victory or loss to offer congratulations or condolences, and sports celebrities were regular visitors at the White House.[34] He even chose a few all-time "All-Star" baseball teams for the Associated Press. He had his image foremost in mind, however, when he carefully selected players to avoid offending ethnic groups. One columnist noted that Nixon "saluted young and old, white and black, Latin and Nordic, lefthanders and righthanders, Catholic and WASP, Jew and American Indian."[35]

The president's concern with image was nowhere more evident than in his sense of history and his place in it. He had a persistent habit of claiming "historic firsts." In 1970, for instance, he sent to Capitol Hill a message on foreign policy; it was, he told reporters, "the first of its kind ever sent to Congress."[36] In England in 1969 he asserted that "for the first time in history, a man occupying the office of president of the United States visited a session of the House of Commons." In Djakarta on July 27, 1969, he told a gathering, "Now, as I stand here today, I realize for the first time in history a president of the United States of America is visiting Indonesia." When he left Djakarta the following day, he said, "This is the first time that I have ever said goodbye to the people of this country."[37]

A keen awareness of image showed in Nixon's love for royalty, the regal, the dignified. He was impressed with the braided ceremonial guards he saw in almost every country he visited on his 1969 trip to Europe. On his return he ordered the Secret Service to spruce up the uniforms worn by the White House police. Some months later Britain's Prime Minister Harold Wilson arrived at the White House to be greeted by a cadre of policemen decked out in dazzling white tunics trimmed in gold braid and buttons. Atop their heads were perched high-crowned, drum major hats; around their waists were strung black leather gun belts. The military tailor hired by the Secret Service explained that he was seeking "a nice police image."[38] But critics were unimpressed. The uniforms, commented *Time* magazine, suggested "by turns, a Ruritanian palace guard, a Belgian customs inspector, and Prince Danilo in *The Merry Widow*."[39] Nixon wanted to "hang tough" and keep the uniforms despite the uproar. But Haldeman persuaded him to accept a compromise; the helmets were stowed away, but the white tunics remained for a while.[40]

Despite his efforts to nurture his image, Nixon could not trust himself to handle the task alone. He was saddled with too many traits that could be viewed as shortcomings in a politician—an aloof nature, a tendency to attribute to his critics the basest motives, a lack of capacity to relax and roll with the punches, physical awkwardness, an inability to engage in small talk. Nixon, said H. R. Haldeman, "was the least dexterous man I have ever known: clumsy would be too elegant a word to describe his mechanical aptitude." According to Haldeman, finding Nixon a tape recorder that he could operate was a "major project." White House aides searched for the simplest machine available and then "had to specially mark the various buttons so that Nixon could handle the simple recording process without mixing things up."[41] On Veteran's Day 1969, Nixon visited a hospital in Washington, D.C., and told a one-eyed Vietnam veteran, "All you need is one. You see too much, anyway."[42]

To avoid such embarrassments and to create and maintain a positive image of himself, Nixon leaned heavily on expert help; he, meanwhile, functioned primarily as a maker of policy, dispatching prescriptive memoranda such as this one to Haldeman, dated September 22, 1969:

In memoranda in the future, I shall use the letters PR whenever I am referring generally to a project I want carried out on the PR [public relations] front. . . .

PR. Every Monday, I want a week's projection as to what we anticipate will be the major opposition attacks so that we can plan our own statements with those in mind. . . .

I have reached the conclusion that we simply have to have [a] full-time PR Director, who will have no other assignments except to bulldog these three or four major issues we may select each week or each month.[43]

But it was Haldeman himself who was functioning, and continued to function, as the PR director, the overseer of the president's image; Haldeman, the advertising man, who knew more than anyone else what it took to make Nixon appear warm and human, strong and decisive. He knew because he had constructed that image, had taught Nixon to appear that way, had sold the "new" Nixon to the public the same way he had peddled bug spray, floor wax, toilet cleaner, "un-cola," and "Snarol" the snail killer.[44] He and Nixon, said Haldeman, discussed "at very great length—questions of public relations."[45] After their talks Haldeman organized groups of dispersers and issued his instructions. "We have to get the word out about his personal attributes," he said in a typical meeting of high-level staff members, "the way he exercises power, the way he handles the workload—he knows, quite cold-bloodedly, that this will aid his ability to lead when times are tough. That's why we have to build equity now—Ike did it. John Kennedy did it, better than anybody. So should Nixon."[46]

Eisenhower and Kennedy may have done it, but they did not have the kind and quality of help that was available to Nixon and Haldeman. By the end of his first term, according to one congressional report, Nixon had the largest presidential staff in history. Some 55 persons were listed as advisers, 600 were carried as White House staff, and 5,395 worked for the Executive Office.[47] Over 50 of these were media men. Many had helped package Nixon in the 1968 campaign, and they followed him into the White House, where they became the most important figures in his administration. They had spent their lives in advertising, broadcasting, public relations, and the news business. Some had made careers out of manipulating the media, and they knew their jobs well.[48] In addition to Haldeman the foremost image makers included five who had worked for the J. Walter Thompson advertising agency: Ronald Ziegler, Dwight Chapin, Larry Higby, Kenneth R. Cole, Jr., and Bruce Kehrli.[49]

Nixon's media experts watched over his every action and weighed his every word. They had two functions, to protect and promote. As a result of their efforts the picture that emerged was one of a wise president who was never ill, never discouraged or troubled, who knew he had his people—the silent majority—behind him, who was in complete control of all situations and was never wrong. The following are just a few examples of the art of image protection in action:

- When Richard Nixon referred to some college students as "bums," communications director Herb Klein told the country the president had been misinterpreted.[50]

- When Nixon, with his attorney general at his side, declared that Charles Manson was "guilty, directly or indirectly, of eight murders without reason"—even as the cult leader was standing trial—there was no admission of error, no immediate correction. There was, instead, a ham-handed attempt by Ronald Ziegler to change the record about what the president had said.[51]

- At Haldeman's insistence, television cameramen were limited to silent filming of Henry Kissinger until late 1972. Explained Kissinger, "The White House public relations people . . . were convinced that my accent might disturb Middle America."[52]

- A group of blind men visited the Oval Office and demonstrated for Nixon how they could "feel" the design of the presidential seal in the carpet. The president impulsively fell to his knees and began rubbing his hands over the carpet with his eyes closed, and official White House photographers snapped several pictures. Haldeman witnessed this genuinely touching scene and immediately proscribed release of the photographs on the grounds that they depicted Nixon in an undignified posture.

- An in-depth marketing survey prior to the 1972 election allegedly revealed that people were repelled by the name *Nixon*; it had something to do with the "Nix" or the "x," the image makers thought. The survey results meant that Nixon's name could not be used in the title of any campaign organization. So after hours of discussion, and at the suggestion of William Safire, the Committee to Re-Elect the President came into being. It quickly became known as CREEP.[53]

The image makers not only protected the president's public appearance; they also attacked. They planned briefings for congressmen and other prominent people; they conducted sales campaigns for Nixon and his programs; they carefully analyzed every request for a meeting, an interview, or information for its promotional benefits. The publicity crusades began even before Nixon assumed office. In a memo to Safire, dated December 16, 1968, John Ehrlichman wrote:

It has been suggested to me that we capitalize upon the work habits of the President-elect; long hours of work, delayed dinners, 18-hour days, late reading, no naps, perfunctory and very short lunch and breakfast times (frequently 5 or 10 minutes);
    No time for exercise except walking to and from;
    Also his make-up as evidenced by his selection of Cabinet and staff: that he is unafraid of being surrounded by brain power; that he selects bright people; that he is intolerant of stupidity. . . .
    When he goes to Florida next week, he will carry bulging briefcases of work; he is a voracious reader who seldom indulges in reading personal stories about himself but limits himself to reading on the issues;
    In 22 years in public life, he has never singled out a critical writer for personal criticism since he has deep respect for the craft.
    His television habits run to the documentary and entertainment, rather than news. He seeks news in perspective and seldom spends his time with the instant news broadcasts since he has found them to be frequently inaccurate.
    His suspicion of "instant news" will bring about a removal of the news tickers and the multiple television sets from the White House.[54]

The major public relations planning was done by a gathering of aides—referred to variously as the Plans Committee, the Planning Group, the PR Group, or the Image Factory—who assembled at least once a week to discuss how best to present a favorable image.[55] One of their projects was a protracted effort to convince the nation that Nixon was a warm and happy man. It came at the height of Senator Edmund Muskie's popularity—when the Maine Democrat was being touted as a presidential contender and was being hailed as a "warm" figure—and the blitz lasted for weeks[56] In a span of two months in early 1971 Nixon held two press conferences, met with a selected group of women reporters to talk about his family, gave two exclusive interviews, went on the NBC "Today" show, and was interviewed by ABC's Howard K. Smith.[57] The image makers, meanwhile, confided to reporters that their man was in fine shape, confident, optimistic and "tracking well."[58]

Nixon's media team lost no opportunity to polish his image. When the first American astronauts walked on the moon, the media experts suggested that Nixon place a telephone call to the astronauts, that he sign a plaque to be left on the moon, and that he arrange a pending, around-the-world trip to include a visit to the astronauts' mid-Pacific landing site. Officials at the National Aeronautics and Space Administration were not infatuated with the proposals, but H. R. Haldeman impressed them with the urgency of the White House requests. When Nixon spoke to the astronauts through the window of a quarantine chamber aboard the aircraft carrier *Hornet*, he got carried away and declared, "This is the greatest week in the history of the world since the Creation." Billy Graham later admonished him for being "a little excessive."[59]

College students and their antiwar attitudes frequently gave the White House image merchants reason to crank up their publicity machine for attacks and counterattacks. In the aftermath of the Kent State tragedy, as student demonstrations broke out across the country, a group of several hundred hard-hatted construction workers decided to turn the tables. They waded into a crowd of student protesters on New York's Wall Street and, as police stood aside, lashed into the demonstrators with pipes and wrenches. Screaming that Mayor John Lindsay was "a commie" and "a fag," they marched to city hall where they forced city employees to raise the flag that Lindsay had ordered to be flown at half-staff as part of a day of reflection in memory of the dead students. From there they went across the street to Pace College where they thrashed the students they found in the lobby of the main building.

Nixon and the White House image men were deeply impressed. Apparently reasoning that he could win votes in the heartland by associating with the construction workers, the president instructed Charles Colson, his liaison with blue-collar organizations, to invite the hard-hat leaders to visit the White House. The construction men paraded into the Oval Office wearing their hard hats and flag pins and gave the president an honorary hard hat inscribed "commander-in-chief."[60] Later, a reporter asked Ronald Ziegler how the hard hats could get in to see the president so easily, when not even Congressmen could get past the East Gate. Ziegler replied only that it was "kind of a loaded question."[61]

There was one man whose image Nixon worried about almost as much as he fretted about his own—the late John F. Kennedy. The fact that he was no longer around did little to deter Nixon's habit of comparing himself with the suave and witty Bostonian who had defeated him in 1960. According to Haldeman Nixon had a "fascination of" and "enduring envy for" the Kennedys and was frustrated because his own carefully constructed image never seemed to match JFK's:

"Nixon took pains with his public image; he dressed neatly and conservatively, handled himself calmly in public, made all of his ceremonial appearances in good style and humor—and yet, no matter what he did, he seemed to come across as flat, unattractive, unappealing. Jack Kennedy had only to stand up to project a charismatic image of 'class.' "[62]

This acute concern for the Kennedy image led the White House publicists into a major public relations blunder. The Kennedys had always been perceived by the public as lovers of the sea. Countless pictures of the clan frolicking in the ocean and sailing off Hyannisport had appeared over the years. Nixon too loved the water. He had been a navy man; he owned homes on the coasts of Florida and California; and he was fond of swimming. It just was not right, reasoned Nixon's image makers, for the Kennedys to appropriate the seas. At San Clemente on a summer day in 1970, photographers were notified that a photo opportunity had been arranged. They were escorted up a cliff near the Nixon home, and their attention was directed to a solitary figure strolling in the surf below. It was Nixon. "Good Christ," someone exclaimed, "he's wearing *shoes.*" Indeed he was wearing street shoes. The photographers pointed their cameras and snapped away, and the "Sea Shot" was born. It was heartily derided by Nixon's adversaries, who had known in their hearts that he was the sort of waxwork who would not enjoy the feel of sand and sea between his toes.[63]

Such bungling on the part of the image peddlers was unusual but not unknown. One of their most serious slip-ups occurred during the 1970 congressional campaign. While stumping in San Jose, California, the presidential party encountered a group of 2,000 demonstrators, and their protests spurred Nixon to climb on the hood of a car and flash a V-sign. The crowd began jeering and booing and let loose a fusillade of rocks, eggs, and vegetables. Nixon viewed the incident as a perfect illustration of the law-and-order message he had been preaching, and two days later, he lambasted the rock throwers in a fiery speech in Phoenix.[64] The Nixon men purchased a videotape of the speech from a local television station, but the black and white film turned out to be fuzzy and of generally poor quality. Yet on election eve the Madison Avenue team beamed it across the nation on all three networks. The same evening Senator Edmund Muskie delivered a calm appeal to voters on behalf of the Democratic party. The contrast with the president's shrill performance was striking, and the whole affair was universally adjudged a setback for Nixon.[65]

Nixon's February 1972 historic visit to mainland China—the first official contact in twenty years between the two countries—was a virtually flawless display of the television end run. Every element of the tactic was used to perfection. The traveling press was kept ignorant of important news; the image makers arranged photo opportunities and timed key events to coincide with prime-time viewing hours in the United States; Nixon was kept cloistered from the press while the staged proceedings were beamed back home by a satellite orbited for that purpose. For Nixon and Haldeman, who masterminded the affair, their "Journey for Peace" was a dazzling public relations victory. As one White House aide put it: "The China trip was Bob Haldeman's master-piece, his Sistine Chapel."[66]

Print reporters began to get an idea of the secondary role they would play when Ronald Ziegler released the list of correspondents who would be permitted to make the trip. Only eighty-seven slots were available; of these print journalists and photographers were awarded but forty-four. Twenty-two correspondents represented all of the nation's daily newspapers; six were from the wire services; six were from national magazines. Pointedly excluded were reporters from *Newsday* and the *Boston Globe*, both of which had frequently published stories critical of Nixon. Three slots went to columnists (Joseph Kraft, a moderate, William F. Buckley and Richard Wilson, both conservatives); and one magazine slot was assigned, incredibly, to the *Reader's Digest*, which rarely covered the White House but was very friendly to Nixon. The forty-three remaining press slots were assigned to the broadcast media. Eighteen were correspondents, the remainder technicians and cameramen. Since an advance crew of sixty-eight technicians was already in Peking, broadcast representatives outnumbered the print press by almost three to one.[67] The China trip thus promised to be a television spectacular, and Ronald Ziegler confirmed the suspicions when he told a UPI correspondent, "After all, it is a picture story."[68]

The presidential jet landed in Peking at 11:30 A.M., or 10:30 P.M., Eastern Standard Time, in the United States. It was, a *Time* magazine writer commented, "an excellent hour for a presidential candidate seeking re-election to make a television appearance."[69] Henry Kissinger and Secretary of State William Rogers had been instructed a dozen times to remain on the plane until Nixon had alighted and shaken Premier Chou En-lai's hand. Haldeman wanted the president to share this moment in the television spotlight with no one. But, said Kissinger, "Haldeman left nothing to chance. When the time came, a burly aide blocked the aisle of *Air Force One*" while Nixon bounded down the steps.[70] So the entire world was treated to a sight many had thought impossible—the old Red-baiter, Richard Nixon, descending from a plane in Peking to be greeted by the premier of Communist China.

The television commentators, however, were stunned. There was no hoopla, no bands, no pomp, no pageantry. With nothing else to cover they mused over the question of whether there was "an air of excitement" in Peking. Back in New York NBC's Edwin Newman analyzed the president's reception and Chou En-lai's greeting. "It did seem to be a cordial handshake," he said.[71]

As soon as Nixon had settled in his quarters, he received an invitation to meet with Chairman Mao Tse-tung. They met that afternoon, and following this occasion, press secretary Ronald Ziegler reached the acme in his career of withholding news. Reporters asked him about the tone of the meeting. No comment. How was Mao's health? No comment. How long did Nixon and Mao shake hands? No comment. Where was Mao's home? No comment. Did the two leaders partake of any refreshments? It would be "fair to assume that tea was served."[72]

Accommodations for the press were good. The Chinese had constructed a press center in the Palace of Nationalities, adjacent to the Hotel of Nationalities where reporters were given spare but comfortable rooms. The press center contained all the needed supplies and facilities except sufficient copy paper and wastebaskets and came complete with a bowling alley, a basketball court, and waitresses to serve tea.[73]

Reporters may have had little to write of substance, but the cameras rarely ceased clicking and rolling, and the picture story unfolded for the home viewers according to plan. Sports fans were treated to displays of gymnastics; those who preferred the performing arts saw clips of a ballet, *The Red Detachment of Women*.[74] Meanwhile, Ronald Ziegler handed out copies of Mr. and Mrs. Nixon's observations as they moved about the countryside. At the ancient Ming tombs, Nixon was moved to note that the emperors had "spoons as well as chopsticks." During a snowfall as they were touring Peking's Forbidden City, Nixon turned to a Chinese official and informed him, "It snows like this in Chicago." At Hangchow, Nixon told Chou En-lai that the scenery "looks like a postcard."[75]

It was at the Great Wall of China, however, that Ziegler put on the most awesome display of his talent. Helen Thomas described the moment:

The president and Mrs. Nixon walked a few steps in each direction, looked up at the mountains, admiring the winding snake that was a wall, and appeased the pre-positioned photographers with smiles, gestures and banter. It occurred to Ziegler that reporters might also record this moment for history's sake. While the presidential party was having a tea break, Ziegler singled out what he thought was a safe reporter and said, "If you ask the President how he likes the Great Wall, he will be prepared to answer." Sure enough, when the president emerged, he was asked on cue, "Sir, how do you like the Great Wall?" "I must conclude that the Great Wall is a great wall," he said.[76]

The stage-managing for television continued even after the presidential party left China. White House television specialist Mark Goode scheduled a long layover in Anchorage, Alaska, to permit the plane to land in Washington at the peak of prime time. Goode then set up a podium, used "The Spirit of '76"—the re-christened presidential airplane—as a backdrop, and gave the Nixon party a welcome-home celebration the nation's television viewers would not soon forget.[77]

The Nixon administration's campaign to take its message directly to the people was but one phase of its total effort to end run the national press corps. The second phase consisted of the use of propaganda and public relations techniques to reach the silent majority through local leaders and hometown press. Administration representatives fanned out to all corners of the country, speaking before almost any audience that would have them; special interest groups were showered with literature and appeals for support; editors, reporters, and broadcast journalists were peppered with pro-Nixon material and accosted by administration representatives and briefing teams.

This well-conceived, comprehensive, and, in many aspects, unprecedented program was directed by Herb Klein, who first worked for Nixon as an unpaid aide in the young congressman's 1948 bid for re-election. Then a reporter for the *Alhambra (California) Post-Advocate*, Klein climbed the ranks in the politically conservative Copley newspaper chain and in 1959 became editor of its flagship paper, the *San Diego Union*. During this period he took five leaves of absence to help in Nixon's campaigns.[78]

Klein was quiet of temperament, low-keyed, unexcitable. Over the years with Nixon he managed to juggle his two, antithetical responsibilities—simultaneously pleasing Nixon and the press—with remarkable dexterity. He did it so well, in fact, that he incurred the suspicion—some said the wrath—of Haldeman. Klein was too easy-going for Haldeman, too lenient and conciliatory. He could forgive and forget, even admit his own mistakes. He believed the best way to combat a negative story was to "put out the complete data very early. I think laying your cards on the table as quickly as possible is the best way of getting past something."[79] In Haldeman's eyes this was a negative attitude. Besides, Klein was a former newsman and enjoyed the company of journalists. He believed in persuasion and in being persuaded, the soft sell. Haldeman was a disciple of the hard sell. He defined public relations, according to William Safire, as "the use of techniques to badger, bully, bribe, entice, and persuade people to your 'side,' which could be accomplished only by organizing and orchestrating and hammering away." For these reasons Haldeman convinced Nixon after the 1968 victory to name Ziegler the presidential spokesman and designate Klein director of communications for the executive branch. To ensure that he retained control of the Klein staff, Haldeman saw to it that one of his acolytes, Jeb Stuart Magruder, was installed as Klein's deputy.[80]

It was to Magruder that Haldeman usually turned when he wanted to perpetrate an end run that called for a devious touch. On February 4, 1970, he sent Magruder a memorandum ordering him to get to work on "the mobilization of the Silent Majority" to combat press criticism:

We just haven't really mobilized them, and we have got to move now in every effective way we can to get them working to pound the magazines and the networks in counter-action to the obvious shift of the establishment to an attack on Vietnam again. Concentrate this on the few places that count, which would be NBC, TIME, NEWSWEEK, and LIFE, the NEW YORK TIMES, and the WASHINGTON POST. Don't waste your fire on other things.

Next point, and this is also highly urgent priority. The State of the Union evoked a tremendous number of very strong editorials praising the content, delivery, etc. Now we need, very quickly, a well-edited, well-packaged, compellingly-presented mailing piece that summarizes the highlights of those editorials, especially the ones from surprising sources like Reston of the TIMES, so that we can get out to our people especially the reaction that the country's newspapers have had to the President's address.[81]

In late 1970, Nixon held a press conference, and Haldeman ordered Magruder to whip up some response laudatory of the president and critical of the press. Magruder's reply, dated December 11, revealed that an outside group had been organized and a letter-writing system had been set up:

Based on this morning's meeting we have begun moving on the following:

1. Ten telegrams have been drafted by Buchanan. They will be sent to TIME and NEWSWEEK today by 20 names around the country from our letter writing system. Copies are attached.

2. Letters to Osborne and Sidey will be sent tomorrow. The letters, as drafted, follow the line of the samples delivered to us.

3. Letters to the editors of the TIMES, POST, STAR, CHICAGO DAILY NEWS, ST. LOUIS POST DISPATCH are being prepared and sent.

4. Nofziger is having satements placed in the CONGRESSIONAL RECORD. Once they appear, they will be printed and distributed together with favorable columns to editors, publishers, business leaders, and other opinion leaders.

5. Nofziger has contacted Victor Lasky, who has agreed to run a column. Nofziger will also contact Lawrence, Kilpatrick and Paul Martin.

6. The NEW YORK TIMES Op Ed page statement is being drafted by Keogh. Nofziger is also preparing a draft. Klein is probably the best signatory. A call is in to Salisbury concerning placement of the piece.

7. In reviewing the comments of the editors and publishers contacted last night, it is our view that most will run favorable editorials, and that it might be counter productive to exert White House pressure.[82]

Shortly after the 1972 elections, rumors began to circulate that Klein would soon leave Nixon's employ. Klein was being isolated more and more from the Oval Office and the man he had loyally served for twenty-five years. "You've just not got to let Klein ever set up a meeting again," Nixon fumed to Haldeman at one point. "He just doesn't have his head screwed on. You know what I mean. He just opens it up and sits there with egg on his face. He's just not our guy at all, is he?" On June 6, 1973, Klein cleaned off his desk and moved on.[83]

As part of a general scheme to reorganize the government and centralize power in the White House, Nixon and his aides decided that Ronald Ziegler would assume Klein's duties. The office of director of communications would continue to exist under the new plan, but overall supervision would shift to the White House, and Ziegler would become the information chief for the entire executive branch.[84] But this project, like so many others, sank slowly into the Watergate morass, and the communications shop remained intact in the capable hands of Klein's deputy Kenneth Clawson.[85]

In the four and one-half years that he was Nixon's communications director, however, Herb Klein developed the most sophisticated publicity operation ever assembled for a president. His job broke down into three parts: he was a press pacifier and door opener for reporters in search of information; he coordinated the activities of public information offices throughout the executive branch; and he was the chief public relations officer for the administration. He also acted as a liaison between the White House and the Republican National Committee, but this was more a part of his job as the administration's PR man than a separate function.[86]

When Klein's appointment as communications director was announced, it elicited editorial comment that he would be a "minister of information" and a "communications czar." He declared he would prove the critics wrong; "truth," he proclaimed in a burst of euphoria, "will be the hallmark of the Nixon administration." He saw his task, he said, as "extending the flow of news."[87] Klein proved true to his word. Whenever a reporter had difficulty obtaining information, a call to Klein usually opened the door. Newsmen were surprised with his performance, and his reputation reached the point that a mere threat to "call Herb" proved sufficient, in many cases, to convince a stubborn information officer to cooperate. Washington journalists also gave Klein high marks for making officials available for interviews. He constantly urged administration functionaries to cooperate with the press; according to one report he arranged one hundred television and newspaper interviews for cabinet-level officials in his first two months.[88]

In his role as Nixon's press pacifier, Klein attempted to convince his former colleagues that the administration was not as antipress as it appeared. He continually promised, for example, that Nixon would pay more attention to press conferences. Early in the first term Klein predicted the president would hold televised press conferences every week or ten days.[89] Although it soon became apparent that reporters would be fortunate to see the president once every few months, Klein continued to hold out hope. As Nixon began his second term, the communications director declared that now they were "past a lot of these negotiations" with the Chinese and Vietnamese, Nixon would be meeting the press more frequently.[90]

When Vice-President Agnew began attacking the press, Klein attempted to appease reporters. Samuel Archibald, director of the Washington office of the University of Missouri's Freedom of Information Center, reported in July, 1970, that "Herb Klein . . . has used his contacts with the editors, publishers and broadcast station owners to play Tweedledee to . . . Agnew's Tweedledum. After Agnew's second blast at the information industry, Klein called a number of his former colleagues together for a White House dinner and told them he deplored Agnew's excesses and assured them the attacks were only political sound and fury. The friendly meeting may or may not have deflected the editorial return fire to Agnew's attacks, but it was a clever public relations ploy."[91] When Clay T. Whitehead, director of Nixon's Office of Telecommunications Policy, called on local television affiliates, in effect, to censor network news, Klein was quick to let reporters know that there was someone in the administration who was not in complete agreement. Whitehead, said Klein, had used "a number of phrases I don't want to associate myself with."[92]

Klein's second task, that of coordinating the information that flowed out of the executive departments, was the role that was least understood, primarily because it was performed behind the scenes. The job of overseeing the information functions of the entire executive branch was difficult for many reasons. More than 6,000 public information officers were working for the federal government during the Nixon years, and most were civil service employees. Such jobs are nonpolitical, and it was not easy to force their endorsement of a particular White House position. Some 200 of the information jobs were filled with political appointees, however, and these officials jumped when Klein called.[93] The task became a bit easier, moreover, after Klein saw to it that former colleagues and friends were appointed to the top information jobs at the Departments of Interior, Commerce, Agriculture and Health, Education and Welfare. He also had some influence on the selection of others.[94]

As a way of keeping track of what was going on throughout the executive branch, Klein assigned each of the members of his staff— which averaged between eighteen and twenty persons, including secretaries—to oversee the public information activities of particular departments and agencies. Each day information specialists from the various agencies telephoned the appropriate Klein aide and reported on the news releases they expected to circulate. Occasionally the procedure resulted in a change of plans for the lower-echelon information officials. In 1969, to cite one example, Labor Secretary George Shultz was prepared to release information about manpower programs. But after Klein's shop was informed, arrangements were made for Shultz to announce his plans at the White House.[95] At times, according to one report, Klein's aides even prepared press releases for departmental information specialists; this was done apparently only when a project was deemed potentially harmful to the administration if not handled with extreme care.[96]

The departmental information chiefs also were required to submit weekly reports outlining the events they expected to occur in the weeks ahead. Klein tried to meet with the public information specialists at least once a month for general discussion of their problems and publicity efforts.[97]

By far the most important of Klein's three tasks was his role as chief public relations officer for the administration, and it was in this aspect of his job that he was most innovative. Strangely, however, the apparatus he set up to publicize the Nixon regnancy, particularly the manner in which the operation was financed, was largely ignored by the press. Indeed Nixon had been in office for months before reporters began to understand what Klein was doing; it was well over a year before they fathomed the extent to which he was doing it. While reporters were marveling over how nice it was of "old Herb" to "open doors" for them, old Herb was finessing them out of their pads and pencils. In retrospect it is obvious that Klein's extensive publicity operation did not simply evolve; he and Nixon worked out the details well in advance of the 1968 election. Before Nixon was sworn in, Klein talked about the job he was to assume: "It's one that we [Nixon and Klein] discussed for a considerable time and we had it under consideration as we worked in the 1968 campaign. . . . We worked in this manner in the campaign. . . . We felt it was successful there, and we feel that as a result of the discussions we've had since, we have been able to fully structure this in a way which will be highly applicable to modern government."[98]

What exactly was this new job to be? It was many months before the specifics were known. In his memoirs Richard Nixon acknowledged that he had assigned Klein to "stay in touch with the media in the rest of the country, bring their reports to me, and get my ideas out to them."[99] In other words, Klein was to deal with journalists who worked west of the Appalachians—the hinterlands press. Because these reporters were not on the scene in Washington, they were less informed about issues and events than their colleagues in the capital; they were flattered to receive mail from the White House and susceptible to the propaganda techniques practiced by the Nixon publicists.

Less than two months after he was named director of communications, Klein began sending materials to the hinterlands press. Some four hundred editorial writers, for example, received information on postal reform; a short while later hundreds of editors received a packet of material concerning the antiballistic missile system.[100] The most ambitious public relations machine ever assembled for a president had been switched on.

Throughout Nixon's tenure the mailings remained a primary weapon in the PR arsenal. Hundreds, occasionally thousands of the kits were mailed each week. In some instances the editors of all eight thousand of the nation's weekly newspapers received a particular kit. Some mailings were addressed to writers in special fields, others to women's publications or the black press. A typical mailing contained press releases, excerpts from news conferences, presidential statements and messages, poll results, magazine or newspaper articles, and columns. They were always chosen to cast the administration in a favorable light. The "fact kits," as they were sometimes called, were usually accompanied by a cover letter signed by Klein.[101]

In 1969 kits containing Nixon speeches on neoisolationists and campus protestors were sent out. When Nixon began pushing for cabinet reorganization in the winter of 1971, Klein mailed informational packets to 3,827 publishers, editors, and broadcast officials. In this case the material was prepared in question and answer form. "Can these 'super departments' be made manageable?" asked one question. Yes, and General Motors and the American Telegraph and Telephone companies were cited as "large but manageable organizations" that "handle complex and complicated tasks in an efficient and effective manner." Other packages went out on such topics as revenue sharing, illegal drug trafficking, the economy, and the budget.[102] Early in 1971, Klein was favorably impressed by a Joseph Alsop column which defended the incursion in Laos and charged that Arkansas Senator J. William Fulbright and other antiwar critics were "eager to be proved right by an American defeat in war, and will loath being proved wrong by U.S. success in Southeast Asia." Klein included the column in a mailing; in his cover letter, he held it to be "timely and interesting."[103]

Another Klein innovation was the creation of administration briefing teams, which toured the country to extol Nixon's programs. Similar briefings were held in Washington as well. So many groups of congressmen and reporters were invited to the White House for briefings on the president's "New American Revolution" that insiders jokingly suggested the Roosevelt Room, where most of the meetings were held, ought to be renamed the "NAR Room."[104] But Klein put the Nixon show on the road. In the summer of 1969 he organized a group of Budget Bureau and White House staff members to explain Nixon's welfare proposals, also known as the family assistance plan. Similar teams toured the nation to explain postal reform and proposals to eliminate the draft.[105]

Klein often made use of the weekly projection reports sent to him by the departmental information chiefs to book appearances for prominent administration officials. James Hagerty, the former press secretary to President Eisenhower and later an ABC network executive, told a *New York Times* reporter that anytime a cabinet officer traveled to Seattle, the local ABC affiliate received a call from Klein's office "two weeks before the trip . . . offering an interview."[106]

A new twist was added to Klein's end runs in 1970 when he began organizing regional briefings—featuring top-level policy men such as Henry Kissinger and occasionally the president himself—for reporters around the country. In June 1970 after Nixon withdrew U.S. troops from Cambodia, Klein arranged a private briefing at San Clemente for thirty-eight editors and news executives. Nixon began with a brief speech; he was followed by Henry Kissinger, Lieutenant General John W. Vogt, Jr., then operations director for the Joint Chiefs of Staff, and William H. Sullivan, deputy assistant secretary of state for East Asian and Pacific affairs, all of whom defended the Cambodian maneuvers. A second regional briefing was held in New Orleans in August 1970 to discuss Middle East policy. A similar session was staged in San Clemente again a few days later, and another one was held in Chicago. In July 1971 Nixon and an entourage of associates held a briefing in Kansas City, Missouri, for 141 midwestern journalists.[107]

The regional briefings met with mixed results. After a briefing on the situation in Southeast Asia, an editor with the *Arizona Star*, David Brinegar, said he still favored withdrawal from Vietnam but "in the future, I probably will not attack Nixon for the nation's policy—I'll view it historically as part of the American scene."[108] An "eastern editor," however, felt a San Clemente briefing "wasn't worth the money to go out there just to hear the administration say the same old thing." He added: "We're trying to make [it] evident to Mr. Klein that we're not in his pocket."[109]

With the help of the plans committee, which he frequently presided over, Klein developed additional methods of reaching beyond the Washington press corps. He inaugurated chain call campaigns in which businessmen and special interest groups were alerted to positive poll results and asked to pass the message on to their friends and colleagues. He and his aides routinely canvassed editors, publishers, and broadcast executives for their reactions to presidential speeches; if the results were positive, they were made known. He dispatched fact kits to special groups, such as blue-collar workers and black, Jewish, and ethnic organizations. He encouraged prominent administration officials to write bylined articles in major publications.[110]

The entire Klein operation, in the view of many Washington reporters, was little more than blatant propagandizing. Klein hotly denied any suggestion he was a minister of propaganda, insisting the material he sent out was fact, not opinion. "If I just gave my opinions," he told me with a hint of irritation in his voice, "it would be a selling job. But we deal in statements of *fact*, and that's a different case."[111]

The mailings Klein sent out contained carefully selected articles and editorials that reflected opinions and not facts, and the curious manner in which the briefing tours and mailings were financed suggested that the Nixon men themselves believed their public relations effort was not entirely free of political propagandizing. For many of the tours and most of the mailings were underwritten by the Republican National Committee. At least sixteen fact kits containing Nixon speeches and statements were printed during the president's first two years at taxpayers' expense, but they were mailed by the party.[112] At some point the Republican party began paying for stationery as well. Kenneth Clawson was asked how this came about and replied, "Herb made the policy at the very beginning."[113] When White House briefing teams departed for the hinterlands to inform the nation about the Nixon welfare reform proposals, the Republican party again bore some of the expenses.[114]

Klein maintained that he was simply trying to lighten the taxpayers' burden and at the same time avoid any suspicion of propagandizing with public funds. But such tactics were essentially devious: the briefing teams did not advertise the fact that they were accepting expense money from the party, nor did the White House stationery purchased by the Republicans for the distribution of Klein's fact kits carry any hint that the mailings were political in nature. As far as the recipients knew, it was all official White House business.[115]

Private financing was also arranged for other Klein activities. Some special interest groups were encouraged to place newspaper ads extoling Nixon programs. In another case tax-exempt foundations financed a White House conference for government, business, labor, and educational leaders.[116]

Richard Nixon, Herb Klein, and James Keogh admitted, in so many words, that the director of communications operation was specifically and carefully designed, in Keogh's words, as an "end run around the national news corps."[117] This prompts the question: Where did the idea for this public relations apparatus originate? Was there a precedent for the Klein operation?

One of Nixon's idols was the twenty-eighth president of the United States, Woodrow Wilson. Significantly, perhaps, it was Wilson who devised the first, large-scale public relations effort that was clearly designed as a means of bypassing the press to deliver a message directly to the electorate. This was the famous Committee on Public Information, or the Creel committee.[118] A comparison of its structure and methods with the Klein operation strongly suggests that Richard Nixon knew something about Wilson's committee.

Eight days after the United States declared war, Wilson placed veteran newsman George Creel in charge of the public information committee. Throughout the rest of the war this was the vehicle that Wilson used most often to transmit information to the public. Even his secretary (there were no press secretaries at the time) stopped the daily news conferences he had been holding for reporters.

Ostensibly the purpose of the Creel committee was to motivate the country to support the war effort, but Creel deliberately chose to associate his information with the president, and the committee quickly turned into what historian Elmer Cornwell terms "a kind of embryonic 'propaganda ministry' for the National Executive."

The array of devices Creel invented to deliver the Wilson message to the public was prodigious. There was, for example, the official bulletin, which contained information about government actions and proceedings. It was posted in military camps and in 54,000 post offices, and was sent to government officials, publicity agents, and editors. Here again, wrote Cornwell, "the President was seeking a means of bypassing the press and getting verbatim information into the public's hands." Creel also produced and distributed posters and pamphlets. Some 75 million pieces of literature, it was estimated, were disseminated, a large portion of which were reproductions of presidential statements and speeches. A handbook was prepared for Boy Scouts instructing each to become "a dispatch bearer from the Government at Washington to the American people all over the country." The Scouts, in turn, attempted to dispatch messages to every home in the nation. In just one campaign over 5 million copies of a Flag Day speech by Wilson were delivered by the Scouts.

Another Creel innovation was the "Four-Minute Men" speaking program. Every week state and local chairmen were provided with a topic and a bulletin of information, including appropriate quotations and suggestions for phrasing. The chairmen distributed the material to their respective speakers, who organized four-minute speeches. They then ventured forth into motion picture houses, theaters, and anywhere else they could find an audience and delivered their messages. Speakers of different nationalities were picked to speak before ethnic audiences; some 75,000 speakers were eventually used, delivering over 1 million talks, reaching an estimated audience of 400 million. In some 90 percent of the speeches, the president was mentioned or quoted. Citizens were reminded of the need to back Wilson's moral leadership. In at least one instance the Four-Minute Men read a Wilson speech verbatim.

Creel also devised a brochure, the "National School Service," which was mailed twice monthly to school teachers across the country. Each issue was crammed with war news, quotations, articles, and suggestions that teachers could use to get a war message across to their students. Some 600,000 teachers received the National School Service free of charge; the message in each issue, it was estimated, reached 20 million homes.

During the war Congress was critical of the Creel committee but tolerated it on patriotic grounds. When the war was over, Wilson disbanded the committee. Creel reluctantly ceased his efforts but not before he dispatched some subtle commendations of the League of Nations.

The similarities between the Creel committee and the Klein shop are obvious. Many of the public relations devices Creel used were duplicated by Klein—the speakers, the presidential speeches mailed to editors, and other techniques. The major difference between the Creel operations and Klein's was the fact that Creel's propaganda could be excused as patriotic excess in time of declared war. Klein had no such excuse, but he managed to put together a public relations campaign that was at least as imaginative as the one created by George Creel and the Committee on Public Information.

6

Intimidation: "The Game Has to Be Played Awfully Rough"

As he waited to be sworn in, Richard Nixon dwelled on the problem of how to deal with the press. "I was prepared to have to do combat with the media in order to get my views and my programs to the people," he wrote in his memoirs.[1] Put another way, he was planning the third major element of his grand strategy for handling the news media: diminishment of the press's credibility with public criticism and the generation of fear with threats.

At least two incidents occurred prior to Nixon's inauguration that presaged what lay in store for journalists who challenged his version of events. During the last week of the 1968 campaign the *New York Times* reported that vice-presidential candidate Spiro Agnew had bene-fited from land deals with wealthy speculators while he was governor of Maryland. The *Times* also charged that Agnew had not told the truth about the inheritance of some bank stock. Agnew was furious. The "Governor," as he was then called by the Nixon men, was pon-dering what to do about the editorial attack when a teletype message was delivered to Agnew's campaign manager, George White. It was from the Nixon camp, and it was signed by Patrick Buchanan:

You might score some real yardage in the South with a good blast at the New York Times. Down there they are the essence of the New York, ultra-liberal, left-wing establishment press that has beaten on the South for years. Suggestions.

1) The Governor tear hell out of them for deliberate and vicious libel, demand an apology, ask if they are "man enough to give it."

2) The Governor then say that the Times is squealing because RN tore hell out of them. That the Times is willing to play low-level dirty politics; but they belly-ache when they have to pay the price. Then use Truman's quote. "If the editorial board of the New York Times

can't stand the heat, maybe they ought to get out of the kitchen."
They can dish it out; but they can't take it.

3) The Governor could needle hell out of them by saying after his
blast and demand for apology that "Actually those fellows who write
editorials for the Times aren't so bad. They just put their foot in their
mouth a little too often."[2]

Agnew did strike back. He issued a statement citing several errors
allegedly made by the *Times*. Nixon backed him up in a heated statement he issued during an interview on "Face the Nation." And the
Nixon-Agnew Campaign Committee placed a full-page ad in the *New
York Times* refuting the newspaper's charges. But Nixon and Agnew
were elected a few days later, and the issue was rendered moot.[3]

On December 23, 1968, John Ehrlichman wrote a memorandum
to William Safire suggesting that the president elect was contemplating
revenge against his perceived enemies, including those in the Fourth
Estate: "RN requests that a research paper be developed which includes
a recapitulation of the typical opposition smears of Richard Nixon
back through the years, including the more vicious press comments."[4]
It was vintage Nixon: he had been elected to the highest office in the
land yet could not bring himself to forgive and forget. As David Halberstam observed, "Now that he was president, he would make them
pay; he would not coopt them; that was too easy. Rather he would
cut them off, crush them."[5]

But during the initial months of the first term his plan to end run
the press worked so well that he did not need to punish it. He maintained his personal peace of mind by avoiding journalists and reading
only what his staff deemed worthy of his time. He delivered his message
directly to the people while his aides fed reporters a diet of harmless
information. But as the weeks passed and the president's traditional
honeymoon ended, the criticism about Nixon's isolation and his policies,
especially his Vietnam war strategy, began to intensify.

Around September of that first year Nixon's attitude toward his
journalistic critics began to harden. On September 13 the president's
news summary noted that a newsletter written by syndicated columnists
Rowland Evans and Robert Novak had contained "some of the most
negative comment on the Administration to date." Nixon immediately
dispatched a note to Herb Klien: "1. Get some tough letters to these
guys from subscribers. 2. Be sure they are cut off."[6] That same month
Frank Shakespeare stood before the annual convention of the Radio-
Television News Directors Association in Detroit and told the broadcasters they ought to be adding a little right-wing ballast to their
allegedly liberal ships.[7]

On October 17, 1969, Jeb Stuart Magruder sent to H. R. Haldeman a memorandum entitled "The Shot-gun versus the Rifle." It revealed that Nixon had ordered his aides on twenty-one occasions between September 16 and October 17 to retaliate against what he believed were inaccurate or unfair press reports. "Yesterday," wrote Magruder to Haldeman, "you asked me to give you a talking paper on specific problems we've had to shot-gunning the media and anti-Administration spokesmen on unfair coverage." Magruder continued:

It is my opinion this continual daily attempt to get to the media or to anti-Administration spokesmen because of specific things they have said is very unfruitful and wasteful of our time. . . .

The real problem that faces the Administration is to get to this unfair coverage in such a way that we make major impact on a basis which the networks-newspapers and Congress will react to and begin to look at things somewhat differently. It is my opinion that we should begin concentrated efforts in a number of major areas that will have much more impact on the media and other anti-Administration spokesmen and will do more good in the long run. The following is my suggestion as to how we can achieve this goal.[8]

Magruder recommended that the Federal Communications Commission set up an official monitoring system to keep track of network news coverage; that the Justice Department's antitrust division "investigate various media"; that the Internal Revenue Service "look into the various organizations that we are most concerned about"; and that the White House "begin to show favorites within the media." There was also this suggestion: "Utilize Republican National Committee for major letter writing efforts of both class nature and a quantity nature. We have set-up a situation at the National Committee that will allow us to do this, and I think by effective letter writing and telegrams we will accomplish our objective rather than again just the shot-gun approach to one specific Senator or one specific news broadcaster because of various comments."[9]

The atmosphere in the White House had clearly become polluted with an anti-press mephitis. This Nixon enemy would have to be confronted directly. The only questions that remained to be answered were, Who would do it, and when? According to Agnew's press secretary, Victor Gold, "They had already decided in the White House to have a speech made attacking the networks, and they had been considering over there who should make the speech for maximum impact. It was decided that Agnew should do it. . . . He had strong feelings about the press, which went back to his days in Baltimore. He disliked the *Baltimore Sun*. When he was nominated in 1968, the

Washington Post compared that to the nomination of Caligula's horse, and he felt the networks and the press had made him look like a fool in the 1968 campaign."[10]

The chain of events that led up to Agnew's emergence as the administration chief press kicker began when Ronald Ziegler announced on October 13, 1969, that Nixon would be making a major statement on Vietnam. During the ensuing three weeks there were press reports that the president would reduce bombing raids, withdraw troops, and offer a cease-fire. When the dramatic moment came, however, he declared his intention to continue U.S. participation in the war until North Vietnam agreed to negotiate an "honorable peace" or until the South Vietnamese were capable of defending themselves, and he called on "the great silent majority of my fellow Americans" to back him up.[11] Network correspondents, in their traditional postspeech analysis, characterized the address as "nothing really new" and "nothing of a substantial nature." ABC, much to the chagrin of the White House, brought out the grand old man of American diplomacy and the Democratic party, Averell Harriman, who gently asserted his opposition to the president's "Vietnamization" plan.[12]

Nixon and his media team smoldered with rage. Thousands of telegrams supporting the president's position poured into the White House, and many were critical of the journalists who had commented on Nixon's speech. The media team discussed what to do, and Pat Buchanan banged out a memorandum to the president suggesting an open attack on the networks, which Nixon quickly approved.[13]

By this time Spiro Agnew had gained a reputation for being the point man of the administration's assault team. He had displayed a lust for battle and a talent for shrill rhetoric only a month before, on October 19, 1969, when he traveled to New Orleans to attack antiwar demonstrators. "A spirit of national masochism prevails," he said on that occasion, "encouraged by an effete corps of impudent snobs who characterize themselves as intellectuals."[14] Agnew had thus demonstrated he was "the right man," in Nixon's words, to take on the press.[15]

On November 13 Agnew's press secretary, Herbert Thompson, informed the networks that the vice-president would be making a major address concerning their profession that evening at the Midwest Republican Conference in Des Moines. Executives at each network read advance copies of the speech and independently decided to accord it prime-time coverage.[16] When the time came, Agnew mounted the podium and lashed out at television journalists. President Nixon's November 3 speech, he charged, had been subjected to "instant analysis and querulous criticism." The reporters, he asserted, had "made clear their sharp disapproval" of Nixon's address "by the expressions on their faces, the tone of their questions, and the sarcasm of their responses." He continued:

Every American has a right to disagree with the president of the United States, and to express publicly that disagreement.

But the president of the United States has a right to communicate directly with the people who elected him, and the people of this country have the right to make up their own minds and form their own opinions about a presidential address without having the president's words and thoughts characterized through the prejudices of hostile critics before they can even be digested.[17]

This, it appears, was what was really bothering the president and his media team: news commentators were interfering with Nixon's control over his message. They were explaining it to viewers, putting it into context, comparing it to what had gone before.

Agnew had much more to say. He ridiculed the "gaggle of commentators" and "tiny and closed fraternity of privileged" journalists who worked in New York City and Washington, D.C., and who were talking "constantly to one another, thereby providing artificial reinforcement to their shared viewpoints." Although he disavowed any notion that he was calling for government censorship of network news shows, he pointedly noted that television stations enjoyed "a monopoly sanctioned and licensed by government" and suggested, "perhaps it is time that the networks were made more responsive to the views of the nation and more responsible to the people they serve."[18]

The Agnew tirade was fraught with shortcomings, the most glaring of which was the dearth of specifics. It was one thing to claim the networks were biased, another to offer evidence. And when Agnew did provide examples, he invariably had his facts wrong. The Nixon speech, for example, was not subjected to instant analysis. Network commentators were provided with copies of the address two hours in advance and had been briefed on it by Nixon's chief foreign affairs adviser, Henry Kissinger. Not a single prominent network commentator, moreover, came from the eastern establishment. David Brinkley hailed from North Carolina, Chet Huntley from Montana, Howard K. Smith from Louisiana, Eric Sevareid from South Dakota, Harry Reasoner from Iowa, Frank McGee from Oklahoma, and Walter Cronkite and Dan Rather from Texas. It was true, of course, that they were not elected, but they were subject to the most basic laws of supply and demand: if they failed to perform adequately, they would soon have been voted off the air by their viewers and employers.

Agnew also charged that when President Kennedy "rallied the nation in the Cuban missile crisis, his address to the people was not chewed over by a round-table of critics who disparaged the course of action he had asked America to follow." Once again he was wrong. Kennedy's speech was "chewed over" by eight newsmen on three networks on October 22, 1962. At one point Agnew alluded to a report of the House Commerce Committee, which charged—said the vice-president—that television coverage of the riots of the 1968 Democratic convention in Chicago "worked an injustice on the reputation of the Chicago police." He ignored the report of the National Commission on the Causes and Prevention of Violence, which stated that "police violence was a fact of convention week."[19] There were other major errors too, but they were overwhelmed by Agnew's harsh, bellicose, threatening tone. Said CBS president Frank Stanton, "Because a federally licensed medium is involved, no more serious episode has occurred in government-press relationships since the dark days in the fumbling infancy of this republic when the ill-fated Alien and Sedition Acts forbade criticism of the government and its policies on pain of exile or imprisonment."[20]

In the weeks following Agnew's broadside network executives spent countless hours debating whether the vice-president was speaking for himself alone or also for the president. Agnew insisted his stated views were his own; Ziegler adhered to the same line. During a press conference on December 9 Nixon was asked about the vice-president's critique of the news business. In his response a smug Nixon danced a fandango around the truth: "The vice president does not clear his speeches with me. . . . However, I believe that he rendered a public service in talking in a very dignified and courageous way about a problem many Americans are concerned about, and that is the coverage by news media and in particular television news media of public figures."[21] But few professional journalists believed they were hearing the full truth. ABC correspondent Bill Gill pointed out, "Anyone who has spent one full week covering news at the White House would know that a vice president doesn't belch until he is burped in the Oval Office."[22]

In the wake of Agnew's speech reporters began to perceive the outline of a carefully orchestrated scheme of intimidation. It was soon learned that Klein's aides had called local broadcasters around the country the day of the president's November 3 speech and asked what editorial comment was planned.[23] FCC Chairman Dean Burch, appointed just two weeks before Agnew's speech, also called the networks and demanded transcripts of the commentaries that had followed

Nixon's Vietnam address. Such a move by the regulatory agency was unprecedented, and the network executives were understandably upset. Then Dan Rather reported other calls: Klein and Ziegler had asked broadcasters to supply them with the details of commentaries they made after future presidential speeches. And Paul O'Neil, a member of the Subversive Activities Control Board, had made inquiries about plans for editorial responses to the administration's activities.[24] Three days after Agnew's speech, furthermore, Klein went on the CBS television program "Face the Nation" and told an astonished panel of reporters that if the press did not take steps to correct its shortcomings "you do invite the government to come in."[25]

The uproar that followed Agnew's initial outburst convinced Haldeman and Ziegler that the administration should hold its fire for awhile, but Buchanan argued they should continue, and the president acceded.[26] One week after his Des Moines appearance, Agnew went to Montgomery, Alabama, where he assured the nation's largest newspapers they would not be ignored. The American people "should be made aware of the trend toward the monopolization of the great public information vehicles and the concentration of more and more power in fewer and fewer hands," he said. He continued, "A single company in the nation's capital, holds control of the largest newspaper in Washington, D.C., *and* one of the four major television stations, *and* an all-news radio station, *and* one of the three major national news magazines — all grinding out the same editorial line — and this is not a subject that you have seen debated on the editorial pages of the *Washington Post* or the *New York Times.*"[27] Agnew moved on to the *New York Times*, citing instances of what he believed were poor editorial judgment. But again his diatribe was devoid of evidence. The "facts" he did cite, furthermore, were not facts at all. He said, for example, that all of the subsidiaries of the Washington Post Company — the *Post*, WTOP-TV, *Newsweek*, and WTOP radio — were guilty of "grinding out the same editorial line." This was not true. One of Nixon's Supreme Court nominees, Clement Haynesworth, was supported by the *Post*, opposed by WTOP-TV; the *Post* had never editorialized against U.S. involvement in Vietnam, which *Newsweek* had; the *Post* editorially urged the resignation of Supreme Court Justice Abe Fortas, whereas the other subsidiaries did not.[28]

Agnew also claimed the "monopolization of the great public information vehicles" was "not a subject that you have seen debated on the editorial pages of the *Washington Post* or the *New York Times.*" In fact, the *Times* had published an editorial on March 13, 1969, urging newspapers *not* to seek exemption from antitrust laws. The vice-president accused the *Times* of ignoring a display of congressional support of Nixon's Vietnam policy. The truth was that the story did not make the Washington edition, which Agnew apparently read, but was published in subsequent editions. The same subject was also covered on four days immediately thereafter.[29]

In sum, Agnew's case against the press fell to pieces on close examination. If there was a blatant bias among the media, he failed to show it. His tirades, moreover, indicated that his gripe was not against the press as a whole but against those he perceived as liberals. It was noteworthy that he attacked only two newspapers for putative monopolization; yet in the city in which he spoke, the *Montgomery Advertiser* and the *Alabama Journal* were both published by the same company. Both adhered to a political credo similar to the vice-president's and were therefore presumably adjudged wise.[30]

During the next few months Agnew reserved what he called his "pithies and pungents" for demonstrators and "intellectuals" and avoided direct confrontation with the press.[31] But on February 23, 1971, the CBS network broadcast a documentary, "The Selling of the Pentagon," which revealed the enormity of the Defense Department's effort—in the words of one observer—to "glamourize combat and maintain among the civilian population a pervasive sense of danger that can find relief only in a military solution."[32] The documentary disclosed, among other things, that the Pentagon's total public relations budget was probably close to $200 million a year; that it continued to use outdated propaganda films of the cold war; that millions of dollars were spent to stage tours and "firepower demonstrations" for VIPs; that a team of lecturing colonels traveled around the nation delving into the forbidden foreign affairs aspects of the Vietnam war, and much more. The CBS effort was a splendid display of investigative reporting, but the network had made some errors in editing, and this provided critics with ammunition for a sustained attack against the program and CBS.[33]

Such a vulnerable target could not be ignored by the administration's press critics, and Agnew's major contribution to the assault on CBS came in Boston on March 18 in a speech before the Republican Middlesex Club. The vice-president charged that "The Selling of the Pentagon" was "a subtle but vicious broadside against the nation's defense establishment," a perfect example of "the widening credibility gap which has simply been reported, not created, by this . . . vice president."[34] He avoided specific criticism of "The Selling of the Pentagon," but instead launched into an attack on previous CBS documentaries: "Considering the serious charges leveled recently by the

CBS television news organization against the public affairs activities of the Department of Defense, the matter of the network's own record in the field of documentary-making can no longer be brushed under the rug of national media indifference."[35]

He criticized "Project Nassau," a documentary of an aborted Haitian invasion, which was never aired, and he claimed CBS had engaged in deceptive practices in the filming of a 1968 documentary, "Hunger in America." The network, said the vice-president, had shown a baby to be dying of malnutrition when in fact it was dying from meningitis. He quoted from an FCC report that allegedly chastized CBS for its duplicity but failed to mention additional, pertinent portions of the FCC order, which stated that "Hunger in America" had been a laudable performance.[36] Furthermore Agnew had not bothered to obtain CBS's side of the story. "When we filmed the baby," said producer-writer Peter Davis, "hospital authorities told us it was dying of pre- and post-natal malnutrition." And CBS president Frank Stanton pointedly noted that President Nixon himself had praised "Hunger in America" when it was aired.[37]

The CBS network responded to the chorus of criticism with a re-broadcast of "The Selling of the Pentagon." But this time the network also aired a series of rebuttals by its critics, including Agnew. The vice-president, however, demanded the privilege of editing his remarks. CBS refused, and Agnew told a regional press conference in St. Louis that he was "totally dissatisfied" with the network's latest performance. "It's rather unusual to give you the right of rebuttal," he said, "and not allow you to decide what you're going to say in rebuttal."[38]

The arsenal of weapons the vice-president used to cow the press included more than simple bombast. In some instances, he barred reporters from covering his appearances; in other cases he dictated who could cover him and who could not. When Agnew went to St. Louis in March 1971 where he lambasted CBS for airing "The Selling of the Pentagon," press credentials to cover the regional news conference were handed out by the publisher of the conservative *St. Louis Globe-Democrat*. As a result reporters from the more liberal *St. Louis Post-Dispatch*, the *Globe-Democrat*'s chief rival, were denied seats. After a heated debate newsmen who had been left out were allowed to sit around the walls of the room while the others sat at a table with the vice-president. Questions were permitted only from the eleven reporters around the table. Agnew's press secretary, Victor Gold, instructed the outcasts along the wall that they could only report on the event, not participate in it. The next day the Agnew-approved *Globe-Democrat* reported that "it was a no-holds barred meeting with newsmen. No restrictions were imposed by Agnew on what type of questions could be asked." There was no mention in the story of the restrictions on who could ask the questions. Ironically, Agnew consumed half the press conference censuring the press—at the same time he was managing the news.[39]

The aim of the Nixon-approved Agnew onslaught was to let the press know what the silent majority thought about the news they were getting. They could not have chosen a more propitious moment in the nation's history. In an August 1969 survey for *Time* magazine pollster Louis Harris found that 90 percent of those he surveyed who read newspapers felt they were "sometimes unfair, partial and slanted"; 75 percent believed that "the real story in Washington is behind the scenes and only a small part ever gets into the news." A third of those questioned distrusted television news.[40]

There is little doubt that Nixon and Agnew struck a vein of antipathy for the press among reasonable, middle-class Americans. An ABC poll conducted shortly after the Des Moines speech showed that of 559 adults interviewed, 51 percent were substantially in agreement with Agnew, 33 percent disagreed, and 16 percent did not know or had no opinion. However, the *Alfred I. duPont-Columbia University Survey of Broadcast Journalism* for 1969–1970 reported that "despite this weight in favor of Agnew [in the ABC poll], only one quarter felt that the news media had been unfair to the administration, while three-fifths felt they had *not* been unfair and should *not* ease up. Sixty-seven percent felt they wanted commentators to continue their prompt analysis and comment after presidential speeches."[41]

The poll results seemed to reflect, therefore, a general dissatisfaction with the press but appeared to refute Agnew's allegation that the great "silent majority" felt journalists were biased against Nixon. The question that begged answering, then, was: From what element of the population did the tremendous support for Agnew's arguments come? Who wrote the thousands of supporting letters and telegrams that the White House claimed to have received?

If the letters sent to the president were similar to those received by television stations and the networks, then it can be said that a portion of Agnew's support came from the far-right fringe of American society. Much of the correspondence sent to the press was clearly hate mail. The Columbia University School of Journalism analyzed some of the letters received by one network and reported: "Eleven percent were anti-Semitic ('He [Agnew] got his pound of flesh off you Jew boy,' 'V.P. Agnew expressed my views 100 percent. We are tired of the news being presented to us from a *Jewish point of view.* Replace some of the Jewish reporters with good Americans.') Ten percent were anti-black ('We are tired of the Niggers having all the time they want. I understand you have a Nigger newsman. You liberals in the East just can't be trusted with the news.' 'You damn Jews have been getting away with a lot of crap, and it took the vice president to stop it. . . . All we see are *Niggers* and *Jews.*')"[42]

CBS's Mike Wallace learned what sort of audience Agnew was playing to when he conducted a grim interview with one of the soldiers who had taken part in the My Lai massacre in Vietnam. This is how Wallace explained it in a November 1969 broadcast of the CBS show, "60 Minutes": "Last night on the 'CBS Evening News' I interviewed a young man who fought in Vietnam. . . . He said he had shot old men, women, children, and babies in cold blood. Since that broadcast we've received hundreds of messages about it. The overwhelming majority condemn CBS News for putting the interview on the air. One viewer had written: 'Either Wallace is a massively unsophisticated reporter or is simply pimping for our anti-war feelings to his own purposes. Perhaps what Agnew means by "effete Eastern snobs" is the contempt Wallace shows for the public and its sensitivities.' "[43]

Was the Agnew onslaught part of a Nixon administration conspiracy to intimidate and subdue the press? In early 1972 the *Columbia Journalism Review* commented editorially that "the observer draws back from the notion of a press suppression plan in view of the sheer lack of pattern, the clumsiness and pettiness" of various incidents.[44] But the *Review*'s editors and many other observers failed to consider that a broad attack on the press did not have to be patterned. However haphazard the intimidation campaign appeared to be, it fit very well into the larger scheme: keep the press ignorant of meaningful information, take the message directly to the people, reduce press interference with that message through relentless intimidation. The purpose of attacking the press, therefore, was to reduce its credibility and to keep it sidetracked and on the defensive; a secondary goal was to get journalists to tell the Nixon story the way Nixon wanted it told.

After Richard Nixon had resigned, it was easily seen that there had existed a plot—unprecedented in its magnitude and organization and in the energy with which it was perpetrated—to intimidate and manipulate the press. For those who refused to accept the documentary evidence, there were erstwhile insiders like William Safire to give witness:

Was there a conspiracy, as Walter Cronkite of CBS solemnly charged, on the part of the Nixon Administration to discredit and malign the press?

Was this so-called "anti-media campaign" encouraged, directed, and urged on by the President himself?

Did this alleged campaign to defame and intimidate Nixon-hating newsmen succeed, isolating and weakening them politically? And did it contribute to the us-against-them divisions that then cracked back at Nixon after his election victory?

The above questions are slanted so as to elicit a ringing response of "Nonsense!" But the answer to all these questions is, sadly, yes.[45]

The man most responsible for maintaining the intense tempo of the administration's attacks on the press was Patrick J. Buchanan. He did not make the press policy; this came from the president, and it was enthusiastically implemented by the chief of staff, H. R. Haldeman. But of all the president's close advisers, Buchanan was most deeply committed to reducing the press to a transmission belt for presidential messages.

Although he was educated in and worked in the profession of journalism, Buchanan was essentially a political animal, a conservative ideologue who saw a liberal behind every typewriter and was determined to purge them even if it meant sacrificing the First Amendment to do it. He was so unconcerned with the freedom of speech and press that he would have banned criticism of Nixon's statements: "My primary concern is that the President have the right of untrammeled communications with the American people. When that communication is completed, what he has had to say should not be immediately torn apart or broken down even before the American people have had a chance to make their own judgment about what he said."[46]

Because he supervised the preparation of the president's daily news digest, Buchanan was able to maintain a close watch over the press. He was apparently designated the White House monitor in early 1970 after previous efforts to establish a press surveillance system proved inadequate. On January 21, 1970, Jeb Magruder recommended in a memo to H. R. Haldeman that a new method he devised and that either Buchanan or Herb Klein take command of it. Buchanan was the better choice, wrote Magruder, because the Klein shop "relates directly with the press" and "has a tendency to go along with them rather than institute counter action." Noted Haldeman, "I'll approve whatever will work—and am concerned with results—not methods."[47] While his staff kept watch over the print press, Buchanan monitored the network news shows. Klein and his aides reinforced the Buchanan operation by monitoring the wire service tickers and the network shows, which they could view simultaneously on a remote-control, three-set console.[48]

The White House watch on the press had one central purpose: to provide ammunition for the relentless campaign of intimidation. As Magruder stated in a memo to Haldeman's aide, Larry Higby, "We will continue to hammer at press favoritism on a regular basis. We will ask the Vice President to make this a standard fare while he's on the stump in the congressional campaigns. We will keep tabs on examples of partisan press treatment and feed them into the Vice President (and Cabinet officers on the stump) on a regular basis."[49] Higby expressed it more candidly: "What we are trying to do here is to tear down the institution."[50]

The Nixon administration employed both defensive and offensive tactics to intimidate and manipulate the press. Included in the former category were demands for corrections and equal time, censorship, gag rules for executive branch employees, and attempts to plug leaks of information, which came to be known in the Nixon White House as "plumbing."

In 1971, for example, a Klein aide who specialized in television, Alvin Snyder, monitored a late night talk show hosted by Dick Cavett on the ABC network and saw three guests speak in opposition to the Supersonic Transport program. Two days before the SST vote in the Senate, Snyder called Cavett's executive producer, and "suggested" they air the other side of the controversy by allowing the appearance of William Magruder, the administration's "program manager" for the SST. The producer asked if he could put SST opponent Senator William Proxmire of Wisconsin on the same show to add a little balance. Snyder gently allowed that "it would be fairer" if Magruder went on alone. ABC relented. "Hi," Cavett said as he greeted his audience the following evening. "My name is Dick Cavett—and we will make equal time available to those who think it is not."[51]

Until the Cavett episode, Snyder had succeeded in masquerading as the administration's television "ombudsman"—the public relations liaison with the networks. He did not "advise" the president on the use of television, he told me in a March, 1971, interview. He did not maintain a "watch" over the networks; he was involved in "setting up interviews" and "coordinating" newsmen's requests, he said. "Broadcasters have never had this kind of service before," Snyder said. "They need help in order to do a better job of telling the story of this administration."[52]

Nixon's associates routinely issued gag orders to those they thought might divulge information to the press. When Clark Mollenhoff resigned from his White House job in May 1970, both Haldeman and Erlichman reminded him that "as a lawyer for the president, I was bound by the lawyer-client relationship against disclosing information I had received while on the White House staff."[53] In 1971 Attorney General John Mitchell tightened Justice Department guidelines on contacts with the press by forbidding subordinates from discussing with reporters "most aspects" of civil cases. In criminal cases the ban would begin "from the time a person is the subject of a criminal investigation" and not from the time a person was indicted or arrested, as was previously the case.[54] Mitchell also threw his department's support behind the attempts of various federal agencies to fight the Freedom of Information Act of 1966, which provides that U.S. citizens, with certain exceptions, must have access to government reports and records. During the first Nixon term the Justice Department went to court over forty times in efforts to deter the release of information requested under the law.[55]

A number of federal agencies, including the U.S. Postal Service, the National Science Foundation, and the Public Health Service, warned employees in 1971 not to associate with reporters.[56] At about the same time officials at the Bureau of Labor Statistics of the Labor Department were ordered to cease providing their customary interpretive briefings for reporters. For twenty years BLS statisticians had held the briefings to analyze for newsmen their complicated price and employment figures. During the first few months of 1971, however, the experts' opinions differed with the rosy picture the White House was trying to paint. So Labor Secretary James Hodgson solved the public relations problem by eliminating the briefings.[57]

Of all the defensive tactics employed by the Nixon team against the press, none was pursued more vigorously—or earned more lasting infamy—than the unremitting effort to plug leaks and punish leakers. When a transgressor was unearthed, the retribution was often harsh. In late 1968 Air Force efficiency expert A. Ernest Fitzgerald revealed to Congress that overruns on the C-5A transport program could amount to $2 billion. Fitzgerald later lost his job. He said he was fired; the Pentagon said his job had been eliminated as an economy measure. The White House was delighted. "We should let him bleed, for a while at least," wrote Alexander Butterfield in a memorandum to H. R. Haldeman. "Fitzgerald is no doubt a top-notch cost expert, but he must be given very low marks in loyalty; and after all, loyalty is the name of the game."[58]

During Nixon's first five months in the White House, the New York and Washington newspapers printed twenty-one stories that Nixon believed jeopardized the national security. He was determined to stop the leaks and discussed what could be done with FBI Director J. Edgar

Hoover and Attorney General Mitchell. The result was the president's decision that national security adviser Henry Kissinger would supply Hoover with the names of all those who had access to information that was leaked; the FBI would then, in Nixon's words, "take the necessary steps—including wiretapping—to investigate the leaks and find the leakers."

On May 9, 1969, a *New York Times* story revealed that American B-52s had been bombing targets in Cambodia for two months, but the raids had been kept secret from Americans on the grounds of national security. Nixon and Kissinger were furious.[59] With the president's approval Kissinger asked Hoover to "make a major effort" to find the source of the story. Kissinger called Hoover four times that day and, in the final conversation, told the FBI director that the White House would "destroy whoever did this, if we can find him, no matter where he is."[60] By early 1971 the FBI had installed wiretaps on the phones of seventeen people: seven members of Kissinger's staff, three State and Defense Department officials, four reporters, and three members of the White House staff.[61] Despite the prodigious effort no leakers were located, and Nixon himself pronounced the surreptitious program "a dry hole. Just globs and globs of crap."[62]

Richard Nixon's *Memoirs* gives this prosaic introduction to what would become one of the major battles in his war against leakers: "On Sunday morning, June 13 [1971], I picked up the *New York Times*. In the top left-hand corner there was a picture of me standing with Tricia in the Rose Garden. *Tricia Nixon Takes Vows* was the headline. Next to the picture was another headline: *Vietnam Archive: Pentagon Study Traces 3 Decades of Growing U.S. Involvement.*"[63] It was the first installment of what would become known as the Pentagon Papers, a seven-thousand-page, highly classified Defense Department study of the Vietnam conflict up to 1968. The papers reveal how the United States, through several administrations, deliberately became involved in and escalated an armed conflict that would cost 57,000 American lives. At first, Nixon was unexcited by the disclosures. The official Pentagon history appeared to indict the Johnson and Kennedy administrations and had nothing to do with him. But Henry Kissinger was livid. According to H. R. Haldeman, "Kissinger told the president he didn't understand how dangerous the release of the Pentagon Papers was. 'It shows you're a weakling, Mr. President. . . . The fact that some idiot can publish all of the diplomatic secrets of this country on his own is damaging to your image, as far as the Soviets are concerned, and it could destroy our ability to conduct foreign policy. If the other powers feel that we can't control internal leaks, they will never agree

Jimmy Carter, July 1979. (Associated Press)

Richard Nixon. (Associated Press)

President Gerald Ford meets
the press in the old Executive
Office Building, December 2,
1974. (Gerald R. Ford Library)

Ronald Reagan, May 1983.
(Associated Press)

Ronald Reagan razzes the press
at a White House News Photographers' dinner, May 1983.
"I've been waiting years to do
this," said the president.
(United Press International)

to secret negotiations.' " Apparently Nixon was still unconvinced, so Kissinger tried another tack: the man primarily responsible for leaking the documents, Daniel Ellsberg, was a "weirdo." Ellsberg had taught at some of Kissinger's seminars at Harvard; he was, said Kissinger, a drug user who had strange sexual tastes. That was enough for Nixon; something had to be done.[64]

The president decided, he later wrote, that "it is the role of government, not the *New York Times*, to judge the impact of a secret document." He ordered Attorney General Mitchell to go to court to stop the *Times* and other publications from printing the Pentagon Papers. He also ordered the Justice Department to seek indictments against Ellsberg for stealing government property and possessing classified documents; a Los Angeles grand jury returned the indictments against Ellsberg on June 28. "While I cared nothing for [Ellsberg] personally," wrote Nixon, "I felt that his views had to be discredited. I urged that we find out everything we could about his background, his motives, and his co-conspirators, if they existed." But he did not trust J. Edgar Hoover, who was friendly with Ellsberg's father-in-law, to do the job, so he decided to launch his own antileak operation.[65]

First, Nixon sent for Haldeman. According to the chief of staff, "I was called into his office, and ordered to confront personally every single Cabinet officer and agency head, brutally chew them out and threaten them with extinction if they didn't stop all leaks in the future. 'You're going to be my Lord High Executioner from now on,' Nixon told me."[66] Haldeman ordered one of his assistants, Gordon Strachan, to conduct a study of leaks and set up a monthly reporting system. Several weeks later Strachen came back with his report: eleven cases had been studied and weighed for "possible Haldeman action as 'Lord High Executioner' to stop leaks."[67]

Meanwhile Nixon had summoned John Erlichman and had instructed him, "If we can't get anyone in this damn government to do something about the problem [leaks] that may be the most serious one we have, then, by God, we'll do it ourselves. I want you to set up a little group right here in the White House. Have them get off their tails and find out what's going on and figure out how to stop it."[68] Thus was born the Special Investigations Unit, later renowned as "The Plumbers." Observed William Safire: "For the second time, a hatred of the press— a need to 'stop the leaks' and to teach the leakers a lesson—caused Nixon to go over the brink, to lose all sense of balance, to defend his privacy at the expense of everyone else's right to privacy, and to create the climate that led to Watergate."[69]

Erlichman named his friend and assistant, Egil "Bud" Krogh, to head the Plumbers unit; Krogh hired an ex-FBI agent, G. Gordon Liddy. David Young, a Kissinger assistant who had done some leak plugging in the national security shop, was also picked to work on the unit. The Plumbers set up an office in the basement of the Old Executive Office Building and equipped it with an alarm system, combination safes, private phone lines, and wall charts for keeping track of their various projects.[70] They had been organized for only a short while when they were joined by former CIA operative E. Howard Hunt, who came highly recommended by Charles Colson.[71] For the next few months the Special Investigations Unit chased leakers from coast to coast. On Labor Day weekend, a Plumbers team burglarized the Los Angeles office of Dr. Lewis Fielding, Daniel Ellsberg's former analyst.[72] They also probed leaks to *New York Times* reporters Tad Szulz and William Beecher and columnist Jack Anderson before the unit was disbanded late in 1971 or early in 1972.[73]

Given the hatred that Nixon and his associates felt for leaks and leakers, it is ironic that they were not above engaging in the practice themselves. Nixon ordered an intensive investigation of Senator Edward Kennedy's Chappaquiddick accident, for example, so the findings could be used to smear him. "I suspected that the press would not try very hard to uncover it," he wrote. "Therefore I told Ehrlichman to have someone investigate the case for us and get the real facts out."[74]

One night during the Watergate period *Washington Post* reporter Bob Woodward met his now-celebrated anonymous source, Deep Throat, in a Washington parking garage and asked about leak-plugging efforts at the White House. Replied Deep Throat, "That operation was not only to check leaks to the papers but often to manufacture items for the press. It was a Colson-Hunt operation. Recipients include all of you guys—Jack Anderson, Evans and Novak, the *Post* and the *New York Times*, the *Chicago Tribune*. The business of Eagleton's drunk-driving record or his health records, I understand, involves the White House and Hunt somehow. Total manipulation—that was their goal."[75]

Another moving force behind the administration's push to plug leaks, Henry Kissinger, was also a practiced leaker. In his first meeting with the National Security Council staff on inauguration day, he instructed his subordinates: "The most important thing is that all of you instantly are to sever your relations with the press. I observed from reading the *New York Times* and the *Washington Post* that the Johnson administration was the leakiest ship afloat. That will not happen here: The penalty is being fired. If anybody leaks in this administration, I will be the one to leak. You are not to talk to the press at all. In certain instances I may ask you to establish contact with the press."[76] And that is the way he went on to play the game. When stories were leaked that reflected poorly on him, he would lay a dragnet for the transgressor. At the same time he would leak with such aplomb that he could openly joke about it. He frequently said that he planted stories of his impending resignation "to lift the morale of my staff."[77]

Kissinger was the master of the backgrounder—press briefings wherein newsmen can report what is said but cannot attribute the source. Sometimes the backgrounders would be held in a semiformal White House setting, and Kissinger would stroll in and begin the session with a funny line: "Does anyone have a question for my answers?" While flying to summit meetings or negotiating sessions, he would saunter into the press section of the plane and hold forth at length—on background, of course.[78]

As a result of his deft maneuvering of journalists and his ability to make them feel he was indispensable, Kissinger was rarely called to task for his shortcomings: his failure to address international economic issues, his refusal to consider human rights matters, his courting of the world's most oppressive dictators. Even the *New York Times* suppressed stories at Kissinger's behest, and he was described by the nation's top news weeklies as the "Merlin of American diplomacy" (*Newsweek*) and possibly "the greatest [Secretary of State] in U.S. history" (*Time*).[79]

By far the most important and most frequently used press intimidation tactic was the attack in all its forms—direct, indirect, overt and covert. On different occasions the assaults were aimed either at the press in general or against specific targets.

The public antipress campaign spearheaded by Vice-President Agnew was trivial when compared to what was going on in the privacy of the White House. On September 15, 1972, Haldeman and John Dean were meeting with the president in the Oval Office when the conversation turned to the "enemies" who were trying to wreck the Watergate cover-up. Dean remarked that he had been keeping notes on "lots of people who are emerging as less than our friends." The president leaned forward and said, "I want the most comprehensive notes on all those who tried to do us in. They didn't have to do it. . . . No—they were doing this quite deliberately and they are asking for it and they are going to get it. We have not used the power in this first four years, as you know. We have never used it. We have not used the bureau [FBI] and we have not used the Justice Department, but things are going to change now."[80]

The "enemies list" memoranda, which finally came to light during the Senate Watergate hearings, addressed "the matter of how we can maximize the fact of our incumbency in dealing with persons known to be active in opposition to our administration. Stated a bit more bluntly—how can we use the available federal machinery to screw our political enemies." The lists contained the names of over fifty active journalists.[81]

The question of whether the Nixon administration "used the power" of the federal government against his enemies prior to September 1972, will be addressed later in this chapter. Suffice it to say, for now, that numerous schemes were certainly considered. In his infamous "shotgun versus the rifle" memorandum of October 17, 1969, Jeb Magruder suggested that the Justice Department, Internal Revenue Service and Federal Communications Commission be turned loose on the press. He wrote another "Confidential/Eyes Only" memo on July 17, 1970 and called it "Tentative Plan—Press Objectivity." Among the recommendations were these:

Have (FCC chairman) Dean Burch "express concern" about press objectivity in response to a letter from a Congressman. . . . Have outside groups petition the FCC and issue public 'statements of concern' over press objectivity. . . . Have a Senator or Congressman write a public letter to the FCC suggesting the "licensing" of individual newsmen, i.e., the airwaves belong to the public, therefore the public should be protected from the misuse of these airwaves by individual newsmen.[82]

Frequently, the media team hauled out the rifles and took aim at specific targets. At various times, they stalked such occasional prey as *Time*, *Newsweek*, *Life*, ABC's Howard K. Smith, NBC's John Chancellor, the *Chicago Tribune*, and Rowland Evans and Robert Novak.[83] *Time*'s Washington bureau chief, Hugh Sidey, was declared persona non grata and denied the privilege of riding on *Air Force One*.[84] Prize-winning investigative reporter H.L. Schwartz III of the Associated Press, *New York Times* reporters Neil Sheehan, William Beecher, and Tad Szulc, and the *Boston Globe* and *Newsday* were censured or probed. On March 27, 1973, according to the White House transcripts, John Ehrlichman recalled for Nixon the steps that had been taken to plug leaks to Szulc: "We had an active and on-going White House job using the resources of the bureau (FBI), the agency (CIA) and the various department security arms with White House supervision."[85] Sheehan—who played a central role in the *Times'* acquisition of the Pentagon Papers—and his wife, Susan, were investigated by a Boston grand jury. No indictments were returned, and the Sheehans were never called on to testify, but the preparation of a legal defense reportedly set the *Times* back $25,000.[86]

Newsday's primary transgression was a six-part series of investigative reports about the shady business investments of the president's friend, Charles G. "Bebe" Rebozo. A team of *Newsday* reporters, headed by Robert Greene, spent the spring and summer of 1971 in pursuit of the story. Nixon's media team heard about the newspaper's probe, and subsequently the reporting team ran into numerous roadblocks thrown up by the Departments of Defense and Interior, the General Services Administration, and the White House itself. *Newsday*'s investigators showed up for interview appointments to find that FBI agents had already been there.[87] Inside the White House John Dean supervised an investigation of *Newsday*'s activities by Jack Caulfield; at one point they considered planting rumors that *Newsday* was looking into Rebozo's activities because some of its editors and reporters were "Kennedy loyalists." They toyed with the idea of filing antitrust charges against the *Los Angeles Times*, which is owned by the same publishing firm that owns *Newsday*.[88] After the series appeared, wrote William Safire, "the president made it plain to Ron Ziegler that *Newsday* was to get nothing, not even the normal courtesies extended to similar news outlets."[89] Robert Greene was called in for a tax audit by the New York State Internal Revenue Division, an act instigated by the White House.[90] The tax authorities also went through the returns of *Newsday*'s publisher, William Attwood, and its editor, David Laventhal, as well as the paper's fiscal records. *Newsday*'s White House correspondent, Martin Schram, was denied the most routine privileges.[91]

The newspaper which became the White House's prime target, however, was the *Washington Post*. One of the first overt signs of the administration's enmity for the Capital's premier newspaper came in Vice-President Agnew's Montgomery, Alabama, speech in November, 1969. Six months later, the following "talking paper" was sent—the sender was not identified—to Jeb Stuart Magruder:

1. Put someone on the Washington Post to needle Kay Graham (the publisher). Set up calls or letters every day from the viewpoint of I hate Nixon but you're hurting our cause in being so childish, ridiculous and over-board in your constant criticism, and thus destroying your credibility.

2. Nofziger should work out with someone in the House a round robin letter to The Post that says we live in Washington, D.C., read the D.C. papers, but fortunately we also have the opportunity to read the papers from our home districts and are appalled at the biased coverage the people of Washington receive of the news, compared to that in the rest of the country, etc.

A few days later, Magruder reported to Haldeman that the suggestions had been implemented.[92]

In 1971 the *Post* obtained and began printing excerpts from the Pentagon Papers, and the administration went to court to force it (and the *New York Times*) to cease publication of the stories. Shortly after, according to Katherine Graham, Deputy Attorney General Richard Kleindienst sent the *Post* a message which threatened "us with a campaign against the press and with criminal prosecution" if the "sensitive" portions of the Pentagon Papers were not returned. If the criminal charges were successfully prosecuted, Kleindienst suggested, the parent Washington Post Company could lose the licenses of its three television stations.[93]

During the summer and fall of 1972, as the *Post* continued its series of exclusive stories on the Watergate burglary and the Nixon campaign organization's political sabotage against the Democrats, the White House began turning up the heat. The president's appointments secretary, Dwight Chapin, took note of a story linking him to dirty-trickster Donald Segretti and pronounced it a "collection of absurdities." John Ehrlichman blasted the *Post*'s Segretti story as "hearsay about four times removed." Ronald Ziegler dismissed the Segretti story and others as tales he would "not dignify with comment." At White House behest Congressman Clark MacGregor, Republican of Minnesota, called a televised news conference and denounced the *Post* for "using innuendo, third-person hearsay, unsubstantiated charges, anonymous sources, and scare headlines."[94] In late October, Republican National Committee chairman Robert Dole appeared before the Maryland State Central Committee in Baltimore and delivered a twenty-minute broadside that contained fifty-seven references to the *Washington Post*.[95]

The very next day, the *Post* published a Bob Woodward–Carl Bernstein story which stated that Hugh Sloan, the former treasurer of the Committee to Re-Elect the President, had testified before the Watergate grand jury that H. R. Haldeman was one of five people who controlled the campaign funds for political espionage and sabotage. The story, it later turned out, contained one error: Even though Haldeman did help control the funds, Sloan had not named him before the grand jury. At the White House, Ziegler was about ten minutes into his morning briefing when a reporter asked, "Ron, has the FBI talked to Bob Haldeman about his part in allegedly managing a secret slush fund for political sabotage?" For the next thirty minutes, Ziegler tore into the *Post* with abandon: "This is shabby journalism by the *Washington Post* . . . based again on hearsay . . . a distorted headline that was based totally on hearsay and innuendo . . . a vicious abuse of the journalistic process."[96] Ziegler continued his routine denials of the *Post*'s Watergate stories for the next few weeks. Then, on Friday, December 15, the press secretary took punitive action.

Post society reporter Dorothy McCardle, a sixty-eight-year-old grandmother who had covered the social life of five First Families, arrived at the White House that day to attend a reception. She was informed that a pool of five reporters had been chosen to cover the event, and she was not among them. It had long been customary to permit the local papers in Washington to cover all White House social functions, but Mrs. McCardle faithfully accepted Ziegler's new rule and returned Saturday night to cover a black-tie dinner. Again, she was excluded. On Sunday, she was barred from the White House worship service. On Monday, she was forbidden from covering a Christmas party for children of foreign diplomats.[97]

Pressed for an explanation, Ronald Ziegler said the White House was concerned that other publications had not had the "opportunity" to cover the social scene at the Executive Mansion. "We intend to spread it around more," he said. With tongue tucked firmly in cheek, Benjamin Bradlee issued a statement: "We are delighted to hear from Mr. Ziegler that no newspapers are being excluded from the pools which cover the White House social events. The *Washington Post* has been excluded from the last four social events, including the party Monday afternoon for diplomats' children. That seems to defy the odds, but we hope we will have the chance to bring firsthand reports to our readers again soon."[98]

But Ziegler was determined to make his new "pool policy" work. On January 5, 1973, he summoned thirteen male reporters and formed a pool to cover a White House reception for new members of Congress. The men had never covered such social events before, and most of them did not wish to start at that late point in their careers. Many of those who chose to report the affair went scampering after society reporters for pointers on how it was done.

The great pool affair was, in the opinion of some observers, one of the most petty acts of revenge the Nixon administration attempted to perpetrate on the press. It lasted until Nixon's second inauguration, when Ziegler quietly ceased enforcement of his new rule.[99]

On the Sunday that Mrs. McCardle was turned away from the White House worship service, *Washington Post* reporter Carl Bernstein attended a dinner where he talked to a friend who was a reporter for the *Star-News*. The friend said he had been told by Charles Colson in early November that "as soon as the election is behind us, we're going to really shove it to the *Post*. All the details haven't been worked out yet, but the basic decisions have been made—at a meeting with the President."[100]

Colson may have been referring to an Oval Office meeting on September 15 during which, according to White House transcripts later prepared by the House Judiciary Committee, John Dean brought up the *Washington Post*'s investigation of Watergate. The following conversation ensued:

PRESIDENT: The main thing is the *Post* is going to have damnable, damnable problems out of this one. They have a television station . . . and they're going to have to get it renewed.
HALDEMAN: They've got a radio station, too.
PRESIDENT: Does that come up, too? The point is, when does it come up?
DEAN: I don't know. But the practice of non-licensees filing on top of licensees has certainly gotten more . . . active in . . . this area.
PRESIDENT: And it's going to be God damn active here.
DEAN: (Laughter) (Silence)
PRESIDENT: Well, the game has to be played awfully rough.[101]

Actually, the Washington Post Company owned three television stations, two of which were in the state of Florida. About three months after the president's Oval Office conversation with Haldeman and Dean, the licenses of both Florida stations were challenged. In Jacksonville three groups sought the license of WJXT-TV; one of them was led by George Champion, Jr., who had served as the finance chairman of Nixon's 1972 campaign in Florida. In Miami the principals of the challenging party included two law partners of former Senator George Smathers of Florida, a close friend of Nixon. The Miami station, WPLG-TV, had also been challenged in 1970 by a group that included former business partners of Bebe Rebozo. That challenge had been dropped after seven and one-half months, at a cost to the Post company of $67,000 in legal fees.[102] Reporters asked Ziegler whether the administration's displeasure with the *Washington Post* was in any way related to the challenges of the parent company's broadcast licenses. "No, absolutely not," replied the press secretary.[103]

Beginning in 1969 several syndicated columnists also became the targets of White House intimidators and manipulators. Nixon himself leveled the sights on Joseph Kraft, a pundit the president admired until the columnist began asserting that the administration's efforts to negotiate an end to the Vietnam war were futile. So Nixon decided to tap Kraft's telephone. According to Haldeman the president wanted to know who was leaking to the columnist.[104] Nixon claimed he wanted

Kraft tapped because he "was in direct contact with the North Vietnamese"; it was thus a question of the "national security."[105]

The FBI did not want to do the job, so Nixon ordered Ehrlichman to get a tap installed on Kraft's Georgetown home. Ehrlichman turned to Jack Caulfield, who hired another investigator, John Ragan. Together they propped a ladder against Kraft's house and planted a bug. There was just one problem: the Krafts were in Europe, and the sleuths overheard no one but their maid speaking in Spanish. At the president's request Kraft was tracked down in Paris, where the French authorities, at the behest of the FBI, tapped the telephone in the columnist's hotel room.[106] "Unfortunately," wrote Nixon in his *Memoirs*, "none of the wiretaps turned up any proof linking anyone in the government to a specific national security leak."[107]

The individual newsman most hated by Richard Nixon and his media team was internationally syndicated columnist Jack Anderson. His name was scrawled on a blackboard in the basement sanctum occupied by the Plumbers as Public Enemy Number One.[108] Wrote Charles Colson: "At the White House we considered him (Anderson) our arch nemesis."[109]

The White House–directed harassment of Anderson apparently began in late 1970 when Haldeman ordered Jack Caulfield to find out who was leaking classified information to the columnist and his reporters. Caulfield reported the results of his probe in February 1971 and concluded, "I . . . suggest that an overt firing of a person directly connected with a leak would go a long way toward making the ability of the Andersons of the world to gain White House information both difficult and hazardous."[110] Shortly after, Anderson reported, FBI and Defense Department security agents seized on the leak of a military story and went to work with interrogations and lie detector machines: "The authorities selected as the sacrificial lamb a bespectacled, $13,500-a-year Pentagon employee named Gene Smith. He was hounded, badgered, threatened and cursed until his health was affected. His neighbors were asked nasty questions about his loyalty, his associates, his drinking habits. At last, he was hauled before a federal grand jury in Norfolk, Virginia, and questioned under oath. U.S. Attorney Brian Gettings concluded from the inquisition, however, that Smith was the wrong man."[111]

In one investigation federal authorities seized the toll records for all calls made from Anderson's office and home and from the homes of his reporters during July 1971. As the columnist described it: "The Bell System—whom we—not the White House—pay for our costly long distance charges, gave the FBI all our records without a whimper.

By the time Ma Bell had stopped giving away our secrets to the FBI, the administration had the toll records for our office [and the homes of] Joe Spear, Brit Hume, Les Whitten, and Whitten's 18-year-old son. Les Whitten III. They also seized the records of a Kensington, Md., technical writer named Charles Elliott. His crime, it seems, was to carry the same name as an intrepid young reporter then on our staff, Chuck Elliott."[112]

The Defense Department often participated in probes of the columnist, according to former Pentagon investigator W. Donald Stewart, who revealed he had been instructed to investigate Anderson on numerous occasions in 1971 and 1972. He was given "every resource in the book" to nail the columnist's sources, Stewart said; one investigation cost an estimated $100,000.[113] At one point, White House Plumber David Young ordered Stewart to establish that Anderson, a teetotaling Mormon and the father of nine children, had been involved in a homosexual affair with another Nixon enemy. Said Stewart: "When I said I wouldn't do it, Young got mad. 'Damn it, damn it, the president is jumping up and down and he wants this and we're always telling him everything can't be done!' "[114]

The Plumbers joined in the campaign against the columnist in late 1971, shortly after Anderson printed top-secret documents which revealed that Nixon had secretly favored Pakistan in the war then raging with India. One of the documents quoted a remark that Henry Kissinger made to colleagues in the White House Situation Room: "I am getting hell every half-hour from the President that we are not being tough enough on India. . . . He wants to tilt in favor of Pakistan."[115] To Nixon the embarrassing leak was intolerable. The Plumbers were summoned and instructed to find the leaker. They soon discovered something else: a young navy yeoman on the staff of the navy's liaison officer to the National Security Council apparently had been copying and leaking top secret documents to the Joint Chiefs of Staff. Put another way, the Pentagon was spying on the White House. The yeoman denied that he was leaking material to either the Joint Chiefs or to Anderson, but the White House took no chances. Nixon admitted, "We had him transferred to a remote post in Oregon and kept him under surveillance, including wiretaps for a time, to make sure that he was not dispensing any more secret information. It worked: There were no further leaks from him."[116]

The Plumbers' next encounter with Anderson came just a few weeks later, when the muckraking columnist disclosed the contents of a memorandum that had been written by Dita Beard, a Washington lobbyist for the International Telephone and Telegraph Corporation.

In colorful language, Mrs. Beard had revealed that ITT was planning to underwrite the 1972 Republican convention to the tune of $400,000 in return for the settlement of several antitrust suits. The Justice Department had abruptly agreed to the settlement in July, 1971. At the time, the Senate Judiciary Committee had already approved Richard Kleindienst's nomination as the new Attorney General, but he was involved in the ITT affair and he asked that a special Senate Judiciary Committee hearing be called so that he might defend his honor. The hearings dragged on for months and turned into a public relations debacle for the administration.[117]

The president called on Charles Colson to guide the adminstration through the ITT crisis, and he immediately set about to prove that the Dita Beard memo was a forgery. E. Howard Hunt was dispatched to Denver to see Mrs. Beard, who had allegedly fallen ill and had retired to a hospital there. Before he left, Hunt visited his old employer, the CIA, to pick up voice changers and a ridiculous-looking red wig; then he was off to Denver, where he obtained Mrs. Beard's denial that she had written the memo. Hunt wanted her to fly East, said H. R. Haldeman, where she would "tell reporters that she hadn't written the memo, then collapse. Whether she was to collapse in front of the microphones, or while riding in a cab, was not made explicit."[118] Colson, buoyed by Hunt's report, obtained the original Beard memo from the Senate Judiciary Committee and sent it to the FBI for tests. ITT's own chemists, in the meantime, had concluded that the Beard memo was phony, thus lending credence to her denial. Suddenly, the lady lobbyist—who had heretofore been portrayed by the White House as a broken-down old drunk—was resurrected as a hard-working mother and career woman. On March 20, ITT triumphantly released the results of its tests on the Beard memo. Four days later, J. Edgar Hoover announced the FBI's findings: The memo was probably authentic. Nixon and his minions were crushed. Jack Anderson was vindicated.[119]

But the columnist would soon learn that coming out ahead in one skirmish with the Nixon White House did not a victory make. Unbeknownst to Anderson at the time, agents of the Central Intelligence Agency were even then following him and the members of his staff. The surveillance operation, referred to by the CIA as Project Mudhen, began in January 1972 and eventually involved eighteen automobiles and twenty agents. It was blatantly, flagrantly illegal.[120]

Anderson became aware in late March that he was being watched, but he thought at the time that the culprits were agents of the Internal Security Division of the Justice Department. He later discovered they were CIA operatives and filed requests under the Freedom of Information Act for all records related to the project. The hundreds of documents he received outlined a massive, probably unprecedented, effort on the part of the CIA, whose operations are limited by law to foreign lands, to identify and presumably punish his sources of information.

The CIA team labeled itself SUGAR and assigned codenames to the columnist and his staff: Anderson, the non-drinker, was BRANDY; his veteran confidential assistant, Opal Ginn, was SHERRY; his chief associate, Les Whitten, was CORDIAL; his reporters, Brit Hume and Joe Spear, were EGGNOG and CHAMPAGNE respectively.[121] Teams of agents were given radio cars and assigned to follow the members of the Anderson shop everywhere they traveled. Maps of their neighborhoods were obtained, observation points were selected, and surveillance was set up on their homes. A SUGAR team rented space— they called it a NEST—in a building across the street from the columnist's office and photographed Anderson and his associates as they came and went. Handwritten and typed logs kept by the CIA agents revealed such observations and occasional ironies as these:

- Subject (CHAMPAGNE)—spouse leave in VW-FN1018 (previously identified) and proceed to bus stop near McRory parking lot. Contact lost when VW near busses. VW located @ residence @ 0740. Sub. was driving and had white shirt and tie.
- BRANDY maintains a rather irregular work schedule but is consistent in automobile routes traveled from residence to downtown Washington, D.C. . . . He is a fast and somewhat careless driver and often violates speed limits and related traffic procedures.
- Phase I coverage of CHAMPAGNE has indicated that CHAMPAGNE and his spouse appear to be maintaining a rather routine pattern of professional activities.
- CORDIAL is youngish in physical appearance but seems possessed of a great deal of nervous energy. He operates his personal automobile in a fast, impatient manner and will deviate from normal routes in order to avoid minor traffic delays.

Toward the end of March, the SUGAR team noted that "when BRANDY was spotted walking to his office . . . he appeared extremely 'tail conscious.' He kept looking around, sideways, behind his shoulder, and his gait was slower than usual." Anderson had, indeed, spotted the surveillance team. At one point, he dispatched one of his children to photograph the CIA automobiles that were lurking around his home. As the agents described it in a memorandum, "As they (the agents) were preparing to leave at 0915, a station wagon with an unidentified female driving pulled into the lot. She brought up a camera, rested it on the dash and through the front window took a picture of Agent (deleted) car (see attached sketch, position #1). She then continued around the circle, stopped behind Agent (deleted) car and took a picture of the rear . . . (see attached sketch, position #2). The camera appeared to be a 35 millimeter with a 50 millimeter lens."

Shortly thereafter, the operation was closed down. In the beginning, SUGAR had confidently predicted that "the coverage will result in a viable revelation of BRANDY organization contacts and procedures." After three months of surveillance and the expenditure of thousands of dollars, the agents concluded that the "operation failed to establish the existence and/or identity of any individual who might have been supplying Anderson, Whitten, Hume, or Spear with classified government data."

At about the same time that the CIA gave up, E. Howard Hunt was reassigned to the anti-Anderson beat. In March, 1972, according to Hunt's later testimony before the Senate Select Committee on Intelligence, he and G. Gordon Liddy met with a retired CIA doctor in a Washington restaurant to discuss hallucinogenic drugs. Hunt and Liddy, it seems, were working on a scheme to smear a drug on Jack Anderson's steering wheel or to put some funny pills in his medicine bottles in order to chemically influence the columnist to "make a fool out of himself" on his radio program, his television show, or on the lecture platform. The plan was dropped for a number of technical reasons, Hunt testified.[122]

A chain of events which led to the arrest of Les Whitten also began during November, 1972, when a group of militant Indians occupied the Bureau of Indian Affairs building in Washington and made off with seven thousand cubic feet of documents. Toward the end of November, according to Whitten, he was contacted by sources who were interested in making some of the stolen papers available for publication. After a series of meetings with the sources, during which Whitten had to convince them he was knowledgeable about the plight of American Indians, many of the documents were made available.

Stories based on the papers soon began appearing in the Anderson column—much to the chagrin of the FBI, which had mounted a massive search to locate the documents. After a number of the stories were published, Whitten learned from Hank Adams—a Washington-based Assiniboine-Sioux who had been acting as an intermediary between the militant Indians and the government—that three cartons of the documents were going to be returned. This event promised to make a good story, so Whitten asked to go along. On the morning of January 31, 1973, Whitten and Adams marked the boxes of documents with the names of FBI agent Dennis Hyten, and walked out to load them into Whitten's automobile. At that point, FBI agents stepped forward, snatched Whitten's notebook out of his hand, and marched the men off to jail in handcuffs. Other Indians were later arrested.

Slowly the story began to unravel. The Indians around Adams had been infiltrated by an undercover agent who apparently had informed the FBI—now under White House control through Acting Director L. Patrick Gray—that the documents were at Adams' apartment and that Jack Anderson himself would be there. The G-men got Whitten instead, and after eight hours in custody—five behind bars—he emerged to relate the circumstances of his arrest. Concerned that the evidence would be destroyed, he had asked FBI photographers to take pictures of the cartons marked with the agent's name. "This camera don't work for photographs like that," Whitten was told.[123] Two weeks after the arrests, Whitten, Adams, and Anderson appeared before a federal grand jury to tell their story. The jury refused to return an indictment, and the government dropped its charges.[124]

About a week later, Anderson discovered the reason Whitten was arrested in the first place. In connection with the investigation of Whitten, the FBI had again subpoenaed the office and home telephone records of Anderson and his staff from the early summer of 1972. This seemed strange, since the occupation of the Bureau of Indian Affairs hadn't taken place until November. Then Anderson learned that FBI agents had been dialing the numbers—some of them unlisted and otherwise unobtainable—on the telephone records, apparently in an attempt to track down his sources of information.[125]

The campaign to intimidate and manipulate the three major television networks continued almost unabated throughout the five and one-half years of Nixon's tenure. Actually the war on the networks had begun behind the scenes almost a month before Vice-President Agnew's November 1969 Des Moines speech when Jeb Magruder recommended enlisting the services of the Justice Department, IRS, and FCC against the broadcast press. Magruder was back in July 1970 with his "tentative plan on press objectivity." The White House, Magruder suggested, should "raise the . . . question of objectivity and ethics in the media as an institution. To do this, we will have to turn objectivity into an issue and a subject of public debate." He offered his recommendation for follow-up action, some of which involved the FCC, its chairman Dean Burch, and the licensing of broadcast journalists. Among Magruder's other suggestions concerning television news operations were these:

• Arrange a seminar on press objectivity with broadcast executives and working newsmen. Attempt to have this televised as a public service. . . .
• Make this issue a major item at the Radio-Television News Directors Convention this Fall and at the next NAB [National Association of Broadcasters] meeting. . . .
• Have Rogers Morton go on the attack in a news conference. . . . Have him charge that the great majority of the working press are Democrats and this colors their presentation of the news. Have him charge that their [sic] is a political conspiracy in the media to attack this Administration. . . .
• Produce a prime-time special, sponsored by private funds, that would examine the question of objectivity and show how TV newsmen can structure the news by innuendo. For instance, use film clips to show how a raised eyebrow or a tone of voice can convey criticism. . . .
• Form a blue-ribbon media "watchdog" committee to report to the public on cases of biased reporting. . . .
• Through contacts in the ASNE [American Society of Newspaper Editors] and NAB, bring up the question of a "fairness pledge" for members.[126]

In fact the summer of 1970 marked a high point in the networks' attempts to be "fair" and "objective." The major networks were attempting to find some practical means of balancing Nixon's numerous nationwide appearances by showing an occasional Democrat. But permitting someone of differing views the opportunity to respond to Nixon was the antithesis of the White House definition of "fairness."

In June 1970, after Nixon had been dominating the airways for eighteen months, CBS president Frank Stanton announced that his network would inaugurate a series of prime-time programs, "The Loyal Opposition," during which the political party not in office would be permitted to air its views. On July 7 Democratic National Committee chairman Larry O'Brien went on the CBS network with a rebuttal to previous Nixon speeches on such issues as crime, civil rights, the economy, and the Vietnam war. The White House media men were apoplectic, and the Republican National Committee immediately demanded equal time. The FCC fairness doctrine requires broadcasters to provide "reasonable opportunity for the presentation of contrasting viewpoints on controversial issues of public importance," but the regulatory agency had never been able to come up with a clear and consistent interpretation of what it means. In this case it agreed with the Republican National Committee and ordered CBS in August to air a Republican response. The network appealed the decision to the courts.[127]

Inside the White House, Nixon and associates decided the time had come to put the networks on notice that such programs as "The Loyal Opposition" would not be tolerated.[128] In September 1970, Charles Colson met with CBS board chairman William S. Paley and president Frank Stanton, NBC president Julian Goodman, and ABC president Leonard Goldenson and vice-president James Hagerty. On September 25 Colson reported the results of his trip in a memorandum to Haldeman:

1. The networks are terribly nervous over the uncertain state of the law, i.e., the recent FCC decisions and the pressures to grant Congress access to TV. They are also apprehensive about us. . . . The harder I pressed them (CBS and NBC) the more accommodating, cordial and apologetic they became. Stanton for all his bluster is the most insecure of all.

2. They were startled by how thoroughly we were doing our home-work—both from the standpoint of knowledge of the law, as I discussed it, but more importantly, from the way in which we have so thoroughly monitored their coverage and our analysis of it. . . .

3. There was unamimous [sic] agreement that the President's right of access to TV should in no way be restrained. Both CBS and ABC agreed with me that on most occasions the President speaks as President and that there is no obligation for presenting a contrasting point of view under the Fairness Doctrine. . . . NBC on the other hand argues that the fairness test must be applied to every presidential speech but Goodman is also quick to agree that there are probably instances in which Presidential addresses are not "controversial" under the Fairness Doctrine and, therefore, there is no duty to balance. . . .

4. They are terribly concerned with being able to work out their own policies with respect to balanced coverage and not have to have policies imposed on them by either the Commission or the Congress. ABC and CBS said that they felt we could, however, through the FCC make any policies we wanted to. (This is worrying them all.)

5. To my surprise CBS did not deny that the news had been slanted against us. Paley merely said that every Administration has felt the same way and that we have been slower in coming to them to complain than our predecessors. He, however, ordered Stanton in my presence to review the analysis with me and if the news has not been balanced to see that the situation is immediately corrected. . . .

6. CBS does not defend the O'Brien appearance. Paley wanted to make it very clear that it would not happen again and that they would not permit partisan attacks on the President. They are doggedly de-termined to win their FCC case, however; as a matter of principle,

even though they recognized that they made a mistake, they don't want the FCC in the business of correcting their mistakes.

7. ABC and NBC believe that the whole controversy over "answers" to the President can be handled by giving some time regularly to presentations by the Congress. . . . In this regard ABC will do anything we want. NBC proposes to provide a very limited Congressional coverage once or twice a year and additionally once a year "loyal opposition" type answers. . . . CBS takes quite a different position. Paley's policy is that the Congress cannot be the sole balancing mechanism and that the Democratic leadership in Congress should have time to present Democratic viewpoints on legislation. (On this point, which may become the most critical of all, we can split the networks in a way that will be very much to our advantage.)

Conclusion

. . . The networks badly want to have these kinds of discussions. . . . They told me anytime we had a complaint about coverage for me to call them directly. Paley said that he would like to come down to Washington and spend time with me anytime that I wanted. In short, they are very much afraid of us and are trying hard to prove they are "good guys."

These meetings had a very salutary effect in letting them know that we are determined to protect the President's position, that we know precisely what is going on from the standpoint of both law and policy and that we are not going to permit them to get away with anything that interferes with the President's ability to communicate.

Paley made the point that he was amazed at how many people agree with the Vice President's criticism of the networks. He also went out of his way to say how much he supports the President, and how popular the President is. When Stanton said twice as many people had seen President Nixon on TV than any other President in a comparable period, Paley said it was because this President is more popular.

The only ornament on Goodman's desk was the Nixon Inaugural Medal. Hagerty said in Goldenson's presence that ABC is "with us." This all adds up to the fact that they are damned nervous and scared and we should continue to take a very tough line, face to face, and in other ways.

As to follow-up, I believe the following is in order:

1. I will review with Stanton and Goodman the substantiation of my assertion to them that their news coverage has been slanted. We will go over it point by point. This will, perhaps, make them even more cautious.

2. There should be a mechanism (through Herb, Ron or me) every time we believe coverage is slanted whereby we point it out either to the chief executive or to whomever he designates. Each of them invited this and we should do it so they know we are not bluffing.

3. I will pursue with ABC and NBC the possibility of their issuing declarations of policy (one that we find generally favorable as to the President's use of TV). If I can get them to issue such a policy statement, CBS will be backed into an untenable position.

4. I will pursue with Dean Burch the possibility of an interpretive ruling by the FCC on the role of the President when he uses TV, as soon as we have a majority. . . .

5. I would like to continue a friendly but very firm relationship whenever they or we want to talk. I am realistic enough to realize that we probably won't see any obvious improvement in the news coverage but I think we can dampen their ardor for putting on "loyal opposition" type programs."[129]

Jeb Stuart Magruder in 1969 had raised the possibility of "utilizing the anti-trust division [of the Justice Department] to investigate various media." The idea tantalized Nixon and his media men, and in December 1971 Herb Klein visited the network chief executives and passed on what they interpreted to be a message. According to a subsequent sworn statement by Julian Goodman, "I recall being surprised that [Klein] raised the subject of a possible antitrust suit. I do not recall the precise words used by Mr. Klein, but I do recall that he said in substance that there was something bubbling under the surface at the Justice Department in the way of an antitrust suit against the networks. . . . I concluded from what Mr. Klein said . . . that the purpose of (the) visit was to deliver a message."[130]

Indeed it was. In April 1972 the Justice Department filed antitrust suits against the three major networks on the grounds that they monopolized the production of prime-time television programs and thus denied the audience "the benefits of free and open competition." Television critics generally hailed the move as laudatory, and indeed it might have been had the suits been filed under different circumstances.

For one thing the administration was under fire because its decidedly benign treatment of ITT in the settlement of three antitrust suits had come to light. The theory was thus tendered that the Nixon men were seeking to allay the implication that they were mollycoddling big business.

Second, and more likely, the networks were sued just as the 1972 presidential campaign was gearing up. This curious timing could well have served to put the networks on notice that the White House would be watching their newscasts in the weeks ahead and that the enthusiasm with which the antitrust suits would be pursued would be commensurate with the type of treatment the administration was given. Such a theory was rendered more plausible by the fact that the suits had been under consideration by the Justice Department for years. One suit had been prepared under the aegis of Secretary of State William Rogers when he was President Eisenhower's Attorney General; another had been worked up for the Johnson administration by Attorney General Nicholas Katzenbach. In both instances, the prospective suits were shelved. Indeed, the antitrust suit that was eventually filed against the networks was first prepared, according to some reports, in 1970; but Nixon had wanted to execute it "at another time" and it had been postponed by the Attorney General until April, 1972—seven months before Nixon had to face the voters.

If, as some observers believed, the administration was treated kindly by the networks during the campaign, it was not without good reason.[131]

During the first eighteen months of the administration, the network that the White House most loved to hate was NBC. This was apparently due to the president's own prejudices: During the 1968 campaign, according to Frank Shakespeare, Nixon was "way down" on NBC.[132] His negative feelings were reinforced when the July 17, 1970, issue of *Life* magazine carried an article about the imminent retirement of NBC anchorman Chet Huntley in which the newsman spoke about the presidents he had known. He rated Lyndon Johnson his favorite but was highly critical of Nixon, of whom Huntley said, "The shallowness of the man overwhelms me."[133] To the White House media maestros this was proof that the press was contaminated with Nixon haters. It was also perceived as an opportunity to get that message across to the country. In his July 16 "tear down the institution" memo to Magruder, Haldeman aide Larry Higby wrote:

As I indicated to you the other day, we need to get some creative thinking going on an attack on Huntley for his statements in *Life*. One thought that comes to mind is getting all the people to sign a petition calling for the immediate removal of Huntley right now.

The point behind this whole thing is that we don't care about Huntley—he is going to leave anyway. What we are trying to do here is to tear down the institution. Huntley will go out in a blaze of glory and we should attempt to pop his bubble.

Most people won't see *Life* Magazine and for that reason I am asking Buchanan to draft a statement for the Vice President [the words *Vice President* were scratched out by someone and the name *Finch* substituted] to give. We should try to get this statement on television. Obviously there are many other things that we can do, such as getting independent station owners to write NBC saying that they should remove Huntley now; having broadcasting people look into this due to the fact that this is proof of biased journalism, etc.[134]

By the next day Magruder had prepared a lengthy plan for Haldeman and Klein. It was the perfect opportunity, he suggested, "to extend these questions [about Huntley] to cover the professional objectivity and ethics of the whole media and to generate a public re-examination of the role of the media in American life." He recommended several specific actions that should be taken against Huntley: leak his letter of apology to Nixon, plant a story about the incident with a friendly columnist, generate a "massive outpouring of letters-to-the-editor," and "position an appropriate writer" to prepare an article for *Life*.[135]

Shortly after the Huntley episode Charles Colson reminded the network executives who was in charge, and thereafter the administration's displeasure with NBC remained relatively routine, until the 1972 election. In one of his few public appearances during the campaign, Nixon flew to the West Coast where he lambasted Democratic candidate George McGovern—without deigning to name him—for his proposed economic, defense, and welfare programs. The traveling press was not permitted to sit in the audience as the president spoke; they had to watch the events on Sony monitors set up in press rooms. After Nixon's speeches most reporters filed routine stories quoting the president's allegations without qualification. One exception was a national correspondent for NBC, Cassie Mackin. While in Los Angeles she filmed a summary story, which she began with the observation that "the Nixon campaign is, for the most part, a series of speeches before closed audiences, invited guests only." She continued, "On defense spending and welfare reform, the two most controversial issues in this campaign . . . the two issues that are almost haunting George McGovern, there is a serious question of whether President Nixon is setting up straw men by leaving the very strong impression that McGovern is making certain proposals which in fact he is not." A film clip then showed Nixon making vague references to "some" who did not care whether the United States had the world's "second strongest" navy, army, and air force. Then Mackin came back on and said, "The president obviously meant McGovern's proposed defense budget but his criticism never specified how the McGovern plan would weaken the country. On welfare, the president accuses McGovern of wanting to give those on welfare more than those who work, which is not true. On tax reform, the president says McGovern is calling for 'confiscation of wealth,' which is not true. . . . When all is said and done, it's like Mr. Nixon says, he is the president and it is the power of the presidency that makes it possible to stay above the campaign and answer only the questions of his choice."[136]

Before NBC's news program was over, Herb Klein and Kenneth Clawson telephoned the network's president, Julian Goodman, and NBC news chief Reuven Frank. "She, in effect, called the president a liar," fumed Clawson afterward. "We didn't ask that she be fired or

removed from covering [Nixon] or reprimanded. We didn't ask anything. We just wanted to register our protest that she was inaccurate."[137]

The White House didn't have to ask anything; the message was
very clear. Cassie Mackin was reassigned, over her protests, to the
Los Angeles bureau. She needed some "film training," network executives told her.[138]

By early 1970 another network was moving to the top of the White
House hate list. Once CBS attained that singular position, it would
occupy it without competition for the remainder of Richard Nixon's
days in the White House.

After Vice-President Agnew excoriated network news operations at
Des Moines, it had been CBS which most vigorously defended the
media. Agnew's assault, said CBS president Frank Stanton, was "an
unprecedented attempt . . . to intimidate a news medium." Richard
Salant called Agnew's speech "terribly disheartening" and predicted
it was only the beginning of a general assault.[139]

It was—for CBS especially. Ten days before Agnew's Des Moines
speech, CBS broadcast a film depicting a South Vietnamese soldier,
without provocation, stabbing to death a North Vietnamese prisoner.
The atrocity, the film showed, had been witnessed by unmoving American military advisers. Eleven days later the Pentagon requested the
network's outtakes; news chief Richard Salant claimed the unused film
was as "sacrosanct" as "a reporter's notebook" and refused to comply.

On April 12, 1970, the *Des Moines Register* ran an exclusive story on
its front page under the banner headline, "Probe TV's Atrocity." The
story related the details of a Pentagon investigation of the CBS story
and the Defense Department's contention that the network's film was
phony. A month later syndicated columnist Richard Wilson, who also
headed the *Register*'s Washington bureau, published a column citing
CBS's failure to cooperate with the Pentagon as evidence the film was
faked. The feeling inside the Nixon administration, Wilson wrote, was
that CBS had perpetrated "a bald fraud" on the public.[140]

At this point CBS began to suspect a campaign of intimidation. A
few months earlier Nixon had appointed the *Des Moines Register*'s highly
regarded investigative reporter, Clark Mollenhoff, as a deputy counsel
to the president. Mollenhoff would serve as a presidential ombudsman
to "direct and conduct continued investigations to assure follow-through
action on corruption and mismanagement and apprise the president
of any questionable operations within his own administration."[141] White
House reporters had heard rumors, however, that Mollenhoff would
also be charged with investigating reporters unfriendly to Nixon. Significantly, it seemed, it was the *Register* that broke the news that the

CBS atrocity story was being investigated by the Pentagon; Richard Wilson, moreover, was Mollenhoff's former boss. CBS believed that Mollenhoff was the moving force behind the unfriendly reports.

The network then learned that syndicated columnist Jack Anderson had obtained a White House memorandum accusing CBS of "irresponsibility" and was going to publish it on Friday, May 22. So on Thursday night, CBS once again aired the atrocity story. "What follows is unusual for CBS evening news," said Walter Cronkite, and in the next seven minutes the story was outlined in great detail. It was obvious that CBS had filmed an authentic event. The next day Ziegler denied that an investigation of CBS had taken place but refused further comment.[142]

Years later, Mollenhoff said he had simply been doing his job and that CBS had wrongfully accused him: "I was trying to keep on top of the Pentagon. I was saying, 'let's not have any coverups.' CBS was trying to link Nixon and the White House with the Pentagon's efforts, and they called me. And I called the Pentagon and asked them to send me their reports. It was turned around to say that there was a White House-directed investigation of CBS. But I was trying to make sure the Pentagon wasn't lying. Nobody even suggested to me that I do this. It wasn't political. It was my desire to make sure the Defense Department didn't come through with a lot of lies. CBS just got its facts screwed up."[143]

Throughout the remainder of 1970 and into 1971 the network's troubles seemed to multiply. A few weeks after the controversy over the atrocity story died down, the White House became exercised over the "Loyal Opposition" series. In February 1971 Herb Klein visited CBS to complain about a "60 Minutes" segment on the career of Vice-President Agnew.[144] That same month the network aired "The Selling of the Pentagon" and once again found itself in the vortex of a maelstrom. At about the time the controversy over "The Selling of the Pentagon" reached its peak, CBS reporter Morley Safer went to Vietnam to report on the progress of Nixon's Vietnamization program. U.S. military officers in Saigon forwarded a memo to their colleagues in the field to warn them that "the word is to be cautious and that Safer is not merely covering the war but has an ulterior motive." Safer was denied military transportation and had to return without a story.[145]

In the spring of 1971 the Nixon media team began zeroing in on individual correspondents. John Ehrlichman traveled to New York in April for an appearance on the CBS "Morning News" show and afterward went to the Plaza Hotel for breakfast with Richard Salant and correspondent John Hart. Suddenly, according to Salant, the conversation turned to the network's aggressive White House correspondent: "In the middle of nice, samll-talk conversation, he [Ehrlichman] suddenly lit into Dan Rather and called him a hatchet man and told me how unhappy they were with him. There were only two things I felt I ought to do, aside from telling him I thought Dan Rather was great. One was to make it public, and the other was to let Dan Rather know that he was now assured of being the White House correspondent as long as he ever wants to. But I can't guarantee that if the White House or somebody like Ehrlichman pulled the same stunt with some other broadcaster, the other broadcaster would react the way I did."[146]

In August 1971 CBS newsman Daniel Schorr arrived at his office to find an FBI agent waiting for him. Schorr was being considered for a "position of confidence and trust" in the Nixon administration, the agent said, and a routine background investigation was being conducted. Strangely, the possibility of a position with the Nixon administration came at a time when the president's media team was at odds with Schorr over the stories he had been reporting. In June 1970 he had exposed the failure of a Nixon plan to distribute food to the needy, and Senator Robert Dole had taken to the floor of the Senate to denounce Schorr for making "false and misleading statements." Six months before Schorr had quoted Dr. James Fletcher, director of the National Aeronautics and Space Administration, as saying that President Nixon harbored secret reservations about the Safeguard antiballistic missile system. Nixon himself publicly labeled the story as "totally without foundation in fact." The day before the FBI probe began, the president had promised, in a speech before the Knights of Columbus in New York, that he was going to see to it that parochial schools received federal aid; Schorr had reported there was "absolutely nothing in the works" to help the schools. That story had prompted a Charles Colson call to Frank Stanton and an "invitation" for Schorr himself to come by the White House for a briefing on "the facts."

In early October Schorr ran into Frederick V. Malek, the top White House personnel recruiter, at a dinner party and asked him if he would clear up the mystery. For what job did the White House need the services of Daniel Schorr? Malek, said the correspondent, "expressed complete surprise and ignorance, even to inquiring when the investigation had occurred." The White House aide promised to check on the job offer and call Schorr; the call never came.

When the story was finally broken, Ronald Ziegler allowed that Schorr had been considered for a position "in the environment area." Malek, who six weeks earlier had never heard of the job offer, backed

Ziegler up. But the FBI report, Malek said, had never been forwarded to the White House. Senator Sam Ervin, chairman of a subcommittee on constitutional rights, subsequently held hearings on the Schorr incident. White House witnesses, on the advice of presidential counselor John Dean, refused to appear, but FBI Director J. Edgar Hoover sent word that "the incomplete investigation of Mr. Schorr was entirely favorable concerning him, and the results were furnished to the White House." At the Executive Mansion, the report, which had never been received there, suddenly became a "preliminary report, which . . . has subsequently been destroyed."

By early 1973 Schorr had become convinced that he had been the object of deliberate harassment and wondered whether it had subtly chilled his usually aggressive approach to his work:

I am left now to ponder, when a producer rejects a controversial story I have offered, whether it is because of the normal winnowing process or because of my troublemaking potential. Even more am I left to wonder, when I myself discard a line of investigation, whether I am applying professional criteria or whether I am subconsciously affected by a reluctance to embroil my superiors in new troubles with the Nixon administration. . . . My employer, with millions at stake in an industry subject to regulation and pressure, is sensitive to the government, and I am sensitive to my employer's problems.[147]

During the Senate Watergate investigation the story of a mix-up and a cover-up finally began to unravel. Eventually the full truth was known: Nixon, angry over Schorr's negative report on his plan to help parochial schools, had exploded to Haldeman, "I want an FBI check on that bastard. And no stalling this time."[148] By the summer of 1974, the full details of the Schorr episode were known and were an embarrassment for a president fighting for his political life. But on June 4, 1973, it was still a source of amusement for Nixon. On that day, he was reviewing his still-secret tapes in the hope of finding something that would destroy John Dean's upcoming Senate testimony, and, over the earphones, he heard himself instructing Dean the previous March to stick to the line that the FBI had been used "only for national security purposes."

"Yeah," said Nixon to Alexander Haig and Ronald Ziegler, who were with him in the Oval Office. "The only exception, of course, was that son-of-a-bitch, Schorr. But there—actually it *was* national security. (Laughs) We didn't say that. Oh, we didn't do anything. We just ran a name check on the son-of-a-bitch."[149]

In late 1972 CBS officials again incurred the wrath of the White House. A segment on the CBS "Evening News" of Friday, October

27, summed up the Watergate break-in and the espionage activities that had occurred during the campaign. It ran for an unprecedented fourteen minutes and helped to turn the Watergate scandal into a national story. Anchorman Walter Cronkite promised his viewers that a second part of the story would run soon.

Charles Colson watched the Friday evening show and seethed. The following morning he tried and failed to reach Frank Stanton, then telephoned network chairman William Paley. For almost an hour Colson excoriated CBS in vulgar, abusive language. Paley summoned his executives and let it be known that he had doubts about the segment that had already run and strongly hinted that part two should be aborted. The news division resisted, and eventually a compromise was reached: part two would be cut from fourteen minutes to eight. It ran on Tuesday, October 31.[150]

A few weeks after the election syndicated columnists Rowland Evans and Robert Novak reported that because of the CBS Watergate stories, "sentiment is building within the White House staff for a partial resumption of the . . . anti-media campaign, with CBS News as a special target."[151] In fact Charles Colson had already called Frank Stanton. He had lambasted CBS at length, claiming the network "didn't play ball" during the first term and would now pay the price. "We'll bring you to your knees in Wall Street and on Madison Avenue," Colson shouted. The five affiliate stations owned by the network would be taken away. "We'll break your network," Colson vowed.[152]

When the Nixon media team fired its next big salvo at the networks, it was not aimed strictly at CBS. The cannon, however, was pointed in the general direction of New York; it was loaded with grapeshot, and it was right on target.

On December 18, 1972, the director of the White House Office of Telecommunications Policy (OTP), Dr. Clay Thomas Whitehead, delivered a major policy statement to the Indianapolis chapter of Sigma Delta Chi. The location was deliberately chosen to demonstrate that the administration was shunning the eastern establishment press and directly addressing middle Americans. His message was simple: the White House was going to see to it that local television stations around the country began vetoing the "biased" news they were being fed by the networks. If they did not, Whitehead said, they could very well be left out in the cold come license renewal time. In the opinion of many experts the Whitehead speech was the most insidious assault on the First Amendment since Agnew's speech in Des Moines.[153]

The speech appeared to mark a radical change of philosophy for Whitehead who, until his Indianapolis address, had staunchly advocated the elimination of the Fairness Doctrine, that ill-defined bane of broadcast journalism which was forever being re-interpreted by the FCC. Suddenly, the Fairness Doctrine became the Holy Writ; and the King Richard Version called for local stations to enforce it on pain of being put out of business if they did not: "There is no area where management responsibility is more important than news. The station owners and managers cannot abdicate responsibility for news judgments. When a reporter or disc jockey slips in or passes over information in order to line his pocket, that's plugola, and management would take quick corrective action. But men also stress or suppress information in accordance with their beliefs. Will station licensees or network executives also take action against this ideological plugola?"[154]

Whitehead proposed a bill to amend the Communications Act of 1934 that would have broadcasters demonstrate they were "substantially attuned to the needs of the community . . . irrespective of where the programs were obtained."[155] Just in case his audience failed to grasp the meaning of these vaguely worded phrases, Whitehead offered an interpretation: "Station managers and network officials who fail to act to correct imbalance or consistent bias from the networks—or who acquiesce by silence—can only be considered willing participants to be held fully accountable by the broadcaster's community at license-renewal time."[156]

Whitehead's message was truly a mind-boggling assault on the First Amendment. The administration was attempting to enlist an army of surrogates to do what Nixon could not: censor the networks. There was even the offer of an enlistment bonus. The administration, said Whitehead, was prepared to meet the local broadcasters' frequently expressed desire for a lengthier licensing period: the three-year term of a broadcasting permit would be extended to five years.[157]

The radio and television community was stunned. Nixon had established the OTP in 1970 to act as a policy-making instrument in the increasingly complex field of communications. By 1973 it had a staff of sixty-five and a budget of $3 million.[158] Broadcasters and other observers had been skeptical about the new agency's vaguely defined role from the beginning; with Whitehead's Indianapolis speech, their suspicions were confirmed.

"It appears that young Clay Whitehead is to provide us with 'four more years' of Nixon's war on the networks," said FCC commissioner Nicholas Johnson, himself a frequent and caustic critic of the broadcasting industry.[159] "Whitehead may talk in vapid generalizations about 'bias' and 'imbalance,'" Johnson said to another interviewer, "but the clear implication, on the Alice-in-Wonderland theory that 'words mean what I say they mean, 'is that the individual stations will be expected only to correct the real or imagined 'bias' of anti-administration news and comment."[160] Former CBS president Fred Friendly called the Whitehead proposal "the most dangerous thing to come along in fifty years of broadcasting."[161] Senator Sam Ervin saw it as "a thinly veiled attempt to create government censorship over broadcast journalism."[162] Even syndicated columnist James J. Kilpatrick, an articulate conservative who backed Nixon on most issues, joined in the chorus of criticism: "If the Nixon administration will yak a little less, perhaps the station managers and viewers, having won some improvement [from the networks], will strive for a little more."[163]

For all the rhetoric about making local television officials more responsible to their communities, the Nixon administration had long been attempting to create tension between the networks and their affiliates. When the ax finally fell, broadcasters were shocked but not surprised. Well over a year before the Whitehead speech, CBS news president Richard Salant had told ACLU investigator Fred Powledge, "After Agnew, we had much more concerted criticism from the affiliates. I've always been convinced— although Herb Klein denies it— that there has been a deliberate effort on the part of the administration to exploit the natural abrasions between the affiliates in the first place. Their notion of news, you know, is different from our notion of news."[164]

There was one broadcasting "network" that Richard Nixon could directly influence, and he did it with abandon. It was the public television system, some elements of which the administration all but strangled. Here again the chief executioner was Clay T. Whitehead.

Before 1967 public television existed in the form of educational television, or ETV, financed completely with private funds. The 1967 Public Broadcasting Act replaced the old ETV with the federally funded Corporation for Public Broadcasting (CPB), whose fifteen-member board was appointed by the president. This private, nonprofit corporation was created to distribute the federal funds to production centers, to local stations, and to the Public Broadcasting System (PBS). PBS was itself a corporation; its members were individual stations, and it was controlled by a board of directors, who were in turn controlled by station managers. The PBS was thus a kind of cooperative that functioned as the stations' network to commission and distribute funds and programs. The public television system was still financially dependent on such outside sources as foundations and corporations, but the federal money imparted a sense of security to the system and permitted it to experiment with ideas that might not appeal to corporate donors.

The CPB was specifically designed to act as a buffer between the government and the broadcasters and thereby remove politics from programming. To reduce governmental influence further, the CPB was to be financed on a long-term basis. A financing system was not set up before President Johnson left office, however, and this left the fate of the public television system largely in the hands of Richard Nixon, who did not approve of the direction in which it was going.

The CPB was donating heavily to the PBS and leaving the selection and development of programs largely in its hands. The power of the PBS had grown, and it had begun putting great emphasis on news and public affairs. By 1971 some 30 percent of public television's prime-time programs were devoted to public affairs, as opposed to 2 percent for the commercial networks. Many of the documentaries and news programs were produced at a public TV production center in New York City and at the National Public Affairs Center for Television (NPACT) in Washington, D.C.[165] The eastern seaboard location, in Nixon's eyes, gave public television an eastern liberal slant. "Colson went after the networks," said a former official in the Office of Telecommunications Policy. "But the one who seemed to care the most about public broadcasting was Nixon himself."[166] A group of commercial broadcasters, in a White House meeting arranged by Herb Klein, heard the president express "unhappiness over the development of public TV" and an abhorrence for "using government funds in programming."[167]

Public television officials were aware of Nixon's views. They were also practiced in dealing with the politicians who controlled their purse strings. In the first years of its existence public television had been funded on an annual basis and therefore was always subjected to political pressures. After the Nixon administration moved in, however, the chill intensified.

Bill Greeley, a reporter for *Variety* magazine who specialized in covering television, told ACLU investigator Powledge that the CPB was now doing only that which is "especially pleasing to the Nixon administration." In 1971, Greeley noted, "the hard-hitting documentaries and the muckraking are gone. . . . They're clearly shying away from controversy."[168]

Indeed they were. The effects of a hostile administration in Washington could be seen not only in the bland diet of programs that began to come over the public television network in the months after Nixon became president; it could also be seen in the day-to-day changes that were made in programming and scheduling. A humorous skit in which comedian Woody Allen would appear as a bumbling Henry

Kissinger was pulled off the schedule a day before it was to be aired. A segment of "The Great American Dream Machine" was dropped because it dealt with the politically sensitive issue of FBI informers.[169]

Try as they might to placate the president, however, public television executives were unable to meet Nixon's standards. He did not approve of "The Great American Dream Machine," an innovative program presented in an unconventional magazine format that frequently touched on public affairs. He did not like documentaries such as "The Banks and the Poor,' which vividly portrayed the tricks used by money lenders to bilk an unsuspecting public. And he undoubtedly fumed when public television aired the views of those who disagreed with his Vietnam policies, as was done at a public station in New York on the day Nixon announced the mining of Haiphong Harbor.[170]

If the president needed any further convincing that public television was peddling "ideological plugola," it came when the NPACT hired former NBC reporters Robert MacNeil and Sander Vanocur, both of whom, Nixon believed, had liberal tendencies.

When Vanocur was signed up by the NPACT in September 1971, Nixon aide Jon Huntsman dashed off a "confidential, eyes only" memo to several colleagues, including H. R. Haldeman: "The above report [that MacNeil and Vanocur had been hired] greatly disturbed the president, who considered this the last straw. It was requested that all funds for Public Broadcasting be cut immediately. You should work this out so that the House Appropriations Committee gets the word."[171]

Other White House aides joined the fray. Ehrlichman suggested the administration eschew Congress: "The best alternative would be to take over the management and thereby determine what management decisions are going to be made. Obviously, this is an uphill fight, but seems to me to be the only feasible path to accomplish your ends."[172] Peter Flanigan, a White House emissary to the business community, argued that there was no way to purge completely the CPB of liberals, but there was still hope: "This administration does have an opportunity to establish, by legislation and otherwise, structures and counterbalances which will restrain this tendency in future years and which, as a political matter, it will be difficult for other administrations to alter."[173]

Clay Whitehead, in a 1979 interview, said there were two schools of thought in the White House: one group wanted to do away with public broadcasting; the other wanted to keep it alive but stop the distribution of "slanted public affairs commentary." The best way to accomplish this, it was thought, was to decentralize the system and funnel more money into local broadcasting operations.[174] This was the message Whitehead delivered to a convention of the National Association of Educational Broadcasters in Miami on October 20, 1971. The public television system, he said, would never obtain ample financing from the Nixon administration as long as it chose to remain in its present state. "To us," said Whitehead, "there is evidence that you are becoming affiliates of a centralized, national network." Programming, he went on, should be a local matter, but it was being dominated by the CPB and the PBS, and they were trying to win ratings contests with commercial broadcasters. If the public broadcasters could not "fulfill the promise" intended for it — as defined by the Nixon administration — "then permanent financing will always be somewhere off in the distant future."[175]

In private, Whitehead pursued public television with more pragmatic tactics: he launched a campaign to vilify the system's two errant liberals, Robert MacNeil and Sander Vanocur. "We planted with the trade press the idea that their obvious liberal bias would reflect adversely on public television," Whitehead notified Haldeman in November. "We then began to encourage speculation about Vanocur's and MacNeil's salaries." In the coming weeks, Whitehead continued, "We will quietly solicit critical articles regarding Vanocur's salary coming from public funds (larger than that of the vice president, the chief justice, and the cabinet) and his obvious bias." Under pressure from the White House and inquiring reporters, the CPB did release the salary figures — $65,000 per year for MacNeil, $85,000 for Vanocur. After a year of controversy over his income and political views, Vanocur resigned from the public television system in January 1973.[176]

In his public appearances, Whitehead became increasingly specific about the administration's real motives. On January 12, 1972, he was interviewed on National Public Radio and said, "There is a real question as to whether public television, particularly I guess really the national federally funded part of public television, should be carrying public affairs and news commentary, and that sort of thing."[177] On February 2, 1972, Whitehead commented before the Senate subcommittee on Constitutional Rights, "No citizen who feels strongly about one or another side of a matter of current public controversy enjoys watching the other side presented, but he enjoys it a good deal less when it is presented at his expense. His outrage — quite properly — is expressed to, and then through, his elected representatives who have voted his money for that purpose."[178]

Thus it became clear to all but the most casual observer: the talk of decentralization and serving local interests was largely euphemistic. Taking the responsibility for programming away from the production centers in New York and Washington was a means of diluting the effectiveness of public affairs programs. Nixon did not want another network airing stories about him, so he determined to do away with public affairs programming on public television, even if it meant destroying the institution itself.

The White House submitted its own bill for financing public television; it called for a one-year budget of $45 million, most of which would be channeled not through the CPB but directly to local public television stations.[179] Congress balked, however, and passed a bill allocating the CPB a two-year allotment of $155 million. At the White House Patrick Buchanan organized a protest by administration officials and advised Nixon to veto the bill, which he did on June 30, 1972. The CPB was forced to struggle along on its previous budget of $35 million.[180]

Reaction among concerned public television executives was swift. Hartford Gunn, president of PBS, lamented that "public broadcasting might have to make a compromise in its news coverage in order to get stable financing. The question is: Is there a price here for survival? And can we afford to pay that price?" Said James Day, chief of the New York production center, "If you want to weaken public television, the fastest way to do it would be to put more money into local broadcasting and less into national. Whitehead's position gives me nausea."[181] And public TV newsman Robert MacNeil noted trenchantly that some prominent Republicans defined "bias" as "any attitude which does not indicate permanent genuflection before the wisdom and purity of Richard Milhous Nixon."[182]

MacNeil's comment was on target, for Nixon had been noticeably uncomplaining when public television's public affairs facilities had been used to his benefit. When the president engaged in a nationally televised conversation with network journalists in January 1971 public television reporter Nancy Dickerson participated without objection from Nixon.[183] Prior to the political conventions in 1972 PBS officials decided to spend $2.75 million for "gavel-to-gavel" coverage of both affairs, but the CPB overruled the proposal on grounds it was too costly. During the Democratic convention, therefore, public television broadcast only a ninety-minute preview and a thirty-minute wrap-up each evening. Just before the Republican convention, however, the CPB found enough money to broadcast the entire affair. Public television cameras were "fixed on the podium" and the Republican event, in the words of the PBS, was given "live, uninterrupted, television-of-record coverage." Commented *Washington Star-News* reporter Robert Walters, "No mention was made of how happy President Nixon and his White House associates might be about the prospect of having their convention—a legitimate exercise in partisan political propaganda—transmitted directly to the electorate without the meddling of any newsmen who might question the value of what was being presented."[184]

By October 1972 CPB president John Macy had resigned and Nixon had appointed enough members to the corporation's governing board to gain a majority. To replace Macy Nixon chose Henry Loomis, a fifty-three-year-old bureaucrat who had spent seven years as director of Voice of America. When asked by a reporter if he would accept the appointment at the CPB, Loomis asked, "What the hell is it?" He admitted he had never watched public television but he was soon offering criticism like a pro. Loomis said he particularly disliked "instant analysis": "Frankly, I think 'instant analysis' is lousy because the commentator who is sitting there hasn't had a chance to think."[185] He did not have high regard for any public affairs programming on public television. Instead, he averred, the industry should aim to please "minorities," whom he defined as "people who love ballet, people interested in adult education, children, Orientals, blacks and chess players."[186]

The best way to seize control of public television and exorcise it of its liberal bias, Whitehead once told Nixon, was to "take more effective control of the CPB board."[187] That had been accomplished by October 1972, and the administration began pursuing a policy that was the precise opposite of its previous proclamations: instead of localizing the system, the White House pushed it toward centralization. Within three months of Loomis's appointment, the CPB board had stripped the PBS of its power to determine programming. The White House, Whitehead later admitted, began pushing its own ideas about programming: "There were efforts to get certain people off certain talk shows, to cancel programs, to get certain programs on that were favorable to the administration."[188] The schedule announced for 1973–1974 was almost devoid of public affairs programming. Conservative William F. Buckley's program, "Firing Line," would be off the air. Bill Moyers, former press secretary to President Lyndon Johnson, had been anchoring a program, "Bill Moyers Journal"; it would no longer be seen. Gone would be the popular news show, "Washington Week in Review." In doubtful status was "The Advocates," a program that aired opposing views on controversial issues.[189]

The first half of 1973 saw the CPB and the PBS engage in a fierce power struggle. The corporation chairman, Thomas B. Curtis, resigned with an angry letter to Nixon which charged that "Mr. Whitehead and others" had interfered by calling "individual members of the

Board privately without my knowledge" and "altering the delicate negotiations in progress with the . . . PBS organization." By May 31 the two corporations had reached a compromise agreement and, in essence, Nixon had achieved what he had been seeking. The CPB would retain a voice in program selection, but local station managers would have much greater influence over the schedule; local production projects would receive greater funding at the expense of national efforts. As a result the NPACT budget was severely slashed, and it eventually folded; public affairs programming on the public television system, with some notable exceptions, was watered down.[190]

In 1974 Whitehead executed another of his turnabouts, but this time, inexplicably, he turned in the right direction. He developed a plan for long-term financing of public television that would insulate the system from political pressures. But Nixon, caught up in the Watergate affair, would have none of it. "I have been informed," Whitehead wrote to then chief of staff Alexander Haig, "that the president has disapproved the long-range funding proposal for the Corporation for Public Broadcasting . . . and wants to end public broadcasting or submit a very limited budget proposal."[191] Apparently, however, Haig and Whitehead were able to persuade the president that the system had been shaped to his liking. In mid-July, shortly before he resigned, Nixon sent to Congress a proposal that would adequately finance public television for a five-year period.[192]

This is the appropriate point to reexamine Richard Nixon's disclaimer of September 15, 1972. "We have not used the power in this first four years," he said to H. R. Haldeman and John Dean at that time. "We have not used the bureau and we have not used the Justice Department, but things are going to change now."[193] The question must be asked whether the president was stricken with amnesia on that day. The antimedia assaults of Spiro Agnew, Charles Colson, and Clay Whitehead were not examples of "using the power"? And what of the Plumbers, the wiretaps, the FBI investigation of Daniel Schorr, the arrest of Les Whitten, the CIA surveillance of Jack Anderson and his staff? The IRS-inspired tax probes of Robert Greene and *Newsday?* Indeed it seemed at times as if the entire federal government had been turned loose on the press. Even the Department of Transportation joined the battle after the Senate in 1971 turned down the supersonic transport program. The SST program manager, transportation official William Magruder, visited a Dallas convention to warn against "journalistic jingoism." The press, he lamented, would never "automatically" rally behind any cause, even if "expert opinion" determined it to be "good for an industry or even the nation."[194]

It is apparently true that the IRS initially balked at doing political dirty work for the White House. One of the documents that John Dean submitted to the Senate Watergate Committee was an unidentified, undated "IRS Talking Paper," which noted: "I.R.S. is a monstrous bureaucracy, which is dominated and controlled by the Democrats. The I.R.S. bureaucracy has been unresponsive and insensitive to both the White House and Treasury in many areas. In brief, the lack of key Republican bureaucrats at high levels precludes the initiation of policies which would be proper and politically advantageous. Practically every effort to proceed in sensitive areas is met with resistance, delay and the threat of derogatory exposure." The "talking paper" then offered several suggestions for the training of IRS Commissioner Johnnie Walters: "Walters should be told to make the changes in personnel and policy which will give the Administration semblance of control over the hostile bureaucracy of I.R.S. . . . Walters must be made to know that discreet political actions and investigations on behalf of the administration are a firm requirement and responsibility on his part. We should have direct access to Walters for action in the sensitive areas and should not have to clear them with Treasury."[195]

When Clark Mollenhoff joined the Nixon administration as an ombudsman in the summer of 1969, the president instructed him to get together with IRS officials and work out a system for gaining access to tax returns. At one point presidential political aide Murray Chotiner handed Mollenhoff a list of contributors to the Democratic party with instructions from Haldeman to "have them investigated by Internal Revenue."[196]

In July 1970 Nixon became upset with the muckraking magazine *Scanlan's Monthly* and ordered John Dean to coordinate a federal investigation of the publication. "As part of this inquiry," Nixon said, "you should have the Internal Revenue Service conduct a field investigation on the tax front." Dean thought a tax probe was dangerous and unnecessary, and he asked Murray Chotiner for advice on how to say no to Nixon. Chotiner responded, "John, the president is the head of the executive branch of this damn government. If he wants his tax collectors to check into the affairs of anyone, it's his prerogative. I don't see anything illegal about it. It's the way the game is played." Dean later mentioned his predicament to Jack Caulfield, who said it was no problem, then called the IRS and asked the tax men to look into the financial affairs of *Scanlan's* owners.[197]

None of these abuses of the public trust could have been accomplished without the acquiescence, and probably the active assistance, of high IRS officials. When it was discovered in 1973 that the White

House enemies list had been given to the IRS with instructions to "undertake examinations" of those on it, a House committee investigated and found "no evidence" that anyone on the list had been subjected to a tax audit "as a result of White House pressure on the IRS."[198] At about the same time, however, the American Civil Liberties Union surveyed 189 persons on the enemies list; 28 percent of the respondents reported tax audits, a far higher percentage than the national average in similar tax brackets during the same period.[199]

Many prominent journalists, moreover, were subjected to tax audits during the Nixon years. In addition to Robert Greene and William Attwood, they included Jack Anderson, Jules Witcover, and *New York Post* editor James Wechsler.[200]

The Federal Communications Commission, under the leadership of former Republican National Committee chairman Dean Burch, also demonstrated occasional willingness to be used by the Nixon White House as an antipress weapon. In November 1969 the FCC chairman personally telephoned the three networks to ask for transcripts of the commentaries that followed Nixon's silent majority speech. He did it, he later admitted to a CBS official, at the request of the White House.[201] In 1970 the FCC ruled that CBS had to make time available to the Republican party to rebut a Democratic "loyal opposition" presentation. Two years later the commission declared that the Democratic National Committee had no right to respond to a series of televised Nixon speeches.[202] Burch's most egregious breach of sound judgment came in the wake of CBS's refusal to cooperate with Congressman Harley Staggers's investigation of "The Selling of the Pentagon." Burch drafted a letter to Staggers that decried the press's "sheer hubris—overweening pride . . . that leads to the knee-jerk response of closing ranks against the critics." He also threatened, according to published reports, that the government would step in if broadcasters did not put their house in order. The full FCC, however, vetoed Burch's letter and in its place sent word to Staggers that the procedures CBS used were matters of judgment and therefore beyond the agency's purview.[203]

The Justice Department also cooperated in the Nixon assault on the press. The case can be made that never in the history of the nation did the public's own lawyers issue so many subpoenas, file so many suits, or initiate so many investigations to prevent the people from knowing what their government was doing or to punish those who had the temerity to suggest that the president and his associates were possessed of shortcomings. The FBI unhesitatingly investigated Daniel Schorr, arrested Les Whitten, subpoenaed Jack Anderson's telephone records. The bureau's experts installed the wiretaps, requested by Nixon, on at least four newsmen.[204]

Lesser officials in the Justice Department also took to threatening the press. At the 1972 convention of the American Society of Newspaper Editors, Justice Department official Kevin T. Maroney told the gathering that if they continued to act as if they were "entirely free to determine for themselves what was proper to publish," they would encounter "interminable mischief." In case the editors missed his point, Maroney reminded them that the Espionage Act and certain other state and federal laws forbade the receipt of "stolen property."[205]

The Justice Department also collaborated with Nixon in his scheme to file a major antitrust suit against the television networks during an election year. And when Nixon decided he wanted to submit his own ideas to Congress about the revision of the U.S. criminal code, Justice Department attorneys drafted some antipress provisions that, in the eyes of numerous legal experts, would have virtually obliterated the First Amendment. The plan, which many journalists came to call "Nixon's Revenge," was merged with another proposal in 1974 and became Senate Bill 1 (S. 1). It would have made it a crime for a government employee to give a document to unauthorized persons, including reporters; journalists could also have been prosecuted for accepting such a document. Journalists and their sources could have been jailed and fined for communicating unclassified "national defense information" if it were determined to be prejudicial to the safety or interest of the United States or advantageous to a foreign nation. The leak or publication of classified information would have been a crime even if the information was not properly classified.[206]

Attorney General John Mitchell displayed his talent for suppression in a direct fashion in June 1971 when he and other lawyers in the Justice Department, on Nixon's orders, moved to restrain publication of the Pentagon Papers, and, with the cooperation of the courts, managed to stop the presses for the first time in U.S. history.

The Pentagon Papers affair began on Sunday, June 13, 1971, when the *New York Times* published the first in a series of articles based on a forty-seven-volume classified history of the Vietnam war assembled under the auspices of the Department of Defense. The series promised to reveal how the United States, through several administrations, deliberately became involved in and escalated the conflict in Southeast Asia. A second installment appeared, with accompanying documents, the next day. That evening the *Times* was asked by the Justice Department to cease publication of the series on the grounds the stories revealed "information relating to the national defense of the United

States." The newspaper's top officers "respectfully declined," and a third installment was published the next day. That night the Justice Department obtained a court order enjoining the *Times* from further publication, pending a court hearing.

On Friday morning, June 18, the *Washington Post* was on the streets with stories based on the Pentagon Papers. Again the Justice Department sought a restraining order, but this time it was refused. The *Post*'s second installment ran on Saturday. The government appealed and eventually obtained an injunction. Again the presses fell silent. Meanwhile the *Boston Globe* came out with a Pentagon Papers story. The newspaper was swiftly enjoined from further publication. In subsequent days the *Chicago Sun-Times*, Knight Newspapers, *Los Angeles Times*, *St. Louis-Post Dispatch*, *Christian Science Monitor*, and the Long Island–based *Newsday*, in John Mitchell's words, got "in the act." Of these, only the *Post-Dispatch* was prohibited from publication.

On Saturday, June 19, the U.S. District Court in New York City ruled in favor of further publication by the *New York Times*, but the restraining order was continued to permit the U.S. Court of Appeals to review the government's case; it was then bounced back to the district court. In Washington both the district court and the appellate court ruled in favor of the *Post*. Subsequent appeals by both newspapers and the government took the cases to the Supreme Court, which voted to consolidate them, continue the ban on publication, and hear evidence. On Saturday, June 26, the court heard the arguments. On Wednesday, June 30, the verdict was announced—six to three in favor of the newspapers. The presses rolled once again.

The celebrations in newsrooms across the country, however, were short-lived, for the victory had been a pyrrhic one. The Nixon administration had succeeded in persuading the courts to restrain publication for fifteen days—an event that had never happened before and, therefore, could only be considered a step backward. The opinions of several of the Supreme Court Justices, furthermore, left many journalists feeling much less secure than they had felt before the Pentagon Papers case.[207]

The Justice Department never sought to prosecute the newspapers involved in the Pentagon Papers affair, but federal attorneys did harass Beacon Press, a Boston publishing house that printed a four-volume set of Pentagon Papers obtained by Democratic Senator Mike Gravel of Alaska. The Justice Department investigation of Beacon was little more than a "fishing expedition." FBI agents secretly examined the bank accounts of Beacon Press and its parent body, the Unitarian Universalist Association; many officers and employees were interrogated, and Beacon spent $50,000 for legal advice. The government, however, never filed charges.[208]

One of the most effective weapons in the president's war with the press was also developed with the approval, and in some cases the active cooperation, of the Justice Department: the use of the general subpoena to force journalists to testify before courts and grand juries and to confiscate their notes, film, photographs, outtakes, travel vouchers, and expense accounts, regardless of any guarantee of confidentiality the reporters may have given their sources.

Before the 1968 riots at the Democratic convention in Chicago, reporters often testified in open court and frequently cooperated with the police to help them solve crimes. On most occasions, however, a reporter testified simply to verify the authenticity of what had been printed or broadcast. The assistance given the police was usually in criminal cases, not the political cases that became so prevalent after 1968. In the aftermath of the Chicago riots, however, the situation changed. A presidential commission, prosecutors, defendants, and grands juries began to subpoena unprecedented quantities of film, notes, and photographs. Again reporters went out of their way to cooperate, largely because the confidentiality of news sources was not compromised. Hundreds of thousands of dollars were spent to duplicate film and photographs; none of the costs were repaid.

The wave of subpoenas continued to grow. *Life*, *Time*, and the Chicago newspapers were told to produce their unpublished materials dealing with the radical Weathermen. *New York Times* reporter Earl Caldwell was ordered to produce his notes on his dealings with the Black Panthers. *Fortune* magazine was subpoenaed to produce the material it had collected while preparing an investigative article on a businessman who was being prosecuted in an antitrust action.[209] In the twenty months between January 1969 and July 1971, CBS and NBC alone were served with 122 subpoenas, 52 issued by government attorneys.[210]

Reporters began complaining that their First Amendment rights were being violated and their relationships with confidential sources were being compromised. Jack Landau, director of public information for the Justice Department, negotiated between John Mitchell and the American Society of Newspaper Editors and eventually drafted a set of guidelines on press subpoenas, which were promulgated by the attorney general in August 1970.[211] "In the future," Mitchell promised, "no subpoenas will be issued to the press without a good-faith attempt by the Department of Justice to reach a compromise acceptable to both parties prior to the issuance of a subpoena."[212] But shortly after

Mitchell's promise, CBS newsman Mike Wallace and his producer, Paul Loewenwater, were subpoenaed to produce the outtakes of a filmed interview with Black Panther leader Eldridge Cleaver. *Times* reporter Earl Caldwell was also served with a second subpoena.[213]

Nevertheless, between August 1970 and March 1973 only eight federal subpoenas were issued to newsmen. Then the Watergate scandal broke open, and the tempo began to pick up. In October 1973 Attorney General Elliot Richardson proclaimed an order declaring that no journalist could be subpoenaed, arrested, questioned, or indicted without the personal approval of the attorney general.[214] A few days later Richardson was fired, and the federal subpoenas continued. By May 8, 1975, an additional fifty-four requests for subpoenas against 107 newsmen had been approved, and another twenty-two had been issued without the attorney general's prior approval. In many cases reporters had already agreed to supply information to the government but had insisted that formal subpoenas be served in order to make it clear that their cooperation was not voluntary.[215]

Thus another device that served to dilute the rights of free speech and free press was approved and adopted by the Nixon administration. The development of this weapon, however, would have been impossible without help from the judiciary. In his *Memoirs*, Richard Nixon declared, "I consider my four appointments to the Supreme Court to have been among the most constructive and far-reaching actions of my presidency."[216] They were also the actions that—in the opinion of a great many newsmen—justify Richard Nixon's perpetual enshrinement in journalism's Hall of Infamy. He is gone, but his legacy lingers to haunt the press.

By the fall of 1971 Nixon had appointed Chief Justice Warren Burger and Justices Harry Blackmun, Lewis Powell, and William Rehnquist, all of whom, in varying degrees, reflected his conservative philosophy. Their shallow regard for the rights of journalists under the First Amendment became apparent on June 29, 1972, when the court legitimized the use of subpoenas to demand information from newsmen.

The landmark case, *Branzburg* v. *Hayes*, also known as the "Caldwell decision," began in 1968 when a thirty-four-year-old black reporter for the *New York Times*, Earl Caldwell, gained the confidence of the Black Panther party and began to report their story from the inside. When he wrote of the guns the Panthers were collecting, he was subpoenaed by a federal grand jury in San Francisco investigating the black militants. He was advised by legal experts and colleagues to comply; he refused and was cited for contempt.

Caldwell's reasoning was based on his experiences in the civil rights movement. He had been on the Memphis motel balcony with Dr. Martin Luther King, Jr., when the civil rights leader was shot. He had reported the riots in Dayton and Cincinnati, Ohio, in Los Angeles, Sacramento, Chicago, Detroit, and Newark. He had followed militant leader H. Rap Brown across the country. He was friendly with Panther leader Eldridge Cleaver and his wife, Kathleen. He knew the Panthers, he said, to be something more than their popular image as black police killers. "The party trusted me so much," Caldwell wrote, that when he met with them, he "did not have to ask permission to bring along a tape recorder." He reasoned that he could not testify against those who had trusted him and to whom he had promised his confidence. Indeed he said, even to appear before a grand jury would ruin his relationship with his sources.

Moreover, Caldwell wrote, the federal government used the subpoena as a technique of harassment. He was first interrogated by the FBI when he reported the fact that the Panthers were hoarding guns. He refused to cooperate and for a while was left alone. Then in late 1969, he was again approached by the FBI:

They wanted to pick my brain. They wanted me to slip behind my news sources, to act like the double agents I saw on old movie reruns on TV. . . .

Finally, Wallace Turner, chief of the *Times* bureau in San Francisco, arranged for an assistant, Alma Brackett, to take all my calls. The FBI even had women call. It went on like that for months, until one day an agent told Mrs. Brackett that, if I didn't come in and talk to them, I'd be telling what I knew in court. That's when they subpoenaed me. They asked for all of my tape recordings, notebooks, and other documents covering a period of more than fourteen months—and let me know that if I did not come in with everything, I would go to jail.[217]

Caldwell appealed his contempt citation and received a favorable decision from the U.S. Court of Appeals for the Ninth Circuit.[218] With the approval of Attorney General Mitchell, the Justice Department took the case to the Supreme Court, which consolidated it with two others. One was that of *Louisville Courier-Journal* reporter Paul Branzburg, a Harvard Law School graduate who in 1969 had been permitted to witness and report on the manufacture of hashish by drug dealers; he had written another story concerning drug use in Frankfort, Kentucky. A grand jury had demanded the identity of the central characters in his stories, and he had refused to divulge the information. The third case involved Paul Pappas, a television reporter-photographer in New Bedford, Massachusetts. Pappas had been given a conditional invitation to visit Black Panther headquarters in New Bedford, and he had refused to tell a grand jury what he had witnessed.

On June 29, 1972, the Supreme Court returned its decision: the reporters did not have a First Amendment right to refuse to cooperate with the grand juries. Writing for the majority, Justice Byron White stated that "fair and effective law enforcement aimed at providing security for the person and property of the individual is a fundamental function of government, and the grand jury plays an important, constitutionally mandated role in this process." Thus, White concluded, "On the records now before us, we perceive no basis for holding that the public interest in law enforcement and in ensuring effective grand jury proceedings is insufficient to override the consequential, but uncertain burden on news gathering which is said to result from insisting that reporters, like other citizens respond to relevant questions put to them in the course of a valid grand jury investigation or criminal trial."[219]

The majority, which included Nixon appointees Chief Justice Burger and Justices Lewis Powell, Harry Blackmun, and William Rehnquist, declared that the problems a pro-press ruling would create for the courts overrode the significance of the First Amendment: "The administration of a constitutional newsman's privilege would present practical and conceptual difficulties of a high order. Sooner or later, it would be necessary to define those categories of newsmen who qualified for the privilege, a questionable procedure in light of the traditional doctrine that liberty of the press is the right of the lonely pamphleteer who uses carbon paper or a mimeograph just as much as of the large metropolitan publisher who utilizes the latest photocomposition methods."[220]

In his dissenting opinion Justice Potter Stewart accused the Court of harboring a "crabbed view" of the First Amendment; its ruling, he wrote, invited government authorities at all levels "to undermine the historic independence of the press by attempting to annex the journalistic profession as an investigative arm of government."[221] Characteristically, Justice William O. Douglas held to his view that freedom of the press is an absolute right: "The intrusion of government into this domain is symptomatic of the disease of this society. As the years pass, the power of government becomes more and more pervasive. It is a power to suffocate both people and causes. Those in power, whatever their politics, want only to perpetuate it. Now that the fences of law and tradition that have protected the press are broken down, the people are the victims. The First Amendment, as I read it, was designed precisely to prevent that tragedy."[222]

In the eight months that followed the Caldwell decision, judges, attorneys, and grand juries across the country unleashed an unprecedented barrage of subpoenas on newsmen. More than thirty-five journalists refused to comply and were cited for contempt; over a dozen reporters were put behind bars.[223] The first to go to jail was a thirty-six-year-old investigative reporter for the *Newark Evening News*, Peter Bridge.

In May 1972 Bridge reported that a member of the Newark Housing Authority Commission, Pearl Beatty, had been offered a $10,000 bribe to influence her vote on a particular issue. An ambitious public prosecutor, Joseph Lordi, decided he wanted to know the name of the unidentified person who had made the bribe, and he summoned Bridge before a grand jury. The newsman refused, on the grounds that it would threaten confidential sources who had verified the story, to reveal more information than had been published. He was cited for contempt. The case wound its way to the Supreme Court, which in October refused to delay Bridge's imprisonment while he prepared a petition for a full review of his case.[224] He was jailed for twenty-one days until the grand jury that had issued the subpoena disbanded.[225]

Shortly after Bridge was released, another reporter, William T. Farr of the *Los Angeles Times*, was jailed for contempt—months after he had originally refused to reveal confidential sources to a judge. During the murder trial of Charles Manson—the cult leader who was convicted of killing actress Sharon Tate and four other persons—Farr obtained the confidential statement of a potential witness who had related the details of future murders the clan had planned to execute. California Superior Court Judge Charles H. Older learned of Farr's pending story and called him in to talk about it. The judge informed Farr that he did not have to answer any questions because of a California law which extended to newsmen the "privilege" of keeping their sources confidential. Farr refused to reveal the information, and he published the story despite Older's stern warning not to. The sequestered jury never saw it.[226]

Later, Farr left the *Los Angeles Herald Examiner*, where he was working at the time, and took a job in the office of the Los Angeles County District Attorney. Judge Older then called Farr in, informed him that since he was no longer a newsman he was no longer protected by the California "shield" law, and demanded to know the identity of the reporter's sources. Again Farr refused to comply. He was cited for contempt—even though he was again a working reporter, this time for the *Los Angeles Times*. Farr, said Older, was "a martyr without a cause."[227] The State Court of Appeals and the California Supreme

Court sustained the lower court ruling; the U.S. Supreme Court refused to hear the case. On November 16, 1972, Farr was ordered to jail until he revealed his sources.[228] He remained behind bars for forty-six days until he was finally released pending his appeals.[229] For the next five years, Farr was constantly in and out of court as one party after another attempted to learn the identity of his sources, or, barring that, send him off to jail again.[230]

During the 1972 trial of the seven men eventually convicted in the break-in of Democratic National Committee headquarters at Washington's Watergate complex, the *Los Angeles Times* published an interview with a prosecution witness, Alfred C. Baldwin III, an ex-FBI agent who told of being hired to monitor wiretaps at the Watergate. One of the defense attorneys asked U.S. District Judge John Sirica for permission to subpoena the tape recordings of the interview; the judge agreed. But the reporters who had conducted the interview, Jack Nelson and Ronald Ostrow, claimed they had turned the tapes over to their editors in Los Angeles. Sirica then ordered the *Times* Washington bureau chief, John Lawrence, to produce the tapes. Lawrence refused and was jailed for two hours until released on appeal. Finally Baldwin himself released the *Times* from its pledge to keep unpublished information confidential, and the tapes were handed over to the court.[231]

Later reporter Nelson accused the federal government of deliberate harassment. The authorities, he said, "upon learning of the interview, tried to block publication first by prior restraint, threatening to withdraw Baldwin's immunity from prosecution if the story appeared." They then beseeched Sirica to issue a gag rule, which he did. "The prosecutors," said Nelson, "told Baldwin he faced possible prosecution and a contempt of court proceeding if the story appeared." The *Times* printed the interview. "Six days after the Baldwin story appeared," said Nelson, "Earl J. Silbert, the chief prosecutor, told me I would have to produce the tapes. He said, 'If we don't subpoena you, the defense will.'" The defense did subpoena the recordings, and the federal prosecutors stipulated they had no objection.[232]

During 1972 and 1973 the Caldwell, Bridge, Farr, and Lawrence cases prompted a movement in Congress to enact a "shield" law that would grant journalists the "privilege" of withholding confidential information and the names of confidential sources. By the beginning of February 1973 ninety-one members of Congress and seventeen senators had either submitted such a bill or cosponsored one. Several major problems soon emerged, however, the chief of which was whether to grant an absolute privilege or a qualified one. Most newsmen who testified before the Senate and House committees considering the bills favored either an absolute privilege law or none at all on the theory that any qualified privilege would limit the absolute rights they felt they already had in the First Amendment. Another major stumbling block in assembling the bill concerned the definition of a journalist. Who among the thousands of people involved in disseminating information was to be given the privilege of withholding confidential sources? Campus reporters? The underground press? And how should qualification be determined? Would journalists have to be certified in some way?[233]

Sam Ervin of North Carolina, then the Senate's foremost constitutional lawyer and chairman of the subcommittee considering the Senate privilege bills, was convinced the Supreme Court had erred in the Caldwell case. The Congress, he felt, had to fill the gap:

Congress must attempt to be as wise as the drafters of the First Amendment two hundred years ago. A press which is not free to gather news without threat of ultimate incarceration cannot play its role meaningfully. The people as a whole must suffer. For to make thoughtful and efficacious decisions — whether it be at the local school board meeting or in the voting booth — the people need information. If the sources of that information are limited to official spokesmen, the people have no means of evaluating the worth of their promises and assurances.[234]

The Nixon administration had little sympathy for congressional efforts to write a shield law. In a letter to Robert G. Fichenberg, chairman of the freedom of information committee of the American Society of Newspaper Editors, President Nixon declared there was no need for privilege legislation "at this time." The guidelines on subpoenas proclaimed by the Justice Department were sufficient, the president said. Besides, the states could do the job; Congress should exercise caution because the "merits of enacting such laws must be carefully weighed against the dangers inherent in the administration and exercise of such a privilege."[235]

Herb Klein simplified the Nixon position by stating that the administration "does not oppose" granting protection to reporters. "We just think," he said, "it's a mistake to rush in with a federal shield law" before the situation had been carefully examined. Klein also argued that relief for journalists ought to be sought "where the problems arise — in the states."

Such an approach, however, ignored the fact that it was state laws that had created many of the problems for the press. Reporters in New Jersey and California were jailed despite the fact that these states had shield laws on the books. The Nixon men well knew, said some critics, that relegating the problem to the states was a virtually foolproof method of ensuring that it would not be solved.[236]

The movement to create a federal law that would protect a journalist's confidential sources continued into 1974. But newsmen who testified before various committees were divided on how it should be written, and a congressional consensus was never reached. The nation's attention turned to Watergate and, except for the introduction of an occasional bill after a particular Supreme Court antipress ruling, the proposal has been all but forgotten.[237]

Meanwhile, many First Amendment cases have wound their way to the Burger court in the years since Richard Nixon resigned, and freedom of the press has been diluted in such important areas as confidentiality of sources, libel, judicial gag orders, prior restraint, and police encroachment on newsrooms and journalists' records.

Scattered throughout this chapter have been descriptions of incidents that suggest that, by the beginning of 1973, the press was reacting to the intimidation campaign in ways that satisfied Nixon and his media team. The CBS network had dropped its "loyal opposition" series and had cut its second Watergate show in half after hearing from Charles Colson; NBC had transferred Cassie Mackin to Los Angeles after she incurred the wrath of the White House; the public television system had dropped controversial shows and commentators and watered down its public affairs programming. Were these isolated occurrences? Or had the press pulled its punches when the White House growled?

Journalists generally abhorred the suggestion that they responded to the Nixon administration's antipress campaign in the manner the White House wanted them to. There is considerable evidence, however, that indicates this was precisely the case. One prominent figure who charged that the press knuckled under to Nixon was consumer activist Ralph Nader. The White House press corps, Nader said, was "a mimeograph machine" for the administration's pronouncements. What the president declared, said Nader, "the press reports. There is absolutely no news judgment." As a remedy Nader suggested assigning investigative reporters to the White House and rotating the assignments.[238]

Another who made similar charges was Fred Friendly, once the president of CBS. Attacks on the press, he alleged in May 1970, caused newsmen to shun probing reports and to concentrate instead on the trivial. He continued, "The journalist fails when he allows himself to be diverted by the tactics of a skilled sleight-of-hand artist, like the vice president. Mr. Agnew is so good at it that Wednesday's [May 20,

1970] *New York Times* felt it necessary to devote four front-page columns, including a picture, to the vice president beaning the director of the Peace Corps with a tennis ball, while burying on page 29 a major report on sulfur dioxide which affects us all."[239]

Many working journalists agreed with these assessments. The White House attacks, said *Chicago Daily News* bureau chief Peter Lisagor, "created kind of a psychological undertow that forced some people in our business to pull their punches, to be a little more cautious than they might be justified in being." Allan Otten of the *Wall Street Journal* claimed the Nixon men "have succeeded to a considerable degree in intimidating some people, particularly in the broadcasting field, and making other people lean over backwards to give them a much fairer shake than they sometimes deserve."[240] CBS news president Richard Salant agreed that the administration's assaults "made us all edgy. We've thought about things we shouldn't think about."[241]

The Nixon White House, as Ralph Nader charged, especially approved of news organizations that objectively transmitted the president's messages. "This is pretty much what the wire services do and do well," wrote Ben Bagdikian, "which is why they are always pointed to by the White House media watchers as the perfect model of journalism."[242] Wire service officials, of course, did not look on themselves as transmission belts for Nixon's pronouncements. In their view they reported facts while striving for the elusive goal of "objectivity." The professional journalist, Associated Press president Wes Gallagher once said, is one who is impartial and objective: "It is the journalist's task to be a clear, cool, objective voice bringing reason to an inflamed and confused world. The strident, partisan voices in today's society contribute heat but no light to a society drowning in problems. They are not in short supply. Someone must make sense out of the heated rhetoric. Someone must search for the facts—all the facts—not just those that fit his point of view, and present them to the public."[243] But the Associated Press, ever mindful of the thousands of hinterlands editors it served who shared the conservative viewpoints of Nixon and Agnew, was known to suppress well-documented stories uncomplimentary to the administration. I was witness to one incident in which an AP reporter brought a story to syndicated columnist Jack Anderson because the wire service's editors felt it treated Nixon too harshly. The story was reinvestigated, rewritten, and published.

The Nixon administration's attempt to force the testimony of journalists with subpoenas was—and still is—the tactic that most threatened to destroy freedom of the press. A reporter's sources are the one treasure he cannot live without, and sources tend to dry up when they feel their identities may be exposed. Reporters themselves begin to avoid stories that they think might cause problems for them or their sources. After newsman Peter Bridge was jailed, for example, two high-level municipal employees in Newark were fired. "They were suspected—that's right *suspected*," wrote Bridge, "of being sources of information to me, as a reporter." What disturbed Bridge even more, however, was the reaction of some of his peers in his jailing: "Some of my colleagues . . . have told me that they have pulled their own punches on some stories because of what was happening to me. They have not told the whole truth because they do not want to go to jail. . . . So the public is already suffering from the current anti-press trend by government agencies. It is being robbed of the full truth because of the intimidation of the press by government officials who are supposed to be representing that same public."[244]

Following the Supreme Court's Branzburg (Caldwell) decision and the imprisonment of several newsmen, a California reporter who had heard of possible corruption in his state legislature called a lobbyist to confirm the story. Demanded the lobbyist, "If I answer that question, will you go to jail to protect me?" A radio reporter in California obtained a promise of help on a bail-bond scandal story from a government employee. When the reporter called for the information, however, he found the man had heard of the Caldwell case. "As far as I'm concerned," the erstwhile source said, "I haven't even spoken to you." [245] *Philadelphia Inquirer* reporter Kent Pollock was working on a bribery story involving a state official when the Caldwell decision came down. An attorney who represented one of Pollock's main informants called to say there would be no more cooperation from his client. Said Pollock, "The ultimate effect of this trend will be the death of a tradition in America—that of the press as a watchdog. This cannot be tolerated by those who love the freedoms of democracy." CBS News was working on a story about welfare and wanted to interview an Atlanta woman who "cheated" the system. She asked for a pledge that CBS would protect her anonymity, the network's lawyers said they couldn't, and the interview was killed.[246] The *Boston Globe*'s assistant managing editor, Timothy Leland, anticipated grand jury subpoenas from a planned investigative series. "We spelled this out to one or two reporters whom we wanted to work on the story," he said. "They considered it combat duty and backed out."[247] Reporter Les Whitten was asked if his being jailed for "possession" of the "Indian Papers" had affected his relationship with his sources. "The Indians won't talk to me anymore," he replied. "They're afraid the FBI will be listening."[248]

One of the most disturbing results of the White House assault on the press was its negative effect on broadcast journalism, the medium that was the special target of the Nixon men. Broadcast executives are a nervous breed to begin with—and understandably so since their right to operate their stations is dependent on government-issued licenses. Two days after Vice President Agnew's Des Moines speech, the city of Washington, D.C., was the scene of some of the largest antiwar demonstrations in history. Some half-million citizens marched peacefully by the White House. The networks, however, gave the event scant notice. Eight months later comedian Bob Hope came to town to lead the celebration of an Honor America Day. This time the network journalists were out in force, devoting hours of coverage to what FCC Commissioner Nicholas Johnson called "the apple pie view of America." Johnson also noticed other discrepancies that heralded, he said, the beginning of the "Age of Agnew" in journalism: "Picking up the spirit of the times, ABC Sports banned halftime coverage of the Buffalo-Holy Cross football game because it had to do with the 'controversial' subject of peace but provided a nationwide audience for the chairman of the Joint Chiefs of Staff to say a few words on behalf of war at the halftime in the Army-Navy game."[249]

The sports department at ABC was not the only bureau that showed signs of nervousness. At ABC News officials began flashing the word *commentary* across the screen whenever anything was broadcast that could possibly be construed as opinion.[250] In 1970, shortly after *New York Times* reporter Earl Caldwell was subpoenaed by a California grand jury to testify about the Black Panthers, ABC sent a producer to Oakland to work on a documentary about the Panthers. The group's leaders, anxious about the Caldwell affair, asked ABC to sign an agreement that it would resist, up to the Supreme Court if need be, the surrender of its outtakes. The network refused and was forced to complete the documentary without any interviews with members of the Black Panther party.[251] In early 1974, ABC cancelled a Dick Cavett show that featured interviews with radical leaders Jerry Rubin, Tom Hayden and Rennie Davis on the grounds that it violated the Fairness Doctrine. It was, protested Cavett, a "landmark precedent in program censorship." An interview he did with Vice President Gerald Ford, said Cavett, "was overwhelmingly positive about the Nixon administration and American institutions," yet he hadn't heard a whimper from ABC.[252]

At CBS, the network that most courageously resisted the Nixon administration's attacks, officials purchased a fifteen-minute special entitled "The Sixties" for use on "60 Minutes." But it was cancelled shortly before air time. NBC picked it up and eventually ran it in edited form. The producer, Chuck Braverman, charged the networks thought it too offensive in the wake of Agnew's criticism.[253] In June 1973 CBS chairman William Paley, acting virtually on his own, eliminated instant analysis, which had so thoroughly irritated Spiro Agnew. The decision upset many CBS reporters, who viewed it as a White House triumph over the network. Five months later, with Nixon reeling from the Watergate scandal, instant analysis was reinstated.[254]

Affiliate stations across the country underwent an even greater retrenchment than the networks. Even before Clay Whitehead's onslaught, according to CBS anchorman Walter Cronkite, his network's affiliates began demanding less analysis and criticism. Some of the local stations began overlaying a slide on the screen stating that what the viewer was witnessing was "CBS News Network Analysis" or "This does not represent the views of this station."[255] In early 1973 CBS scheduled a prize-winning anti-Vietnam war play, "Sticks and Bones," and promptly began hearing from its affiliates. With just a few days until air time, some 80 of the network's 184 affiliate stations announced their intentions not to carry the play, and CBS threw in the towel. The cancellation, wrote Washington *Evening Star* critic Frank Getlein, represented "the first major triumph of the White House policy toward ideas on commercial television as enunciated by Clay T. Whitehead."[256] The president's telecommunications chief himself was asked what he thought of the network's surrender to its affiliates. "This is a good example of how the process ought to work," he said[257]

At Dallas–Fort Worth, station WFAA announced it would use "Support Your President" station breaks. WFAA anchormen began sporting flag lapel pins similar to those worn by Nixon and his associates. In Seattle KIRO-TV labeled itself the "good news" station and began promoting its "fairness." KIRO, stated the station's ads, "tells your side of the story." In another case, the *Alfred I. duPont-Columbia University Survey of Broadcast Journalism* reported, "KHVH Honolulu instituted a Citizens Editorial Board to discuss and evaluate the handling of the news. The station did not, it was quick to explain 'intend to accept policy from the board, but merely criticism. Hopefully this criticism will bridge the gap of understanding between us.' Eight months later, the board had yet to meet. According to duPont's Honolulu correspondent, 'Lawrence S. Berger, president of KHVH, was unable to find the right kind of balance of people to serve on this board. Only right-wing activists were eager to serve.'"[258]

The calculated campaign of intimidation also wrought a chilling effect on journalists, especially broadcast newsmen. Stories that might have been reported in 1968 were not reported in 1972 because avoiding a controversial story was the easiest way to avoid trouble. In other words the use of intimidation techniques was another way of effecting prior restraint—censorship in advance. Bill Monroe, then the Washington editor of NBC's "Today" show, explained the subtleness of the chilling effect: "We . . . know there are stations that don't do investigative reporting. There are stations that confine their documentaries to safe subjects. There are stations that do editorialize, but don't say anything. There are stations that do outspoken editorials, but are scared to endorse candidates. My opinion is that much of this kind of caution, probably most of it, is due to a deep feeling that boldness equals trouble with government, blandness equals peace."[259]

All three major networks were offered huge chunks of the Pentagon Papers in 1971, and all three rejected the opportunity. At CBS, reporters actively pursued Daniel Ellsberg, the man with the papers. They finally caught up with him in Boston, and Walter Cronkite flew up for an exclusive interview. The questions, however, focused on Ellsberg himself and rarely touched on the great issues involved. Ellsberg offered CBS a two-foot high stack of the Pentagon Papers, but the network refused to broadcast the contents. CBS officials denied their decision was rooted in their concern for their government-licensed radio and television stations.

NBC officials explained they did not air the papers because Ellsberg insisted they do it immediately on receiving the papers. Had they accepted Ellsberg's terms, one NBC representative said, it would have been tantamount to "press agentry for Ellsberg." When Ellsberg offered to appear on NBC, following his CBS interview, he was turned down. The reason: "Ellsberg had answered almost all of the questions we would have asked." The network finally ran stories based on the papers, after the Supreme Court had ruled in favor of the newspapers.

ABC refused a thousand pages of the Pentagon Papers because it was "not a very good television story." The network was also advised by its lawyers that it may have been held in contempt if it "published" the papers in cities where newspapers had been enjoined.[260]

The results of their campaign to silence the press often had the Nixon men smiling. In April 1970, just five months after Agnew's Des Moines speech, Herb Klein addressed the convention of the National Association of Broadcasters and claimed that television coverage of the administration was "more fair" in the post-Agnew months. He cited the practice of labeling commentary as evidence.[261] It was obvious to White House insiders, wrote William Safire, that their antipress activities forced the networks to tone down criticism of presidential speeches. After Agnew went on the warpath, said Safire, television officials "saw the light or felt the heat, and the trend toward commentators' immediate rebuttal soon slowed."[262] And a smug Patrick Buchanan told journalist Julius Duscha, "We of course don't take credit for the CBS Spectrum commentators or the wide range of opinion on the *New York Times* op-ed page . . . but consider CBS's Spectrum. They've got Jeffrey St. John and Stan Evans on the right, Stewart Alsop in the middle, and Murray Kempton and Nick von Hoffman on the left. This is a balanced run of commentary which is a by-product of the vice president's criticism of the networks."[263]

The signs were many, in sum, that journalists consciously and unconsciously succumbed to the Nixon cannonade. But the most convincing evidence was the manner in which the press covered the 1972 elections. Indeed, some experts believe, the Nixon campaign was a virtually flawless case study of media manipulation.

Watergate: "I Hope You Give Me Hell"

The three major elements of the grand strategy to manipulate the press were followed to the letter in Richard Nixon's 1972 campaign. The scenario for Nixon's reelection called for him to act the role of an above-the-battle president while his representatives toured the countryside extolling his virtues and excoriating the opposition candidate, George McGovern. As Nixon later wrote:

I planned to spend the month and a half following the Republican convention in the White House doing my job. . . .
  Senator Bob Dole of Kansas, the highly articulate Chairman of the Republican National Committee, and various members of the Cabinet and the administration would travel throughout the country as presidential "surrogates," talking about our general record and achievements as well as their own specialized issues. Ideally, one surrogate would precede McGovern's appearance in each major city and another would follow him as soon as he left.[1]

Nixon thus articulated two elements of the grand strategy: he would remain isolated from the national press while he and his associates executed end runs with television and propaganda techniques. A campaign of intimidation was begun, but it was soon aborted, largely because the previous four years had already created a cooperative press.

In the 1972 presidential race, exactly as they had done in 1968 and during the entire first term, the Nixon men supplied journalists with statements, handouts, and all the bloody marys they could drink. But with a few notable exceptions, the press failed to put the president to the test that major candidates were expected to pass. One reason was that he did not give them the opportunity.

The most perspicacious reporters began to get an idea of what was to come during the convention in Miami Beach. They were unwelcome at most events, especially social affairs attended by the party's wealthy contributors.² At convention headquarters in the Fontainebleau Hotel, Nixon's public relations team pumped out "news releases" with numbing regularity, but most of the information they passed on was so routine that it rarely resulted in an article or broadcast item. On a typical day, reported David Broder of the *Washington Post*, the propaganda team arranged four events, only one of which received any coverage.³

The man who pulled the strings behind the scenes in Nixon's 1972 campaign was the ubiquitous H. R. Haldeman. He helped organize the Committee for the Re-election of the President, placed his own surrogates in key positions within the organization, and was in constant telephone contact with them. Under his guidance, reported *Newsweek*, the campaign became "the cocoon of 1968 carried to its logical development—a closet candidacy that hardly required Mr. Nixon's leaving the White House at all."⁴

Between August and November Nixon pursued what was described as a "limited campaign." He was, after all, the president, as his spokesmen kept informing the nation. He had affairs of state to attend to. The truth was that he ensconced himself in the White House and refused to come out except for occasional one- or two-day campaign forays in key states. Dan Rather became so frustrated that he ended one report, "Dan Rather with the Nixon campaign at the White House."⁵ When Nixon did campaign, his appearances were carefully selected, as were his audiences, to ensure friendly receptions. Admission was usually by ticket only, and hecklers and demonstrators who managed to infiltrate Nixon's rallies were sometimes soundly thumped and dragged off by police and Republican vigilantes. After one such donnybrook, Nixon praised the show of force: "I have seen tonight the blue uniforms of the police. Give them the backing and respect they deserve."⁶ The traveling press rarely got near the president and usually had to be satisfied with a view of him over closed-circuit television monitors set up in press quarters.⁷

In September, for example, Nixon traveled to New York City to address a $1,000-per-plate fund-raising dinner. The event, telecast by closed-circuit television to dinner guests in twenty-eight other cities, earned the Republicans an estimated $7 million. Reporters covered the event, but their stories were based on what they saw on television sets from a room two hundred feet from the ballroom where Nixon spoke. At one point *Washington Star* reporter James Doyle jumped up and shouted at the monitor: "This is terrible! This is awful shit. I just want to take a look at him! Is he alive? How do I know he's alive?"⁸

By late October Nixon had visited just nine states; his longest campaign swing had lasted only three days, and this trip had spanned the continent from New York to California.[9] His refusal to meet the press or freewheel on the campaign trail eventually elicited from a frustrated George McGovern the charge that Nixon was hiding in the White House. The Nixon team's response was quick and remarkably monolithic. "He is attending to the matters of the presidency," said press secretary Ronald Ziegler. "How can you expect a man to be president and candidate at the same time?" said Vice-President Agnew.[10]

With the president in seclusion the press was forced to turn to his spokesmen, who were brimming with innocuous information but were taciturn on subjects that were taboo. Ronald Ziegler spent a good portion of the campaign issuing denials. He denied that thousands of dollars in contributions from the dairy lobby had influenced the administration's sudden decision to increase government price supports for milk.[11] At one briefing alone Ziegler was asked twenty-nine questions about alleged White House involvement in the Watergate affair, and he answered each with some variation of "no comment."[12]

In October the *Washington Post* reported that the president's appointments secretary, Dwight Chapin, had hired an old college classmate, Donald Segretti, to sabotage the Democratic campaign with dirty tricks, and Ziegler was faced with the dilemma of how to respond to journalists' questions. He met with several White House aides to rehearse his answers. Chapin suggested that Ziegler should say, "I am not going to dignify desperation politics." John Ehrlichman offered this response: "We just don't take as seriously as you do these campaign pranks. Some of you for your own purposes have blown these into something that is not there." When he finally faced the press, Ziegler was prepared with an array of non-answers. The Segretti stories, he claimed, were "fundamentally inaccurate" and based on "hearsay, innuendo, guilt by association." He also asserted that Chapin enjoyed the president's trust and was not being pushed out of the White House. Chapin later resigned.[13]

Ziegler's major task on the road and aboard the president's plane was to act as a buffer between Nixon and the press. The large majority of the traveling reporters had to ride in a separate press plane; on the presidential jet the seven-or eight-person pool was relegated to a rear compartment and instructed to remain there unless invited forward. Such overtures were rare and were usually extended only for a three-bump interview or a photo opportunity.[14]

Even when following Nixon on the ground, reporters saw little of him. From the plane he hopped into his automobile and was off again.

Newsmen climbed into press buses and joined the motorcade far behind the lead car. Behind the president's limousine, typically, was a Secret Service car; then came automobiles carrying political dignitaries, a number of pool cars carrying White House aides and pool reporters, several small trucks bearing television cameramen, and finally the press buses. Since those who had to tell the country what was going on could not see what was going on, someone up front had to describe the action by a radio hookup. The person who performed this chore rode in Ziegler's car and thus was called the "Z-pooler."[15]

Nixon held only two press conferences between the Republican convention and the November election. The first, on August 29, was billed as a "political" news conference as a way of reinforcing the notion that the president was refusing to exploit his position for selfish purposes and would respond to political questions only when he stepped out of the presidential shoes.[16] Nixon met the press again on October 5 but said little worth writing down. He would not reply to charges of corruption in his administration. He would not comment on the Vietnam peace negotiations. No, he would not campaign a great deal because he had to stay around to veto legislation that would otherwise result in a tax increase. As for the Watergate burglary, a grand jury had handed down some indictments in that case, and he had once been criticized for declaring Charles Manson guilty before he was officially determined to be so, and, he ended, "I know you would want me to follow the same simple standard by not commenting on this case."[17]

Nixon faced a problem in his convention of 1972: since he and Spiro Agnew had the nominations wrapped up, it promised to be the most boring show of the year. The desire to put on a well-organized and interesting performance was reinforced by the disorderly convention held by the Democratic party. To Nixon it was "a political shambles" dominated by "women, blacks, homosexuals, welfare mothers, migrant farm workers," and other practitioners of "new politics." George McGovern had appeared on the final night to accept the nomination at 2:48 A.M.—"prime time on Guam," noted Nixon. The Republicans, he determined, would show the country how to put on an interesting convention. How he and his media team succeeded is the story of one of the most spectacular end runs they ever executed on the press. They converted the convention hall, and in some respects the city of Miami Beach, into one gigantic television studio. Reporters, like millions of viewers across the country, were little more than spectators.[18]

At the convention hall, an $80,000 podium, designed by the art director for a television show, "The Dating Game," was constructed to resemble a Greek column. The floor in front of the microphone was built to be raised or lowered so that all speakers would stand at the exact height of President Nixon. Above the podium three twenty-seven-foot screens were installed for film and slide presentations. For the benefit of those in the first few rows of the audience, four television sets were set up to rise on hydraulic lifts from the first tier of the podium.[19] A staircase was strategically placed to permit the speakers to make their entrances on camera. And an air-conditioning unit was installed in the podium to relieve the president and others of the embarrassment of sweating in front of the entire nation.[20]

The convention proceeded on schedule with the precision of a drill team exhibition. Throughout the proceedings delegates were kept attentive for the nationwide television audience with slide shows and films about Nixon, Pat Nixon, and other Republican heroes. A continuous stream of movie stars and other prominent figures marched forth to pay homage to their man in the White House. All events unfolded so perfectly that reporters began to suspect there was a script—and indeed one did turn up. Delivered by mistake to a few reporters, it outlined each event and allowed for "spontaneous" demonstrations, all timed to last a prescribed number of minutes. When enough ballots were cast to give Nixon the nomination, the script called for convention chairman Gerald Ford, then a congressman from Michigan, to say, "I am informed that . . ." Then, noted the script, it was time for the "Demonstration—Nixon Now."[21]

All went as planned, and thousands of balloons floated to the floor. A few minutes later the delegates looked up in surprise to see Nixon appearing live on the gigantic screens above them. For as he was being nominated in one part of the city, Richard Nixon was being driven to Miami Beach's Marine Stadium where a youth rally—emceed by entertainer Sammy Davis, Jr.—was in progress. From a command trailer at convention hall, Nixon was cued when to make his entrance at the rally, and he jumped out to tumultuous applause for a live television appearance just a few minutes before the late evening news shows.[22]

It may have been disheartening for the reporters who were outflanked by the Nixon men. But as far as the star of the show was concerned, it was a smash hit. "It's just been wonderful," Nixon told the man who directed the perfectly timed affair. "It's like no convention has ever been in the world."[23]

Ostensibly the Nixon campaign was managed by the Committee for the Re-election of the President (CRP), housed in a well-secured building near the White House. In truth, however, the campaign was run from the executive mansion, and it was dominated by the Nixon media men. Haldeman was at the top of the pyramid. His chief strategist was Patrick Buchanan, who analyzed McGovern's positions on the issues, assembled "assault books" of material used in attacking the Democrat, and dreamed up the "lines" that were hammered into the public consciousness by Nixon's surrogates. The primary executioner of Buchanan's strategems was Charles Colson, who coordinated many of the activities of "attack groups" based in the White House, at the CRP, and the Republican National Committee and on Capitol Hill.[24] Each morning members of the White House attack group pored through information gleaned from press accounts and the reports of their own spies in the Democratic camp and devised ways to keep the heat on McGovern. They then passed their battle plans on to the other attack groups and to Nixon's surrogates.[25] To handle the routine advertising chores the Nixon image merchants created their own advertising agency, the November Group, headed by Peter Dailey, an advertising executive from Los Angeles. "There is only one candidate in this election, not two," Dailey told a *Miami Herald* reporter. "There is the incumbent. The president. Mr. Nixon. And then there is the only candidate, McGovern."[26]

Overall the Nixon reelection team spent only about $5 million for television advertising and far less for promotion in all its forms than had been anticipated. Much of the money originally earmarked for the broadcast media was used to finance a series of radio and television speeches by Nixon in the closing weeks of the campaign.[27] One of the major reasons the CRP could spend less on a paid advertising campaign was because Nixon and most of his surrogates were public officials, and thus their activities were routinely covered by the networks.

After a Labor Day break at the Western White House, for example, Nixon stopped in San Francisco for what was billed as a nonpolitical appearance. While there he took a forty-five minute ride on a Golden Gate ferry, where he conferred with his Citizens Advisory Council for Environmental Quality. Prior to the president's arrival the White House advance men contacted the transit manager and requested that certain portions of the ferryboat be repainted so it would provide a good backdrop for television coverage of the president.[28]

After five years of practice, in short, the television end run had been virtually perfected. "We're being finessed out of our boots," said *Chicago Daily News* reporter Peter Lisagor. "We're just sitting on the bench while the administration dribbles the ball past us."[29] Concurred Theodore White, "It was easier to cover the president on campaign in 1972 by staying home and watching television with the rest of the people—which was the way the president wanted it."[30]

Each stop on Nixon's campaign schedule appeared to be designed to bolster his image. For example, he twice flew to the flood-devastated town of Wilkes-Barre, Pennsylvania, to tell the citizens, many of them homeless, what he was doing to bring them relief.[31] In September, Nixon swooped down upon a festival of Italian-Americans in Mitchellville, Maryland.[32]

It was important, the media men felt, to continue to project the image that an overwhelming majority of the American people supported the president's Vietnam war policy, even if it meant stretching the truth. After Nixon decided to mine Haiphong harbor in May 1972, the CRP placed a phony advertisement in the *New York Times* suggesting that many independent citizens supported the president and were willing to pay thousands of dollars to express their opinions. In addition the CRP activated its letter- and telegram-writing network to ensure that the mail coming into the White House was overwhelmingly favorable to Nixon. A former mail clerk at the CRP also revealed that the Nixon campaign organization had rigged a poll, sponsored by a Washington, D.C., television station, to make it appear that respondents supported Nixon's moves in Vietnam. The television station had printed a ballot in Washington newspapers asking readers and viewers to declare their opinions toward the mining of Haiphong harbor. CRP employees purchased several thousand newspapers, clipped the ballots, and cast them in favor of Nixon. Then, concerned that someone might notice that the CRP trash contained a ton of newspapers, all missing the Vietnam ballot, Nixon's campaign officials ran them through their document shredder.[33]

The president's men worried about the images projected by prominent Democrats almost as intensely as they fretted about Nixon's. As early as March 1971 chief political strategist Patrick Buchanan established a watch on each of the major Democratic contenders. While Buchanan was pondering strategy, other White House aides concentrated on more pragmatic matters designed to alter the opposition's public image: Three espionage and two sabotage operations were set up in the various Democratic camps. Presidential political aide Murray Chotiner hired two journalists, Seymour Freidin and Lucianne Cummings Goldberg, to travel with Democratic candidates and file reports on their statements and activities.[34] At the CRP Jeb Magruder supervised an operation known as "Sedan Chair," which was designed to spy on and annoy Nixon's opponents.[35]

The third espionage and sabotage operation was rooted in Richard Nixon's anger and humiliation over having been harassed throughout his career by political prankster Dick Tuck. As the 1972 campaign approached, Nixon wrote in his *Memoirs*, he "insisted to Haldeman and others on the staff that in this campaign we were finally in a position to have someone doing to the opposition what they had done to us. They knew that this time I wanted the leading Democrats annoyed, harassed and embarrassed—as I'd been in the past." Haldeman thus hired a lawyer named Donald Segretti, who had attended the University of Southern California with White House aides Dwight Chapin and Gordon Strachan. Segretti's job was to conduct a "black advance" program.[36]

Using funds provided by Nixon's lawyer and campaign aide, Herbert Kalmbach, Segretti recruited a group of agents and in the summer of 1971 launched his own campaign of dirty tricks, most of them directed against Edmund Muskie. At one point the senator had discussed his reluctance to select a black running mate, so Segretti and one of his agents placed this ad in a college newspaper: "Wanted. Sincere gentleman seeking running mate. White preferred but natural sense of rhythm no obstacle. Contact E. Muskie."[37]

During the New Hampshire primary Segretti's hired hands posed as representatives of a Harlem-for-Muskie committee and telephoned residents of Manchester in the middle of the night to solicit votes. In Florida letters accusing Senators Hubert Humphrey and Henry Jackson of sexual improprieties were written on Muskie stationery and mailed out. At a Washington fund raiser in April 1972 Muskie's campaign workers were dumbfounded when $300 worth of liquor, cakes, flowers, and two hundred pizzas arrived unordered. A dozen African diplomats arrived in limousines hired in the name of Muskie's organization. Two magicians showed up, one from the Virgin Islands, to entertain children who were not present.[38]

After the Democratic convention Nixon's dirty tricksters went to work on McGovern's image. Antiwar demonstrators who harassed Nixon were described as McGovern supporters who were being financed by communists and foreigners. Indeed there is some evidence that when no protesters were expected at a Nixon function, his advance team hired some. When McGovern appeared on the ABC show "Issues and Answers," he found himself answering questions sent over by an aide to Herb Klein. On another occasion someone called the CBS network and attempted to cancel a McGovern broadcast about Vietnam;

McGovern aide Frank Mankiewicz claimed he had no evidence but suspected a Republican trick.[39]

While the media team's major efforts during the campaign were directed toward the manipulation of television, the president's chief public relations man, Herb Klein, sold the president to the public in other ways. His normal duties—keeping the hinterlands press informed with "fact kits" and organizing briefings by teams of administration spokesmen—were left to others as he campaigned actively for Republican candidates.[40]

A slightly different form of the propaganda end run was created when Nixon appointed thirty-five "surrogate candidates" to stand in for him at appearances throughout the country. Using suggestions from the various attack groups and coordinated by Charles Colson, the surrogates ripped into anything said by George McGovern and other prominent Democrats and topped them with claims and charges of their own. National security adviser Henry Kissinger and Secretary of State William Rogers predicted peace in Vietnam at every turn. Secretary of Defense Melvin Laird blasted the Democratic candidate's positions on military matters. Agriculture Secretary Earl Butz accused McGovern of "witch-hunting" and "making smear charges." Attorney General Richard Kleindienst criss-crossed the country speaking about "the accomplishments of the Justice Department" while insisting his speeches were "nonpolitical but partisan." Treasury Secretary George Shultz criticized McGovern's tax reform proposals. Labor Secretary James Hodgson abandoned his field of expertise altogether to accuse McGovern of perpetrating a "cruel hoax" on the American people by making "rash promises" to "bring our prisoners home" from Vietnam.[41]

In their effort to be "objective" and "balanced," newsmen gave the surrogates coverage equal to that accorded McGovern. "I'm running against Nixon," the frustrated Democrat complained, "not Melvin Laird or Earl Butz." He continued, "I think when a presidential candidate is given a minute and a half on network television that it's unfair to put some second-stringer on for a minute and a half on the Republican side. Let the president come out and talk for himself."[42]

In June 1972 *Newsweek* magazine reported that Nixon's campaign strategists were planning to make the "liberal" press an issue in their drive for the reelection of the president. Nixon's top-level advisers, it was said, had already held strategy meetings to plan their assault on the press.[43] *Newsweek*'s report was right on target. There had been discussions among the Nixon media men about bludgeoning the press, particularly the networks, into submission. Included in Patrick Buchanan's campaign plan of March 14, 1972, for example, there was this section, entitled "Accuracy in Media":

Suggest establishment of a "Fair Coverage Committee" or "Equal Time Committee" which might be located in the RNC, which would "clock" precisely the positive and negative coverage of presidential and vice presidential candidates on the networks. If we are getting anything more than "equal time," this committee can remain silent; if we get anything less than equal time . . . then send a memorandum to John Mitchell who should get on the horn to the network president and point this out, indicating that if it is not corrected, and equal time is not provided—this will be made an issue in the campaign, and the subject of legislation in the coming congress.[44]

By early June Nixon was upset at what he perceived to be the disparate press treatment accorded him and McGovern. After lengthy consultation with Carles Colson about the Democratic candidate's "love affair" with the press, the president fired off a candid memorandum to Patrick Buchanan: "It is very important in terms of the final campaign that the media be effectively discredited."[45]

In late July, however, the situation abruptly changed. During the California primary Democratic candidate Hubert Humphrey openly attacked a number of the more radical programs proposed by George McGovern, and the press, belatedly convinced of McGovern's strength among the electorate, joined in. This confused the Nixon men, who had expected the "liberal" press to be kind to the liberal McGovern. The president's advisers, including former newsmen Ken Clawson and John Scali, began to argue that as long as the press was spotlighting McGovern's shortcomings, the Nixon camp should call a moratorium on its war with the media.[46] The president, said William Safire, was astounded.[47] The White House signaled its pleasure with a truce, fittingly announced by the administration's preeminent press critic, Vice-President Agnew, in Portland, Oregon, on July 22. Before a joint convention of the National Newspaper Association and the Oregon Newspaper Publishers Association, Agnew declared, "The substance of my remarks is that we all, whether government official or editor, might do well to forgo harangue and cliche in favor of discussion based on reason and public interest. There is a place for the press and the government to coexist with respect to each other and yet to maintain that vital and delicate adversary relationship that is so vital to the maintenance and preservation of a free society. I think that we can bring that about with mutual cooperation."[48]

With some exceptions the administration's truce with the press remained in effect until after the election, but a few insiders were careful to warn that it could only be considered temporary. Patrick Buchanan observed that the moratorium "doesn't mean that some of us have abandoned or will abandon some of our cherished assumptions about the press."[49] Even as Buchanan spoke Nixon and his key enforcers were taking names. The president, according to John Dean, ordered that a list be kept of reporters who gave him "trouble" during the campaign and vowed the offenders would be "taken care of" after the election.[50]

In the opinion of many political observers the press generally gave the president a free ride during his run for reelection. Among the many reasons was the fact that Nixon stayed out of the line of fire by secluding himself in the White House. McGovern did his part by keeping reporters diverted with what seemed to be an unending string of blunders. But the most important factor apparently was the fear that gripped the news industry after three years of doing battle with the Nixon administration. Press critic Ben Bagdikian studied the election-year coverage and concluded, "A sample study of leading papers and network specials during the presidential campaign makes it clear that the Nixon administration's three-year war against the news media has succeeded. There has been a retrogression in printing newsworthy information that is critical of the administration and a notable decline in investigation of apparent wrongdoing when it is likely to anger or embarrass the White House. This, coupled with the shrewd manipulation of the media by Nixon officials, has moved the American news system closer to becoming a propaganda arm of the administration in power."[51]

The newspaper coverage, however, was not as poor as that of the television networks. Traditionally during presidential elections the networks run several documentaries designed to examine the issues. The president's favorite network, ABC, ran no specials at all during the 1972 campaign. CBS, which had averaged seven political specials in campaigns since 1960, aired but two in 1972. "The answer," wrote Bagdikian, "appears to be the Nixon-Agnew attack on the networks."[52]

What was not written or televised about Nixon, in sum, was more telling than what was. Few stories appeared during the campaign about the ITT scandal, for example, or the deception practiced by the administration during the Indo-Pakistan conflict of 1971. And the president succeeded in hiding out in the executive mansion with a minimum of concern on the part of the press. On the few occasions he ventured out, he avoided situations in which he could have been questioned about issues and events. When he did answer queries, reporters treated him with deference.

George McGovern, on the other hand, received a drubbing at the hands of the press. One commentator for the *Washington Post* observed, incredibly, that McGovern was responsible for his own poor coverage because he was too candid. Wrote Stephen Isaacs:

George McGovern may complain about it [his coverage], but he is the principal cause for it. For the past 22 months that he has been an announced candidate for the presidency, he has always insisted on an "open" campaign. Even now a reporter can walk up to him and ask him almost any and every question, and he will try to answer it. He insists that his staff do the same, no trickery, no appearance of guile. This is one of the things that attracted so many of his young staffers in the first place. It is, in fact, a basic tenet of his campaign strategy.

In other words, instead of being commended for his honesty and openness, McGovern was faulted for it. The implied suggestion was that he should have been more secretive. Isaacs also made the tacit admission that McGovern's poor treatment was a direct result of the three-year campaign of harassment by the Nixon men. Reporters were not necessarily afraid of Nixon, Isaacs seemed to be saying, but they felt they had something to prove to him:

One suspects . . . that the reporters—or at least many of them—are over-compensating for their own biases. Many of them, particularly in the writing press, resent the cold treatment they have received from the White House over the last four years, they have been stung by Mr. Nixon's going to the public over their heads—directly via the tube, from the TV theater in the White House. They like McGovern's openness.

But they remember Mr. Agnew's attacks on the press in 1969. They don't want to go "in the tank" for George McGovern, just because they happen to like the guy. Even more, they seem often to go out of their way to show they are fair, unbiased.[53]

In short, the Nixon men had conjured up journalism's bogeyman—objectivity—to scare the press into an excoriation of George McGovern. Few newsmen were able to perceive that their pursuit of this elusive goal was resulting in unfair treatment of the Democratic candidate.

Perhaps no incident was more examplary of Nixon's talent in keeping the press on a string than the manner in which he handled the press during a visit to Liberty Island to dedicate the new American Museum of Immigration and make a pitch for the ethnic vote. His audience was largely a crowd of school children who had been bused and boated in. Reporter Richard Reeves reported the event:

There were even real live protesters there, about six of them, shouting, "Stop the bombing," while most of the crowd chanted, "Four more years!" When the dissonant shouts began, the president stopped speaking for a moment, then said: "Ladies and gentlemen, I would only suggest that on your television screens tonight, in addition to showing the six there, let's show the thousands that are over here."

The television cameras swung dutifully away from the demonstrators, police removed the six protesters, and the reporting of the 1972 campaign of Richard Nixon moved smoothly along.[54]

The only problem that remained was to ensure that the networks received the film in time to make the evening news shows. The Nixon men had a solution for this too: they volunteered to have it delivered, and the film was flown to the mainland by helicopter. Commented one television executive, "When the administration doesn't want us to film something, we damn well can't. But if they want, they can be marvelous at helping with the logistics of film. They've got almost unlimited facilities, of course."[55]

On November 7, 1972, nearly 61 percent of those Americans who went to the polls cast their votes for Richard Nixon. His historic 18 million vote margin gave him, in his opinion, the "new majority mandate" he had been seeking, and he began planning some changes. One thing he would do, he later wrote, would be to remind the press who was boss: "During the first term I . . . had had to observe the official fiction that the president and the media do not have a fundamentally adversary relationship. Now in the second term, however, I planned to let them know that I would no longer uncomplainingly accept their barbs or allow their unaccountable power to go unchecked."[56]

The barb that rankled him most in the postelection weeks was criticism of his decision to resume the bombing of North Vietnam during the 1972 Christmas season. It especially irritated him that Henry Kissinger was treated more kindly by the press and that Kissinger's role in the bombing decision was downplayed.[57] In late January a peace agreement was initialed, and Nixon decided, in his own words, that it was time he "took off the gloves" and took on the press.[58] The opportunity came when he was asked, during a January 31 news conference, what he would to to heal the wounds that had rift the nation: "Well, it takes two to heal wounds, and I must say that when

I see that the most vigorous criticism or, shall we say, the least pleasure out of the peace agreement comes from those that were the most outspoken advocates of peace at any price, it makes one realize whether some want the wounds healed. . . . As far as this administration is concerned, . . . we finally have achieved a peace with honor. I know it gags some of you to write that phrase, but it is true."[59]

The arrogance reflected in that angry statement was typical of the attitude that pervaded the White House after the 1972 election. The Democrats had attempted, and failed, to make the Watergate affair an issue; the president and his top aides were confident that the scandal could be contained to include only the original burglary, for which seven men had been indicted. When James Reston of the *New York Times* suggested to Kissinger that the time had come to reconcile the differences between the press and the White House, the national security adviser retorted, "It will not come from this House until the press acknowledges it was wrong."[60] In February Kissinger made plans to travel to mainland China and North Vietnam, and Ziegler announced that "because of the facilities we have available in terms of transportation and because of the nature of Dr. Kissinger's trip, we decided we could not provide transportation to members of the press." Then why was Herb Klein accompanying Kissinger, Ziegler was asked. Responded the press secretary, "He is along to deal with any communication matters that come up, primarily to make sure that no communication matters come up."[61]

A few weeks later during hearings to confirm him as director of the FBI, L. Patrick Gray III dropped a bombshell: at the request of the White House appointments secretary, Dwight Chapin, the president's personal attorney, Herbert Kalmbach, had funneled upward of $40,000 in campaign funds to dirty trickster Donald Segretti. Until then Chapin had denied any involvement with Segretti, and a reporter asked Ziegler, "Which man is lying?" Said Ziegler, "I have nothing new to respond to you with, but it is that type of question that solidifies my position not to comment."[62]

There was good reason for such cheek: the press was on the run. Clay Whitehead had recently warned network affiliate owners they might lose their licenses if they did not censor the news programs coming out of Washington and New York. Charles Colson had threatened to bring CBS to its knees in Wall Street. And the *Washington Post* was feeling the heat from several directions. For ten months the *Post* had pursued the Watergate story, and this had provoked Nixon's promise to create "damnable, damnable problems" for the newspaper. And now with the president safely ensconced in the White House for four more years, those problems had begun. The licenses of the Post company's two Florida television stations had been challenged by Nixon's friends; its society reporter, Dorothy McCardle, had been frozen out of the White House; its chief competitor, the *Washington Star-News*, was being fed exclusives.[63] Then on February 26 came another devastating blow: the *Post*'s publisher, Katherine Graham, its managing editor, and three reporters, along with several newsmen from the *New York Times*, the *Washington Star-News*, and *Time* magazine, were subpoenaed by the CRP in connection with several civil suits and countersuits.[64]

In short, as William Safire later wrote, "in the month of February, 1973, [Nixon] had his foot on the 'liberal establishment press's' neck."[65] The administration had "won the battle" against the press, James Reston told the Minnesota Newspaper Association, "at least in the public's mind."[66] NBC president Julian Goodman warned that "some federal government officials are waging a continuing campaign aimed at intimidating and discrediting the news media, and the public has expressed very little concern."[67] And certainly Benjamin Bradlee, executive editor of the *Washington Post*, knew the press was on the ropes. "The First Amendment is in greater danger than any time I've seen it," he said during an appearance on the Dick Cavett show on March 22, 1973.[68]

Little did Bradlee know, as he spoke those words, that Richard Nixon's star had already burned its brightest and would, in less than twelve hours, begin collapsing upon itself.

U.S. District Court Judge John J. Sirica, a sixty-nine-year-old, rock-ribbed Republican, had scheduled March 23, 1973, as the day he would pronounce sentences on the seven men who had been convicted in the Watergate burglary conspiracy. Sirica had a reputation for issuing harsh sentences—indeed, he had, over the years, earned the sobriquet "Maximum John"—and he had made it plain that he did not believe the federal prosecutors had gotten to the bottom of the Watergate case. The sentences he would hand down, therefore, were expected to be severe. And thus did one of the conspirators, James McCord, become persuaded that he would spend fewer days behind bars if he supplied some of the information the judge had been seeking. Three days earlier McCord had sent Sirica a letter, and moments after court was convened on that Friday, the judge read it aloud:

In the interests of justice, and in the interests of restoring faith in the criminal justice system, which faith has been severely damaged in this case, I will state the following to you at this time which I hope may be of help to you in meting out justice in this case:

1. There was political pressure applied to the defendants to plead guilty and remain silent.

2. Perjury occurred during the trial in matters highly material to the very structure, orientation, and impact of the government's case, and to the motivation and intent of the defendants.

3. Others involved in the Watergate operation were not identified during the trial, when they could have been by those testifying.[69]

More than any other single event the McCord letter marked the turning point in the president's relations with the press. Suddenly the White House was no longer credible. Nixon fought—ferociously, viciously—for fifteen months. He tried every trick, every tactic in his press-manipulation manual. But this time, the appeasement, the evasion, the intimidation didn't work.

Throughout the long months of the crisis Nixon attempted to adhere to the first principle of the grand strategy for press manipulation that had served him so well during the first term: the national press was nonessential. The people could be reached directly by television and with modern propaganda techniques. There was no need to filter his messages through the Washington press corps. His spokesmen could keep newsmen happy with creature comforts and preoccupied with piffle. He soon discovered, however, that the press could not be ignored; people were reading, watching, and listening to reports about the Watergate scandal. And he soon determined that the press was indeed essential, as an enemy, a scapegoat.

But he tried to appease and avoid journalists. His penchant for privacy became an obsession after March 1973. While in Washington he spent few hours in the Oval Office, preferring instead his sanctuary in the Old Executive Building. Trips up and down the Potomac River aboard the yacht *Sequoia* became more frequent.[70] His door was guarded zealously by Haldeman and Ehrlichman until they resigned on April 30, 1973; afterward the new chief of staff, Alexander Haig, and press secretary Ronald Ziegler became the gatekeepers.[71] The Nixon family spent as little time as possible in Washington. Between his inauguration in January, 1973, and Thanksgiving of that year, the president remained in the capital only four out of forty-four weekends.[72]

On his frequent trips to the presidential retreats, Nixon took great pains to stay out of the public eye. During a three-week sojourn at San Clemente over the 1973 Christmas holidays, for example, he secluded himself in his office and den and surfaced only for the wedding of his physician, a trip to Palm Springs, and an occasional automobile ride with Bebe Rebozo. "They're gloomy, gloomy out there," said one visitor to the San Clemente complex. "They're sitting around blaming all their troubles on the liberal press and wondering what's going to happen next."[73]

Reporters went to Camp David with the president in late January 1974 and discovered that the press trailer had disappeared. "I'm told it is at Camp David," said the befuddled deputy press secretary, Gerald Warren, when asked where it had gone. Two weeks later the reporters were notified that their trailer had been relocated to a public campground a half-mile from the mountain retreat.[74]

The efforts of Nixon and his media team to shun newsmen during the months of Watergate were exhaustive, often ludicrous, and sometimes saddening. Among the more memorable incidents were these:

- While flying to New Orleans for a speech before the Veterans of Foreign Wars in late August 1973, Nixon was informed by the Secret Service that an assassination attempt might be made against him. As the distressed president approached the convention center where he was to speak, reporters tagged along behind him. Nixon suddenly stopped, grabbed Ronald Ziegler by the shoulders, spun him around, and angrily shoved him toward the group of newsmen. "I don't want the press with me," growled Nixon. "You take care of it." White House staff members insisted that the episode had never occurred, but CBS cameras had captured it on film.[75]

- On October 20, 1973, former *Los Angeles Times* publisher Norman Chandler died of cancer. Twice in the preceding months, Richard Nixon had scheduled a visit with his old friend and supporter at his country home, some fifteen minutes from San Clemente. The president never showed up.[76]

- In early November 1973 a White House press assistant announced that reporters were forbidden to observe the president's helicopter taking off from the White House or landing at Camp David.[77]

- During the waning months of his presidency Nixon virtually disappeared from sight. Time and again he listened to the secret tape recordings of White House conversations. At 6:00 P.M. on August 8, 1974, the night he announced to the nation his intention to resign, he notified the Secret Service that he wanted to walk from his Old Executive Office Building hideaway to the White House without being seen. Reporters found themselves locked in the press room for twenty-three minutes. Later that evening they were instructed to leave the premises, and the White House doors were bolted and guarded as Nixon and his wife wandered through the Executive Mansion for one last look.[78]

Ziegler's keep-them-comfortable-but-keep-them-ignorant technique of controlling newsmen also began to fail as the Watergate stew thickened. Prior to the release of the James McCord letter Ziegler had reigned like a monarch over the press corps that followed the president. He cleared reporters' appointments and thus controlled all access to White House newsmakers. Questions about possible White House involvement in the Watergate burglary and campaign irregularities were routinely and haughtily turned aside. But in the wake of L. Patrick Gray's Senate testimony and the McCord letter, reporters pounded Ziegler with increasing hostility. During March 1973 the press secretary parried 478 questions about the Watergate scandal.[80] At times he seemed on the verge of crying; he fidgeted and pounded his lectern with rolled-up papers. Once he snapped: "You don't have to accept this rationale. You can giggle if you like."[81]

By mid-April Nixon and his chief advisers had become aware that presidential assistants John Dean and Jeb Magruder might cooperate with federal investigators in return for immunity from prosecution. The president decided to seize the initiative; on April 17 he visited the White House press room and read this short statement:

On March 21, as a result of serious charges which came to my attention, some of which were publicly reported, I began intensive new inquiries into this whole matter. Last Sunday afternoon the attorney general [Richard Kleindienst], the assistant attorney general [Henry Peterson] and I met at length in the Executive Office Building to review the facts which had come to me in my investigation and also to review the progress of the Department of Justice investigation. I can report today that there have been major developments in the case concerning which it would be improper—to be more specific now, except to say that real progress has been made in finding the truth.[82]

With a stiff smile, Nixon departed, and the assembled reporters closed in on Ziegler. Were previous statements and denials of White House involvement in Watergate now "inoperative"? In a miscue that would come to haunt him, Ziegler picked up the language:

The other statements that were made were based on information that was provided prior to those events which have been referred to in the president's statement today. Therefore, any comment which was made up until today or previously was based on that activity. This is the operative statement.

The way to assess the previous comments is to assess them on the basis that they were made on the information available at the time. The president refers to the fact that there is new material; therefore that is the operative statement. The others are inoperative.[83]

At the regular press briefing the next day, Clark Mollenhoff, who had left Nixon's employ in July 1970, tore into Ziegler: "Do you feel free to stand up there and lie and put out misinformation and then come around later and say it's all 'inoperative'? That's what you're doing. You're not entitled to any credibility at all."[84]

Twelve days later, after a series of damaging Watergate revelations, Nixon appeared on national television to announce the resignation of H. R. Haldeman, John Ehrlichman, John Dean, and Richard Kleindienst. The following day Ziegler was asked by a reporter whether an apology to the *Washington Post* was in order. Responded a now contrite press secretary: "In thinking of it all at this point in time, yes, I would apologize to the *Post* and I would apologize to Mr. Woodward and Mr. Bernstein. . . . We would all have to say that mistakes were made in terms of comments. I was over-enthusiastic in my comments about the *Post*, particularly if you look at them in the context of developments that have taken place"[85]

Ziegler maintained a humble mien for a short while, but the crush of events and the hard, insistent questions they engendered from reporters soon had him in a snappish mood again. During the daily briefings newsmen hooted and jeered at his comments. "If I said something wrong, I'll retract it," puled Ziegler during one angry exchange. Shouted a reporter, "If you said something *right*, retract it." The questions had taken on a "sadistic quality," commented Peter Lisagor of the *Chicago Daily News*, "but they come from a frustrated, outraged and indignant press corps." Agreed UPI's Helen Thomas: "We have more nerve now. The evasion we accepted before we will never accept again. We realize that we did a lousy job on Watergate. We just sat there and took what they said at face value."[86]

Pundits of different political persuasions began to call for Ziegler's dismissal. "I don't believe the White House is best served by Ziegler," wrote conservative columnist James J. Kilpatrick. "The word 'inoperative' is going to follow him the rest of his life."[87] Observed James Reston of the *New York Times*, "Ron Ziegler, the president's press secretary, who is under attack for misleading the press on Watergate, is apparently going to resign or be transferred to another job. He is a symbol of past troubles. . . . He is too vulnerable and too visible."[88]

Several of Nixon's confidants, including domestic counselor Melvin Laird, chief of staff Alexander Haig, and ex-Treasury Secretary John Connally, were urging him to oust Ziegler.[89] Nixon, however, believed that dismissal would be tantamount to a confession of wrongdoing; therefore the press secretary was elevated into Nixon's inner circle, given the title of assistant to the president, and put in charge of all

White House communications. Thereafter Gerald Warren conducted the daily press briefings, and Ziegler stepped forth only to censure the president's critics or to make major announcements.[90] After Nixon's State of the Union message in January 1974, for example, Ziegler emerged to announce that the public response was "substantial" and was running about five to one in favor of the president.[91] The next day he took the podium in the press briefing room to declare that he and Nixon had had enough of Watergate and were putting it behind them:

It is the position of the president and my position as White House spokesman that we will answer questions on the business of government and the positions we take on issues.

But it is the very firm determination—indeed, it is a fact—that we are not going to proceed day in and day out through 1974 answering questions and consuming ourselves with Watergate affairs.

You can ask what you will . . . but the answer is that I have nothing to say.[92]

In the spring and summer of 1974 Ziegler devoted many of his special appearances to attacks on the House Judiciary Committee, which was considering whether to impeach the president. When the committee's chief counsel, John Doar, finally urged Nixon's impeachment on July 19, Ziegler fumed that Doar had been conducting a "kangaroo court" and was "a partisan and has been a partisan from the beginning." And the committee itself had made "a total shambles out of what should have been a fair proceeding."[93] Nothing that Ziegler said or did, however, could stem the now rampaging press. He had prevaricated and stonewalled too many times; he could not be believed. His mere presence, wrote Hugh Sidey of *Time* magazine, "triggers in reporters a salivation of distrust [and] suggests that the White House considers [any] new issue so touchy it is sending out its top deceiver. Get ready to be misinformed."[94]

The brunt of the journalistic anger, however, was borne by the bespectacled, pipe-smoking deputy press secretary, Gerald Warren. He attempted to turn aside the gibes with a few verbal thrusts of his own, but the White House press corps would not be placated. A typical exchange, this one concerning the president's taxes, occurred on April 8, 1974:

Q: You used the figure $148,000 and some odd dollars as the amount of the 1969 assessment. Where did you get that figure?
A: It was given to me by the president's tax counsel.

Q: The Joint Committee's figure is something like $170,000. Is there a difference of some $40,000?

A: . . . Really this is the last question I'm going to answer on this —

Q: You haven't answered one yet.

A: (Long pause) Does anyone want to continue with this briefing? I really, Adam [Clymer, of the *Baltimore Sun*], feel a bit offended by your comments this morning. I'm giving you the White House's position. I'm not asking you to agree with it.[95]

On the evening that President Nixon announced he would resign, Ziegler attempted to make his peace with the press. Some newsmen thought his farewell speech magnanimous; others resented it as the epitome of hypocrisy. He said, "We have been through many difficult times together, and we have been through many historic times together. I know that I will remember the good ones, and I hope you will, too. I would just like to conclude by saying that whatever our differences have been, I believe that there are no simple answers to the complex questions that this period poses, but above all, I think I take away from this job a deep sense of respect for the diversity and strength of our country's freedom of expression and for our free press."[96]

During the Watergate months President Nixon held steadfastly to his conviction that the formal press conference was an institution of little merit. Facing reporters in such a situation was too dangerous: he could not control the questions that were asked, and the risk of making mistakes was great. This was especially true of queries about the Watergate scandal and related incidents, areas in which he was particularly vulnerable. Between March 1973 and August 1974, therefore, Nixon held only six regular press conferences. On three other occasions he submitted to questions before various groups, sessions that could best be described as quasi-press conferences. In each instance, it appears, Nixon had ulterior motives: to demonstrate that he was emotionally strong and in control, or to confront the press and convince the public that he was under assault by a journalistic mob.

By and large, however, he adhered to the principle he had lived by during the first term: the national press was nonessential, and therefore press conferences were nonessential. After a March 15, 1973, meeting with reporters — when he agreed to cooperate with Senator Sam Ervin in his Watergate investigation as long as the senator avoided "hearsay . . . guilt by innuendo . . . guilt by association" — Nixon held no news conferences for five months.[97] In the interim, reported *Newsweek*, the president's aides let it be known that the acrimonious exchanges during the daily press briefings had persuaded Nixon "not to hold a news conference until the press corps improves its manners."[98]

Over the following months the question of which party—the president or the press—was more contentious became a toss-up. Some reporters who asked questions at press conferences were clearly hostile, sarcastic, and rude. But the record shows they were goaded by a president who was more interested in provoking public sympathy than in imparting information:

August 22, 1973: Alarmed over stories alleging that his emotional health was deteriorating, Nixon's aides hastily summoned the press for a news conference. The president began, with quivering voice and shaking jowls, by announcing that Secretary of State William Rogers would resign and be replaced by Henry Kissinger. Then the assembled reporters launched into a barrage of questions about Watergate. Nixon, deliberately it seemed, called on such outspoken antagonists as Clark Mollenhoff and Dan Rather. Rather prefaced his query by saying, "I want to state this question with due respect to your office." Retorted Nixon, "That would be unusual." "I would like to think not, sir," replied the nonplussed Rather. "You are always respectful, Mr. Rather," said the president. Obviously pleased with his performance as the underdog, Nixon halted the proceedings to remind the viewing public that his enemies were dwelling on Watergate: "We have had 30 minutes of this press conference. I have yet to have, for example, one question on the business of the people, which shows you how we are consumed with this. I am not criticizing the members of the press, because you naturally are very interested in this issue, but let me tell you, years from now people are going to perhaps be interested in what happened in terms of the efforts of the United States to build a structure of peace in the world."[99]

One of the president's aides described Nixon's mood after the press conference as "jubilant."[100] The press was less ecstatic. Nixon's strategy, commented *Newsweek*, "was to throw himself quite deliberately to the press corps' meanest wolves."[101]

September 5, 1973: Buoyed by his August 22 performance Nixon called another meeting with the press thirteen days later. The president, deeply tanned but heavily made up, kicked the conference off by lecturing Congress on economic and energy matters. Then he was asked about charges that he had financed his personal property in Florida and California with campaign funds and had realized private benefits from improvements to the properties that had been paid for by the federal government. Nixon bristled. He had ordered an audit, he said, the results of which "gave the lie to the reports that were carried, usually in eight-column heads in most of the papers of this country—and, incidentally, the retractions ended back up with the corset ads for the most part." A few minutes later he was asked whether a reported lack of confidence in his leadership was a problem. He responded, "It is rather difficult to have the president of the United States on prime time television—not prime time, although I would suppose the newscasters would say that the news programs are really the prime time—but for four months to have the president of the United States by innuendo, by leak, by, frankly, leers and sneers of commentators, which is their perfect right, attacked in every way without having some of that confidence being worn away."[102]

Afterwards, a White House spokesman asserted that anyone who detected resentment in Nixon's anti-press remarks was "paranoid."[103]

October 3, 1973: The president was asked if he had given any thought to who might replace Spiro Agnew should the vice-president—then under investigation for possible violations of tax and bribery laws—decide to resign. Absolutely not, replied Nixon. He "would hope," furthermore, that Agnew "would not be tried and convicted in the press and on television by leaks and innuendo and the rest." Nothing was more harmful to an accused person, Nixon went on, "than to be tried and convicted in the press before he has an opportunity to present his case."[104]

October 26, 1973: As he stood offstage waiting for a television producer's cue to enter the East Room, Nixon was seething. The three weeks since his last press conference had been fraught with grave events: Vice-President Agnew had resigned on October 10; two days later the U.S. Court of Appeals had upheld Judge John Sirica's ruling that secret tape recordings of White House conversations had to be surrendered to Watergate special prosecutor Archibald Cox; on October 20, in what had been dubbed the "Saturday Night massacre," Cox had been fired and Attorney General Elliot Richardson and Deputy Attorney General William Ruckelshaus had resigned; on October 23 and 24 twenty-two bills calling for an impeachment investigation had been introduced in Congress; on Thursday, October 25, in the midst of the Arab-Israeli war, Henry Kissinger had announced that U.S. armed forces around the world had been put on a general alert because of the possibility that the Soviets might take military action in the Middle East.[105]

The president asked the television producer, Sid Feders of CBS, how much time was left before the press conference was due to begin.

"Fifteen seconds, Mr. President," said Feders.

"I'm glad you people are accurate about some things," snapped Nixon.

A few seconds passed. "Mr. President, it's time," said Feders.

"O.K., here we go," said Nixon. And then: "Cronkite's not going to like this tonight, I hope."[106]

The fourth question was posed by Dan Rather of CBS, who wanted to know Nixon's thoughts when he heard calls for his impeachment or resignation. The president, visibly agitated, responded, "Well, I'm glad we don't take the vote of this room, let me say. And I understand the feelings of people with regard to impeachment and resignation. As a matter of fact, Mr. Rather, you may remember that when I made the rather difficult decision—I thought the most difficult decision of my first term—on December 19, the bombing by B-52's of North Vietnam, that exactly the same words were used on the networks—I don't mean by you, but they were quoted on the networks—that were used now: Tyrant, dictator, he has lost his senses, he should resign, he should be impeached."[107]

A few minutes later a reporter asked the president whether the shocks of recent events were having a negative effect on the nation. Nixon pounced on the question. The intensity of the "shocks," he implied, were largely the fault of the "electronic media." He continued:

I have never heard or seen such outrageous, vicious, distorted reporting in twenty-seven years of public life. I am not blaming anybody for that. Perhaps what happened is that what we did brought it about, and therefore, the media decided that they would have to take that particular line.

But when people are pounded night after night with that kind of frantic, hysterical reporting, it naturally shakes their confidence. And yet, I should point out that even in this week, when many thought that the president was shell-shocked, unable to act, the president acted decisively in the interests of peace, in the interests of the country, and I can assure you that whatever shocks gentlemen of the press may have, or others, political people, these shocks will not affect me in my doing my job."[108]

Toward the end of the press conference, Nixon called on Robert Pierpoint of CBS.

"Mr. President, you have lambasted the television networks pretty well," said the correspondent. "Could I ask you, at the risk of reopening an obvious wound, you say after you have put on a lot of heat that you don't blame anyone. I find that a little puzzling. What is it about the television coverage of you in these past few weeks and months that has so aroused your anger?"

"Don't get the impression that you arouse my anger," said Nixon.

"I'm afraid, sir," said Pierpoint, "that I have that impression."

A smile creased Nixon's face. "You see," he said, "one can only be angry with those he respects."

As Nixon finished his answer to the next question, he suddenly returned to the exchange with Pierpoint and attempted to soften his disdainful remarks by drawing a distinction between "reporters" and "commentators": "Let me say, too, I didn't want to leave an impression with my good friend from CBS over here that I don't respect the reporters. What I was simply saying was this: That when a commentator takes a bit of news and then, with knowledge of what the facts are, distorts it, viciously, I have no respect for that individual."[109]

The booming voice of Clark Mollenhoff, representing the *Des Moines Register* and *Tribune*, rose above the din: "Mr. President!"

"You are so loud," said Nixon, "I will have to take you."

"I have to be," thundered Mollenhoff, "because you happen to dodge my questions all the time."

"You had three last time," said Nixon.

Mollenhoff asked his question: "Could you explain the rationale of a law-and-order administration covering up evidence, *prima facie* evidence, of high crimes and misdemeanors"—and Nixon gave a curt answer. He then turned and abruptly stalked off as Frank Cormier of the Associated Press shouted the traditional "Thank you, Mr. President" at his retreating back.[110]

November 17, 1973: On the first stop of a five-day barnstorming tour designed to bolster his image, Nixon stopped at Disney World in Orlando, Florida, for a "press conference" before four hundred members of the Associated Press Managing Editors Association. The forum was carefully chosen to give the impression that the president was voluntarily subjecting himself to an inquisition by his accusers in the press. In truth White House correspondents were forbidden to participate and were forced to sit silently as their desk-bound, less aggressive, and less knowledgeable superiors asked the questions.[111]

The editors were very much aware, however, that Nixon wanted to use them as props in a staged show, and they spent two days preparing questions and a system that would ensure that follow-up queries were asked.[112] The questions were sufficiently pointed, but Nixon managed to say a lot without saying anything. Gesturing awkwardly, he touched on such subjects as the wiretap he had ordered on his brother's telephone, his income taxes, his decision to boost milk-price supports. At one point, he declared, "People have got to know whether or not their president is a crook. Well, I'm not a crook. I've earned everything I've got."[113]

That remark would plague him for the remainder of his months in office. It "was not a spur-of-the-moment statement," Nixon later wrote, because he felt is was necessary to defend himself in plain language. "But it was a mistake," he said. "From then on, variations of the line 'I am not a crook' were used as an almost constant source of criticism and ridicule."[114]

February 25 and March 6, 1974: At two news conferences within a nine-day period, during which seven of his former aides were indicted for their involvement in Watergate and related offenses, an articulate but nervous Nixon coolly and confidently addressed questions about the energy situation, the economy, international affairs, the Watergate scandal, the congressional impeachment investigation, and his personal finances. Correspondent Sarah McClendon outshouted the other reporters and posed a shrill query about Veterans Administration chief Don Johnson. "Well," responded Nixon, "if he isn't listening to this program, I will report to him just what you said." The assemblage erupted in laughter, and a smiling president broke in with another quip: "He may have heard even though he wasn't listening to the program."[115]

During both press conferences Nixon seemed to resist the temptation to berate the press. He slipped only once—on March 6—while responding to a question suggesting he had forbidden the granting of immunity to his erstwhile aides as a means of deterring his former counsel, John Dean, from testifying. Immunity would be improper, said the president; moreover Haldeman, Ehrlichman, and Colson had been testifying openly because they were convinced of their innocence. He continued, "Under these circumstances, while they have been convicted in the press over and over again, while they have been convicted before committees over and over again, they are now before a court, and they are entitled to, they will receive from me and, I think, from every fairminded American the presumption of innocence that any individual is entitled to, because a court of law is the proper place for such matters to be decided."[116]

Overall, however, the president projected an image of confidence and self-assuredness. Commented the *Washington Post* following the February 25 conference, "Mr. Nixon last night showed himself to be very much the man in charge, very much the president of the United States."[117]

March 19, 1974: The president reverted to his old form when he flew to Houston for a nationally televised question-and-answer session before a convention of the National Association of Broadcasters. Although it was billed as a news conference, the event was in reality a staged show, the third public relations appearance he had made within four days. On March 15, he had answered questions from a friendly audience of businessmen at Chicago's Executives Club, and the following evening he had appeared at the Grand Ole Opry in Nashville where he had played the piano and twirled a yo-yo.[118]

The Houston audience, composed of affiliate owners, broadcast executives, salesmen, and local Republicans, admitted by ticket, was strongly stacked in Nixon's favor. At first the White House had insisted that only queries from the audience would be entertained, but NAB officials had argued that the press be allowed to ask questions as well. It was finally agreed that the queries would be posed by a group of local news directors and White House correspondents, who would be seated on a stage facing Nixon.[119]

If the president was in a foul mood on that Tuesday, he had ample reason. The day before Judge Sirica had ordered that secret materials compiled by the Watergate grand jury be turned over to the House Judiciary Committee. And on that morning Senator James Buckley of New York had become the first conservative Republican to call openly for Nixon's resignation.[120]

As the conference got underway, it became obvious that the president was once again playing his beat-the-press game. He returned to the subject again and again. When asked how he felt about his press coverage, Nixon set his jaw and growled, "The president should treat the press just as fairly as the press treats him." A Tennessee reporter wanted to know if Nixon planned more appearances designed to show the human side of his personality. "I left my yo-yo in Nashville," said the president with a scowl. "I am not going to be diverted by any press criticism—fair or unfair—from doing the job I was elected to do," he said at another point.[121]

Just a few moments before the conference was due to end, Nixon responded to a question that he had cooperated fully with the Watergate grand jury and the special prosecutor. In the press section several hands shot in the air. A monitor pointed to Dan Rather, and, as he stood, a round of applause mingled with boos filled the hall.

"Mr. President . . . thank you, Mr. President," said the newsman. "Dan Rather of CBS News."

Nixon, the applause and jeers ringing in his ears, jabbed at Rather: "Are you running for something?"

"No sir, Mr. President," Rather shot back. "Are you?"

The second the words were out of his mouth, the newsman knew he had played directly into Nixon's hands. But as Rather later explained, he had simply reacted without thinking: "Keep in mind that we were dealing in milliseconds. When the president said, '*Are you running for something?*' I thought to myself, well, I don't quite know what he means by that. If I had been allowed half a day, or even half a minute, to think, my response *might* have been different. But in those sandspecks of time I only had long enough to think, well, you don't want to stand here simply mute. And so I said, '*No sir, Mr. President, are you?*' "[122]

The incident stirred up a storm of controversy. White House insiders, Rather was told, were delighted because the president now had an easily identifiable symbol—Rather himself—of the press's antagonism toward him.[123] Many of the correspondent's colleagues, on the other hand, were less than thrilled. Rather had been "gratuitous," said *Washington Post* editorial page editor Philip Geyelin, and his performance tended "to confirm in the public mind what the president says about TV newscasters."[124]

The Houston conference was Richard Nixon's last as president of the United States. On the day he decided to quit the office, he met with Alexander Haig and Ronald Ziegler in his Old Executive Office Building retreat to work on his resignation speech. Afterward, as they made their way across the White House grounds to the residence, Nixon noticed several reporters watching them. He turned to Ziegler. "One thing, Ron, old boy," he said. "We won't have to have any more press conferences, and we won't even have to tell them that either!"[125]

In his struggle for political survival Nixon attempted to end run the national press with the same evasive tactics that had served him so well throughout his first term. White House experts used sophisticated propaganda techniques to get the president's point of view before special interest groups and the hinterlands press. Nixon himself abused his welcome in the nation's living rooms with a continuous series of television appearances obviously designed for public relations purposes. He was on television so often that he wore makeup much of the time. Dan Rather once ran into Nixon and the president of the Congo conversing on a White House driveway; the African leader, reported Rather, was totally confounded by Nixon's appearance: "There was President Nixon, wearing heavy television makeup, and the president of the Congo, a very strong robust man who spoke nothing but French, and his interpreter. The president of the Congo could not take his eyes off Nixon's face. It was obvious that he was thinking, What is that stuff?"[126]

One of the most memorable of the Nixon broadcasts occurred on April 30, 1973, when the president announced the resignations of

Haldeman, Ehrlichman, Attorney General Richard Kleindienst, and White House counsel John Dean. It was a genuinely painful moment for Nixon, but he managed to convince many of the millions who watched that it was just another staged event contrived to win sympathy.

Half an hour before the televised speech, UPI reporter Helen Thomas ran into Nixon on the White House grounds. The president grabbed Thomas' hand and pleaded: "I know we don't have the same religion but will you say a prayer for me?"[127] As he sat before the cameras, an American flag pin adorned his lapel; a bust of Abraham Lincoln was at one side, a picture of his family at the other.[128] "I want to talk to you tonight from my heart," Nixon began and went on to praise Haldeman and Ehrlichman as "two of the finest public servants it has been my privilege to know" and to blame the Watergate affair on those who had been delegated to handle his 1972 campaign. But, he continued, "In any organization, the man at the top must bear the responsibility. That responsibility, therefore, belongs here, in this office. I accept it." He praised the system that had exposed the scandal— "a determined grand jury, honest prosecutors, a courageous judge . . . and a vigorous free press." There would be "no whitewash at the White House," he said. He had but 1,361 days left in his term, he said, and he wanted them to be "the best days in America's history, because I love America . . . God bless America and God bless each and every one of you."

A few minutes after the broadcast, Nixon walked into the White House press room, alone and unannounced, and stood in the shadows at the unlit podium. "Ladies and gentlemen of the press," he said to the few reporters who were still there, "we have had our differences in the past, and I hope you give me hell every time you think I'm wrong. I hope I'm worthy of your trust."[129]

But Watergate would not go away. On May 22, 1973, Nixon issued a four-thousand-word statement, purported to be a complete account of the scandal.[130] On August 15 he once again went on national television, forswore any personal involvement in Watergate, and decried the double standard of his critics. The Watergate wrongdoings, he said, had been perpetrated by enthusiastic underlings whose belief in a higher cause was similar to that of the civil rights protesters of the 1960s. But the above-the-law attitude of the latter, Nixon pouted, had been "praised in the press and from some of our pulpits as evidence of a new idealism." He implied that the democratic process itself was under assault and proclaimed his "constitutional responsibility to defend the integrity of this great office against false charges."[131]

Month after month the litany of denials was chanted over the airways. In November the White House announced the president would deliver a major television address on the energy crisis. An hour before he went on the air on November 7, Nixon scribbled some notes on the back of his text. His own staff was surprised when, at the close of his energy speech, he looked directly into the camera and addressed the numerous demands for his resignation: "I have no intention whatever of walking away from the job I was elected to do. As long as I am physically able, I am going to continue to work sixteen to eighteen hours a day . . . . And I am confident that in those months ahead, the American people will come to realize that I have not violated the trust that they placed in me."[132]

In January 1974 Nixon delivered a prime-time State of the Union message and asserted that "the time has come to bring [the Justice Department's] investigation and other investigations on this matter to an end. One year of Watergate is enough." Press secretary Ronald Ziegler, who had not conducted the daily White House briefings for months, stepped forward to hammer home the theme: "The president is determined not to be consumed for another year by Watergate."[133]

Three months later a desperate president and his media men executed one of the most audacious television end runs they had ever attempted. Behind Richard Nixon, as he peered intently into the television cameras on Monday evening, April 29, stood a stack of leatherbound notebooks, embossed in gold. They contained, he informed his millions of viewers, transcripts of secretly recorded White House conversations in which he had participated between September 15, 1972 and April 27, 1973. He was turning them over to the House Judiciary Committee in response to its subpoena for the actual tape recordings. More than that, he was also releasing this mountain of material to the general public. "Because this is an issue that profoundly affects all the American people," he said, "in addition to turning over these transcripts to the House Judiciary Committee, I have directed that they should all be made public—all of these that you see here." At one point, he waved an arm toward the gigantic stack of notebooks and declared that "never before in the history of the presidency have records that are so private been made so public." As he spoke, the television cameras swung from his face to the transcripts and back again.

It was a hoax. The transcripts turned over to members of the Judiciary Committee were contained in a single volume of 1,254 pages, roughly the thickness of a big-city telephone directory. The pile of transcripts featured during Nixon's televised speech was a stage prop.

And when the House Judiciary Committee later released its own transcripts of several key White House conversations, it turned out that the Nixon edition had been edited to make the president and his associates appear less culpable.[134]

Nevertheless White House spokesmen continued to claim that the full story of Watergate was contained within the transcripts released by the White House, and not one line had implicated "the president of the United States . . . in a criminal act to obstruct justice." Nixon's chief Watergate attorney, James St. Clair, abandoned his usual reticence and agreed to an on-the-record interview with a group of reporters. A few days later he appeared on NBC's "Meet the Press," where he acknowledged that the transcripts had been released in the hope that everyone would "come to a feeling of confidence that this is the full and complete story." On the same Sunday White House chief of staff Alexander Haig argued the administration's case on ABC's "Issues and Answers." Nixon hit the stump with speeches in Arizona, Washington State, and Oklahoma.[135]

The attempts to end run the press with direct appeals to the public failed, and Nixon lurched toward his final hour. Even that painful moment, he determined, would be a television extravaganza. On Thursday evening, August 8, 1974, he delivered a televised resignation speech, as he put it, "to America and the world." The following morning the First Family marched onto the stage in the East Room for Nixon's farewell remarks to the cabinet and staff before live cameras. When Pat and Tricia learned that this last emotional act was going to be played out before millions of viewers, they became upset. As Nixon described it, "It was too much, they said, that after all the agony television had caused us, its prying eye should be allowed to intrude on this last and most intimate moment of all. 'That's the way it has to be,' I said. 'We owe it to our supporters. We owe it to the people.' "[136]

From the beginning the White House had viewed the Watergate scandal as a problem that could best be overcome by projecting the proper image. Charles Colson once suggested to Haldeman that Nixon hire a good criminal lawyer to guide him through the Watergate morass. "You lawyers are all alike," responded the president's chief of staff. "This is a public relations problem. We've got too many lawyers now."[137]

The campaign to depict Nixon as a wholesome, honest, healthy, happy president who was in complete control of his job never ceased. His physician, Walter Tkach, described for the press a president who "never overeats" and "never overdrinks" and was in "excellent" condition.[138] On the occasion of Abraham Lincoln's 165th birthday in February 1974, Nixon astonished a crowd at the Lincoln Memorial by showing up and offering some obvious comparisons with one of America's greatest presidents: "It is quite clear that no president in history has been more vilified during the time he was president than Lincoln. . . . Lincoln had that great strength of character never to display [hurt], always to stand tall and strong and firm no matter how harsh or unfair the criticism might be."[139]

A carryover from the first term was the image team's practice of attempting to associate Nixon with men of the cloth. On February 1, 1974, the Rev. Sun Myung Moon was ushered into the White House to see Richard Nixon. Moon hugged Nixon and prayed for him. "Don't knuckle under to pressure," said the South Korean preacher to the president as he was preparing to leave. "Stand up for your convictions." The White House later issued a statement thanking Reverend Moon for his support of the president.

Nixon had good reason to be grateful: Moon claimed he had been given a direct order from God to support the American president. The revelation had come, he said, after a 1973 evangelical tour of the United States, and he promptly called on the 500,000 members of his Unification church to rally behind Nixon.[140]

When all else failed and when the Watergate pressures became particularly intense, Nixon and his entourage hit the road. A presidential trip served two purposes: it was a good escape, and it was good for the image because it reminded the public that here was a president who was doing what he was elected to do.

When the Watergate clamor became a cacophony of censures, charges, and demands in the spring of 1974, for example, Nixon packed his bags. In April he flew to Paris to attend a memorial service for President Georges Pompidou, got carried away by the friendly crowds that greeted him, and pronounced the national day of mourning "a great day for France." He returned to the United States and took off immediately for a tour of Xenia, Ohio, which had been leveled by a tornado. The following day he was in Michigan campaigning for a Republican congressional candidate.[141]

A few weeks later he was off on a speaking tour of the western states. From June 12 to June 19 he toured Egypt, Saudi Arabia, Syria, Israel, and Jordan. He was home barely six days before he took off for a summit meeting with Soviet premier Leonid Brezhnev.[142] From Moscow the two leaders flew to Yalta, on the Black Sea, for a stay at Brezhnev's magnificent dacha.

Yalta, of course, had been the scene of the 1945 conference between Stalin, Churchill and Roosevelt, where the Allied victors had divided up Europe, much to the advantage of the Russians in the eyes of some conservatives. The White House media men were deeply concerned that Nixon's opponents at home would paint this meeting as a second Yalta Conference. But with the help of the Soviets, a solution was found: Brezhnev's villa, it turned out, was actually in a neighborhood called Oreanda. So the neighborhood suddenly became an official town, and the meeting became the "Oreanda Summit."[143] On his return to the United States Nixon spent only nine days in Washington before he took off for a two-week stay in California.[144]

From the beginning to the end of the Watergate period, Nixon and his image merchants seldom wavered in their conviction that the scandal was essentially a public relations problem. Even after Haldeman departed the White House, the media team continued its search for a "public relations solution." Beginning in early November 1973 at least four distinct PR campaigns were launched to convince an increasingly skeptical public that their president was pure.

Operation Candor began on November 7 when Nixon ended his televised energy speech with the abrupt declaration that he would not resign and was "confident" that the American people would soon realize he had "not violated the trust that they placed in me." In eight meetings over the next six days the president met with 234 Republican senators and representatives and 46 Democratic leaders. He asserted his innocence in all Watergate matters and vowed he would produce from his tape recordings, notes, logs, and other documents evidence that would be "totally exculpatory." On November 12 he issued a statement repeating the same promises publicly.[145]

Nixon then embarked on a tour to take his "I-am-not-a-crook" message to the people. He spoke to 4,000 Washington, D.C., realtors, held a press conference at Disney World, addressed a crowd in Macon, Georgia, and met with nineteen Republican governors in Memphis. "Are we going to be blindsided by any more bombs?" demanded Oregon Governor Tom McCall of the president at that gathering. "If there are any more bombs, I'm not aware of them," responded Nixon. The next day the president's attorneys informed Judge John Sirica that an eighteen-minute section of one of the subpoenaed tape recordings—covering a June 20, 1973, meeting between Nixon and Haldeman—had been mysteriously erased.[146]

Another bomb was armed and began slowly ticking on December 8 when Nixon released a comprehensive package of tax returns, audits, and documents in a desperate effort to lay to rest rumors, engendered by a series of news reports that he had paid negligible taxes in 1970 and 1971, that he was a person of questionable honesty. The public furor that erupted when it was revealed that the president had paid only $5,964 in income taxes for the three years 1970 through 1972 was muted somewhat by Nixon's promise to will his San Clemente estate to the public and to permit the Joint Congressional Committee on Internal Revenue Taxation to render a judgment on his returns.[147] (The bomb exploded in April 1974 when the committee released a 994-page analysis of Nixon's tax returns and asserted that he owed $476,431 in back taxes. The Internal Revenue Service, which had independently conducted its own audit, delivered to the White House a back-tax bill for $432,787.)[148]

Around mid-December 1973 Nixon's resolve to be candid began to dissipate. Decisions to release the transcripts of some presidential conversations as well as a series of White Papers on various scandals were reconsidered. By December 19, when the Senate Watergate Committee subpoenaed a thousand documents and the tapes of four hundred of Nixon's conversations, the White House was once again prepared to do battle. The subpoenas, fumed a presidential spokesman, were "a grotesque fishing expedition." Another Nixon assistant was more explicit: "We will tell the committee to go screw itself."[149]

Thus did *Operation Candor* evolve into *Operation Fight Like Hell*, a short-lived, half-hearted campaign designed to demonstrate that Nixon was putting Watergate behind him, was performing his tasks well, and was prepared to stick it out, no matter how protracted the battle. The new public relations thrust began with Nixon's State of the Union declaration that "one year of Watergate is enough." Delegations of congressional leaders were then summoned to the White House to hear the president's war whoop: "There is a time to be timid. There is a time to be conciliatory. There is a time to fly and there is a time to fight—and I'm going to fight like hell."[150]

Loyal Republicans began seeking out opportunities to spread the gospel of Nixon's innocence; others openly attacked Nixon's opponents on Capitol Hill; still others began leaking stories of their own.[151]

The president also launched a personal Fight-Like-Hell offensive. He stopped off in Huntsville, Alabama, on February 18, to participate in an Honor America Day rally with Governor George Wallace. In what he termed a "what's right with America speech," Nixon suggested to a crowd of 20,000 that support of their president was the epitome of patriotism. He also managed to get in a few licks against the press:

In the nation's capital, there is a tendency for partisanship to take over from statesmanship. In the nation's capital sometimes there is a tendency in the reporting of the news—I do not say this critically, it's simply a fact of life—that bad news is news and good news is not news.

And as a result, those of us who work there and try to develop the policies of the nation may get a distorted view of what is America and what it is really like. It is there that you hear more than any other place in America that America is sick, that there is something wrong with America that cannot be corrected. . . .

I thank you for reminding all of America that here in the heart of Dixie we find that the heart of America is good, the character of America is strong, and we are going to continue to be a great nation.[152]

In mid-March the media team's emphasis shifted once again. *Operation Fight Like Hell* became *Operation Friendly Persuasion*, and Nixon began seeking opportunities to defend himself in public forums. During this period he addressed a group of Chicago business executives, twirled a yo-yo at the Grand Ole Opry in Nashville, and engaged in a question-and-answer session before the National Association of Broadcasters convention in Houston. "The idea of the media campaign," said one insider, "is to create as many doubts as possible about the charges against the president."[153]

When all of the PR gambits failed, the media team returned to its tried-and-true strategem: the president's enemies, especially the press, were conspiring to destroy him. This final coordinated campaign to find a PR solution, which might be called *Operation Counterattack*, began on April 29, 1974, when Nixon went on national television and announced that he was releasing 1,254 pages of transcripts of presidential conversations to the press and to the House Judiciary Committee, which had subpoenaed the actual tape recordings. In short he was going to fight, and he would let the American people be the judges.

The judgment, from the beginning, was that Nixon was a loser. The presidential conversations were laden with shallow comments and "expletives deleted." All three television networks ran special reports on the transcripts; some shows offered "dramatic readings," with newsmen reading the words that had been spoken by Nixon, Haldeman, John Dean, and others. Remarked CBS commentator Eric Sevareid, "These pages constitute a moral indictment without known precedent in the story of American government. . . . There are minimal references to truth but innumerable conjectures about the most salable publicity techniques for defending themselves."[154]

In late May the White House media maestros began attacking the House Judiciary Committee for allegedly initiating news leaks. As the days wore on, the charge became a chant. The House Judiciary Committee lawyers were similar to "hired guns," said Nixon aide Dean Burch, and the chairman, Peter Rodino of New Jersey, "seems to have lost control" of his subordinates.[155] The news leaks, charged Ken Clawson, were part of "a purposeful effort to bring down the president with smoke-filled room operations by a clique of Nixon-hating partisans."[156] Patrick Buchanan observed that the leaks amounted to a campaign of "nameless, faceless character assassination" against the president.[157] Ronald Ziegler charged that Judiciary Committee chief counsel John Doar was conducting a "kangaroo court."[158]

As the media team's attention focused on the committee, the press was not forgotten. On July 17 Buchanan laid into "the big media" for allegedly giving "enormous, positive and favorable publicity to movements associated with the far left," which included, he said, "the anti-war movement, the civil rights movement, the consumer movement."[159]

In the spring of 1973 the office of communications was wheeled to the Watergate front. It was now presided over by thirty-seven-year-old Ken W. Clawson, the pudgy, cantankerous former *Washington Post* reporter who had been hired as a deputy to Herb Klein in February 1972 but who had actually taken his orders from Charles Colson, whose "can-do" style closely paralleled Clawson's own. Although Klein resigned on June 6, 1973, Clawson retained the title of deputy director of communications until January 30, 1974, when he was finally accorded full honors. A self-confessed "Nixon superloyalist," Clawson pursued all of the Herb Klein functions—press pacifier, coordinator of public information officials, and public relations manager for the executive branch—with more enthusiasm and panache than had Klein.[160] In his role as press pacifier and door-opener, for example, Clawson eagerly served as a sounding board for complaints. Following a Nixon press conference, he routinely telephoned as many as forty newspaper editors to get their comments and criticisms concerning the presidential performance.[161]

As a White House reporter for the *Post*, Clawson had been frustrated by the unwillingness of many Nixon aides to make themselves available to the press. After he joined the Nixon camp, he persuaded chief of staff Alexander Haig to allow him to set up interviews for small groups of reporters with top officials. An experiment was conducted at San Clemente during the summer of 1973; some eighty sessions were held within a ten-day period. They were pronounced a success, and Clawson was given permission to continue the program. The meetings, held three to five times a week in Clawson's well-appointed room in the Old Executive Office Building, proved popular and soon became known among journalists as "Cocktails with Clawson." As fifteen or twenty invited reporters settled back in cushioned chairs to question the guest, they were served soft drinks, chips, dip, and occasionally alcoholic beverages. The list of officials paraded before the press was impressive: Nixon's Watergate lawyer James St. Clair, Patrick Buchanan, and presidential counselors Ann Armstrong and Dean Burch, to name but a few.[162] Clawson's clambakes were generally appreciated, but some newsmen who were rarely invited claimed he discriminated against Nixon's more outspoken critics. Other journalists dismissed the sessions as public relations tomfoolery and refused to attend. "The idea that the credibility of their people can be improved by putting them in comfortable chairs is ridiculous," said the *Boston Globe*'s Washington bureau chief Martin Nolan.[163] His point was superlatively illustrated in May, 1974, when Clawson hauled out White House speechwriter and resident Jesuit, Father John McLaughlin, to defend the tone and morality of Nixon's expletive-laden transcripts. "The conclusion that they are amoral or immoral," said the priest to an audience of doubting Thomases, "is erroneous, unjust and contains elements of hyprocrisy."[164]

Another of Clawson's jobs—coordinating public information activities throughout the executive branch—was made a little easier when, shortly after Nixon was sworn in the second time, the White House moved to replace career public information officers with "responsive" appointees. In various federal agencies the careerists were demoted to second-in-command positions, instructed to handle routine chores, and told to refer sensitive inquiries to their new bosses. All of the replacements possessed sound Republican credentials.[165] The public relations director for the Committee to Re-elect the President, Ann L. Dore, for example, was appointed to the top information position at the Environmental Protection Agency. Another CRP press officer, Arthur L. Amolsch, was named director of public information at the Federal Trade Commission.[166]

The office of communications under Clawson's direction also continued the practice of providing the hinterlands press with news releases, handouts, and policy statements. As the president's Watergate problems deepened, the information kits grew increasingly vicious. One package mailed in the spring of 1974 contained five pages of quotations from members of the House Judiciary Committee on the subject of impeachment; the statements were carefully selected to imply that the committee was biased against Nixon.[167] The propagandistic nature of the fact kits was tacitly acknowledged in January 1974 when the Justice Department reluctantly paid the Postal Service $10,240 for the bulk mailing of an anticrime speech the president had delivered in March, 1973. At White House behest the speech had been reproduced with funds from the Republican National Committee and mailed under government frank to 64,000 people in envelopes and with cover letters supplied by the Justice Department.[168]

In November 1973 Clawson organized a surrogate program, similar to the one used so effectively in the 1972 election campaign, under which administration officials and prominent presidential friends sought every opportunity to speak out in Nixon's favor. The surrogates featured such personalities as Julie and David Eisenhower, presidential counselors Anne Armstrong and Melvin Laird, Father John McLaughlin, HEW Secretary Caspar Weinberger, Commerce Secretary Frederick Dent, and Labor Secretary Peter Brennan. Clawson arranged speaking dates for the surrogates and pressed the television networks to interview them.[169]

Some examples of the surrogates at work:

• December 15, 1973: Commerce Secretary Dent delivered a Nixon-as-Lincoln speech to a Support Our President rally in Los Angeles. He warned the "misguided political partisans" who were trying to destroy the president that "the American people can take just so much. When their innate sense of fair play tells them that these vile attacks on our president have gone too far, there is going to be an outpouring of support for him such as this nation has rarely seen."[170]

• May 11, 1974: Julie and David Eisenhower held a press conference in the East Garden at the White House. Watergate, said the president's daughter, was a "third-or fourth-rate burglary" and the whole affair had been brought on by enthusiastic aides trying to win "brownie points" with her father.[171]

• July 18, 1974: Rabbi Baruch Korff, founder and president of the National Citizens Committee for Fairness to the President, sponsored a pro-Nixon rally in Washington, D.C. Some 1,500 enthusiastic Nixon supporters, many of them sporting "Get Off the President's Back" buttons, heard speeches, prayers, and a song written for the occasion entitled "We Need Nixon." A Baptist minister exhorted the Almighty to visit His wrath on journalists and other "opportunists" who were "the enemies of world peace." A number of prominent surrogates appeared and Nixon himself telephoned his appreciation from San Clemente. "We love you dearly," said Rabbi Korff to the president as he hung up the telephone and brushed away a tear.[172]

For four years, Nixon and his media men had berated the press as liberal and biased, and by 1973 the drumfire had grown a bit tedious. But journalists, villains to millions of Americans, made ideal scapegoats, so throughout the Watergate period the threats and imprecations grew even more intense. And the president led the chorus.

Richard Nixon

Many of Nixon's verbal broadsides were delivered during press conferences: the September 5, 1973, charge that he was being condemned by "innuendo, by leak, by . . . leers and sneers of commentators"; his October 26 blast at "outrageous, vicious distorted reporting"; his March 19, 1974, are-you-running-for-something confrontation with Dan Rather. But he was equally obstreperous behind the scenes. On April 27, 1973, for example, he huddled with Ronald Ziegler and Assistant Attorney General Henry Petersen to discuss Watergate stories that had been appearing in the press. Ziegler remarked that *Washington Post* reporter Bob Woodward was even then working on a story that would cite grand jury testimony that had allegedly implicated the president in a Watergate cover-up. Nixon exploded. He ordered Ziegler to "take a hard line" and to instruct White House staff member David Gergen to tell Woodward, "Anything on that, they better watch their damned cotton-picking faces."[173] Three months later journalists began questioning how Nixon had managed to obtain his 29.9-acre estate on the California coast, and once again the president erupted in rage. He summoned Ziegler and ordered him to denounce the reports as "unfounded, malicious and scurrilous." Ziegler did what he was told and added these words: "These types of stories continue to run, the innuendo and the suggestions continue to fly out of this environment, and it is unjust, it is unfair, and it is not in my mind relevant to our way of life in this country for this type of smear charge to be made against the President of the United States. . . . I would say that the president is appalled by these consistent efforts being undertaken in the malicious—I don't know whether you can say libelous in terms of the president—but these constant efforts to suggest that there has been in any way wrongdoing associated with the purchase of this property."[174]

In an early October turnabout Nixon paused in his press criticism to extol the profession of journalism. "The freedom of the press is one of the proudest and most zealously guarded aspects of our national heritage," he said in a statement in honor of National Newspaper Week. This event, he continued, was "an annual reminder of the intrinsic value of unfettered journalism in our lives." But less than three weeks later, Nixon broke the peace with his October 26 press conference, and his cavalier commentary continued unabated into the new year. Following a ninetieth birthday party for Alice Roosevelt Longworth in February, the president observed that the dowager "would have been dead by now" had she spent much time reading the Washington newspapers.[175] The following month, Nixon instructed the Justice Department to draft legislation that would make it easier for politicians to win libel suits. As the law stood, said the president in a radio address, it was "virtually a license to lie" about people who ran for public office. A change was needed, Nixon argued, to encourage "good and decent people" to pursue political professions without fear that they would be subjected to "slanderous attacks on them or their families."[176]

In an interview with Rabbi Baruch Korff on May 13, Nixon was asked to evaluate the White House press corps. The president responded: "There are some, putting it in the vernacular, who hate my guts with a passion. But I don't hate them, none of them. . . . Their philosophies are different, they don't agree with my positions and after all they want to write and take me on. An individual must not turn hatred for hatred."[177]

Spiro Agnew

The scourge of journalists during the first term, Vice-President Agnew, performed only erratically in his press critic role during the early Watergate period. At times he resembled the hawk of old; at other times he was a dove bearing an olive branch. The vice-president offered some conciliatory remarks, for example, during an address before the Maryland Press Club on May 2. His first-term approach had been too harsh, Agnew said, and he had now "intentionally adopted" a different tone. "I do not apologize for the content of my earlier criticism," he continued. "But I freely admit that it could have been stated less abrasively."[178] A week later he addressed an audience at the University of Virginia and assailed the press for its Watergate coverage. He could not deny, he said, that reporters had made a "contribution" by exposing the scandal, but "I think this contribution has been overblown by the over-adulation of some of the media. I applaud the efforts and I applaud the results, but I cannot applaud the techniques being used. It's a very short jump from McCarthyism to what is going on now." He was referring, he said, to the fact that the press was reporting "a great amount of hearsay and a great amount of material from sources without the courage to reveal themselves."[179]

On August 1 Agnew was formally notified by the U.S. attorney in Baltimore, George Beall, of something the vice-president had known since April: he was under investigation for possible violations of tax, bribery, and conspiracy laws. By August 6 the *Wall Street Journal* had heard of the Beall letter, was ready to move a story about it, and requested a statement from the vice-president. A few hours later the *Journal* discovered it had been scooped. Agnew had released a public statement acknowledging that he was under investigation, asserting that he was innocent, and declaring that he would have nothing further to say until the Justice Department probe was complete.[180]

Over the next few days details of the accusations and allegations began appearing in the press. On August 8 Agnew called a news conference to proclaim his innocence once again. Still the stories continued; among other things it was said that as the governor of Maryland, he had accepted kickbacks and cash payoffs from contractors doing business with the state. On August 20 *Time* magazine reported it had "learned that in the view of Justice Department officials in Washington, the case against [Agnew] is growing steadily stronger, and that an indictment appears inevitable." The following day Agnew called another press conference and angrily accused Justice Department officials of trying "to indict me in the press."[181]

The next day, during a San Clemente press conference, President Nixon declared that his "confidence in [Agnew's] integrity has not been shaken" and decried "the outrageous leak of information from either the grand jury, or the prosecutors, or the Department of Justice or all three." Any Justice Department official found guilty of leaking stories about Agnew, said the president, would be "summarily dismissed from government service." He went on: "Convicting an individual in the headlines and on TV before he has had a chance to present his case in court is contrary to the American tradition. Even a vice president has a right to some, shall I say, consideration in this respect."[182]

On September 22 CBS correspondent Fred Graham broadcast a report on a negotiating session that had taken place between Agnew's lawyers and Justice Department attorneys. Quoting an unnamed source "close to the negotiations," Graham reported that Assistant Attorney General Henry Petersen had said, "We've got the evidence. We've got it cold."[183]

Agnew was livid. During a nationally televised speech before a convention of Republican women in Los Angeles, he counterattacked: "In the past several months, I've been living in purgatory. I have found myself the recipient of undefined, unclear, unattributed accusations that have surfaced in the largest and most widely circulated organs in our communications media." Then he zeroed in on Petersen: "The conduct of high individuals in the Department of Justice, particularly the conduct of the chief of the criminal investigations division, is unprofessional and malicious and outrageous."[184]

In late September the Baltimore grand jury began hearing the evidence against Agnew, and the vice-president's lawyers launched an intensive effort to halt the investigation. In an affidavit submitted to U.S. District Court Judge Walter Hoffman, Agnew's attorneys charged unnamed Justice Department officials with "an immoral and illegal attempt to drive the vice-president from the office to which he was elected and to insure his conviction." Meanwhile Agnew's lawyers called several reporters and asked them to identify their news sources; an October 3 the attorneys requested Judge Hoffman's permission to subpoena anyone they believed had knowledge of leaks to the press. Hoffman immediately complied with a court order, and in an extraordinary public session admonished the grand jurors not to be influenced by news accounts of the Agnew probe.[185]

Two days later Agnew's attorneys served subpoenas on nine reporters for *Time, Newsweek,* the *Washington Post, New York Times, New York Daily News, Washington Star-News,* CBS, and NBC, ordering them to appear in federal court in Baltimore on October 11 and to bring with them "all writings and other forms of record (including drafts)" that might contain the names of their sources.[186]

Agnew and Judge Hoffman thus raised a free-press, fair-trial issue of astounding ramifications: Did the Supreme Court's Caldwell decision, which held that a grand jury could subpoena reporters' notes, extend a similar privilege to individuals? Was not the authorization of such a legal dragnet a violation of constitutional guarantees against illegal search and seizure? Such a legal action, if upheld, would probably result in the elimination of investigative reporting.

Executives of the news organizations that employed the reporters subpoenaed by Agnew immediately announced they would resist. The subpoenas, said the *Columbia Journalism Review,* were "in the grand tradition of political attacks on the press in general and of the past practices of the Nixon-Agnew administration in particular—unspecified allegations of falsehood, attributions of malice, resorting to suppressive means." Even *New York Times* columnist William Safire, an Agnew defender, admonished the vice-president for using the law "like a bludgeon to fight the wrong fight—that old grudge fight against the press."[187] The Justice Department itself filed a brief with Judge Hoffman requesting that the subpoenas be quashed on the grounds they were a "fishing expedition" based on "frivolous" grounds. Agnew's attorneys, stated the brief, were "engaged in an attempt to confuse the issue and halt a legitimate investigation by the common defense tactic of trying the prosecutor."[188]

The subpoena question became moot on October 10 when Agnew suddenly appeared in open court before Judge Hoffman and pleaded "no contest" to a charge of evading $13,551.47 in federal income taxes on his 1967 return. Hoffman instructed Agnew that his no-contest plea was "the full equivalent of a plea of guilty." An Agnew attorney then notified the court that "at 2:05 P.M. today, there was delivered to the Secretary of State in Washington a letter from the defendant in which he submitted his resignation." Attorney General Richardson read a statement summarizing the government's extensive case against Agnew—he had accepted more than $100,000 in kickbacks and payoffs from Maryland contractors—and then disclosed that all criminal charges against the vice-president were being dropped in return for his resignation and no-contest plea to the tax evasion charge. Judge Hoffman approved the agreement and sentenced Agnew to three years of probation and a $10,000 fine.[189]

In the wake of his resignation Agnew could not resist one last blast at the press. He requested and was granted network television time for a farewell address. He said:

Late this summer my fitness to continue in office came under attack when accusations against me made in the course of a grand jury investigation were improperly and unconscionably leaked in detail to the news media.

I might add that the attacks were increased by daily publication of the wildest rumors and speculation, much of it bearing no resemblance to the imformation being given the prosecutors.

All this was done with full knowledge that it was prejudicial to my civil rights.

The news media editorially deplored these violations of the traditional secrecy of such investigations but at the same time many of the most prestigious were ignoring their own counsel by publishing every leak they could get their hands on.

From time to time I made public denials of those scurrilous and inaccurate reports and challenged the credibility of their sources. . . .

I repeat and I emphasize that denial of wrongdoing tonight.[190]

Ronald Ziegler and Gerald Warren

The president's official spokesmen, press secretary Ronald Ziegler and his deputy Gerald Warren, denounced the press sparingly after March

1973, but when they did, their words carried an extra weight. Reporters knew that when their mouths moved, Richard Nixon was pulling the strings. Shortly after James McCord's letter was read in open court by Judge Sirica, for example, the *Los Angeles Times* learned that McCord had informed the Senate Watergate Committee that Jeb Magruder and John Dean had been involved in the planning of the Watergate burglary. The Washington bureau of the *Times* asked its White House correspondent, Robert Toth, to obtain a comment from Ziegler, then in Key Biscayne with Nixon. That evening Toth telephoned his Washington colleagues to report on a conversation he had just had with the press secretary:

I'm calling you from a restaurant and Ziegler just came up to my table, which means he had to work very hard to find me because I didn't tell anybody where I was going. I mean, he put in a lot of work to find me. And he said, "We've known each other a long time and been friends a long time, right Bob?" And I said right. "And I've always been very straight with you, right?" Right, Ron. "Okay, I'm being very straight with you now, your boys are doing that story tomorrow about Dean and Magruder, and you have our denial. But I'm saying this now to you as a friend, because we've always been friends, if you print that story, you're flat-ass wrong and we're going to tear your ass apart; we'll leave nothing behind. I'm passing this along as a friend and because I respect you and I don't have to tell you this."[191]

Shortly after Ziegler branded himself with his "inoperative" statement, was converted into an assistant to the president, and virtually disappeared, only occasionally appearing to alert the press to its transgressions.

Gerald Warren, normally the personification of equanimity, also heaved some stones at the press when instructed to do so. During the intimidation campaign organized in the wake of President Nixon's October 26 press conference, Warren scolded White House reporters for two days on their lack of responsibility and "perspective." When asked for "a bill of particulars" to back up his and Nixon's charges, Warren responded, "Sure, we will look into that for you, but when you have an atmosphere in which the president's ability to run the country is being questioned by the news media, when the president's soundness is being questioned by the news media, I think you can realize what we are talking about here."[192]

In late November, 1973, Warren turned his attention to Special Prosecutor Leon Jaworski, who had replaced Archibald Cox just three weeks before. Jaworski's office, chided Warren, had been responsible for two instances of what "might be called leaks," one of which was "staggering."[193] The following day, the *New York Times* charged that Warren's broadside was "just one more resort to the by now familiar maneuver of diverting attention from a White House impropriety by creating the impression that the offense was not in the deed itself but in the telling of it."[194]

Patrick Buchanan

Patrick Buchanan, the pugnacious warrior who was the divine afflatus behind the first-term attempt to pound the press into submission, continued his personal campaign throughout Watergate. "The Watergate crowd cannot hold a candle to its principal accusers in politics and the press," he thundered in a guest essay published by the *New York Times*. He continued: "Nor is one surprised to learn that the publications beating the drums for immediate public disclosure of the most sensitive papers and conversations of the president are one and the same with the publications in the vanguard demanding an absolute shield law to protect in perpetuity the confidentiality of their reporters' notes."[195]

On September 26, 1973, Buchanan testified before the Senate Watergate Committee and scored a clean triumph. Taking the offensive, he accused the committee's staff of orchestrating news leaks. "How can this select committee set itself up as the ultimate arbiter of American political ethics," he demanded, "if it cannot even control the character assassins within its own ranks?"[196]

Three days after President Nixon's angry outburst on October 26, Buchanan went on the CBS "Morning News" program and accused newsmen of creating the confrontation. The mood in the East Room, he charged, "was really like Sunday afternoon in the Tijuana bullring . . . and I thought in that mood the president expressed feelings that he had gathered over a period of time."[197] Buchanan contended that the television networks were too powerful and would benefit from some competition: "Every legal and Constitutional means ought to be considered to break up that dominance, in order to spread it out so that you decentralize power in this area."[198] Several months later Buchanan again hammered his break-up-the-network-dominance theme. "What is good for NBC is not necessarily good for America," he said. He called on large corporations to use their advertising dollars to bring the television networks to heel. And the average citizen could help, he suggested, "by boycotting the products of the advertisers. Better 5,000 letters to the principal advertiser on the NBC Evening

News than 5,000 into the trash can of the news editor." He also took CBS correspondent Dan Rather to task for his malapert exchange with Nixon during the President's Houston press conference. Rather's performance, said Buchanan, was "the epitome of impertinence and insolence to the highest office in the land."[199]

Ken Clawson

As director of the White House office of communications, Clawson regularly watched the evening news shows on the networks and frequently telephoned the anchormen, while they were still on the air, to demand corrections or insertions. "Usually, you can get any of these guys during a commercial," he once said. This practice, in the opinion of Dan Rather, was a blatant effort to intimidate:

They now have a journalistic goon squad operating inside. The idea is to crowd you, to harass you when they can with phone calls complaining about pieces, complaining to other people, calls during the broadcast, "Rather's piece is wrong and we want a correction on the air." If that isn't pressure, what is it? . . .
   Ken Clawson is the current leader of the goon squad. For a long time they did not have anyone around there who knew a great deal about reporting. They knew about advertising. But Clawson (a former reporter for the *Washington Post*) knows the news business from the inside. He's good at what he does. That is, he's a good attacker, which is to say he knows where the vulnerabilities are. He knows who to call. He knows how to crowd you. He understands strengths and weaknesses in the people. He knows the harassment game very well. He's one of the best they've ever had.[200]

In an effort to back up the president's charges that newsmen were guilty of "outrageous, vicious, distorted reporting," Clawson kept a file — which he called "The Press Firestorm" — on his desk. It contained examples, he said, of what Nixon was talking about. During interviews, he often lectured from his journalistic sin list, but he never showed it to anyone.[201]

In March 1974 Clawson launched an assault on columnist Jack Anderson, who had claimed that Nixon possessed a "hidden stash" of tape recordings in the form of Dictabelt recollections of daily conversations. There was nothing secret about the recordings, Clawson avowed; Nixon himself had mentioned them in a statement on November 12, 1973. Fumed Clawson, "The Anderson column personifies the Watergate syndrome which seems to have possessed the Washington press corps, and an exorcist is direly needed. . . . Jack Anderson is at least guilty of amateurish journalism." Asked to define the "Watergate syndrome," Clawson responded, "A propensity to believe without thorough research and checking almost anything. God knows that the people who engage in that kind of crap need an exorcist."[202]

Bruce Herschensohn

Bruce Herschensohn joined the White House staff as a deputy special assistant to the president in 1973 and immediately entered the front ranks of Nixon's antipress commandos. What he lacked in experience he made up in enthusiasm. He was a fanatical believer in his leader's innocence and readily acknowledged "the highest respect" for the disgraced Spiro Agnew. Herschensohn's job, as nearly as it could be ascertained, was to promote the president's cause with speeches and articles and by staying in touch with people attempting to organize support for Nixon.[203]

Herschensohn achieved his greatest notoriety, however, as an antipress polemicist. "The national media is [*sic*] a kangaroo court and the verdict is very clear from the outset," he exclaimed in one of his first public appearances, at a Support the President rally in Albuquerque, New Mexico. Reporters, he went on, were "not just the messengers of the news [but] the news itself. They should be subject to the same scrutiny as they give their target, the president."[204] He moved on to Los Angeles where he charged that the Watergate special prosecutor and the press were engaged in a "vendetta" against Nixon. Herschensohn deplored the "lynch-mob pressure against the highest office in the land," and added, "Since they [the press] cannot prove his [Nixon's] guilt on any charge, they demand he prove his innocence."[205]

By February 1974 Herschensohn had come up with two explanations for the president's problems: the Boredom Crisis of 1972 and the Great Encapsulation Conspiracy. As Herschensohn outlined it for *Wall Street Journal* reporter Fred Zimmerman, Americans were ready for a scandal because they were bored: "The only crime the president is guilty of was creating a boredom crisis at the beginning of 1972. The Vietnam war was over, there was a detente with the Soviets, the domestic situation was okay." Then came the Watergate break-in, which the press used as an "umbrella" under which "all of these other charges were encapsulated, inferring that these other charges are criminal, too." He had been a motion picture executive, Herschensohn said, and he knew all about propaganda techniques. And Walter Cronkite of CBS was a premier practitioner of such black arts. Herschensohn did not like Cronkite's "intonations" and his use of the "hold-frame gimmick"—stopping a motion picture momentarily—which conveyed the subliminal message that the subject of the film was guilty of something. This was "very sharp stuff," said Herschensohn. "I know about it; anybody in the business knows about it."[206]

Clay Whitehead

As the Watergate scandal unfolded, Clay Whitehead, the Office of Telecommunications Policy director who had terrorized the networks and the public television system during the last days of the first term, virtually disappeared from sight. But on June 1, 1973, he addressed the Associated Press Broadcasters Association in New Orleans and declared he was opposed to government regulation of the content of programs. The profession should police itself, he said.[207]

In the midst of the brouhaha that erupted after Nixon's October 26 press conference, the OTP released a study demonstrating the ease with which sixty-seven new television stations could be established in the nation's top one hundred markets. The report frightened network executives, who feared competition with their affiliates, but the timing of the release appeared to be coincidental.[208]

The Bureaucrats

During the early Watergate period the Justice Department continued to intimidate and harass the press with interrogations and arrests. On April 17, 1973, for example, reporter Thomas Oliphant of the *Boston Globe* was aboard an airplane that dropped food and medical supplies to a group of militant Indians who had occupied the village of Wounded Knee, South Dakota, on the Oglala Sioux reservation. Although Oliphant was merely doing his job—he wrote a first-person account of the flight—he was subsequently arrested by FBI agents and charged with conspiracy and aiding and abetting a riot. The case dragged on for two and one-half months before it was finally dismissed on the government's own motion.[209]

On October 4, 1973, as the administration was reeling from a summer of Watergate hearings and the special prosecutor's demands for Nixon's tapes, the Justice Department announced a new policy: no reporter would be questioned, arrested, or indicted without the personal approval of Attorney General Elliot Richardson. Justice Department spokesman John Hushen's remarks seemed to indicate that the administration was seeking to improve relations with the press.[210]

The Justice Department's antitrust division sparked a furor in January 1974 when it formally petitioned the Federal Communications Commission not to renew the broadcast licenses of several radio and television stations in St. Louis, Missouri, and Des Moines, Iowa, on the grounds they were owned by newspaper publishers. License renewals, noted the federal attorneys, "would perpetuate the high degree of concentration in the dissemination of local news and advertising." The licenses in St. Louis were held by the Pulitzer Publishing Co., owners of the *St. Louis Post-Dispatch*, and the Newhouse Broadcasting Corp., owner of the *St. Louis Globe-Democrat*. In Des Moines the licenses were held by Cowles Communication, owner of the two daily newspapers, the *Register* and the *Tribune*.[211]

The antitrust action appeared to be politically motivated. Numerous other communications companies in such cities as Chicago, New York, and Atlanta also enjoyed simultaneous ownership of broadcast facilities and newspapers, but many of these news organs had been generally friendly toward Richard Nixon. The Justice Department chose to move against firms in St. Louis, where the *Post-Dispatch* had always been anti-Nixon, and Des Moines, where the *Register*—and especially its Washington bureau chief, Clark Mollenhoff, had turned against the president because of the Watergate scandal. The Justice Department vigorously defended its action on the grounds that it had been urging the FCC since 1971 to move against the cross-ownership of broadcast facilities and newspapers located in the same city. Said Jack Hushen: "The FCC has been diddling around for three years and has not done anything on it, and the Justice Department simply got tired of waiting. The administration is thought of as anti-media, and it has been especially critical of television reporting, but those criticisms have absolutely nothing to do with our position on this matter.[212]

Washington Post reporter Susanna McBee investigated the matter for two weeks and found "no evidence that the action was ideologically inspired or that it was dictated by the White House."[213] Other expert observers, however, refused to believe the administration's motives were pure. Former FCC commissioner Nicholas Johnson, who was personally opposed to cross-ownership, viewed the action as yet another maneuver in Nixon's "war on the media." A Washington attorney who specialized in broadcast law speculated that the Justice Department was laying the groundwork for similar actions against other Nixon "enemies" whose broadcast licenses had to be renewed shortly.[214]

By 1974 the Internal Revenue Service had ceased the pernicious practice of instigating tax audits against journalists who irritated the Nixon White House. But in January of that year they requested the records of all long-distance telephone calls made from the Washington bureau of the *New York Times* over the preceding seven-month period. The IRS also asked for the records of telephone calls placed from the Maryland home of *Times* reporter David Rosenbaum, who had been investigating the tax problems of one of Richard Nixon's financial angels. Always eager to please the federal government, which watches over its own activities, the Chesapeake and Potomac Company (then the local AT&T subsidiary) disgorged the records of some 2,500 long-distance calls for the IRS.[215]

The telephone company did, however, notify the *New York Times* that it had fulfilled the IRS request, and the paper's publisher promptly served notice that if the records were not surrendered, one or more lawsuits would be filed against the government. Most of the documents were soon delivered back to the telephone company, and after a meeting with lawyers representing the *Times*, IRS commissioner Donald Alexander announced he would "rethink" his agency's policies concerning the use of subpoenas to obtain reporters' records.[216]

At the United States Information Agency, director and former Nixon speechwriter James Keogh ordered the subordinate Voice of America news staff not to broadcast Watergate stories that were attributed to anonymous sources. "My guidance," he said when asked, "has been to cover the Watergate story factually, but do not use rumor, speculation, hearsay or anonymous accusation." He continued, "You have to realize that this is a very sensitive thing for us—the impression that the foreign audience gets. It's difficult for people to understand what we're doing. In some countries, they might get the impression of something conspiratorial about this [the broadcasts themselves]." As a result of Keogh's policy VOA editors killed a story they had prepared from *Washington Post* and *New York Times* accounts of what John Dean had told federal investigators about President Nixon's participation in a Watergate cover-up. Both newspapers had attributed their information to "reliable sources." When the White House subsequently issued a denial, the VOA moved the story, with the denial as the lead. Said Keogh, "If an accusation is important enough to warrant a denial, it's a different thing."[217]

The president's version of events during his Watergate crisis was challenged daily by contradictory news stories. "Watergate joined the issue of credibility as it had never been joined before," observed Benjamin Bradlee and Howard Simons of the *Washington Post*. "White House attacks on newspapers and television quite literally forced the reader and the listener to choose between the White House and the press."[218]

The Washington press corps, in Nixon's view, had turned into an angry mob determined to lynch him. His *Memoirs* are filled with complaints of press abuse. Many Watergate stories were "unfair and misleading," he wrote. Journalists were "fired by personal passion." And, "At some point in the hot, muggy summer of 1973, some of the more influential members of the Washington press corps concluded that I was starting to go off my rocker."[219]

Many of his minions agreed. "The press reporting was harsh," commented Charles Colson, "attacks personal and bitter, political rhetoric increasingly shrill."[220] Speechwriter Raymond Price, himself a former newsman, was even more censorious: "Wrongs had clearly been done, but they were not particularly new or unprecedented. What was new was the sustained intensity of the media coverage, the increasingly open animus, even hate, that suffused it, and the collapse of all bounds of restraint as the psychology of the chase took over, with the pack in full cry in pursuit of a single prey."[221]

The critics found support in some surprising places. From Capitol Hill came the complaint of Senator William Proxmire, Democrat of Wisconsin, that the press was engaged in a campaign of "McCarthyistic destruction" of the president. The Watergate stories that were appearing, said Proxmire, were "grossly unfair" and represented "the press at its worst."[222] Deposed Special Prosecutor Archibald Cox accused the press of arrogating unto itself the responsibilities of "the fourth branch of government." He had "quite a few misgivings," he said, about the way the press was reporting the Watergate scandal.[223]

Even journalists occasionally lamented the quality of the Watergate coverage. The *Times* of London published a lengthy editorial charging that the *New York Times* and the *Washington Post* were impeding the process of justice by "publishing vast quantities of prejudicial matter."[224] Wrote UPI White House correspondent Helen Thomas, "By October of 1973, the Watergate affair had heightened the president's hostility toward reporters, and I will concede that by this time many reporters were harboring resentments toward him."[225]

The public had come to a similar conclusion a few months earlier. A Gallup Poll published in mid-June 1973 revealed that 44 percent of those interviewed believed there had been "too much" news about Watergate. Thirty-eight precent felt the coverage had been "about right." A typical opinion was expressed by a retired businessman: "The press and television somehow have not awakened to the fact that the Watergate movie is over. The lynching party has hanged the bad guys."[226]

If the press did indeed turn on the president and pursue him, the reasons were ample. Wrote Theodore H. White, "By the beginning of 1973 the news system of the United States had been pushed to the wall. Its practitioners had been spied on, intimidated, tax-harassed—and they feared worse. In defending itself by counter-attack, it was defending far more than the news system. It was defending the rights of all Americans; if individual reporters and newspapers and TV outlets were not safe, then no one was safe from the same search and seizure, harassment, tax menace and reprisal to which the news system felt itself subject."[227]

Washington Post executive editor Benjamin Bradlee, fed up with the administration's railing about the press, exploded:

It happens that when the unfair press is lied to over and over and over and over again, it gets to the point where honest men resent the hell out of it. Never mind the personal attacks, never mind the $10 million libel suits. Never mind the challenges to one's television licenses. Never mind the little rocks that come over the wall. Never mind Bill Safire being quoted in *Time* that the name of the game is who can screw the *Post* the most. Never mind that. Just try to do an honest day's work when you go to the administration. But to be told when you ask, "Is it true?"—that the question is character assassination, innuendo, and anyway it's not true, and told again and again that it's not true. And then it's true. That really does something to a man's soul—and to a woman's soul. And to a reporter's soul.[228]

Did such anger, rightful though it was, distort journalists' sense of fair play? Did the press indeed abuse the president during the Watergate period? Were reporters unfair and inaccurate?

In my judgment: occasionally, yes.

Among the countless Watergate stories, inevitably there were some inaccuracies. In the spring of 1973, for example, the *Washington Post* reported that federal prosecutors had been told by "two top officials of President Nixon's Re-election Campaign Committee" that Charles Colson had advance knowledge of plans to bug Democratic offices in the Watergate office complex and urged that the surveillance be "expedited." It was never conclusively shown that Colson knew about the bugging plans in advance.[229] Bob Woodward and Carl Bernstein named three Nixon campaign officials who allegedly had received transcripts of the Watergate wiretaps. No evidence ever surfaced to support that story.[230] ABC correspondent Sam Donaldson, quoting a sole source, reported on March 29, 1973, that James McCord had charged former presidential aide Harry Dent with being "part of a general sabotage and espionage operation directed by the White

House." The story was not true, and Donaldson subsequently apologized on the air.[231] "The truth is," concluded *Washington Post* associate editor Robert Maynard in November 1973, "there's a lot of fast and loose stuff being printed."[232]

There were also some news reports that seem to have been unfair. Perhaps the most outstanding example was the great "slap flap" of November 1973. After his news conference with newspaper editors at Disney World, President Nixon was driven to McCoy Air Force Base, near Orlando, where Air Force One was parked. Just before he boarded, he waded into a small crowd of well-wishers, shook some hands, and had his picture taken while holding an infant. Through the brilliant floodlights, he spotted a small boy and a shadowy figure at the child's side. "Are you this boy's mother or grandmother?" asked Nixon, squinting to see the person he had addressed. "Neither," replied Master Sergeant Edward Kleizo. Nixon leaned forward for a closer look. "Of course not," he said, and he reached up and slapped Kleizo on the face.

The incident was witnessed by two pool reporters, William Eaton of the *Chicago Daily News* and Matthew Cooney of the Westinghouse Broadcasting Company, but they felt it so insignificant that they left it out of the pool report they prepared for the rest of the White House press corps. Eaton, however, mentioned the slap to *Wall Street Journal* reporter Fred Zimmerman, who asked for a demonstration. Zimmerman subsequently reported, in an eighty-one-word story, that the President had "soundly slapped" a man at McCoy Air Force Base. A few correspondents believed the incident was a sign that Nixon's emotions were frayed and filed stories to their own newspapers. As it turned out, Master Sergeant Kleizo was not at all upset by the presidential pat. "He slapped me," said Kleizo, but it was "just an affectionate slap like a father would give a son." He was so pleased, Kleizo added, that "I may not even wash my face again."[233]

Too many words had been devoted to a meaningless incident. But if the reporters involved had treated the president unfairly, the White House media team went them one better. A decision was made to spotlight the matter as a means of discrediting the White House press corps. In a harsh, heavy-handed formal statement Nixon's press office fulminated:

Some members of the White House press corps, solely on the basis of rumor and gossip, distorted a friendly gesture in which the president patted a man on the face into a "slapping incident." The White House feels compelled to condemn this unethical and unprofessional reporting.

This is an example of irresponsible and twisted accounts which have been circulated in recent months, without adequate substantiation and which creates false impressions concerning the president of the United States. The motives of those who generated the rumors and those who wrote these stories can only be explained by the reporters involved.[234]

Nixon and his supporters persistently cited the furor that erupted when he fired Special Prosecutor Archibald Cox as another outstanding example of unfair press coverage. Although the verdict in that case is not as clear as in the Kleizo case, it warrants reexamination.

Shortly after the existence of President Nixon's secret tape-recording system was revealed in July 1973, Cox requested the tapes of eight presidential conversations. The White House refused, and Cox petitioned Judge John Sirica for permission to subpoena the tapes. Sirica's ruling—that he review the tapes and turn over to Cox those that were relevant—was immediately appealed by both parties. On October 12 the U.S. Court of Appeals ruled in Cox's favor. Nixon, meanwhile, had come up with a compromise: the White House would prepare a summary of the subpoenaed tapes, have it "authenticated" by Senator John Stennis, Democrat of Mississippi, and then release the document to Cox. The special prosecutor refused the offer, and an irate Nixon ordered Attorney General Elliot Richardson to fire Cox. Richardson refused and offered to resign, as did Deputy Attorney General William Ruckelshaus. The third-ranking Justice Department official, Solicitor General Robert Bork, agreed to carry out the order.

At 8:22 P.M. on Saturday, October 20, 1973, Ronald Ziegler announced that Cox had been dismissed, that Richardson and Ruckelshaus had resigned, and that the special prosecutor's office was being abolished. The Justice Department, said Ziegler, would resume its investigation of Watergate. Shortly after it was learned that FBI agents had been ordered to surround Cox's office to "protect" the files contained therein.

In the tense, supersaturated atmosphere of Washington, D.C., the public reaction was swift and angry. The television networks interrupted their regular programming with special reports. "The country tonight is in the midst of what may be the most serious constitutional crisis in its history," said NBC's John Chancellor. It was a "stunning development," he continued, and added, "In my career as a correspondent, I never thought I would be announcing these things." Throughout the weekend, television reports about the "Saturday Night massacre" continued. Congressmen, columnists, and correspondents went before the cameras to censure the sudden series of events as a

"Brownshirt operation," a "reckless act of desperation." Nixon had employed "Gestapo tactics"; his actions smacked of "dictatorship." Newspapers soon joined the chorus of criticism. "The desperation of President Nixon's moves . . . makes it plain that neither law nor orderly government process now stand as obstacles to the exercise of his will," editorialized the *New York Times*.[235]

Just outside the White House fence, meanwhile, automobile horns blared as protesters held high "Honk For Impeachment" signs. Telegrams began pouring into the White House and Capitol Hill offices; within ten days a record 450,000 had been processed by Western Union. By Tuesday, October 23, more than twenty resolutions for Nixon's impeachment had been introduced on the floor of Congress.[236]

The adverse public reaction, in the opinion of the president and his associates, was the fault of the press. "It was manufactured fervor," said one White House official.[237] The networks had been "almost hysterical," wrote Nixon in his *Memoirs*. He continued, "Commentators and correspondents talked in apocalyptic terms and painted the night's events in terms of an administration coup aimed at suppressing opposition."[238]

Precisely who painted this image in the public mind, however, is highly debatable. It was Richard Nixon, not newsmen who dramatically fired the special prosecutor just as he was about to gain possession of evidence that could establish whether the president was involved in Watergate crimes. As *Time* magazine put it: "The networks could hardly be blamed for the dearth of responsible people eager to support the president on the Cox dismissal; even many Republicans were critical on that issue. And the notion that it was TV's reporting of the act, rather than the act itself, that caused the furor underscores a basic White House misconception about journalism's role."[239]

Nixon and his associates, it appears, were themselves hitting below the belt when they cited press coverage of the Cox firing as an example of unfair treatment.

They were also perverting the truth when they attempted to portray the press as a monolithic mob dedicated to the deposal of the president. Richard Nixon had his defenders in the Fourth Estate; it just wasn't politic for the president to remind the public of this fact. Syndicated columnist Richard Wilson, for example, excused the foul play in Nixon's 1972 campaign on the grounds that John Mitchell, H. R. Haldeman, and John Ehrlichman were trying to preserve "the kind of system they believed most Americans wanted." Wilson continued, "Which was not what Daniel Ellsberg, the Berrigan brothers, Jane Fonda, the black militants, welfare chiselers and the campus radicals and George

S. McGovern desired. In that mood it was possible to justify means of opposition to the hostile encroachment of hated perceptions which under ordinary circumstances might be avoided."²⁴⁰ On occasion, columnists Joseph Alsop, George F. Will, Vermont Royster and James Reston were also inclined to treat Nixon kindly.²⁴¹ By 1976 even putative liberal Nicholas von Hoffman had joined the ranks of those who subscribed to the theory that Nixon was done in by a journalistic lynch mob: "From the summer of 1973 onward, Nixon increasingly became the object of the kind of universal media attack that we have heretofore pretty much reserved for foreign enemies or obscure domestic Communists. These past three years Nixon has had a worse press than Stalin in the height of the Cold War. The only name for it is hysterical contagion."²⁴²

Such indiscriminate criticism is easily uttered. But the skeptical reader yearns for details. Where is the evidence? Where is the proof? In late 1973 Richard Nixon and his media team were provided with an ideal opportunity to make their case. They failed to do so, and therein, perhaps, lies the best answer to the question of who abused whom.

In his October 26, 1973, press conference President Nixon savagely attacked the press, particularly television journalists. "I have never heard or seen such outrageous, vicious, distorted reporting in twenty-seven years of public life," he fumed and quickly added, "I'm not blaming anybody for that."²⁴³

The National News Council, a fifteen-member group organized in 1973 to monitor the press, immediately offered to investigate Nixon's charges and asked the White House to "furnish specific examples of the distorted reporting."²⁴⁴ On November 29 the council's directors met with Ronald Ziegler and were informed that it would be "inappropriate" for the White House to cooperate. Several days later deputy press secretary Gerald Warren explained that the administration had refused to join in the effort "because we simply don't have the staff or the time."²⁴⁵

As the National News Council's negotiations with the White House continued, other researchers stepped forward with the results of their own investigations. *National Observer* columnist James M. Perry studied the transcripts of CBS news shows broadcast during the ten days immediately following the Saturday Night massacre and determined that "most of the material is pretty bland, pretty straight and pretty sketchy in detail." Perry concluded, "It's hard to believe the president has much of a case. There are a lot of problems with television news coverage (and print coverage, for that matter), but what CBS did between Oct. 19 and Oct. 29 hardly amounted to a 27-year record in viciousness and distortion."[246]

Professor Lawrence Lichty of the University of Wisconsin probed Nixon's allegation that he had been labeled a "tyrant" and a "dictator" by persons interviewed on television in the wake of his December 1972 decision to bomb North Vietnam. "In reviewing nearly 100 live and film reports by network reporters and other material added by anchormen during the period of Dec. 18–31, 1972," wrote Lichty, "I found that the networks neither presented nor quoted anyone saying the president was a tyrant, dictator or that he should resign or be impeached."[247] Three teams of graduate students at the American University, working under the direction of Edward Bliss, Jr., studied videotapes of all network newscasts shown during the two-week period preceding Nixon's October 26 blast at the press. The verdict, said Bliss, was "a clean bill of health" for the networks. A few cases of questionable editorial judgment were turned up, Bliss continued, but "none of the distortions President Nixon was talking about."[248]

The National News Council, meanwhile, grew weary of trying to persuade the White House to cooperate in the council's investigation of the president's charges and issued a public statement:

It would be difficult, if not futile ... for the council to attempt to deduce, from broad and non-specific charges, the particular actions of the television networks that inspired the president's remarks. . . .

We believe it is seriously detrimental to the public interest for the president to leave his harsh criticisms of the television networks unsupported by specific details that could then be evaluated objectively by an impartial body.[249]

Bruce Herschensohn, a deputy special assistant to President Nixon, stepped forward in March 1974 and declared he had compiled some examples of news distortion. In a story about the president's daily news summary, he said in a speech, the *Washington Post* had printed only a two-page index of the forty-five page document, thus giving the impression that the digest presented a sketchy treatment of events. The *Post, Time* magazine, CBS, and ABC had described Dwight Chapin as a "Watergate man" even though he had no part in the actual burglary. NBC had unfairly broadcast four segments of a Henry Kissinger press conference about the October Middle East crisis; all four film clips had depicted Kissinger's responses to charges that American troops were put on alert as a way of diverting public attention from Watergate. And CBS had led an evening newscast with a Watergate story when it should have featured an item about the end of the Arab oil embargo. In an interview with the *New York Times* a few days later, Herschensohn provided some additional examples, and he would deliver the details to the National News Council, he said.[250]

The specifics were never provided, and on May 16, the News Council finally washed its hands of the matter. Ned Schnurman, associate director of the council, said he and Herschensohn had "agreed that by May 1, he would tell us whether he would give us the information. On May 1 he said he still needed more time. We set another deadline of May 8. I called three times, and he didn't return the calls." A *New York Times* reporter later reached Herschensohn at the White House and recorded his response: "At the time, I was terribly busy. The next thing I knew I saw a news release from [the National News Council] saying that a White House official failed to provide the information. I was extremely upset. I never said I would, and that's one of the reasons I'm not going to. To tell you the truth, I had never heard of the National News Council. I had never established that they were the place where the media and the president had agreed to arbitrate complaints."[251]

The solution to the president's "PR problem" was never found. The attempts at image making, the television end runs, the progaganda campaigns, the efforts to appease the press, and to intimidate it— nothing worked. On July 24 the Supreme Court ruled, eight to zero, that Nixon had to surrender the tape recordings of sixty-four conversations to special prosecutor Leon Jaworski. One of them, a recording made on June 23, 1972, revealed that Nixon and Haldeman had discussed the use of the CIA to thwart the FBI's investigation of the Watergate burglary. It was clearly the "smoking gun" that Nixon's defenders had demanded of his opponents. On August 5 the president released the contents of the June 23 tape with the acknowledgment that "this additional material I am now furnishing may further damage my case." The tapes contained information, he said, which was "at variance with certain of my previous statements." But, he allowed, the record "in its entirety, does not justify the extreme step of impeachment and removal of a president." The adverse reaction was overwhelming. Many of Nixon's remaining friends on Capitol Hill declared they had been betrayed; some openly suggested that he resign. Rumors began spreading throughout Washington that this was precisely what he would do.[252]

At noon on August 8 a wan and shaking Ronald Ziegler announced to a crowded press room that the president would make a televised address to the nation at 9 P.M. As they waited, the reporters sprawled across sofas, stretched out on the floor, drained the coffee vending machine.[253] Helen Thomas wandered into Gerald Warren's office and found him in tears.[254]

Outside the White House, a crowd that would soon number two thousand began to gather. Network camera crews, barred from the White House grounds, began setting up in Lafayette Square across the street. As darkness fell, someone ran up to Dan Rather and threw a felt-tip pen at his chest. It was, said Rather, "a member of the Nixon press staff, half out of his head with emotion."[255]

Reporters in the press room watched the president's speech on television. Photographers snapped pictures of the scene, and television cameras filmed the screen on which Nixon appeared.[256] At one point the editor of Nixon's daily news summary, Mort Allin, stormed into the room and shouted: "I hope you guys are having fun getting drunk in your celebration, you (expletive deleted)."

After the president's speech the network correspondents offered their "instant analysis," and most were magnanimous. On CBS Walter Cronkite averred that Nixon had been conciliatory. "Few things in his presidency," remarked Eric Sevareid, "became him as much as his manner of leaving the presidency." Dan Rather was maudlin: "He gave his moment a touch of class . . . more than that, a touch of majesty." Roger Mudd demurred: "From the viewpoint of Congress, that wasn't a very satisfactory speech." On NBC John Chancellor wrapped up the evening's events with this observation: "A president has resigned from his office. Tomorrow, we will have a new president. And the world goes on."[257]

The following morning Nixon, Pat, and Tricia and her husband Ed Cox strode down a long red carpet to the presidential helicopter. Ziegler ran behind them, pointing at the roped-off press and shouting to the White House police, "Hold them back! Hold them back!" At the top of the ramp Nixon turned and, with a grim smile, waved to the crowd on the South Lawn.[258]

As the Nixon party was flying to San Clemente, a *Washington Post* printer ran off a mock advertisement for the paper's "Help Wanted" section. It featured a picture of Gerald Ford against a backdrop of classified ads. Beneath the picture were the words: "I got my job through the Washington Post."[259]

8

Review: "Believe Me, It Reads Well in Peoria"

As the years give perspective to Richard Nixon's tenure in the White House, one fact becomes increasingly clear: in the insidious art of media manipulation, he was truly the grand guru. The men who have succeeded him have acted as if they sat at the master's feet and heard his teachings on what to do and, just as important, what *not* to do in their dealings with the press.

They have learned not to become personally involved in confrontations with reporters. This was one of Nixon's rules too, but he could not restrain himself and thus became an example of the misfortune that can befall a president who permits himself to engage in personal combat with the press.

The post-Nixon presidents have learned that a White House propaganda machine, Nixon's office of communications, is an indispensable tool for end running the national press and convincing journalists who reside west of the Appalachians that the man in the mansion is a compassionate and sagacious leader. Before Nixon was elected, the propaganda apparatus did not exist; it is now a fixture.

The presidents have learned that an in-house news digest is an effective means of maintaining a watch on the press. Richard Nixon created it; it is now considered essential.

The presidents have learned from Nixon the guru a mantra that is endlessly repeated and thought of as the key that unlocks the mysteries of public acceptance and power: television . . . television . . . television.

The use of television and the attendant public relations gimmickery as a means of projecting the image that a president, or a presidential candidate, is indeed presidential did not begin with Nixon. The notion was born in the 1950s, but it was considered vaguely offensive. It gradually gained acceptance and is now considered appropriate, necessary and nothing to be ashamed of.

That was Richard Nixon's major contribution to politicians in their eternal battle with the press: He brought PR out of the closet, put the seal of approval on television and imagery as political tools. Before Nixon took office presidents used television haphazardly and unscientifically and seldom recognized it as a way of evading the meddlesome press. It is now viewed as the primary means of manipulating public opinion directly, without the press filter. Before Nixon image specialists were relatively few in number and lightly regarded; they now rank among a president's most important advisers. They wander through the White House talking about "attitudinal polling," "political communication," "emotionality," and the "sincere mode." They now know how to stage "media events" and time the Festival of the Balloons.

Richard Nixon, in short, devised a highly effective strategy for manipulating the press. That is his legacy and we are wrestling with it today.

Appeasement

If Gerald Ford departed the White House slightly confused about how he got along with the national press, he could be forgiven. The relationship had been a paradox. On the one hand, anything he said or did with respect to the press looked progressive when compared with the record of his predecessor. On the other, Ford faced a press that was often hostile and always suspicious, thanks again to the Nixon experience.

Ford made an extraordinary effort to be accessible to journalists. When he was sworn into office on August 9, 1974, he made a promise that sounded much like a vow made by another president five years earlier. "In all my public and private acts as your president," said Ford, "I expect to follow my instincts of openness and candor with full confidence that honesty is always the best policy in the end."[1] Richard Nixon had promulgated that rule and had promptly disappeared behind his Berlin Wall; Ford by and large proved true to his word. On his second day as president he called a cabinet meeting and urged all present to be more affirmative with the press.[2] To ensure that he would not become too isolated, he attempted to establish a "spoke-of-the-wheel" staff structure in which nine senior assistants shared equal access to the president. But he soon discovered this was too cumbersome and reluctantly appointed a chief of staff to oversee the people and paper that flowed into the Oval Office. Nixon's former top aide, Alexander Haig, performed this function until Donald Rumsfeld took over in late September 1974.[3]

As vice-president Ford had mingled freely with the reporters assigned to cover him. As president he could not mix with them as easily, but he went out of his way to be as accessible and open as possible, a habit that sometimes got him into difficulty. On January 16, 1975, for instance, he attended an off-the-record luncheon at the White House with a small group of *New York Times* editors and columnists and remarked that the CIA had engaged in activities that would "blacken the name of every president back to Harry Truman," including involvement in plans to assassinate several world leaders. The *Times* journalists were ethically bound not to disclose the story, but word of the CIA's activities eventually reached CBS correspondent Daniel Schorr, and he broke the story on February 28, 1975. Revelations about secret CIA operations subsequently dominated the headlines for a year.[4]

In his first months in the White House Ford invited a few reporters to formal dinners for heads of state. Such events usually began with a social reception and ended with entertainment in the East Room, but the president restricted news coverage of the receptions. He liked to "chat privately" with his guests, he said, and he did not approve when reporters who were covering the affairs mingled with the visitors in search of hard news stories. At a May 1975 dinner in honor of Singapore prime minister Lee Kuan Yew, for example, Ford interrupted an inquisitive reporter. "This is not a press conference, no press conference," he snapped, and walked away. The next day press secretary Ron Nessen announced that the president's policy was going to be enforced, and coverage of White House receptions would henceforth be restricted. At the next official function reporters found themselves observing the receiving line and reception from a roped-off area.[5] UPI correspondent Helen Thomas organized a protest, and in August the president relented. Small pools of reporters would be permitted to mingle with guests, provided they kept notebooks and tape recorders out of sight and did not attempt to interview Ford.[6]

Of all the presidents who have served since 1974, none was as evocative of Richard Nixon as James Earl Carter, Jr., but he did not like to hear that. "Equating Carter with Nixon makes Carter so mad that he becomes more like Nixon," remarked journalist Aaron Latham during the 1976 campaign. Perhaps Carter was sensitive about such comparisons because they struck a raw nerve: both men had similar backgrounds (rural/small town), similar family situations (dominating mother), similar psyches (prone to depression), and similar senses of humor (almost none). Both men were cold, aloof loners who surrounded themselves with a small coterie of close friends and associates. Both men made use of a campaign operation that specialized in dirty tricks; Nixon had the CRP and Carter, during his 1970 gubernatorial race in Georgia, had what came to be known as the "stink tank," which specialized in creating a negative image for the opponent.[7] And both men believed the press to be their enemy.

Their antipress attitudes appeared to reflect their insecurities. Nixon saw journalists as elitist easterners who picked on him because he was a poor boy from the West. Carter ascribed unfavorable press treatment to an antisouthern bias. In an infamous 1976 *Playboy* interview the Democratic presidential candidate offered this observation: "There's still a tendency on the part of some members of the press to treat the South, you know, as a suspect nation. There are a few who think that since I am a Southern governor, I must be a secret racist or there's something in a closet somewhere that's going to be revealed to show my true colors."[8]

Even when he was a state senator in Georgia in the early 1960s, observed journalist Reg Murphy, then with the *Atlanta Constitution*, Jimmy Carter believed there was "a conspiracy in the newspaper business to get things wrong. You just dreaded to see Carter coming down the hallway in the legislative session because you never could talk about substantive issues for him wanting to point out little picayune comma faults in stories."[9] From Carter's perspective the truth was the precise opposite. It was reporters who ignored the issues. He made an emphatic point of this in his *Playboy* interview:

Issues? The local media are interested, all right, but the national news media have absolutely no interest in issues *at all*. . . . The traveling press have zero interest in any issue unless it's a matter of making a mistake. What they're looking for is a 47-second argument between me and another candidate or something like that. There's nobody in the back of this plane [the press section] who would ask an issue question unless he thought he could trick me into some crazy statement.[10]

Despite his disdain for the press, Carter made a major effort to get along with journalists. Indeed, the nurturing of newsmen was an important element in his strategy to gain and succeed in the presidency. "Stories in the *New York Times* and *Washington Post* do not just happen, but have to be carefully planned and planted," wrote Carter's chief political strategist, Hamilton Jordan, in a seventy-page memo on November 4, 1972, while Carter was the governor of Georgia. Jordan continued, "The thrust of your national press effort should be that state government is working in Georgia and is solving the problems in meeting the needs of ordinary citizens. . . . Once your name begins to be mentioned in the national press, you will not lack for invitations and opportunities to speak in major groups and conventions." Jordan named more than a dozen journalists who were worthy of Carter's attention and added, "Like it or not, there exists an Eastern liberal news establishment which has tremendous influence. The views of this small group of opinion-makers in the papers they represent are noted and imitated by other columnists and newspapers throughout the country and the world. Their recognition and acceptance of your candidacy as a viable force with some chance of success could establish you as a serious contender worthy of financial support of major party contributors. They could have an equally adverse effect, dismissing your effort as being regional or an attempt to secure the second spot on the ticket."[11]

Throughout his four years in the White House Carter held regular press conferences, met with many editors and correspondents, and spoke with scores of reporters in background sessions. But his efforts were largely mechanical; his heart was not in it. In a 1979 interview a veteran White House correspondent, who asked not to be identified, put it this way: "Much of it is just personality. Ford liked reporters and Carter doesn't. Ron Nessen didn't have to make Ford see reporters, but Jody Powell and Jerry Rafshoon have to make Carter see reporters, because he doesn't like them."[12]

Carter's loner instincts and his desire for privacy made it virtually impossible for him to live up to his promises to be open and accessible to the public and the press. Three months after Carter took the oath of office, *New York Times* correspondent James Wooten reported that the president was resentful of dissent, was often intimidating, and was growing increasingly isolated. An angry Jody Powell questioned twenty White House aides in search of Wooten's sources and issued a stinging denial. "You've got to have some opportunity to defend yourself," he said. "The president has been called a brutal recluse."[13] But reporters remained unconvinced. By the spring of 1976, reported UPI correspondent Wesley Pippert, access to the news in the White House was almost nonexistent. Cabinet secretaries departed the premises without speaking to the press; congressional leaders left by the South Gate, an area barred to reporters; Jody Powell had become as communicative as a brick during his formal briefings and was speaking more often on background.[14] Concluded Terence Smith of the *New York Times*, "The 'open administration' that Mr. Carter pledged in his campaign has always been more of an illusion than a reality. The Carter White

House restricts newsmen's access much as its predecessors did, and the president is only rarely glimpsed in any kind of formal setting."[15]

Access to Carter was also erratic when he was on the road. On the typical trip to the president's home town, Plains, Georgia, reporters had to content themselves by conducting interviews with the president's colorful brother, Billy; by witnessing the First Family's attendance at Sunday church services; and by covering Jody Powell's trivia-laden briefings and photo opportunities.[16]

Camp David afforded even more privacy than Plains for the president, and he relished his visits there as fervently as Richard Nixon had. In August 1978 Carter took Israeli prime minister Menachem Begin and Egyptian president Anwar Sadat to his mountaintop retreat for a thirteen-day summit meeting. Some four hundred reporters, photographers, and television technicians tagged along and set up one of the largest journalistic stake-outs in history. It was also one of the most uneventful. Israeli and Egyptian officials agreed that Jody Powell should be the spokesman for the summit, and he chose to imitate the Sphinx that guards the pyramids at Giza. He held one news conference a day in a makeshift press center at the local American Legion hall and ladled out what he admitted was "rather innocent information."[17] Everyone involved in the negotiations remained behind the fences of Camp David, so newsmen began interviewing the local folk, tourists, and each other. One Israeli journalist questioned a tree and filed his story with a warning to his editors that it was not a scoop: television correspondent Barbara Walters had earlier interviewed the arboreal source.[18]

Unlike Richard Nixon, however, Carter had more sense than to abandon the national press altogether. As one presidential aide put it in 1977, "He knows he can use the press to help him and his programs."[19] Each year he was in the White House Carter made at least one concentrated effort to massage reportorial egos with food, drink, and cozy conversation. In 1977 he invited journalists to partake of wine and cheese around the presidential swimming pool or to drinks on the South Lawn. During the summer of 1978 he held a series of private dinners and breakfasts for journalists at the White House. A year later Carter launched another series of dinner meetings with newsmen.[20] Invitations were generally extended only to journalists and news executives of renown, a fact that irritated some members of the White House press corps. One who was not invited was Curtis Wilkie of the *Boston Globe*, and he had this to say about Carter's private meetings: "He can be very charming when he wants to be. His raw intelligence is as good as I've ever seen. . . . You'd have to be pretty hard-nosed to come out of one of those things feeling negative about him. . . . His 'dog and pony shows' are more for the so-called opinion makers than for the working stiffs—the columnists and the thumb-suckers who go to Georgetown salons and traffic with Henry Kissinger and people like that. . . . They don't traffic in the same circles as the White House press corps."[21]

While aloft in his 1976 campaign plane, Peanut One, Carter occasionally would stroll through the press section and answer questions.[22] Three years later NBC correspondent Judy Woodruff recalled that Carter "was much looser" in 1976. "We got to see him more often, and we could just holler a question at him. There were all sorts of opportunities and he would occasionally pause and talk to us."[23] But after four years of exposure in the White House, the press was not so essential and the president was not so available. There were few casual contacts. Pool reporters were ordered to stay put in the rear of Air Force One, and Carter remained in his forward cabin.[24]

Most journalists appear to appreciate Ronald Reagan about as much as they disliked Jimmy Carter. The reporter who is generally regarded as the most eminent expert on Reagan is Lou Cannon of the *Washington Post*. Said Cannon, "He's a friendly guy. He doesn't make a distinction that when he is with people, that we, the press, are different from anybody else. That's why his people don't want him to speak out at photo opportunities. Too often he gives an honest answer."[25] Other journalists have expressed similarly benevolent attitudes toward Reagan. NBC correspondent Don Oliver has said, "I think Reagan basically likes reporters. . . . He even likes people who have written nasty things about him if he's known them for a while."[26]

During the last two years of his tenure Jimmy Carter chose not to attend the annual dinners of the White House Correspondents Association, and his absences were widely perceived as insults. In the spring of 1981, while recovering from wounds suffered in the attempt on his life, Ronald Reagan telephoned from Camp David to address the eighteen hundred people attending the bash. "I'm happy to be speaking to the White House correspondents' spring prom," he joked. He then delivered a series of one-liners that sent his sophisticated audience into raucous laughter.[27]

As Lou Cannon pointed out, Reagan tends to view reporters as regular people and thus speaks his mind while in their presence. For this reason and because he has a habit of stammering and digressing while speaking spontaneously, his top aides urge him to limit his exposure to journalists, particularly to print reporters. They do not especially like to do this because Reagan is a charming and genial man. But they feel that most of the time he needs to be protected from himself, and so they periodically attempt to isolate him.

During the 1980 primary campaigns, for example, Reagan was usually accessible to the press. There were days when he held as many as five news conferences.[28] But along the way he made too many self-damaging remarks. He told a Mississippi crowd that he favored "states' rights"; he lauded a Mexican revolutionary hero as a "brave American priest"; he referred to Illinois Governor James Thompson as "Governor Dave Thompson."[29] Suddenly, shortly after Labor Day, Reagan's media team went on the defensive. The candidate was advised to pace himself and get plenty of rest. He began to avoid reporters; whenever they got within earshot, press secretary Lyn Nofziger leaped in front of Reagan and shouted, "No press conference. No questions, no questions."[30] Television crews, however, were included in every pool. After all, said one of Reagan's aides, it is "pictures that count."[31] News conferences with the national press were held to a minimum. Once after Jimmy Carter had accused Reagan of avoiding reporters, a press conference was arranged, in the words of one aide, to show Reagan "isn't in hiding."[32] After several weeks of few contacts with the press, during which news accounts seemed to focus less on his shortcomings and more on what he was saying about his policies and about Jimmy Carter, Reagan returned to a state of semi-isolation.[33]

Reagan's habit of swinging between periods of isolation and semi-isolation, which had also characterized his behavior as governor of California, continued after he moved into the White House. Following bursts of bad publicity, his staff gathers around him like a human wall and he disappears for a while; when the coast appears to be clear, the wall dissipates and he begins to make limited appearances in the press room or at photo opportunities. "Reporters covering the White House work within one hundred feet of the Oval Office," Associated Press correspondent James Gerstenzang wrote. "But they can go days, or even weeks, without seeing President Reagan."[34]

In an effort to help elect as many Republicans as possible in the 1982 congressional elections, Reagan's media specialists decided they should get a firmer grip on the presidential image. Early in the year they began cutting back on the president's appearances before reporters. Warnings went out to journalists to cease their practice of asking questions of Reagan during photo opportunities.[35] During the final weeks before the elections, the president virtually disappeared. His last press conference prior to election day was held on September 28. Reporters were barred from witnessing the most mundane presidential activities — bill signing ceremonies, meetings with such groups as the Boy Scouts and the National Venture Capital Association. When Reagan departed Washington to campaign, pool reporters were kept at a distance; if they got close enough to the president to shout questions, he was immediately surrounded by Secret Service agents and whisked away. Observed UPI's Helen Thomas, "These situations come up all the time, and what we do is keep fighting for access. But there is always a tightening up around mid-term. And there is always a lot more management around election time. But this administration has nailed it down to a fine art."[36]

Predictably the day after the elections, Reagan met with reporters for fourteen minutes in the Rose Garden. Predictably news stories began to appear carrying quotes from White House officials who lamented the fact that the president was so secluded. One front-page account in the *Washington Post*, for example, carried the headline "Reagan Aides Fear President Is Too Isolated," and noted that "some White House aides believe his isolation has begun to reinforce the impression of a president who is distant, uninformed or out of touch."[37]

Even when Reagan is in one of his responsive periods, reporting from the White House that he presides over is a demanding task. The press is confined to a designated area in the west wing and not permitted to wander beyond it. All that the regulars can do is place telephone calls from their cramped cubicles and wait for them to be returned. One former White House correspondent said he sometimes felt as if he was trapped in the locker room during a football game. "You hear the crowd, you know something is going on," he said. "When they let you up to see what is going on, you see a lot of activity, but later you find out that was only the half-time show."[38] Said Terry Hunt of the Associated Press: "It is extremely difficult to cover Reagan. There is no access. You never see him except when he is getting in and out of cars or going to or coming from church. You can't wander in the hallways. You can't go anywhere except right here in the press room. All you can do is put out a string of calls and wait for them to call back. Did you ever try to get (presidential counselor) Ed Meese to return a call?"[39]

Shortly after Reagan was sworn in, similar limitations were placed on journalists who visited White House staff members with offices in the Old Executive Office Building. Armed security guards began accompanying reporters to and from their appointments, while other people wearing visitor cards were allowed to wander at will. Previous administrations enforced no such restrictions, and *New York Times* correspondent Terence Smith lambasted the Reagan rules as "hysterical."[40]

To reduce the journalistic clamor for access to the president, Reagan's media team has periodically toyed with a technique that has become known as the mininews conference. With short notice White House reporters are shuttled into the Oval Office for a ten- to fifteen-minute session with the president. He usually begins with an announcement and, under ground rules established by deputy press secretary Larry Speakes, the first question asked the president must focus on his statement. Once a subject is raised it must be completely exhausted before queries will be entertained on other matters.[41] When the mini-conferences were first tried in April 1982, Speakes admonished White House reporters not to abuse them. "You screw it up and it doesn't happen again," he said. "It's as simple as that, I can guarantee you that."[42] The media team was thrilled with the results: the president got the desired messages across and did not have to deal with a wide range of topics.[43]

Television journalists are treated with special deference during mini-conferences. At one session a White House press aide scooted radio and newspaper reporters to the rear of the group so television correspondents could be filmed sitting in front of the president. On another occasion a miniconference was carried live on several networks, and only television reporters were permitted to ask questions.[44] As a result of the special handling broadcast officials are delighted with the mini-conference concept. "He [Reagan] keeps the television news departments in business with the mini-conferences," said NBC's Roger Mudd. "As much as we say we are being used, we would complain if he stopped." Sam Donaldson of ABC expressed a more prosaic point of view: "They want the impression of a president who frequently meets the press, but they are using every device to control it."[45]

Reagan has used a number of other techniques to deliver his messages and demonstrate his "openness" to the public. His office of media liaison keeps a steady stream of out-of-town news executives and editors pouring into the Oval Office. The president also pops into the press briefing room occasionally for short, impromptu news conferences. He has granted interviews to numerous reporters, individually and in small groups.[46] The latter seems to be a favored method of satisfying journalists' demands for access to the president, but it has occasionally backfired. When the first group session was arranged by press secretary James Brady, Reagan got carried away and offered some harsh criticisms of the Soviets and Jimmy Carter. The hoped-for headlines about the economy never appeared, and Brady was warned to call off such meetings, in the words of one White House official, "until he [Brady] gets his act together."[47] In May 1983 Reagan spoke with six reporters in the Oval Office, and the discussion was simultaneously piped into the White House press room. During the course of the interview the president tended to ramble, and he offered several candid revelations about his administration's support for guerrillas who were rebelling against the leftist government of Nicaragua. Several times during the interview reporters in the briefing room laughed openly, and the resulting stories so irritated the president's media specialists that they threatened to put him back into isolation for a while.[48]

Reagan on the road is as inaccessible to the press as Reagan in the White House. During his June 1982 ten-day, five-nation trip to Europe, reporters rarely got close to the president. At each stop they were confined to secluded press centers and fed official versions of the news. The routine was broken only when a journalistic audience was needed for a media event. During a visit to the Vatican, however, the White House image merchants learned that not even their favorite actor can pull off a crackerjack performance every time he goes before the cameras. At a ceremony in the Vatican library, televised live, Reagan spoke about his "pilgrimage for peace" and then sat down while Pope John Paul II delivered a dry homily on the horrors of war. With millions of viewers watching, Reagan's head drooped and he began nodding off to sleep. He quickly caught himself, wiped his face with his hand, and focused his attention on the pope.[49]

In the spring of 1982, Reagan and his wife Nancy accepted a long-standing invitation from good friend and former actress Claudette Colbert to spend a few days at her home on the Caribbean island of Barbados. After the trip was announced, the image team began to fret that it wouldn't look appropriate for the president to be frolicking in the surf while most of the nation he governs was struggling with the final throes of a harsh winter. So they arranged for Reagan to meet with the leaders of five Caribbean countries to discuss the regional economy and added an overnight stop in Jamaica.[50] In his closing toast to Jamaican prime minister Edward Seaga, the president spoke of how hard they had toiled but predicted he would "find it reported fulsomely that we had a lengthy, leisurely vacation while we were here."[51] Reagan then departed for Barbados for a three-day romp in the tropical sun. Reporters were lodged at a safe distance from the Colbert house, and a public beach was blocked off so the Reagans could swim without risk of being photographed. But enterprising television newsmen located a hotel with waterfront rooms that offered a perfect view and filmed Reagan, clad in boxer swim trunks, skipping stones and swimming vigorously in the surf. In an apparent fit of presidential pique, Reagan subsequently cancelled a scheduled photo opportunity.[52]

Nowhere does President Reagan enjoy more splendid isolation than at Rancho del Cielo, his 688-acre spread perched in the Santa Ynez Mountains 2,250 feet above the Pacific, some twenty miles north of Santa Barbara. It is accessible only by helicopter or by a narrow, twisting, one-lane road that is virtually impassable in wet weather. On a typical trip Air Force One lands at a naval base near Santa Barbara, and Reagan switches to a helicopter for the short flight to the ranch. The press corps is usually put up in the oceanfront Sheraton Santa Barbara Hotel and Spa while the White House staff moves into the more fashionable Mariott Santa Barbara Biltmore Hotel. The press and the staff are kept separate for a reason: the less contact, the fewer ungoverned stories hit the headlines.[53] "There are two events," one aide told a reporter during a February 1981 trip. "Arrival and departure."[54]

Secluded on his mountaintop Reagan spends his days riding horses, clearing brush, and chopping wood. A White House photographer snaps pictures for the press, which is totally at the mercy of deputy press secretary Larry Speakes. "All the information in this story was given to reporters by Reagan press aides in Santa Barbara, 20 miles from the Reagan ranch," reported Lee Lescaze of the *Washington Post* on Friday, November 27, 1981. "The president has not been seen except on television since reaching his ranch Monday night."[55]

Even the television coverage of Reagan's ranch excursions is spotty. Network correspondents and technicians have located a vantage point three miles from the Reagan spread from which, using telescopic lenses, they can film the president and his Secret Service bodyguards as they ride horses. Viewers have to accept on faith, however, that Reagan is a member of the party being filmed because the figures appear on the television screen as tiny specks.[56]

In August 1981 the president and Nancy Reagan stayed at the ranch for twenty-eight days, two days fewer than Richard Nixon's summer 1969 respite at San Clemente. At one point he invited the press corps to come up the mountain and watch him sign his tax and budget bills, after which he held an impromptu news conference. Despite the presence of his protective aides, a relaxed Reagan responded to all queries and left his audience laughing. "This is the first morning we haven't ridden," he said. "We decided instead that we'd come out and be ridden."[57]

On a week-long western trip in March, 1982, the Reagans stopped off at their retreat for four days of rest. At one point, he hopped aboard his helicopter for a short ride to a nearby cattle ranch for a concert featuring country-western star Merle Haggard. After a cattle-cutting demonstration, in which a trained horse separates a cow from a herd, the president and his millionaire friends dined on barbequed steak and chili beans and sipped wine and beer. Pool reporters following the president, however, had to witness the repast from a bolted cattle pen into which they had been shepherded. Larry Speakes professed to like the arrangement so much that he wanted to take the cattle pen back to Washington with him.[58]

All of the post-Nixon presidents have continued his practice of monitoring the media with a news summary prepared by members of the White House staff. Gerald Ford, unlike Nixon, used his thirty-five to forty-page daily digest to supplement the dozen newspapers he read every day. The first editor of "The President's Daily News Summary" was Philip Warden, a former reporter for the *Chicago Tribune*. He eschewed the editorial remarks that had pervaded the old Nixon product, brightened up the layout, and added political cartoons. A former editor of the *Reader's Digest*, James Shuman, replaced Warden in April 1975 and immediately began to include in the summary articles critical of Ford and his aides.[59]

In the Jimmy Carter White House a staff of five under the supervision of Jody Powell prepared a weekly summary of the contents of dozens of magazines and a daily digest of the stories that appeared in newspapers and on the network newscasts. All of the latter were also videotaped, edited, and replayed over the White House closed-circuit television system twice a day. The president could request a replay at any time. Carter's news summary staff put a great deal of emphasis on negative stories and this, some insiders suspected, reinforced his conviction that the press was his enemy.[60]

Ronald Reagan's news summary office is supervised by William E. Hart, a retired Air Force noncommissioned officer and former director of communications for the Republican National Committee. Each weekday he and his staff of four or five compile two editions of the daily digest: an early version, which goes to top White House officials and cabinet secretaries, and a later one, which gets wider distribution. Each edition averages around twenty pages in length. Special editions containing actual newspaper clippings are prepared periodically on various issues. At the end of each week a collection of political cartoons is assembled and distributed; Hart refers to this publication as the "Friday Follies."[61]

Despite communications director David Gergen's claim that the digest is not used as a news management tool but for "information purposes" only, White House officials have attempted to kill or deflate stories that were seen by the news summary staff prior to actual publication.[62] There is evidence, moreover, that Reagan's aides intended to use the digest for this purpose from the beginning. Shortly after Reagan took office, press secretary James Brady was asked how the president wanted his news summary prepared. Said Brady:

> He's interested in views of newspapers from across the country without regard to where they fall in the political spectrum, and in fact, having a mix, so that we can see how traditional liberal papers regard this, how traditional conservative papers regard this, and then middle of the road coverage. . . .
> We're going to try to work with a regional media program where newspapers that are known for their coverage in certain areas . . . will be selected and clipped. We'll look at how something is received editorially. We'll be able to spot a trend.[63]

Of all the presidents who succeeded Richard Nixon, Gerald Ford had the most difficulty finding and keeping a press secretary who possessed the requisite mix of talents to keep his subjects in check. The first to hold the position was a newsman of thirty-one years experience, Jerald F. terHorst. He was the Washington bureau chief of the *Detroit News*, had known President Ford for twenty-five years, and was held in high esteem by his professional colleagues. He remained in the job one month. On September 8, 1974, President Ford announced he was granting a "full, free and absolute pardon unto Richard Nixon" for all offenses he may have committed during his term in office, and terHorst, convinced that he could not "in good conscience" support Ford's decision, submitted his resignation.[64]

The deputy press secretary, former Justice Department spokesman Jack Hushen, took over for terHorst while Ford's aides searched for a permanent replacement. They settled on NBC correspondent Ron Nessen, a veteran journalist who had been wounded while covering the Vietnam war. After he was presented to White House reporters by President Ford on September 20, Nessen took the floor: "I hope the White House press corps is ready for another Ron. I am a Ron, but not a Ziegler, I can tell you that. I will never knowingly lie to the White House press corps. I will never knowlingly mislead the White House press corps, and I think if I ever do you would be justified in questioning my continued usefulness in this job."[65]

The well-intentioned Nessen then set about to be as helpful as he could, given the constraints of the job. He reorganized the chaotic, forty-five-person press office staff; he wangled permission for a television pool crew to travel on Air Force One with the president; he arranged for follow-up questions to be asked at press conferences; he published a White House telephone book and an organizational chart; he supplied long on-the-record quotes from participants in the meetings he attended; he hid behind a curtain when President Ford visited a seriously ill and hospitalized Richard Nixon and emerged with a full description of the encounter, complete with dialogue.[66]

But try as he might, Nessen could not get along with a press corps that, in the wake of Watergate and the Nixon pardon, was every bit as abrasive as he was. By early October Nessen had been asked 1,074 questions, 477 of them related to Nixon.[67] The press secretary soon began complaining openly that "nobody has given this president the benefit of the doubt."[68] By early June 1975 Nessen's daily spats with the press had degenerated into donnybrooks. On June 6 he tried to explain why a report on the activities of the CIA, prepared by a commission headed by Vice-President Nelson Rockefeller, had not been released as promised. But the reporters who assembled in the briefing room that day were skeptical. One called Nessen a "liar"; another accused him of conducting a "cover-up." After fifty-five minutes of angry exchanges, Nessen abruptly turned on his heel and marched from the room.[69]

Three days later Nessen suddenly stopped his routine briefing and began reading from a prepared statement. "I think that some people here are too quick to make unsubstantiated charges or implications that I am lying or that my credibility has been destroyed," he said. President Ford had been in office for ten months, Nessen continued, glancing at his notes, and this was "more than enough time for this blind, mindless, irrational suspicion and cynicism and distrust to evaporate." The president "is an honest man," the press secretary continued, "and he is a man of integrity and, as press secretary, I have kept the promise I made the first day I took the job." Newspaper readers and television viewers, he said, "are badly served and, in fact, are misled when suspicions are raised about everything said here when there is nothing to base those suspicions on except blind and irrational mistrust and the cynical thinking habits that have built up over the past ten years."[70] Later in the day Nessen called a meeting of reporters and attempted to soften his earlier remarks. "You all know me by now," he grinned, "and you know I don't have an ideal temperament for this job." He insisted to a *Newsweek* reporter, however, that he had acted correctly and had tried to lance "a boil that has been festering for a long time."[71]

The press secretary had many shortcomings in addition to his hair-trigger temper, according to White House reporters. A major complaint against Nessen was that he often gave inadequate or inaccurate responses to questions. Newsmen thus believed he was not close enough to the president or top White House aides to represent their views competently. For his part Nessen admitted to an occasional lack of information, but this did not mean, he said, that he misrepresented the man he answered to: "The central function of a press secretary is to accurately reflect the president's views. Looking back, I can't think of a single time when I didn't do that. A couple of times, I went to Ford and asked, 'Did I miss a signal somewhere?' He said, 'You've got it exactly right.' "[72]

Jimmy Carter's multipurpose tool for the placation, manipulation, and intimidation of the press was his young, charming, handsome, funny, witty, intelligent, self-effacing, down-home, moody, combative, fearsome, hopelessly disorganized, sometimes arrogant and inveterately foul-mouthed press secretary, Joseph Lester Powell, Jr. He preferred a countrified version of his name—Jody—and, indeed, it seemed to complement his drawling, "ain't"-punctuated speech and unpretentious, good-ole-boy demeanor. Powell invariably conducted his daily briefings with a cigarette in one hand, his frame slouched over the lectern, his vest and collar open.[73]

Pity the reporter, however, who was lulled into thinking Powell was a soft touch. He was mercurial, feisty, loyal to a fault, and seldom hesitated to employ his formidable vocabulary of barnyard words to express his displeasure over unfavorable stories. A typical adjective for a negative report was "chickenshit." A favorite verb for the transgression of asking testy questions was "nitshitting." When Powell was in a good humor, he referred to reporters as "you people"; when slightly provoked, he might address them as "you cynical jerks."[74] During the summer of 1977, numerous stories appeared about the muddled personal finances of White House budget director Bert Lance, and Powell was in high dudgeon. In an interview with a *Time* magazine correspondent, the press secretary compared the newsmen on the Lance beat to a pack of hyperactive bird dogs: "You feed 'em and groom 'em and exercise 'em for six months. And then you finally turn 'em loose and they piss all over the truck and bite roots and eat butterflies. They go crazy."[75]

Powell and Carter had what some observers described as a father-and-son relationship, and for the reporters, this meant that when Powell spoke, they were not getting opinion or speculation. They were hearing words that truly reflected the views of the man in the Oval

Office.[76] But for Powell, what appeared to be an asset was in reality a two-edged sword. Said a wire service correspondent who asked to remain anonymous: "It cuts both ways. Being close, he [Powell] can reflect [the president's] views with great accuracy and authority. But at the same time, being so close, he winds up an advocate much more than just a regular press secretary."[77]

White House reporters were forced to pay grudging respect to Powell's intelligence. Speaking of Carter and Powell, *Washington Monthly* editor Charles Peters observed that "both men are extremely intelligent." Peters continued, " 'Jody is as smart as Jimmy, bright enough to be president himself one day,' is typical of what I've heard about Powell."[78]

In July 1978 because of his lack of administrative talents, Powell surrendered many of his duties to image specialist Gerald Rafshoon and concentrated on the care and feeding of the White House press corps. He could smile, stonewall, joke, explode, and sneer with the best of them, and these things he did daily. A brief look at the press secretary in his many manifestations might be useful:

Powell as provider: Whenever reporters traveled with the president, the press plane was always well stocked with good food and liquor. Buses or rental cars were waiting when the plane landed, and luggage was invariably picked up and delivered before reporters reached their hotels.[79] When Carter embarked on a 24,000-mile overseas trip in November 1977, Powell persuaded him to schedule plenty of free time and an extra day in Paris so as not to exhaust reporters. Tired journalists, Powell argued, would tend to write negative stories.[80]

Powell as sweetness and light: During a breakfast meeting with reporters three days after Carter was elected, Powell vowed "a new beginning" in the relationship between the White House and the press. Smiling and joking, the newly appointed press secretary was as ambrosial as a Georgia honeydew as he contemplated the months ahead: "This administration will have the first chance to make a clean break with what has gone on for the past decade with Vietnam and Watergate . . . There is an inclination not only on our part to want to return the relations between the press and government to a more even keel, but I believe I detect that inclination among the press, too. There is a feeling that things may be a bit out of kilter."[81]

As the months passed, Powell exhibited a lust for combat and a predeliction for biting and sarcastic retort. But periodically he would cast aside his nasty mien and declare he would show tolerance for the journalistic skeptics who questioned the Carter view of events. After one such announcement in July 1979, he told a *Washington Post* reporter he thought "it was to everybody's benefit to get things back to normal. I thought I ought not to do anything that unintentionally would rub things rawer. . . . It was time to spread a little oil on the waters."[82]

Powell as stonewaller: Although Powell was an extraordinarily well-informed press secretary, he did not always deem it appropriate to impart the information to which he was privy. "When stonewalling was called for," wrote Hedley Donovan, "he was a master of saying nothing in a dozen different ways."[83] During one briefing in early 1979, the press corps peppered Powell with questions about Iran, Saudi Arabia, the United Nations, China, Taiwan, Cambodia, Namibia, Mexico, a presidential luncheon, and some insulting remarks about a few of the president's friends that had been uttered by his brother Billy. Virtually every query was met with an "I don't know," an "I can't comment," or an "I can't answer that." When asked about Billy Carter's suggestion that he, Powell, retire to a south Georgia farm, the press secretary responded: "I think I have said on several occasions regarding the comment that I would be better off running a farm in south Georgia is something to which I can hardly take exception, particularly in situations such as I find myself today." A few minutes later a reporter posed "one final question: If you do go back to south Georgia to be a farmer, will you do a good job at it? As well as you have in briefing us with all of this information?" Powell paused, took a drag on his cigarette, and answered: "I don't know."[84]

Sometimes the press secretary crossed the line from stonewalling to dissembling and, on at least one occasion, to outright lying. Throughout the spring of 1980 when Iran was holding American hostages who had been seized when the U.S. embassy in Tehran was ransacked in November 1979, Powell consistently dismissed suggestions that the administration was considering a military rescue mission. At one point he led reporters to believe that the White House would wait until mid-May 1980 before making such a decision. On April 24 a rescue team landed in an Iranian desert but was forced to turn back because of equipment failures. Eight American commandos died when a helicopter crashed into a transport plane. Afterward Powell admitted he had deliberately misled, and occasionally lied to, the press: "I gave responses to questions that I felt were necessary to protect our mission. I'm sure if I went back I could find ways that I could have handled my responses more skillfully. But there's no question that my intent, my motive, was a conscious one. If I had to do it over again, I'd do it."[85] After his confession Powell anticipated that an uproar of protest would force him to resign. But reporters remained curiously mute, and he stayed on.[86]

Powell as farceur: "He gets away with murder by just being so witty and funny," said Fred Barnes of the *Washington Star* about Powell. "You can see it happen, but you also see it works."[87]

Indeed it did. During the 1976 campaign, former Georgia governor Lester Maddox called a press conference and denounced Jimmy Carter as a prevaricator. Responded Powell, "Being called a liar by Lester Maddox is like being called ugly by a frog."[88] Powell participated in a panel discussion during a 1978 convention of the American Society of Newspaper Editors and listened quietly as columnist Jack Germond commented on Jimmy Carter's performance. "There is a perception in the country that Jimmy Carter is in trouble," said Germond and added: "I don't mean the same kind of trouble that teen-age girls get into." "In some cases," responded the press secretary, "at least figuratively, the cause can be the same."[89] When Nancy Collins, a gossip columnist for the *Washington Post*, alleged in 1977 that White House chief of staff Hamilton Jordan "never wears—in fact, has never owned—a pair of underwear in his whole life," Powell replied: "Hamilton Jordan does not wish to respond to questions about his underwear. It is his position that the author of that piece will be the last one to know, one way or the other."[90]

Powell as Momus: Like the Greek god of censure and mockery, Powell seemed to take delight in railing and carping, and it was difficult to discern at times whether he was trying to be cute or whether he was being snide. Observed one person who knew Powell well, "I think that in a very important part of his body psyche, he has a great contempt for the press." John Osborne once noted that Powell "shares with Carter a basic distrust of the media. He is very thin-skinned and it resurfaces now and then."[91]

At a White House briefing in the spring of 1977 a reporter inquired about some of United Nations ambassador Andrew Young's controversial statements on the subject of Angola. "It is difficult to say," Powell responded, "knowing even less about Angola than many people who write about it."[92] A reporter telephoned Powell early in 1977 to ask about the president's nominations to government jobs. Wasn't it true, the newsman wanted to know, that Carter—while promising a new beginning—was really appointing many of the same old Democrats who had been in and out of government for years? "You just keep on talking, Jim," the press secretary said, "and I'll try to think of a euphemism for 'crock of shit.' "[93]

Powell as tartar: The press secretary truly enjoyed swapping insults with reporters, but his biting remarks often devolved into tasteless, angry aspersions. During Carter's 1976 *Playboy* interview, for example, the candidate called Lyndon Johnson and Richard Nixon liars, cheaters, and distorters of the truth and later implied that the magazine was responsible for the "unfortunate juxtaposition." Carter eventually admitted it was his own "mistake," but the confession came only after relentless questioning by reporters. Powell blew up, accused the Carter press entourage of 'nitshitting," and stalked off. A reporter who had not been present later told the press spokesman he was "sorry to have missed your daily snit." Powell smiled and said, "It was no snit. It was a calm and reasonable discourse, on my part, with a couple of assholes of the press."[94]

Powell's snits continued off and on throughout Carter's administration. The press secretary lapsed into prolonged fits of rage when the president's health adviser, Dr. Peter Bourne, was accused of using a fictitious name on a drug prescription, when budget director Bert Lance was forced to resign because of questionable banking practices, and when Hamilton Jordan was reported to have doused a woman's chest with a mouthful of Amaretto and cream.[95] Powell's cynicism seemed to grow worse toward the end of Carter's term. "The last two years strained Powell terribly," said *Time* magazine's White House correspondent Chris Ogden. "He got a lot of defenses up. He got very uptight about reporters."[96] By the time he left the White House, according to some accounts, the press secretary was bitter and angry. Powell put it this way: "After four years, I do find myself with a greater degree of sympathy for presidents in general, Democratic and Republican, and the problems they face in trying to lead the country and explain why they are doing what they are doing. It's reasonable to be concerned that the press, as an institution, is making any president's job unnecessarily difficult and in some cases almost impossible."[97]

Ronald Reagan's press handler, deputy press secretary Larry Speakes, is no Jody Powell. Speakes is not an insider or a stand-up comic, but he is a good provider and a capable stonewaller. He works hard, attempts to be helpful, is accessible to reporters, and is generally regarded by them as a decent and honorable presidential spokesman. "Speakes is good at his job," said Robert Timberg, White House correspondent for the *Baltimore Sun*. "He's pleasant, generally accommodating. I see him for what he is, a spokesman."[98] Lou Cannon of the *Washington Post* concurred: "Larry is underrated. He can be very helpful and he's generally honest."[99]

Operating on the Nixon-Ziegler theory that a contented press is a quiescent one, Speakes pays great attention to the professional and personal needs of journalists. On the Reagan trip to Barbados, for example, he included in the presidential party five technicians who carried portable labs to develop photographs for the press.[100] During Reagan's lengthy vacation at Rancho del Cielo in August 1981, Speakes arranged a sumptuous press reception: tenderloin filets wrapped in bacon, smoked salmon, scampi au Pernod, fettucini Alfredo, oysters on the half shell, escargots wrapped in French dough, and assortments of cheese and fruit.[101]

While the presidential entourage was in California that August, the White House press room was closed for repairs. When they were completed, the old furniture was gone and in its place were neatly arranged theater chairs affixed with plates bearing the names of news organizations with regular correspondents at the White House. The change was made, said David Gergen, in an effort to "produce a more productive atmosphere in the press room." But what Gergen and Speakes were really trying to do, some reporters suspected, was subdue and control journalists to a greater extent by giving the press room an aura of formality.[102]

Speakes conducts two briefings a day: an informal one in his office for a small group of reporters at 9:15 A.M. and the formal session at noon or shortly after for all members of the White House press corps. The noon briefings, he has said, are "so much of a ritual stage play."[103] And they are. In order to force the press to focus on a single issue each day, Speakes enters the newsroom prepared to talk about one subject. When other matters are raised, he goes into a subtle stonewalling act. "Doesn't anyone have a question on a different subject?" he will say. Or, "Is there a serious question anywhere here?"[104]

When the U.S. ambassador to Saudi Arabia, Robert Neumann, resigned for personal reasons in July 1981, rumors circulated that he had been fired for criticizing Secretary of State Alexander Haig on Capitol Hill. Asked about the scuttlebutt, Speakes responded: "You people have been in this town long enough to know what goes on in these things and to draw your own conclusions, and you know what we're going to say from here."[105] On a hot afternoon in August, 1982, Speakes' topic of the day was the president's views on tax legislation. As he was reading some of Reagan's quotes from a meeting with congressmen, a reporter interrupted. "If you really want us to take this dribble down, you've got to go slower," he said. Speakes patiently continued but was stopped again, this time by Sarah McClendon. "Choke it down, Sarah," Speakes said. "I've got a little bit more."

Before the briefing was over, Lester Kinsolving had inquired about President Reagan's stand on necrophilia, bestiality and sodomy. Said an exasperated Speakes: "This is a foolish briefing . . . I tell you what: I challenge any news organization here to reprint this briefing in full in their newspaper."[106]

Unlike Jody Powell Speakes plays his role as enforcer with a gentle touch. His occasional outbursts of anger are mild compared to those of Carter's press secretary. Once ABC's Sam Donaldson insisted on referring to a Reagan proposal for additional taxes as a request for a "tax increase." Speakes corrected him. "Deficit reduction, Sam," he said. Donaldson objected and Speakes cut him off. "This is not a debate society, Sam," said the press secretary. "If you want the facts, I'll be glad to give them to you. If you want to debate, I'll bring on a debater."[107]

The only major grievance that journalists seem to have against Speakes is that he lacks access to President Reagan and his top aides and therefore cannot reflect their views with credibility. "Speakes' access is limited," said Chris Wallace of NBC. "He is only as good as his guidance."[108] AP's Jim Gerstenzang agreed: "Speakes has less personal access to the president [than Jody Powell]. He's well informed to the point the staff wants him to be."[109] Lou Cannon, however, thought that Speakes was speaking with greater authority with each passing month. "His access has improved," Cannon said in June 1983. "He has become a lot better informed, a lot more so in the last three or four months."[110]

In a report published in December 1975 the National Press Club praised Gerald Ford for improving relations between the president and the news media, especially for "restoring regular White House press conferences." At that point he had been in office sixteen months and had held twenty-three news conferences.[111]

Ford's press conference record was testimony to his courage and perseverance: The subject reporters most wanted to talk about in the first months of his term was the one he most wanted to avoid—Richard Nixon. As Ford approached his first meeting with the press, in fact, he was determined to set himself apart: "Throughout my political career, my relations with reporters had been excellent, and I was really looking forward to my first press conference on August 28. Nixon's press conferences—when he'd had them—had often turned into surly, belligerent confrontations which, in my opinion, had demeaned both the president and the press. I was determined to get off to a different start."

To emphasize that Ford was not a Nixon, the president dictated some changes in the press conference format. Reporters were moved closer to the podium from which he spoke; a blue curtain that had been used by Nixon as a television backdrop was removed and the president's lectern was symbolically positioned in front of an open door; Nixon's heavy, bulletproof lectern was discarded in favor of a narrower one.

The news conference, however, did not go as well as Ford had hoped. The reporters in attendance seemed interested mainly in Richard Nixon, and afterward Ford was discouraged. "Was I going to be asked about Nixon's fate every time I met with the press?" he wondered. He had been "hoping to have press conferences every two or three weeks. I realized now that I'd be questioned repeatedly about [Nixon] and his many legal problems."[112] His pardon of Nixon only worsened his problems with the press. At his second press conference, on September 16, he was asked twenty-two questions; fifteen concerned the pardon or the former president's papers and tape recordings.[113]

The Nixon issue eventually dissipated, and Ford went on to become one of the most accessible presidents ever to hold the office. In the twenty-nine months of his tenure he held 39 press conferences, granted 200 interviews, and had 133 other contacts with reporters. According to Ron Nessen, "I don't think I ever suggested an innovation in press relations when Ford didn't say, 'Let's try it.' "[114]

When he took office, Jimmy Carter promised to hold two press conferences a month, but it wasn't simply an overriding passion for the democratic process that compelled him to make the vow. "It is good public policy for Americans to see their leader grilled," explained Carter's media adviser, Barry Jagoda. "It is also good television. People watched the space shots because they knew each time something might go wrong and the astronauts could be burned up before their eyes. We want that kind of authenticity, that sense of natural vulnerability and of being on top of things."[115]

The risk factor was enhanced somewhat by Carter himself. He did not like to prepare for press conferences and refused to conduct practice sessions. Some two or three hours before a news conference was scheduled to begin, he sat down with briefing books assembled under Jody Powell's supervision. About fifteen or twenty minutes before the press conference, Carter met with Powell, Gerald Rafshoon, and other aides to hear the points they thought ought to be emphasized and to clear up any questions he had. The president then strode onto the stage to face his inquisitors, and he invariably laid them low.[116]

The president's political career conceivably hung in the balance, for example, when he stepped in front of the cameras on August 4, 1980, in an hour-long effort to defuse a controversy surrounding Billy Carter. Beginning in 1978 the president's younger brother had struck up a relationship with the radical Arab government of Libya. He had visited that country twice, had hosted Libyan visitors to the United States, and on hearing that American Jews might be unhappy with his actions had riposted: "They can kiss my ass as far as I'm concerned now." Then the Justice Department had learned that Billy had accepted $220,000 in "loans" from Libya and had forced him to register as a foreign agent. Meanwhile the president had asked national security adviser Zbigniew Brzezinski to exploit Billy's Libyan connection to secure Tripoli's help in the Iranian hostage situation. By late July a Senate subcommittee was probing the "Billygate" scandal, and prominent Democrats were searching out ways to deny Carter the presidential nomination at the upcoming convention.

During his press conference the president took questions from twenty-three journalists. He had not known until July 15 that Billy had taken money from the Libyans, Carter claimed. He had indeed sought Billy's help in the hostage crisis and "that may have been bad judgment. I did what I thought was best for our country and best for the hostages, and I believe that's exactly what Billy was doing." He had no authority to order Billy around, said the president. "Billy is a colorful personality," he said. "I love him and he loves me."[117]

Little was disclosed about the Billy Carter affair that was not already known, but the press conference and a ninety-nine-page White House report that was dispatched to the Senate subcommittee seemed to convince the country that Carter and his top aides were innocent of any illegality or impropriety. Of the one thousand telephone calls and telegrams to the White House that immediately followed Carter's performance, over 84 percent were favorable.[118]

Claiming that the Iranian hostage crisis and other matters of state required his total concentration, Carter adopted the Nixon Rose Garden strategy and holed up in the White House during the winter of 1979–1980 while his Democratic opponents, chiefly Senator Edward Kennedy, vied for delegates in the primary elections. The president's sessions with reporters during this period invariably had political overtones. On March 14, 1980, four days before the Illinois primary, he held a prime-time press conference, the first eleven minutes of which were devoted to a statement about his anti-inflation plans. On April 1 he convened a highly unusual 7:18 A.M. news conference to announce that progress had been made toward a resolution of the Iranian hostage crisis. The president's appearance, coincidentally, came just minutes before the voting booths opened in the Wisconsin and Kansas primary elections.[119]

Despite a haughty, even disdainful attitude toward journalists, Carter made mighty efforts to render himself available to the press. They were the efforts of an automaton, but they were efforts. In addition to his fifty-nine press conferences, Carter held fifty-eight meetings with out-of-town news executives and editors, conducted twenty-eight briefing sessions for foreign reporters, and had a multitude of informal contacts with domestic newsmen. All told, his on-the-record meetings with the press numbered nearly six hundred.[120]

Ronald Reagan's abysmal press conference record suggests that he approaches them with more reluctance than any other president since Richard Nixon. Between his inauguration and the midterm elections of 1982, he held thirteen news conferences, precisely the same number as Nixon. Eisenhower convened fifty press conferences in that period during his tenure; Kennedy held forty-four, Johnson (between his inaugural in 1965 and the midterm elections in 1966) held forty-four, and Carter held thirty-nine.[121]

Some of Reagan's critics believe that his disinclination to face the press in formal situations stems from his lack of enthusiasm for the arduous preparation required for the task. Others say he suffers a loss of confidence when reporters zero in on his miscues.[122] There is no question, though, that he considers his press conference confrontations burdensome. When Helen Thomas of UPI closed a September 1982 session with the traditional, "Thank you, Mr. President," Reagan breathed a sigh of relief and replied, "Helen, thank *you*. I thought you'd never say it."[123]

The president's aides seem to share his attitude. Press conferences, said one White House official, are "minefields to be tiptoed through periodically, but not something you hope to get a lot out of politically." Said another aide, "A virtuoso performance at a press conference may impress the press corps and a few sophisticated people. But it's not where most Americans are going to get their estimate of his job performance. Press conferences are more to be looked at from a hazard point of view, because blunders can hurt you more than a virtuoso performance can help."[124] That does seem to be the primary reason for Reagan's lack of ardor for news conferences. When answering questions off the cuff, he tends to speak haltingly, garble his replies, and stumble over facts. In a press conference on January 19, 1982, for example, he defended his unemployment record and cited a number of statistics to bolster his case. Each figure he cited was incorrect. At his next press conference he pulled some papers from his inside suit pocket and waved them at his inquisitors. Referring to the stories that had appeared about the errors he had made a month earlier, he said, "I'd like you to know that documentation proves the score was five to one in my favor." In the following few minutes, he went on to make three misstatements about the history of U.S. involvement in the Vietnam War. He also confused Nicaragua with El Salvador and stated that the United States was supporting covert activities in the former. He quickly corrected the mistake.[125]

For this reason Reagan's media team has taken extraordinary steps to tighten control over the press conference format. Prior to the president's sessions with reporters, he is provided with briefing books on domestic and foreign matters. He is then rehearsed, sometimes twice, with aides playing the role of reporters. Usually Reagan's staff is able to anticipate all but one or two questions that are asked.[126] The sessions have been switched to prime time so television journalists do not have the opportunity to edit the videotapes of his appearances for the nightly news shows; seating assignments are arranged for reporters so the president knows where the "known friendlies" are located; photographs and names of journalists are provided to Reagan so he can call on correspondents of his choice and refer to them by first names. This gimmick backfired, however, in January 1983 when the president pointed toward his audience and called out the name "Bob Thompson." Thompson, the Hearst newspapers' Washington bureau chief, was at home watching the press conference on television. The room fell silent for a few seconds until Reagan called on someone else. A few minutes later the president pointed to a section of the audience and said "Al." There was no "Al" there but another reporter alertly jumped up and asked a question.[127]

Following a disastrous press conference performance on June 16, 1981, Reagan waited fifteen weeks before holding another one. He finally consented to meet the press again on October 1 and began poring over his briefing books several days in advance. He also studied a thirty-eight-page compilation of questions and answers assembled by his staff. On the day before the press conference, David Gergen, Larry Speakes, and several other aides met with the president in the White House cabinet room, fired questions at him for an hour, and critiqued his answers. The process was repeated again that afternoon. At lunch on the day of the conference, Reagan and his media team once again reviewed the responses they wanted to give to the anticipated questions. When the president strode into the East Room to face reporters that afternoon, he demonstrated how a professional actor who has rehearsed his lines can steal the show. Why was it, one newsman asked, that Wall Street seemed to have little confidence in his economic policies? Well, said the president, he just happened to have in his pocket a letter from Security Industries Association president Edward O'Brien proving that Wall Street was in fact behind him, and he proceeded to read the letter. Wasn't he concerned about the effects of his cuts in domestic programs? Well, said Reagan, let's just take a look at the "block" grant programs that were going to replace the old "categorical" grant programs. He held up a thick stack of regulations that were used to administer the categorical grants and compared them to a thin stack, which he said were all the rules needed for his block grants. On and on he went, smoothly citing facts and figures. As the press conference ended with reporters still waving for recognition, Reagan smiled and said, "I always hate to leave those uplifted hands. We ought to have a three-hour press conference."[128]

Overall Ronald Reagan and his media specialists have executed appeasement and evasion tactics with a more masterful touch than any administration that has occupied the White House since television came of age. Witness the testimony of an expert, Jody Powell: "They're doing a damn good job that I frankly did not think you could get away with in this day and time. They've been able to get reporters on the things they want them on and away from the things they don't want them on."[129]

Reagan is aware that he has been enormously successful in his efforts to go around and over the press in order to deliver undiluted messages to the public. In a statement reminiscent of a remark made by John Ehrlichman a decade earlier, Reagan told reporters in mid-1982: "I know that what we've been doing doesn't read well in the*Washington Post* or the *New York Times*, but, believe me, it reads well in Peoria."[130]

Evasion

Gerald Ford was a traditionalist who had served in the political trenches for twenty-five years, but media advisers and image specialists were important members of his White House staff from the beginning. Shortly after he was sworn in, he hired Robert Meade, a producer for CBS News, as a television adviser. As the 1976 elections drew near, a curly-haired, former stand-up comedian and television writer-actor named Don Penny joined the president's staff as a special consultant. A while later advertising specialists Peter Dailey and Bruce Wagner went to work for Ford's campaign organization; they were later replaced by advertising executive James J. Jordan, and he was subsequently supplanted by media experts John Deardourff and Doug Bailey. Another television consultant, William Carruthers, also advised the president during the campaign; Carruthers had once worked as a consultant for Richard Nixon and had directed or produced such commercial programs as "The Newlywed Game" and "The Dating Game."[131]

The media merchants told Ford what to wear, they advised him which events made good television and which did not; they wrote words for him to say and taught him how to say them. They converted Ford into a competent television performer. Considering what they started with—a long-winded mossback politician who, by his own admission, dressed like an undertaker—that was no small accomplishment.[132]

If Richard Nixon brought public relations specialists out of the closet, Jimmy Carter rendered them respectable. He and his media experts made little effort to disguise their activities; they accepted their machinations as normal behavior, showed no remorse or embarrassment. Said NBC News president Richard Wald, "There is a difference with these [Carter] people. It's not that they are doing things that differently than Nixon or Johnson did. It's that they are a new generation and they're less troubled by doing it. They take manipulating television for granted."[133]

Indeed they did, and it started at the top. Jimmy Carter was not a great television performer but he was a skilled one. Although cold and aloof in person, he projected an image of confidence and familiarity, and he possessed an actor's instinct for timing and cadence. "The camera is kind to him," observed David Halberstam, "it heightens his strengths—a strong sense of himself, a good smile, a face wonderfully American, born of a thousand Norman Rockwell covers."[134] One of the president's television advisers, Barry Jagoda, explained that in Carter's case, the camera converted a restrained personality into a normal one: "President Carter has a low key personality, and it tends not to be magnified by television the way others can be. The average guy can come across very ebullient. Television helps bring Jimmy Carter up to perceived normalcy."[135] Carter himself was well aware of his video talent, accepted it, and used it to his advantage. "Mr. Carter is the first occupant of the White House to treat television as an American institution," Barry Jagoda once said.[136]

Wherever Carter traveled a bevy of aides ensured that his activities were properly covered by the networks. On a visit to Yugoslavia in June 1980, for example, a flatbed truck carrying television crews moved out so fast that the cameramen could not film Carter and Yugoslav president Cvijetin Mijatovic, who were traveling behind in a limousine. White House advance man Richard Moore pounded on the roof of the cab and ordered the Yugoslav driver to slow down. The truck sped on. Behind them the presidential limousine stopped and Carter bounded out and plunged into the crowd to shake hands. A photo opportunity was being lost and Moore was furious. He jumped on the running board of the truck and shouted at the driver: "Stop this truck, you son of a bitch, or I will personally rip your lungs out." The matter was eventually straightened out—the driver had been following the radioed instructions of a superior official—and Carter made the evening news.[137]

Detailed plans for the manipulation of television were worked out even before Carter was sworn in. Pollster Patrick Caddell advised the president elect in a seventy-page memorandum that the people were not confident that they knew him and were uneasy. Caddell's solution was to continue campaigning for another ninety days after assuming office. Carter bought the proposal and launched what *Newsweek* magazine dubbed "Operation People."[138] Ideas bounced around the Carter media shop: the president should hold regular "town meetings" with citizens in different localities; he should spend a day and night with an ordinary family in the hinterlands, maybe even attend a PTA meeting with them; he should randomly select some average Americans and invite them to sup at the White House.[139]

One member of the Operation People team, Barry Jagoda, was dubbed media adviser to the president and went about his self-described task of ensuring that the interests of the White House and the networks were "in harmony" with the ardor of a child let loose in a toy store. Before Carter had been in office a hundred days, he had addressed the nation in a "fireside chat," had conducted a televised town meeting in Clinton, Massachusetts, had invited NBC cameras into the White House to record a "typical" working day, and had hosted the first Dial-a-President show, which was broadcast by the CBS radio network and moderated by Walter Cronkite.[140] Jagoda was ecstatic. He weighed proposals for more televised town meetings and additional call-in shows. One of his ideas called for Carter to conduct televised "conversations" with artists and novelists—perhaps a "conversation about alienation" between the president and writer Saul Bellow. "We've got the biggest star in television," Jagoda exclaimed at one point. "Jimmy Carter may be the biggest television star of all time."[141]

The paramount public relations expert in the Reagan White House is Michael Deaver, a forty-five-year-old publicist who worked with the president when he was the governor of California and has been with him off and on since. He is extremely close to both Ronald and Nancy Reagan and protects their interests zealously. Deaver carries the title of deputy chief of staff, but most of his energies are devoted to the Reagan image. He reviews the speeches turned out by the speechwriting staff; before a Reagan appearance he often supervises the placement of television cameras.[142] Deaver seems to be particularly adept in the use of defensive public relations techniques. He is sensitive to charges, for example, that Reagan is a disengaged president who would rather cut brush on his ranch than attend to the affairs of state. When Reagan headed west to host a state dinner for Queen Elizabeth II in late February, 1983, Deaver scheduled several additional official events to give the impression that the president was tirelessly serving the public.[143]

Every morning Deaver reviews the day's schedule with the president's senior staff members. The news event of the day is discussed and photo opportunities are planned. Each Wednesday and Friday Deaver chairs meetings with other White House image specialists and maps out the media strategy for the coming weeks. There is no effort, as there was in the Nixon White House, to keep the media team's machinations secret. Deaver spoke openly of his role to reporter Juan Williams of the *Washington Post*:

You know, I've been in public relations, in public affairs work, and you are always trying to protect your client and show him in the best light. And so you are looking for positive things to do, because you know the press is continually looking for the negative. That is a professional relationship that I understand and the media understand. So we spend a good deal of time trying to show the positive aspects of this administration. . . .

In other words, the press is on a kick, some negative response to this president or this administration, maybe it's foreign policy, maybe it's domestic policy. Okay, what are we going to do about it? And we kick out various ideas from a scheduling standpoint, from a communications standpoint, to get at that. Now that . . . you call that managing the news. I call that defending our record.[144]

The second most important media merchant in Reagan's administration is communications director David Gergen, who seems most adept at offensive public relations strategies and specializes in "long-range planning." Put another way, he ponders how to manipulate events and reporters for the president's benefit. He attempts to put what he calls the proper "spin" on the news and sometimes even reviews the videotapes shot by network camera crews and suggests how they be used on the nightly news shows.[145] Like Deaver Gergen makes no attempt to disguise his motives: "I don't see what goes on here as manipulation. There is a certain sense in which the White House is theater and we put on our show. Particularly with the advent of TV, the White House has become more and more theater, and it is not unnatural that White House staffs over the years have become more and more the station managers. They want to run the show." Gergen, who worked for both Nixon and Ford, attends Deaver's public relations planning sessions, and he once explained how they work: "We sit down with a detailed schedule for the next three or four weeks, and we also have a block schedule for thirty to sixty days. . . . We look at things on the schedule with an eye toward the story line we are trying to develop that week or that month, and other things you put on the schedule because they are good events in and of themselves."[146]

Most of the media team's efforts are directed toward the manipulation of television news. Network correspondents and technicians are handled with great care, much to the chagrin of print reporters. On the evening in July 1980 that Reagan accepted the GOP nomination in Detroit, his advance men led a press pool through the subterranean chambers of the arena to a predetermined vantage point. At one set of locked doors, television cameramen and still photographers were permitted to pass, but newspaper and magazine reporters were barred. "We started pounding on the doors, but we didn't get in," said Laurence Barrett of *Time* magazine. "They don't give a damn about the print people. They were only interested in getting the cameras up there."[147] In the White House, network correspondents are given front-row seats at press conferences and are guaranteed they will be given the opportunity to ask questions of the president.[148] In September 1982 Reagan's aides scheduled a press conference for 8 P.M. on a Tuesday night. Officials at ABC were upset because the news conference conflicted with their successful Tuesday night entertainment programs, and the network's vice-president for news called David Gergen to complain. The White House communications director obligingly rescheduled the president's appearance for 7:30 P.M.[149]

Reagan's television advisers are also adept at using the medium in defensive ways. While traveling with the president on the West Coast in October 1982, for example, they learned that the Commerce Department would be releasing figures showing the unemployment problem was getting worse. Arrangements were hastily made for President Reagan to sign an export-promotion bill while touring Los Angeles harbor. The ceremony originally had been scheduled for the following week in Washington.[150] The day after Reagan delivered his State of the Union address in January 1983, he took off on a quick trip to Boston. Why that particular day? Said David Gergen: "We all wanted to have a trip the day after the State of the Union because the next day the press goes to Capitol Hill for reaction. We had to find a way of keeping the attention on the president."[151]

The star of the show that Deaver and Gergen stage each day is Ronald Reagan. No other politician has ever entered the White House with more experience in playing roles. After graduation from Eureka College in Illinois, he worked as a radio broadcaster. Five years later he passed a screen test and began acting in films. During his twenty-seven-year, fifty-four movie career, he played lawyers, doctors, scholars, scientists, artists, musicians, reporters, athletes, soldiers, lawmen, crooks, and even a Secret Service agent. He learned how to hide his emotions and how to feign them. He learned a sense of timing and pitch, when to pause, nod, and smile. He learned how to shed tears on cue. He polished what he has called "that easy, conversational, persuasive sell."[152]

In 1954 Reagan signed a contract to host a series of television dramas sponsored by the General Electric Co. and to act as a roving spokesman for the company. Over the next eight years, he gave over nine thousand speeches and talks on behalf of the firm.[153] In the mid-1960s he moved into politics and in 1966 won the California guber-natorial race. During the campaign, he told an aide: "Politics is just like show business. You have a hell of an opening, coast for a while and then have a hell of a close."[154]

That, some observers argue, is precisely how Reagan has approached the presidency. *Washington Post* television critic Tom Shales has called Reagan "the first true Prop President, one whose real self is the image on the TV screen and whose shadow self is the man in the White House. Behind the scenes, the counselors take over; out in front of the curtain, Ronald Reagan is wowing the crowds."[155]

Among the many ways the post-Nixon presidents used and continue to use television to wow the crowds are these:

Speeches: When the president speaks before a live audience, he usually receives some sort of television coverage; Gerald Ford was no exception. But he occasionally experimented with the format, and one gimmick he tried was the double-whammy speech. In October 1974 Ford un-veiled a major anti-inflation drive with a nationally televised appearance before a joint session of Congress. The heart of his program would be an effort to mobilize the citizenry through private groups and organizations; everyone would be educated to turn down their ther-mostats, drive less, and clean their plates. The campaign would even have a slogan: "Whip Inflation Now" (WIN). When Ford faced the cameras and the congressmen, he was wearing the first WIN button on his lapel: "Only two of my predecessors have come here in person to call upon Congress for a declaration of war, and I shall not do that. But I say to you that our inflation, our public enemy number one, will, unless whipped, destroy our country, our homes, our liberties, our property and finally our national pride as surely as will any well-armed wartime enemy. I concede there will be no sudden Pearl Harbor to shock us into unity and to sacrifice, but I think we have had enough early warnings. The time to intercept is right now. . . . My friends and fellow Americans, will you enlist now?"[156]

The second half of the twofold television effort came a week later when Ford provided some details in a speech before the annual convention of the Future Farmers of America in Kansas City. He wanted his appearance televised, but the networks refused. Ron Nessen angrily filed a formal request for coverage, and the networks complied. But CBS apologized to its viewers for interrupting regular programs, and a CBS executive served notice on the White House that future requests for coverage would be carefully scrutinized.[157]

Jimmy Carter sometimes took advantage of televised speeches to announce dramatic shifts in policy. The 1980 State of the Union address was just such an occasion. In May 1977 Carter had informed a commencement audience at the University of Notre Dame that the United States was no longer inordinately afraid of communism and could thus attempt to use the power of persuasion, as opposed to military might, to convince the Soviet Union "that one country cannot impose its system of society upon another" by force. When Soviet tanks rolled into Afghanistan in December 1979, Carter appeared to see the invasion as a personal betrayal. In his February 1980 speech he informed the Congress, and his millions of viewers, that if the oil fields of the Persian Gulf were threatened, the United States would be prepared to fight: "Let our position be absolutely clear: An attempt by any outside force to gain control of the Persian Gulf region will be regarded as an assault on the vital interests of the United States of America. And such an assault will be repelled by any means necessary, including military force."[158]

The expertise of Reagan and his media team in using props, graphics, and metaphors was evident from his very first speech, the inaugural address, which was delivered for the first time from a platform erected on the west side of the Capitol building. Reagan faced west toward the majestic Washington monument, the Lincoln Memorial, Arlington National Cemetery, and the grave of John F. Kennedy. In essence the memorials were turned into props, for as Reagan referred to them, CBS cameras cut to shots of them.[159]

For sheer political theater, nothing Reagan could do could surpass his speech on the economy to a joint session of Congress on April 28, 1981, thirty days after a would-be assassin's bullet was removed from his left lung. The president's image specialists were keenly aware of the drama of the moment and wanted it to be "pumped for everything we can." But Reagan instinctively realized that the scene should not be overacted. "I want them [the television viewers] to be able to say at the end that I didn't exploit the shooting," he told his aides. His intuition proved correct. As he entered the chamber, congressmen and dignitaries surged to their feet in wild acclaim. As he spoke, he was interrupted by applause twelve times. He thanked the American people for their support. He praised his wounded press spokesman, James Brady, and the Secret Service agents and District of Columbia policemen who had protected him. He pulled out a letter from a second-grader from New York who had written to the president, "I hope you get well quick or you might have to make a speech in your pajamas." The audience erupted in laughter. And they continued to cheer loudly as Reagan moved on to other subjects, finished, and weaved his way through the crowd to the exit. Haynes Johnson of the *Washington Post* called him a "smash."[160]

Chats and addresses: President Nixon had demonstrated that informal addresses aimed directly at television audiences were valuable end-running and image-molding tools, and Gerald Ford followed his example. In January 1975 he executed a variation of the double-whammy—a fireside chat–formal speech combination on energy and the economy—to salvage his image as a strong leader. The president decided he would prepare the nation for his State of the Union speech with a television address two days earlier. In his autobiography Ford admitted he had his image foremost in mind: "I knew much depended on the way I delivered those two speeches. If I came across as a Chief Executive fully in command of the situation, I could win the support I needed to push my programs through the Congress. If, on the other hand, the public viewed me as weak and indecisive, I would decline in their esteem to a point from which I could not hope to recover."[161]

Ford had a history of fluffing his lines, so his media experts decided he should rehearse. A complete mobile television unit—a truck, two cameras, and technicians to operate the equipment—was rented, and Ford practiced his speech at least six times, then reviewed his performance on videotape. The small, cluttered, cozy Lincoln library on the ground floor of the White House was chosen as the setting, and special noncrackling logs were brought in for the fire. Acting on his media team's advice, Ford changed his position several times as he spoke; he sat at a desk, leaned against it, stood beside it. As he finished his virtually flawless performance, his advisers were ecstatic. "We did it! "We did it!" shouted Ron Nessen. The State of the Union speech, delivered two days later, was received with considerably less enthusiasm.[162]

One of Jimmy Carter's most memorable addresses aimed directly at the television audience was his first: the FDR-style fireside chat delivered as part of Operation People. Although the president planned to discuss several serious subjects, principally energy conservation, he and his aides were clearly more concerned with how he appeared than with what he said. While the chat was being planned, several major debates erupted among the White House image men. What should the president wear? A business suit, a sport coat, and a slacks-and-turtleneck sweater combination were ruled out for various reasons. Finally Barry Jagoda came up with a compromise solution: a beige cardigan sweater, shirt, and tie. Where should the speech be given? The Oval Office and the family living quarters were eliminated and the Lincoln library chosen. So a smiling Jimmy Carter sat in a Chippendale chair beside a three-log fire, his fingers arranged in a church steeple to convey thoughtfulness, and told the American people to turn down their thermostats.[163]

No other president, however, has ever been better at conducting chats with television viewers than Reagan, the Great Communicator, and few have been more adept at using the medium for pure political advantages. Several weeks before the 1982 midterm elections, for example, the White House learned that an announcement would soon be made that unemployment had surpassed 10 percent for the first time since the Great Depression. The speechwriters were called into the Oval Office and given instructions; David Gergen telephoned the Washington bureau chiefs of the three networks and asked them to extend coverage to a "nonpartisan" presidential speech. The fact that the address would be delivered about two weeks before the voters went to the polls, Gergen argued, was coincidental; it would be a genuine news event.[164] Over the objections of top Democratic party officials, NBC and CBS consented.[165] On October 13, after several rehearsals, the president went on the air and declared that his economic programs were working, with the exception of the unemployment problem, which always lagged behind in a recovery. Colorful electronic graphics were used for the first time.[166] Reagan ended his "nonpartisan" speech with the slogan that Republicans had been using in their campaign advertisements: Americans could return to prosperity, he said, by "staying the course." Commented Robert Kaiser of the *Washington Post*, "It was one of the great 'screw you' lines of recent American history."[167]

Interviews: Ford was comfortable with reporters, projected that image during interviews, and therefore used the format frequently. During January 1976, for example, he filmed an interview with NBC's John Chancellor, answered questions for forty minutes on CBS's "Sixty Minutes" show, and appeared on CBS's "Face the Nation" and ABC's "Issues and Answers."[168]

Like all other chief executives Carter participated in many television interviews while in the White House, but it was during the political season that he most adroitly manipulated the format. While other Democratic candidates campaigned for the primary elections in the winter of 1979–1980, Carter remained in the Rose Garden under the pretext of being preoccupied with the affairs of state, chiefly the Iranian hostage situation. But as the inaugural event of the primary season, the Iowa precinct caucuses, approached, he decided he needed a forum to remind the people that he had been leading while other pretenders had been politicking. He explored the possibility of advancing the date for his State of the Union address, but congressional leaders reminded him that lawmakers were in recess and might be reluctant to return early for the purpose of advancing his political fortunes. So Carter accepted a long-standing invitation to appear on NBC's "Meet the Press" on January 20, one day before the Iowa caucuses. The president regarded the interview program as a legitimate news show, explained Jody Powell, and Carter would appear only because he felt "an obligation to keep the American people informed."[169]

One of President Reagan's interviews that showed him at his thespian best came during a Barbara Walters special, "Ronald Reagan, at Home on the Ranch," aired on the ABC network on the day after Thanksgiving 1981. The first half of the hour-long program was devoted to shots of Reagan chopping wood, feeding his horse, and riding in a Jeep. In one scene he stood on a mountain and said, "God really did shed his grace on America, as the song says." Walters then talked with the president about his programs, his associates, his "toughest decisions." He spoke about the attempt on his life and expressed his sorrow that he endangered the lives of those who accompany him outside the White House. Overall observed Tom Shales of the *Washington Post*, the show was "warm, folksy, western, rosy, cuddly, cute" and an "engrossing encounter with Reagan."[170]

Announcements: When a president wishes to say something to the nation, all he has to do is snap his fingers and television crews appear to film it. Most of the time the televised announcement is used to project a specific image or create a particular effect. On July 8, 1975, for instance, television crews at the White House were summoned to film Gerald Ford's announcement that he would be a candidate in 1976. Ron Nessen later revealed why this particular format was chosen for the event: "The statement, delivered from the president's desk, lasted only three minutes. There were no crowds, no campaign hoopla. We staged the event so as to convey the impression of a busy president stealing a few minutes from official business to make a routine announcement of his candidacy, then quickly returning to the burdens of his awesome duties."[171]

During the Billy Carter–Libya scandal Jimmy Carter decided to make a preemptive attack. He appeared in the White House press room and announced he was eager to testify before the Senate subcommittee investigating his brother. He wished to appear "at the earliest opportunity," he said, "the sooner the better." The television networks interrupted their regular programs to carry Carter's announcement live.[172]

Ronald Reagan has used the televised announcement to demonstrate that he is a forceful, decisive leader unafraid of crises. When the nation's air traffic controllers went on strike in August 1981, the president assembled reporters and camera crews in the Rose Garden and announced that the controllers "are in violation of the law, and if they do not report for work within forty-eight hours, they have forfeited their jobs and will be terminated." Two days later he followed through on his threat and fired the striking controllers.[173]

Staged events: As Jimmy Carter's aides were preparing for a presidential roadshow to Latin America in March 1978, *Wall Street Journal* correspondent Dennis Farney asked Barry Jagoda for permission to go along on a preadvance excursion to Venezuela. (The preadvance is an exercise in which White House media specialists, advance teams, and network producers visit a location weeks ahead of the president, preview his every move, and stake out spots where the cameras will be set up.) Jagoda turned the reporter down: "I won't cooperate with you in any way." So Farney took a commercial flight to Venezuela and was waiting when Jagoda and several network producers arrived in a White House jet. The correspondent watched and listened as the preadvance team anticipated Carter's paces. A presidential speech was arranged for 8:25 A.M. (7:25 A.M., Eastern Standard Time, perfect for the networks' morning news and feature shows) in a tiny room in the

Venezuelan capitol. Local officials, however, did not want the American television crews present because Venezuelan cameras might be crowded out. An ABC producer objected: "I understand it's their squalid little congress. But it's our president, and we have a right to cover him." The Venezuelans relented but not without complaint. "We are friendly to Carter," said the director general of information. "We realize his trip is primarily oriented to the audio-visual media, so we try to cooperate with him." But the White House and network officials were bursting with "cultural arrogance," he said. "They think we're stupid Indians. They think we can't do anything right."[174]

Ronald Reagan's presidency is probably the best staged one in history, thanks to his acting abilities and the expertise of his media specialists. While the Reagans were vacationing in California in August 1981, one of his assistants, Joseph Canzeri, arranged a presidential visit to the aircraft carrier USS *Constellation* in the Pacific. It turned into a television spectacular featuring aerial acrobatics and mock bombing runs. A reporter heard about the event a few days in advance and told Canzeri it should take place "in the morning so we can make the deadlines." Canzeri responded, "Why do you think we're doing this?"[175] In August 1982 during a two-day trip designed to bolster Reagan's image as a leader deeply concerned with issues, the presidential entourage stopped off at an Iowa hog farm where Reagan was to be videotaped eating homemade ice cream and discussing agricultural problems with farmers. At the last minute Michael Deaver ordered that all sound equipment be removed. When asked why, he replied that it was a "picture story."[176]

A quintessential stage-managed event occurred on February 4, 1983, the day before President Reagan's seventy-second birthday. David Gergen announced that the president would hold an impromptu mini-press conference, and all television networks decided to carry it live. As Reagan was answering questions, his wife walked onto the stage carrying a birthday cake. The president sliced it, and pieces were handed out to the television correspondents in the front rows. When ABC's Sam Donaldson asked if Reagan had any observations to make on his birthday, Reagan replied that it was "just the thirty-first anniversary of my thirty-ninth birthday." That would have made him seventy years old instead of seventy-two. *Washington Post* White House correspondent Lou Cannon explained how Reagan could have made such a mistake: "The line was born during the 1980 presidential campaign, when Reagan's strategists sought to defuse concern that he was too old by conspicuously celebrating his birthday with a series of parties before his opponents could get around to observing it. Once

Reagan commits a one-liner to memory, it is sure to surface again." The party dragged on, and one by one network officials decided to return to their regular programming. "We put the president on the air because of the news potential, not for cutting a birthday cake," NBC bureau chief Robert McFarland later griped. "We were surprised. We were not happy." Rejoined a White House aide: "They want to run their game shows rather than our game shows."[177]

Local events: The post-Nixon president who best exploited the "local event" format as a gimmick for end running the press and delivering his message undiluted to the public was Jimmy Carter. The vehicle he invented to do this was the so-called "town meeting." Citizens in local areas around the country were assembled in high school auditoriums or other halls, and Carter—usually after pausing to doff his coat and roll up his sleeves—took questions from them. He was at his populist best in such situations—sincere, informal, friendly, personal, a man of the people. He often took the names and addresses of his questioners, promising to write them with more complete answers.[178]

Carter was invariably a hit with his audiences, but that was a by-product. The most important benefit of the thirty-odd town meetings he addressed was the fact that they almost always were accorded saturation coverage by the television and radio stations in the states where they were held. And the networks frequently covered the presidential question-and-answer sessions, often as the lead story, on the nightly news shows.[179]

The questions he was asked at town meetings, Carter often said, were more reflective of the problems of ordinary Americans than the queries presented by the national press corps. Washington reporters greeted this spurious reasoning with incredulity. Hugh Sidey of *Time* magazine put it this way: "There really is a contrived drama here that is pitched to television. These town meetings for a president really are kind of phony in a way. The questions are not that sharp. . . . Some of that is kind of a taveling road show to give him exposure to build his base. They ought to be identified as what they are, not as great sessions of enlightenment."[180]

To prove the point the *Washington Post* listed some of the questions Carter had been asked at town meetings:

• What part of your job is the hardest? What part of your job do you enjoy the most? And do you get dizzy flying in Air Force One? (Bangor, Maine, February 17, 1978.)

• How would you like to be the first president of the United States to honor us by being a member of the Beaver Castle Girl Scouts? (Aliquippa, Pennsylvania, September 23, 1978.)

- I'd like to know if I can have a kiss? (Elk City, Oklahoma, March 24, 1978.)

- I know what I want to say, first of all, is really unprofessional and un—what am I trying to say?—not really related, but I think you're really cute. (Spokane, Washington, May 5, 1978.)[181]

The White House media merchants know that the way in which a president is perceived by the public is just as important as, if not more so, than what he actually says. This means they must strive to see that the president projects a positive image, as well as protect him from anything that could cause the public to view him negatively. Put another way, they employ both offensive and defensive image techniques. The offensive methods can be divided into three general categories.

The president as leader. Looking like a leader requires telegenic mingling with world statesmen. Jimmy Carter's first trip abroad—a post-Christmas 1977 jaunt to Poland, Iran, India, Saudi Arabia, France, and Belgium—was covered by 166 traveling journalists, including 75 network technicians and correspondents. They faithfully beamed the president's activities back to the United States but balked when Barry Jagoda requested that Carter's New Year's greeting from Tehran be covered live.[182] Even when a foreign trip was impossible, Carter found ways to project the image of a leader deeply involved in international affairs. In March 1977, two months after he took the oath of office, he outlined his foreign policy goals before the United Nations. The General Assembly was not in session at the time, but Carter insisted it be convoked to hear his views.[183]

Looking like a leader also calls for displays of stoic disinterest in mundane politics. This was the purpose of the Rose Garden strategy that kept Jimmy Carter in the White House for six months while other Democrats campaigned in the 1980 primaries. He was preoccupied with the Iranian hostage crisis and the Soviet invasion of Afghanistan, he said, and he took steps to make sure the public got the message. In late December 1979 Jody Powell dispatched to the Oval Office a "memo" advising Carter to accept an invitation to debate Senator Edward Kennedy and California Governor Jerry Brown in Iowa. Across the bottom of the memo Carter scrawled his response: "I can't disagree with any of this, but I cannot break away from my duties here, which are extraordinary now and ones which only I can fulfill. We will just have to take the political consequences and make the best of it. Right now both Iran and Afghanistan look bad, and will need my constant attention." The "memo" was then leaked to the wire services.[184]

Like Richard Nixon, Reagan and his aides attempt to make it appear that he is unconcerned with his image. The president is a relaxed man who is comfortable with himself, his associates say; he watches television news and reads the newspapers but is not particularly interested in stories about himself and how he is performing his duties.[185]

Perhaps Reagan is not preoccupied with his image, but his media specialists are. They worry about his casual work habits and his demonstrably vague grasp of key issues. They therefore struggle daily to develop public relations ploys that will establish the image of a chief executive who is immersed in his work and in command. When reporters for a magazine visited the White House to record a "typical day" in the life of the president, Reagan's aides scheduled a ten-hour day for him and loaded his calendar with meetings. "That wasn't a day in the life," one high-level official later joked, "that was a week in the life."[186]

During the summer of 1983 it was disclosed that in 1980 Reagan's aides had been privy to internal documents taken from the Jimmy Carter camp, including a briefing book used to prepare Carter for his nationally televised debate with Reagan. The president dismissed the affair as "much ado about nothing," but congressional and FBI investigations subsequently were launched, and the White House media team began to fear a negative public reaction. Would Reagan be perceived as not in control of his staff or reluctant to become involved in the situation? Something had to be done, and something was. At the daily press briefing on July 8 Larry Speakes informed reporters that Reagan had earlier in the day interrupted a meeting of his senior staff members to order them to cooperate fully with the FBI. "We want to get to the bottom of this and we want it out in the open," Speakes said Reagan said. "It was," the press secretary added, an "eye-to-eye session with his senior staff."[187]

The president as nice guy. When Gerald Ford was sworn in, he realized he had to act immediately to reassure the nation that he was not another Nixon. He informed the Marine band that played at presidential functions to eschew "Hail to the Chief," ordered the removal of all listening devices in the Oval Office, and eliminated the Sunday worship services at the White House. Television crews were invited into the presidential kitchen to film Ford as he toasted his own breakfast muffin. Members of the president's staff and cabinet were asked to suggest the names of individuals with whom Ford could conduct well-publicized telephone chats. This public relations gimmick was formally known as the "Presidential Telephone Call Recommendation Program."

When Ford sat down to make a "spontaneous" call, he was provided with a memorandum of "background notes" and "talking points."[188]

Portraying Jimmy Carter as "just folks" was the major preoccupation of his media team. Shortly after he was elected, Jody Powell announced that Carter wanted to break out of the "rather strange and unnatural world composed primarily of staff and press and other political people" and was instructing a group of associates "to study ways to make the president more accessible to the people of the country and the people more accessible to the president." The public was invited to send ideas to People, P.O. Box 2600, Washington, D.C.[189] During his 1976 *Playboy* interview, Carter took out needle and thread and began repairing a rip in his jacket. "Say, do you always do your own sewing?" asked the interviewer. "Uh-huh," replied Carter as he bit off the thread with his teeth.[190]

Periodically Carter buttressed his image as a people's president by paying calls on the common folk. After his first town meeting in Clinton, Massachusetts, he bunked for the evening with local beer distributor Edward Thompson, his wife, and eight children. The president entered the house, kissed Mrs. Thompson, took off his coat and tie, plopped down on the sofa between two of the daughters, and proclaimed that he felt right at home. After snacks and small talk, Carter retired at 10:30 P.M. At 6:30 A.M. he arose, made his bed, and took a shower. Before he left he wrote notes to the youngest Thompsons' teachers. "Memo to teacher from Jimmy Carter," said one of them. "Please excuse Jane for being late. She had a guest in her house."[191]

Ronald Reagan is a natural nice guy, so there is little need for a concerted effort to portray him as such. His sense of humor tends toward the self-deprecating. During a budget confrontation with Congress in November 1981, for example, he ordered government employees — except for "essential workers" — to close their offices and go home. An interviewer asked him if he were an "essential worker." Reagan replied, "No one told me whether I was or not. I sat there in the office just in case somebody tried to take over."[192]

Although a vigorous effort to promote a nice guy image for Reagan is not necessary, his aides do try to reinforce it from time to time. During the campaign they released posters of the candidate wearing plaid shirt, jeans, cowboy hat, and his characteristic warm, skewed grin. On Valentine's Day 1983, the media team arranged for network camera crews to follow the president as he visited a drugstore to buy some cards for Nancy.[193]

On May 3, 1982, a story appeared in the *Washington Post* about a suburban Maryland black couple who had been awarded damages in a civil suit they filed after members of the Ku Klux Klan burned a cross on their yard. That afternoon, the couple was paid a visit by the president and his wife and a horde of reporters and cameramen. The story of what had happened was courteously relayed to newsmen by Larry Speakes: The president had read the newspaper report, had informed Michael Deaver he wanted to see the couple, and had rushed through his busy schedule so he could find the time. Reagan and his entourage boarded one helicopter, reporters boarded another, and off they went. While the First Couple talked with the black couple, Larry Speakes took notes so he could pass exact quotes to newsmen. "I came out," the president said, "to let you know that this (the cross burning) isn't something that should happen in America." Hugs and kisses were exchanged, a White House photographer took pictures, and the president and his wife departed—precisely one-half hour after they had arrived and just in time for television reporters to make their evening news deadlines.[194]

The president as more noble than his opponent: This approach—similar to Richard Nixon's dump-on-McGovern strategy—is designed to make a president look good by making his opponent look bad. A few weeks before the 1976 elections, for example, some of Gerald Ford's aides began spreading rumors that Carter had been involved in extramarital love affairs while serving in the Georgia state senate. Many reporters heard the gossip, but none found it to be true.[195] When Carter came under intense criticism for remarks he made in his interview with *Playboy* magazine, Ford was quick to inform reporters that he too had been asked by the magazine to sit for an interview but had refused. "I don't think the president of the United States ought to have an interview in a magazine featuring photographs of unclad women," he said.[196]

From the beginning of his political career, Jimmy Carter displayed a predilection for demeaning his opponents, and his media advisers reflected a similar attitude. They were ecstatic when Reagan was nominated to carry the Republican banner in 1980. He was demonstrably probusiness and antilabor; he advocated the relaxation of consumer and environmental protection laws; he had spoken out against welfare and Social Security; and most important, he was a hawk on matters of defense and the national security. All they had to do, Carter's advisers believed, was research and attack Reagan's record; having been handed the ball, the press would run with it.[197]

The barrage began with Carter's acceptance speech at the Democratic convention. Former actor Ronald Reagan, thundered the president, lived in "a world of tinsel and make-believe," a world in which "all problems have simple solutions. Simple—and wrong." Reagan, Carter continued, would launch an arms race that "could put the whole world in peril." The anti-Reagan rhetoric grew harsher as the campaign wore on. In September Carter accused the GOP candidate of being a racist. In October Reagan was labeled a threat to world peace. That same month, with Reagan leading in the polls, Carter suggested to party supporters that the election would decide "whether Americans might be separated, black from white, Jew from Christian, north from south, rural from urban."[198] Wrote *Time* magazine columnist Hugh Sidey: "The wrath that escapes Carter's lips about racism and hatred when he prays and poses as the epitome of Christian charity leads even his supporters to protest his meanness."[199] During his October 28 debate with Reagan, Carter coldly, methodically, and relentlessly pursued the attack. Fourteen times he used such adjectives as *radical*, *ridiculous*, *disturbing*, and *dangerous* to describe the Republican's positions on various issues. On five of his nine turns at the microphone, Carter alluded to Reagan's alledgedly menacing attitudes on the issue of war and peace. The president's debate strategy failed; most major pollsters declared Reagan the winner.[200]

Reagan and his campaign team countered the Carter attacks with some fusillades of their own, but for the most part they lacked an equivalent rancor. "The failed presidency and President Carter's lack of leadership will be major themes of this campaign," said Reagan's chief of staff, Ed Meese, during the GOP convention in July 1980. As the weeks passed Reagan accused Carter of creating "a severe depression in our nation" and adhering to farm policies that were an "unprecedented disaster."[201] In late October Carter told reporters that Reagan did not understand the problems of the presidency, and the Republican candidate shot back by raising the volatile issue of the American hostages in Iran, which he had rarely mentioned before:

Well, you know, for once I agree with him—he's hit it right on the nose. I don't understand why we have had inflation at the highest peacetime rates in history. . . . I don't understand why his answer to inflation was to put two million people out of work. I don't understand why mortgage rates are at fourteen percent.
I don't understand why our defenses have weakened, why American prestige has fallen abroad, why Afghanistan is now occupied by the Soviet Union [and] why there is massive instability in the Persian Gulf region. . . . And lastly, I don't understand why fifty-two Americans have been held hostage for almost a year now.[202]

It was left to Reagan's campaign spokesman, the caustic Lyn Nofziger, to level the cruelest blow at Jimmy Carter. When a completely false rumor spread in September that Reagan had suffered a heart attack, Nofziger was furious. "I'll tell you who started it," he told reporters. "The White House. Now, I'm going to start another rumor. Write this down. Jimmy Carter has the clap."[203]

For all their offensive public relations talents, the media advisers who serve the presidents cannot prevent occasional indiscretions. So they must also practice the defensive arts: protection of the presidential image. It was in this area that the Gerald Ford media team's mettle was truly tested. Ford had an irremediable habit of fluffing his lines, of tripping over his own feet, of walking innocently into awkward situations. He made a farm policy speech at Iowa State University and referred to it as Ohio State. He wrestled with the name of California senatorial candidate S. I. Hayakawa and it came out "hire-a-cow-a." He was presented with a football helmet four sizes too small and twice whacked the top of his bald pate trying to get it on. He tripped on the ramp of Air Force One in Salzburg, Austria, and fell several feet to the tarmac. He bumped his head on helicopter doors and on the side of a swimming pool.[204]

Because of Ford's accident-prone ways, his aides had to maintain what amounted to an around-the-clock, emergency, image-salvaging service. In an effort to demonstrate that the Ford White House was a citadel of good-natured folks, for example, Ron Nessen agreed to act as the guest host for an April 1976 edition of NBC's popular program of satirical comedy, "Saturday Night." The series featured a young comedian named Chevy Chase, who specialized in portraying Gerald Ford as an oaf who bumped into desks, tripped over rugs, and understood little that was said to him. Nessen participated in several skits as Chevy Chase, playing his Ford role, stapled his ear to his head, walked into a flag, affixed his signature to his hand, and attempted to stick a vase of flowers in his lapel.[205]

Because Jimmy Carter was widely perceived as ineffectual and was prone to periodic lapses, his image specialists were also obliged to develop a defensive capability. Shortly after Carter's *Playboy* interview was published, for example, he traveled to San Francisco for his second debate with President Ford. He arrived at the private residence where he was to rest before the debate and discovered that his host was a collector of nude paintings and statuaries. One of his aides, Greg Schneiders, asked the owner of the residence to remove the nudes lest some photographer snap a picture of the candidate looking at them.[206] Even as Americans were lining up at the gas pumps in June

1979, the OPEC cartel announced yet another hike in the price of oil. In a memo to the president White House domestic policy adviser Stuart Eizenstat outlined the problems the crisis was causing and advised Carter to seize the moment and use OPEC as a scapegoat for the nation's economic and energy problems: "I honestly believe we can change this to a time of opportunity. We have a better opportunity than ever before to assert leadership over an apparently insolvable problem, to shift the cause for inflation and energy problems to OPEC, to gain credibility with the American people, to offer hope of an eventual solution, to regain our political losses. We should seize this opportunity now and with all our skill. . . . With strong steps we can mobilize the nation around a real crisis and with a clear enemy— OPEC."[207]

Ronald Reagan's image protectors work arduously to overcome Reagan's seeming inability to stick to the script and his prediliction for using unverified facts and figures as the basis for what some aides call his "parables." While campaigning in New Hampshire in February 1980, candidate Reagan told an ethnic joke about a Pole who took a duck to a cockfight and an Italian betting on it and the duck winning because the Mafia had the event rigged. A reporter who heard about the joke asked Reagan to repeat it, and he did. In the ensuing months, he persisted in shoring up his antigovernment ballyhoo with spurious statistics. Vietnam veterans were not eligible for GI benefits, he erroneously charged. The federal government had 144 regulations on the use of ladders, he claimed; there were, in fact, 2.[208]

August was an especially memorable month for Reagan bloopers. He expressed the opinion that the biblical account of creation ought to be taught in public schools. He irritated officials of the People's Republic of China by calling for close U.S. ties with Taiwan. He defended the Vietnam war as a "noble cause." Holding forth on environmental subjects, he later claimed that trees and volcanoes pollute the air as badly as automobiles and defended man-made oil slicks on the grounds that natural oil slicks had been floating off the coast of California "as long as the memory of man."[209]

There has been no improvement in Reagan's gaffe-prone ways since he entered the White House. In August 1982 he strolled into the Rose Garden with Liberian leader Samuel K. Doe and introduced him to the press as "Chairman Moe." Returning from a trip to Latin America in December 1982, the president declared to reporters that he had "learned a lot." He continued, "You'd be surprised. They're all individual countries." After almost every press conference, the White

House media team has been constrained to correct the president's mistakes or explain points he was trying to make.[210].

The president's image specialists are thus forced to keep their defensive machinery well oiled. They are sometimes disconcerted, for example, by Reagan's passion for vacations. By Labor Day 1982 he had taken 12 extended holidays for a total of 110 days—an average of about a week off for every 5 weeks of work. In an effort to stave off a spate of fun-in-the-sun stories when Reagan traveled to Barbados in April 1982, White House officials invited journalists to take their families along. "We figured it would be a lot harder for them to write vacation stories if they were vacationing themselves," said one of the president's aides.[211] Following a visit with the president in October 1982, Nobel prize-winning economist George Stigler was taken to the briefing room to speak to the press. The seventy-one-year-old University of Chicago professor was a free-market advocate, so he was expected to have nothing but praise for Reagan's conservative "supply-side" approach to the economy. Instead Stigler allowed that the nation was in a "depression" and that supply-side theory was a "gimmick" and a "slogan that was used to package certain ideas." Reporters were still peppering Stigler with questions when a White House press aide interrupted and led him from the stage.[212] When Interior Secretary James Watt decreed that rock-and-roll groups could not participate in the 1983 Fourth of July festivities on the Washington Mall, one of the musical groups precluded was the Beach Boys. The relatively staid ensemble happened to be a favorite of Ronald and Nancy Reagan and they were embarrassed by the deluge of critical news stories about Watt's asinine edict. The president sent for the Interior Secretary, awarded him a fiberglass foot with a hole in it, and directed him toward the waiting television cameras. A sheepish Watt dutifully ate his plate of crow and said Reagan had given him the "award" for "shootin' yourself in the foot."[213]

Each White House office of communications since 1974 has clearly been modeled on the propaganda apparatus invented by Richard Nixon and Herb Klein. Indeed one of Klein's top assistants, Margita White, remained with the Ford administration for a while to see that the communications office ran smoothly.[214] Even before Jimmy Carter was sworn in, Jody Powell summoned Klein to Washington for a private conference.[215] Ronald Reagan's director of communications, David Gergen, worked in the Nixon White House as a speechwriter; he stayed on with Gerald Ford and supervised the office of communications during the 1976 campaign.[216]

The manner in which the office of communications is used to court the hinterlands press through the use of fact kits, regional press briefings, White House briefings, and miscellaneous gimmicks has been detailed. But there is another function that falls within the purview of the director of communications that deserves examination: coordination of executive branch public information officers.

Under the old Klein system, this job was performed by deputies, but Jody Powell apparently wanted to do it himself. Before Jimmy Carter's inauguration Powell drew up a list of candidates for the major PIO jobs and issued an edict that no one not on the list could be hired without first being interviewed by him. One person interviewed for a cabinet-level public affairs position reported that Powell had emphasized the necessity of good relations with the press. But, the interviewee added, Powell "also kept talking about 'close contact' between him and me. I felt I was watching the creation of Jody's own little cabinet."[217]

Powell did indeed maintain close contact with the departmental PIOs. He held regular meetings with them, advised them on the content and timing of announcements, and dismissed charges that he had set himself up as an information czar on the ground that it was important for "the White House and the agencies to be moving along the same wavelength."[218] When Gerald Rafshoon joined the Carter staff in the summer of 1978, he assumed the task of getting the departmental PIOs to march in lockstep with the White House. It apparently proved a difficult undertaking for him: "It just got to the point where you know they [the PIOs] are going to outlast us. We had these PIO meetings and I got to the point where I knew they were going back to their department and ignore everything. They have different priorities. . . . They are interested in survival in Washington. . . . If I had been there in the beginning, I would have formed the PIOs from our organization. To me there's only one name that's going to be on the ballot, Jimmy Carter."[219]

In the Reagan White House PIO coordination is handled by a subdivision of the office of communications called the public affairs section.[220] The true extent of the coordination surfaced in January 1982, when the president's chief of staff, James Baker, dispatched a memorandum to top administration officials to remind them and their subordinates that television appearances and print interviews had to be cleared in advance with the White House.[221] Larry Speakes and David Gergen acknowledged that certain senior officials were required to notify the White House of their television appearances but insisted this was a "coordination process and not a clearance process." Speakes later added that coordination of television appearances by administration officials was done to avoid duplication and insisted that no one had been instructed to clear their newspaper and magazine interviews with the White House.[222]

Intimidation

As closely as Gerald Ford followed Richard Nixon's example in the way he used propaganda, television, and image-shaping techniques to end run the press and take his message directly to the people, there was one way in which the thirty-eighth president was the antithesis of his predecessor: Ford refused to become involved in direct confrontation with the press.

Ford's strongest criticism of journalists came in the wake of his second debate with Jimmy Carter, on October 6, 1976, in San Francisco. "There is no Soviet domination of Eastern Europe," the president blithely declared, "and there never will be under a Ford administration." When pressed to expand on his remark, Ford asserted that Yugoslavia, Romania, and Poland were independent and autonomous.[223] His comments sparked a rash of critical news stories and, as Ron Nessen put it, Ford "broke one of his basic rules of political life and openly criticized reporters." Even so his remarks to a group of New York newspaper and broadcasting executives were hardly in a league with Nixon's diatribes: "I am frankly disappointed that there was not a better, more thoughtful analysis [of the debate] in the news media. Ninety percent of what has been written . . . [involved] one sentence. . . . There was such a concentration on that one point, ignoring virtually everything else, that I think the news media didn't give a full and accurate picture of the substance in many of the questions and many of the answers."[224]

Probably because Ford did not believe in intimidation as a tool for the manipulation of the press, the record of his years in the White House is remarkably devoid of efforts to bludgeon reporters into submission. There were, of course, numerous attempts to influence reporters and editors to print and broadcast stories the way the White House saw them, but there was no conspiracy to intimidate the press, no use of the CIA, FBI, IRS, FCC, or the Justice Department to hound journalists. There were some efforts to plug leaks but no White House plumbers willing to use any tool, even murder, to protect the national security, or the president's political security.

Whatever discipline reporters received during the Ford years was usually meted out by press secretary Ron Nessen. As the 1976 campaign got underway, he became even more discomposed than usual. "I'm tired of taking it on the ear" from reporters, he screamed after one tumultous briefing in September.[225] When John Dean appeared on NBC's "Today" show and charged that Ford had cooperated with the Nixon White House to scuttle an early Watergate investigation in Congress, Nessen telephoned Richard Wald, president of NBC news. They argued for several minutes and finally Nessen shouted: "We are not getting anywhere this way. I am just going to tell you we are going to win this election and you are going to be left with shit on your face."[226]

There was a sustained effort in the Ford White House to stem the flow of unauthorized information to the press. One of the world's most polished leakers, Secretary of State Henry Kissinger, complained in April 1975 that the White House press office was leaking negative stories about him, and Ron Nessen promptly fired one of his assistants, Louis M. Thompson. Nessen later claimed he had planned to dismiss Thompson anyway, but the press secretary let Kissinger believe it had been done to appease him.[227]

Ford and his associates were never renowned for efficacy, however, and the leaks continued. On September 10, 1976, less than two months before Ford would be voted out of office, the deputy White House chief of staff, Jim Cavanaugh, was compelled to lecture Ron Nessen for leaving confidential briefing papers for the president lying around the press office.[228]

Although Jimmy Carter's attitude toward the press was similar to Richard Nixon's, he largely avoided Nixon's mistake of attempting to beat reporters into submission. Indeed, the few efforts he did make to intimidate jounalists were pedestrian compared to those of Nixon. A month after he took office, Carter met with the *Washington Post*'s executive editor, Benjamin Bradlee, in an attempt to convince the newsman he ought to drop a story which disclosed that King Hussein of Jordan had been secretly receiving a million dollars a year from the CIA. Much to Carter's chagrin the *Post* published the story twenty-four hours later.[229] Because he did not like *New York Times* reporter James Wooten, Carter refused to grant that newspaper an exclusive interview until Wooten was removed from the White House beat in March 1978.[230] Once an Associated Press photogragher caught Carter jogging around the White House flower gardens in his shorts; an order was subsequently issued to the president's guards to use force if necessary to keep the press off the grounds while Carter was running.[231]

On occasion Carter found it difficult to contain his contempt for journalists. Several times during the 1976 primary campaigns, he lost

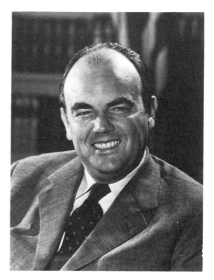

H. R. Haldeman, assistant to
President Richard Nixon, May
1971. (Official White House
photograph)

John Ehrlichman, assistant to
President Richard Nixon,
December 1972. (Official White
House photograph)

Jeb Magruder, deputy director of communications for President Richard Nixon, January 1970. (Associated Press)

Ronald Ziegler, press secretary to President Richard Nixon, March 1969. (Official White House photograph)

Charles Colson, special counsel
to President Richard Nixon,
August 1970. (Official White
House photograph)

Herb Klein, director of communications for President Richard Nixon, May 1971. (Official
White House photograph)

Gerald Ford and press secretary Ron Nessen, December 1974. (Official White House photograph)

Jerald terHorst, press secretary for President Gerald Ford, September 1974. (Associated Press)

Jody Powell, press secretary for President Jimmy Carter, April 1980. (Associated Press)

Nancy Reagan, Ronald Reagan, and press secretary James Brady, January 1981. (Associated Press)

David R. Gergen, director of communications for President Reagan, January 1981. Gergen also served in the administrations of Presidents Nixon and Ford. (Official White House photograph)

Larry Speakes, deputy press secretary for President Ronald Reagan, September 1983. (Associated Press)

his temper and snapped at reporters in his entourage. Once he interrupted a reporter in mid-question: "Do you want to stop talking so I can give you my answer or do you want to go ahead and ask a second question as well?" At a press conference in Peoria, Illinois, Carter offered to answer queries from the national press and then "turn to the more substantial questions from the local press."[232] This was apparently one of his pet peeves: During his 1976 *Playboy* interview he censured the "national news media" for having "absolutely no interest in issues *at all.*"[233] He was sensitive about the "issues" issue, perhaps, because his own pollster, Pat Caddell, had informed him that the "leading Carter negative" in one of his surveys "was the category 'not specific, wishy-washy, changes stands.' "[234]

Four years later Carter was still blaming the press for his own failures and problems. As the 1980 elections approached and it became increasingly apparent that he would not be able to bring home the American hostages then being held in Iran, he pointed the finger at journalists: "One thing that concerns me a lot lately has been a buildup in the American press—television, radio and newspapers—of expectations that the hostages are going to come home early that I don't think are justified."[235]

Carter believed the *Washington Post* was his greatest nemesis among the nation's newspapers. He took time during cabinet meetings to complain about the *Post*'s coverage of his actions. In a letter to Benjamin Bradlee the president groused that the newspaper had given wide coverage to John F. Kennedy's 1962 trade negotiations but had virtually ignored similar efforts by the Carter administration. As did Richard Nixon, Carter fulminated about the *Post* in his diary. On September 1, 1977, for example, he wrote, "The *Washington Post* is conducting a vendetta against Bert [Lance] and has apparently ordered two front-page stories about him each day. This morning, for instance, they had nine separate stories about Lance—headline stories—throughout the paper. In contrast, the *New York Times* didn't mention him."[236]

Although Carter's scoldings of the press were infrequent and relatively temperate, Jody Powell's were not. The press secretary's displeasure was often provoked by the slightest errors or contextual discrepancies. "Powell will complain about anything," said Fred Barnes of the *Baltimore Sun.* "Once he called me several weeks after a story appeared and complained about a quote or something in the fifteenth or sixteenth paragraph. . . . It was an extraordinarily minor point in the story."[237]

One of Powell's favorite targets was NBC White House correspondent Judy Woodruff, who had covered Carter as the governor of Georgia.

While floating down the Mississippi with the president aboard the *Delta Queen*, Powell took offense at one of Woodruff's questions and snapped, "Judy, I know you can't find any place to get your hair done along the river, but you don't have to take it out on me."[238] During a speech in Los Angeles in October 1980, Carter painted Ronald Reagan as a warmonger and Powell was forced to admit the president's charge was an "overstatement." He offered some mitigating evidence in the form of old Reagan quotes on matters of war. ABC and CBS used Powell's material; NBC did not. Aboard the press plane, he set out in search of Woodruff. Curtis Wilkie described the scene: "Employing the tone he uses when he tries to intimidate reporters, Powell told Woodruff he could not believe her network had ignored his material and asked if NBC planned to use it on the *Today* show the next morning. Woodruff . . . calmly told him that a spot on the topic had been filed. She showed no interest in pursuing the argument, so Powell returned to his seat somewhat mollified, but still muttering about the sins and stupidity of the networks."[239]

Occasionally Powell attempted to bully journalists. In September 1977 Rowland Evans and Robert Novak published a column about a telephone conversation between Jimmy Carter and Reverend Billy Graham during which, said the columnists, the preacher and the president discussed Bert Lance's problems and the negative manner in which the press was reporting the affair. In a letter to the *Washington Post* one day later Powell charged that the Evans and Novak column was "virtually a total fabrication."[240] Correspondents of the major news magazines visited Powell's office in July 1979 for their regular weekly briefing and found themselves being instructed to toe the White House line. "I've been talking to other top people around here in the White House," said Powell, "and they have the impression they spend an inordinate amount of time talking to the . . . news magazines. And they're beginning to think that perhaps all this time is a waste of time because their views are not reflected in the news columns." According to Jack McWethy of *U.S. News & World Report*, "Clearly he was trying to intimidate us and it was a very low-key threat that if somehow our stories were not more reflective of the views of the senior staff, our access would be cut off. . . . Losing access to the senior staff at the White House is akin to cutting off your left arm."[241]

The efforts of the Carter White House to plug information leaks could not be described as plumbing in the Nixon sense, for invariably they were directed at suspected leakers rather than at journalists. But the intended effect was intimidation of reporters, albeit indirectly.

In the spring of 1978 the administration launched a government-wide campaign to locate leakers and exert greater control over the distribution of classified information. According to an account in the *New York Times*, "Sources report that high-level concern over the flow of information has become as great as it was in the early months of the Nixon administration."[242]

The crackdown affected me in a personal way. Following a news-gathering trip to Turkey in May 1978, I filed a report for Jack Anderson on a confidential assessment by U.S. ambassador Ronald Spiers of an anti-American speech by Prime Minister Bulent Ecevit. Spiers, in a classified cable to the State Department, had characterized Ecevit's address as "mindless nationalism." Shortly after the story appeared the State Department, on instructions from the White House, ordered an internal investigation to find the persons who had leaked the cable. Anderson then wrote a story about the probe. "Sometimes," he began, "it seems as if Richard Nixon never left town."[243]

A month later Carter himself tried to stem the leaks from Capitol Hill. He called a meeting of congressional leaders and declared that disclosures of unauthorized information from Capitol Hill sources amounted to an "epidemic." As a result, he complained, intelligence sources were refusing to cooperate with the United States, and the national security was in jeopardy. Reporters later pressed Jody Powell for specific examples, arguing that without them the president's case lacked credibility. Powell refused to provide details and fumed, "I really don't give a damn whether you believe it or not."[244]

During the third year of his presidency, Carter's anxiety over leaks appeared at times to devolve into paranoia. On February 5, 1979, CBS State Department correspondent Marvin Kalb reported that administration officials believed the government of Iranian Prime Minister Shahpour Bakhtiar would fall within a few days. Before the broadcast was over, Jody Powell telephoned the network to deny the report. The following morning, presidential aide Phillip Wise called the State Department and rattled off the names of sixteen high-level officials whom the president wished to see that afternoon, along with Secretary of State Cyrus Vance. A grim-faced Carter began the meeting with some words of praise for Vance. Then he began talking about the problem of leaks. As he spoke, his tone became increasingly hostile. Finally he declared, "This leaking has got to stop, and what I am going to do is this. If there are any leaks out of your area, whatever the area may be, I am going to fire *you*. Whether or not that's fair, and I can see where some of you might not think it fair, this has just got to stop. So, leaks from your area, regardless of who is at fault, and *you're fired!"* The president then stalked from the room, Hamilton Jordan and Jody Powell following him.[245]

In October 1979 the *Washington Post* disclosed that high-level administration officials were divided over whether to provide new military equipment to King Hassan II of Morocco. When Carter saw the article, said one official, he "went off the ceiling." He reportedly notified his national security adviser, Zbigniew Brzezinski, that he would like to "get the results" of his subordinates' discussions "before the *Washington Post*." He also let it be known that he would like to have the sworn affidavits of a score of top officials that they were not the source of the leak. Twenty individuals signed affidavits. State Department spokesman Hodding Carter refused. "I don't believe in signing a piece of paper that says I am innocent," he later said. "That's not how things are supposed to work in this country."[246]

There are some individuals in Ronald Reagan's inner circle who would prefer to cross swords with the press. "Sometimes it's easier to have clear-cut enemies," one of the president's more contentious assistants told *National Journal* correspondent Dick Kirschten.[247] The prevailing attitude, however, seems to be one of forbearance: be patient, try to understand that scandals come and scandals go, do not get overly defensive, do not lock horns with the press in any sustained, self-destructive way.[248]

This tolerative viewpoint seems to reflect Reagan's basic personality. He is a sensitive person who occasionally loses his temper, but he is not fundamentally combative and does not hold grudges. "He likes the press," press secretary James Brady told an interviewer a few days after Reagan's inauguration. "He likes them as a group, and he comes in with no ingrained paranoia. I don't think from a media standpoint there's a paranoid bone in his body (or a feeling) that the press is evil and to be avoided at all cost."[249]

Reagan has gone on to demonstrate the validity of Brady's observations in many ways. The president sometimes appears disconcerted, for example, when meetings with the press come to an end and reporters are still clamoring for his attention. "He does seem to be concerned that he will offend the press by not answering their questions," noted Richard Bergholz of the *Los Angeles Times*.[250] While speaking at the White House News Photographers Association dinner in May, 1983, Reagan suddenly stopped, put his thumbs in his ears and wiggled his fingers. "I've been waiting years to do this," he said with a puckish smile as the audience erupted in laughter. The dinner was supposed to be off the record, but a UPI photographer captured the moment and the picture was published around the nation. "I don't care if the cameras were on," Reagan said. "It still got a good laugh,"[251]

Despite his generally benign attitude, Reagan occasionally becomes frustrated with journalists and shows it. Said Lou Cannon of the *Washington Post*:

He's a proud man, he's sensitive about stories that say he doesn't know what he's doing. . . . He's sensitive to things that show him, as a man, in a bad light. He can take policy criticism. He doesn't like you to announce things, he wants to do that himself. After I had published a leaked story, he confirmed it in the next day's mini-conference, then said to an aide, "I can't believe I called on Cannon again. All he prints are leaks."

He gets annoyed, upset. He has an Irish temper. He blows up. Things get difficult for a day or two, then they go away. . . . There is no vendetta mentality here. . . . You have a short, unpleasant period, but they don't try to retaliate.[252]

News stories that Reagan believes to be erroneous especially raise his ire. He once became upset when a columnist and a television correspondent reported he was about to make some changes in his foreign policy team. "All I can say," he snapped at reporters, "is that whoever wrote that report was not only blowing smoke but also doing a disservice to this country."[253] In August 1982 the president got "ticked off," in Larry Speakes' words, by a CBS story about the administration's plans to limit arms sales to Taiwan and telephoned anchorman Dan Rather in the network's newsroom. "The coverage has not been right all day, Dan," he said. "I want you to understand there's been no retreat and no change in our policy. We'll continue to arm Taiwan."[254]

On the whole, however, Reagan has fostered a fraternal relationship with the press and has described his occasional pique as "a little momentary frustration or misunderstanding, but that's all it is."[255]

Even the outbursts of Reagan's press "enforcers" have been infrequent and mild compared to those of Ron Nessen and Jody Powell. When Larry Speakes or one of his assistants "don't like one of my stories, they grumble," said Chris Wallace of NBC. "They let me know they think it's a cheap shot, then things get back to normal."[256]

Among senior White House officials, communications director David Gergen seems to take the most broadminded approach to the press. "There is a constant tendency among presidents," he once observed, "to say that the glass is half-full and the press to say that it's half-empty. That's a built-in conflict—to look at the same set of facts and put a different slant on them."[257] On another occasion he noted that the Reagan administration had "intentionally set out to have a decent and civilized relationship with the press. We are not interested in a war."[258]

Despite his basically amicable attitude, however, Gergen sometimes takes angry exception to negative news accounts. On election night 1982 he telephoned CBS correspondent Lesley Stahl to complain that the network was projecting too great a gain for the Democrats.[259] During his March 1982 interview with the *Daily Oklahoman*, President Reagan cited a local Washington, D.C., television report as an example of the erroneous manner in which the economic recovery was being covered. A few days later the reporter who did the story showed up at the daily White House press briefing and engaged in a heated exchange with Gergen that lasted for half an hour. The president was in error, the reporter argued, but Gergen wanted to discuss only the larger issue—that Reagan "was being portrayed as Scrooge" by television journalists. "We all have trouble in a very complicated world of making sure we have every single fact straight," he concluded. "The question is whether the larger points are right."[260]

Other top-level Reagan associates have occasionally stepped forward to take pokes at newsmen. Deputy chief of staff Michael Deaver once told a *Washington Post* reporter:

The press tends to have a pack-herd mentality. They don't check their facts, a lot of them. . . . There is so much . . . competition to make the big bucks in journalism that reporters are driven to compete. And that is not helpful.

I'm not saying it's a conspiracy. It's more of what I said before. This competitiveness on behalf of editors and producers is what is hurting this country. . . . They destroy every hero. We don't have heroes anymore, we don't have anyone to believe in because they strip them naked.[261]

Presidential counselor Edwin Meese has sometimes cited what he calls "Gresham's Law of Journalism" which, in his words, means that "bad information drives out good."[262] Meese became perturbed in February 1981 when British prime minister Margaret Thatcher visited the White House and ABC's Sam Donaldson, impatiently awaiting her appearance at a welcoming ceremony, yelled for someone to "bring her on out!" Meese instructed a subordinate to notify ABC that Donaldson would henceforth restrain himself or his White House press pass would be revoked.[263] During an appearance on NBC's "Meet the Press" in June 1981, Meese described a government employee who leaks information as a person "who is betraying this country." A journalist who reports such news, Meese added, was no better: "He's equally as guilty."[264]

Leaks are a touchy issue with Reagan and his associates. In January 1982 he opened a press conference with a trenchant thrust at reporters: "I was going to have an opening statement, but I decided that what I was going to say I wanted to get a lot of attention, so I'm going to leak it."[265] At times Reagan's concern over leaks has approached the ludicrous. At a Republican fund-raising event in California in August 1981 he was asked to cite the thing about the presidency that had surprised him the most. "Leaks," he quickly responded. "It's gotten so I address some things in the Cabinet meetings to the chandelier. I'm sure it must have a microphone in it."[266] In March, 1982, a "senior administration official" was quoted as saying that the civil strife in El Salvador was a global problem, that it was being aided and abetted by Cuba and the Soviet Union, and that the United States would deal with it from that perspective. Asked about the reports, Reagan responded: "I always have trouble about wondering who those senior officials are. I haven't met any of them yet."[267] The president was apparently unaware that the remarks had been made by Secretary of State Alexander Haig in a background briefing for reporters and that he had insisted they protect his anonymity by using the standard euphemism "senior administration official." The following day, Larry Speakes claimed that Reagan had known about Haig's briefing all along and that the president's comment had been made "in jest."[268]

Many of the actions the Reagan administration has taken to plug leaks of information to journalists have been described. Investigations have been launched to locate reporters' sources; the classification system has been tightened by executive fiat; the Freedom of Information Act has been narrowly interpreted; journalistic access to top officials has been restricted; polygraph tests have been administered to Defense Department employees in an effort to discourage leaks; public officials and former officials with access to classified information have been ordered to clear their speeches and writings with the government. In short, the fittings and the fixtures have been caulked and tightened — but the faucets still drip. In the words of Lyn Nofziger, "This is the leakiest administration, the leakiest White House I have ever seen in my time in Washington."[269]

Yet despite his extraordinary attempts to control the flow of news, Ronald Reagan is generally viewed by journalists as a good-natured and good-humored leader who bears them no ill will. Paradoxically, however, he has appointed a number of people to high-level posts in his government who seem to regard reporters as piranha and treat them as pariahs. One was James Watt. The staunchly conservative former interior secretary was chatting with David Gergen one day in February 1982 when a reporter walked up. Watt took the opportunity to say he was delighted that President Reagan seemed to be adopting a more austere attitude toward the press. "I'm glad to see he's getting tougher," said Watt, because reporters had been "indecent" and "cruel" and their coverage of the administration had been marked by "pettiness."[270] A few days later, Watt traveled to Capitol Hill to testify before a House Appropriations subcommittee. Two sympathetic Congressmen—Tom Bevill, D-Alabama and John T. Myers, R-Indiana— deplored the criticism Watt had been receiving from environmentalists and the press. As reported by UPI, the conversation went like this:

"We, too, take a lot of flak for being over-concerned about our country," Myers said.

"They kill good trees to put out bad newspapers," Watt replied.

Myers suggested the electronic media are "burning dirty coal" by using electricity to attack Watt "from right to left."

"From left to right—and put 'left' in caps," Watt responded.

When Rep. Lindy Boggs (D-La) suggested newspapers "sometimes" make mistakes, Watt interrupted.

"In this town," he said, "I don't believe anything I see in the newspapers."[271]

Another who tolerates the press poorly is William Casey. The seventy-one-year-old CIA director, who served Richard Nixon loyally as chairman of the Securities and Exchange Commission, once ran into CBS correspondent Ike Pappas at a diplomatic reception and got into a heated exchange about press access to intelligence information. "Who elected you to tell the American people what they should know?" demanded Casey. "When we think they should know something we will tell you about it."[272] As Casey's comments indicate, he has little appreciation for the role that the free press plays in the American system. In March 1981 he petitioned Congress to exempt the CIA completely from the Freedom of Information Act. Two months later he asked Congress to amend existing law to permit FBI agents to conduct surprise raids on newspaper and television newsrooms if the organization involved had published the names of covert agents. A few days later he terminated all CIA background briefings for reporters on the grounds they were a waste of time. In June 1981 he closed down the CIA's office of public affairs and appointed a new assistant to deal with journalists. The appointee said his job could be described as "inverse public relations."[273]

James Edwards is a third example. The Reagan administration's first energy secretary returned to private life in November 1982, but four months after he took office, Edwards traveled to his home state of South Carolina to deliver an address to the Greater Columbia Chamber of Commerce and offered a suggestion about who was responsible for the ills that had befallen the nation:

The liberal media in Washington have too much influence on American thought. And the rest of the press just picks that up, instead of doing their own work.

The *New York Times* and *Washington Post* aren't stalwart, conservative-thinking institutions. They believe in the Ted Kennedys and the Tip O'Neills. They're the ones who got America in the shape it's in today.[274]

Sometimes it seems as if Richard Nixon never left town.

Notes

Chapter 1

1. "Lyn Nofziger on Ronald Reagan and the Press," *Washington Journalism Review* 4:2 (March 1982): 29.

2. "The President-Elect and the Press," *Quill* 64:12 (December 1976): 2.

3. *Washington Post*, February 1, 1977, Sec. A, p. 2.

4. *New York Times*, February 18, 1977, Sec. B, p. 6; *Washington Post*, February 18, 1977, Sec. A, p. 20. The cabinet minutes were never released to the press, but they were leaked, much to Carter's consternation.

5. *Washington Post*, February 18, 1977, Sec. A, p. 20.

6. David S. Broder, "Carter and the Press: 'Hide and Seek,' " *Washington Post*, January 5, 1977, Sec. A, p. 19.

7. *Washington Post*, February 8, 1977, Sec. C, p. 3.

8. "The President's Secret Life," *Newsweek*, June 11, 1979, p. 44.

9. Statement by Frank Cormier, interview, August 1, 1979.

10. Ron Nessen, *It Sure Looks Different from the Inside* (Chicago: Playboy Press, 1978), p. 247.

11. Richard Reeves, et al., "Notes from Our Boys in the Back of the Bus," *New York*, October 25, 1976, p. 38.

12. "Trapped in the Steel Cocoon," *Time*, November 8, 1976, p. 78. Pool reporters are selected to cover events when the rules or physical restrictions prevent the entire press cadre from doing so.

13. Tom Hamburger, "How the White House Cons the Press," *Washington Monthly* (January 1982): 22.

14. "A Talk with Dave Gergen," *Washington Journalism Review* 4:3 (April 1982): 44.

15. John Herbers, "The President and the Press Corps," *New York Times Magazine*, May 9, 1982, p. 75.

16. Lynne Olson, "The Reticence of Ronald Reagan," *Washington Journalism Review* 3:9 (November 1981): 44.

17. John Osborne, "Images," *New Republic*, September 9, 1978, p. 10.

18. "A Talk with Dave Gergen," *Washington Journalism Review* 4:3 (April 1982): 44.

19. *Chicago Tribune*, May 5, 1982, p. 6. The director of the news summary staff, William Hart, later told me he regretted the use of his product in the effort to kill

the Anderson column, primarily because the story that was eventually published was more damaging than the original.

20. Statement by Ron Nessen, personal interview, August 14, 1979.

21. James J. Kilpatrick, "Of Presidents and the Press: What Will Reagan Do?" *Washington Star*, December 27, 1981, Sec. A, p. 9; Sanford J. Ungar, "Reports & Comment: Washington," *Atlantic* (April 1977): 6; "Jody Faces Life," *Newsweek*, September 19, 1977, p. 120.

22. John Osborne, "In Jody's Shop (I)," *New Republic*, March 18, 1978, p. 18.

23. "The President's Boys," *Time*, June 6, 1977, p. 23.

24. Statement by Judy Woodruff, interview, August 3, 1979.

25. Statement by Jack McWethy, interview, August 3, 1979.

26. *Washington Post*, January 7, 1981, Sec. A, p. 3; "Affable Bear," *Time*, January 19, 1981, pp. 19–20.

27. Herbers, "President and the Press Corps," p. 97.

28. United Press International dispatch, *Washington Post*, March 26, 1983.

29. *Washington Post*, October 17, 1982, Sec. B, p. 1.

30. Dom Bonafede, "The Washington Press—It Magnifies the President's Flaws and Blemishes," *National Journal*, May 1, 1982, pp. 768–769.

31. Helen Thomas, *Dateline: White House* (New York: Macmillan Publishing Co., Inc., 1975), p. 261; *Wall Street Journal*, February 28, 1975, p. 1.

32. "President-Elect and the Press," p. 2. James J. Kilpatrick, "Of Presidents and Press: What Will Reagan Do?" *Washington Star*, December 27, 1981, Sec. A, p. 9.

33. *Washington Post*, July 1, 1977, Sec. A, pp. 1, 26.

34. "Talk with Dave Gergen," p. 42; *Washington Post*, May 18, 1983, Sec. A, p. 1.

35. Thomas M. DeFrank, "Fine-Tuning the White House Press Conference," *Washington Journalism Review* 4:9 (October 1982): 27–29. See also *Washington Post*, October 2, 1981, Sec. A, pp. 1, 11.

36. DeFrank, "Fine-Tuning," p. 27; *Washington Post*, August 4, 1982, Sec. B, pp. 1, 6.

37. Curtis Wilkie, "Carter's Televised Presidency," *Boston Globe Magazine*, November 2, 1980, pp. 17, 20.

38. "President McLuhan," *Nation*, February 11, 1978, p. 132.

39. Peter Meyer, *James Earl Carter: The Man and the Myth* (Kansas City: Sheed Andrews and McMeel, 1978), p. 153.

40. "Cruisin' Down the River," *Time*, September 3, 1979, p. 18.

41. *New York Times*, August 17, 1979, Sec. A, p. 15.

42. "Focusing On Carter," *Newsweek*, August 27, 1979, p. 60.

43. *Washington Star*, August 17, 1979, Sec. A, p. 10.

44. United Press International dispatch, *Washington Post*, August 15, 1979.

45. *New York Times*, August 17, 1979, Sec. A, p. 15.

46. Associated Press dispatch, *Washington Post*, August 18, 1979; "Crusin' Down the River," pp. 18–21; "Life on the Mississippi," *Newsweek*, September 3, 1979, pp. 30–31; *Washington Post*, August 22, 1979, Sec. A, pp. 1, 6, 25.

47. *Washington Post*, August 25, 1979, Sec. A, p. 3.

48. David Halberstam, "How Television Failed the American Voter," *Parade*, January 11, 1981, p. 4.

49. Rowland Evans and Robert Novak, "The Leading Man," *Washington Post Magazine*, January 18, 1981, pp. 8–13.

50. Halberstam, "How Television Failed," p. 4.

51. Statement by Lou Gerig, personal interview, June 22, 1981.

52. *Washington Star*, July 14, 1980, Sec. A, p. 5.

53. *Washington Post*, July 14, 1980, Sec A, pp. 1, 15; "A Grand Old Party for the GOP," *Time*, July 28, 1980, pp. 14, 15; "How To Leave Them Cheering," *Time*, July 28, 1980, p. 29.

54. Nessen, *It Sure Looks Different*, pp. 75, 128, 341.

55. Ibid., p. 259.

56. Periscope, "Carter Puts on Weight," *Newsweek*, September 22, 1980, p. 21.

57. *Washington Post*, October 27, 1980, Sec. A, p. 4; "Carter Was Speechless," *Time*, July 16, 1979, p. 9. Carter abruptly cancelled this speech and retreated to Camp David to engage in a lengthy reassessment of his presidency.

58. Hugh Sidey, "Trying to Show His Toughness," *Time*, July 30, 1979, p. 29.

59. "I'll Whip His Ass," *Newsweek*, June 25, 1979, p. 40; "Whip His What?" *Time*, June 25, 1979, p. 45; Eleanor Randolph, "The 'Whip-His-Ass' Story, or the Gang That Couldn't Leak Straight," *Washington Monthly* (September 1979): 50–51.

60. *Washington Post*, September 2, 1980, Sec. A, pp. 1, 3; *Wall Street Journal*, September 4, 1980, p. 1.

61. "Stumping in South Succotash," *Time*, March 29, 1982, p. 27.

62. *New York Times*, January 3, 1983, Sec. A, p. 13; *Washington Post*, January 3, 1980, Sec. A, p. 3.

63. United Press International dispatch, *Washington Post*, June 11, 1982; *Washington Post*, June 12, 1982, Sec. A, p. 10.

64. White House memorandum, April 25, 1983.

65. *Washington Post*, May 28, 1983, Sec. A, pp. 1, 14, May 31, 1983, Sec. C, pp. 1, 4.

66. Richard Cohen, "Achievement," *Washington Post*, June 2, 1983, Sec. B, p. 1.

67. John Osborne, "Ford's Image Machine," *New Republic*, March 1, 1975, p. 10.

68. Statement by Ron Nessen, personal interview, August 14, 1979.

69. *Wall Street Journal*, January 10, 1975, p. 1.

70. James Stevenson, "A Reporter At Large: Moving In, Moving Out," *New Yorker*, December 27, 1976, p. 48. "Advance" refers to those who visit a site where the president will be ahead of time to prepare routes, arrange for lodging, and even pinpoint locations for network cameras.

71. John Osborne, "In Jody's Shop (I)," *New Republic*, March 18, 1978, p. 18. See also Sanford J. Ungar, "Reports & Comment: Washington," *Atlantic* (April 1977): 12; "Jody Powell," *Quill* 69:2 (February 1981): 14; "Polishing the Carter Image," *U.S. News & World Report*, August 8, 1977, p. 16.

72. *Washington Post*, January 29, 1979, Sec. B, p. 9; Dom Bonafede, "Has the Rafshoon Touch Left Its Mark On the White House?" *National Journal*, April 14, 1979, pp. 588–593.

73. Ungar, "Reports & Comment" p. 10; "Things You Never Asked," *Time*, November 27, 1978, p. 20.

74. "President Carter Speaks on the Record," a Report Prepared for Editors and News Directors by the Office of Media Liaison, The White House Press Office, January 1979.

75. Michael Baruch Grossman and Martha Joynt Kumar, *Portraying the President* (Baltimore: Johns Hopkins University Press, 1981), p. 92.

76. "Talk with Dave Gergen," p. 41.

77. *Washington Post*, February 15, 1981, Sec. A, pp. 1, 17.

78. Ibid., May 2, 1981, Sec A, p. 5.

79. *New York Times*, January 18, 1976, Sec. E, p. 4.

80. Nessen, *It Sure Looks Different*, p. 169.

81. "Nessen's Complaint," *Newsweek*, July 7, 1975, p. 43.

82. Nessen, *It Sure Looks Different*, pp. 167–168. See also "Image Maker with His Hands Full," *U.S. News & World Report*, January 12, 1976, p. 27.

83. *Wall Street Journal*, October 25, 1974, p. 1.

84. *Washington Post*, January 8, 1976, Sec. A, p. 3.

85. *New York Times*, February 13, 1976, p. 7. The House Ethics Committee, which had never investigated a congressman, launched a seven-month probe of the leak, and Schorr was threatened with a contempt of Congress citation when he refused to disclose his source. But the matter was dropped in September 1976, and Schorr's source was never disclosed. See Daniel Schorr, *Clearing the Air* (New York: Berkley Publishing Corporation, 1978), pp. 184–253.

86. "New Policemen to Battle Abuses," *Time*, March 1, 1976, p. 12.

87. Meyer, *James Earl Carter*, p. 144.

88. Reuters dispatch, *Washington Post*, July 21, 1980.

89. Blake Fleetwood, "The Resurrection of JFK," [*MORE*] 6:3 (March 1976): 24.

90. Ibid. See also Meyer, *James Earl Carter*, pp. 122–124.

91. Dom Bonafede, "Beat the Press," *National Journal*, December 9, 1978, p. 1988.

92. TRB, "Carter's Press," *New Republic*, November 20, 1976, p. 4.

93. "Playing Catch-Up Ball," *Newsweek*, November 3, 1980, p. 34.

94. Lewis W. Wolfson, "The President and the Press: The First Report Card," *Quill* 65:10 (October 1977): 14.

95. Victor Lasky, *Jimmy Carter: The Man and the Myth* (New York: Richard Marek Publishers, 1979), p. 235.

96. Benjamin Stein, "If You Liked Richard Nixon, You'll Love Jimmy Carter," *Penthouse* (November 1976): 64.

97. United Press International dispatch, *Washington Star*, August 30, 1979.

98. *Washington Post*, August 17, 1980, Sec. A, p. 3. See also "Jack Anderson's Rescue Mission," *Newsweek*, September 1, 1980, p. 67.

99. United Press International dispatch, *Pittsburgh Press*, August 16, 1980.

100. *Atlanta Journal and Constitution*, April 5, 1981, Sec. A, pp. 1, 12.

101. ABC World News Tonight, October 21, 1980.

102. Statement by Phil Gailey, personal interview, January 12, 1981.

103. Statement by a White House correspondent, interview, August 18, 1979.

104. Statement by Chris Ogden, personal interview, April 24, 1981. Powell himself thought this theory was far-fetched. "If I ever intimidated anyone by talking to them," he once said, "it was not apparent in anything they later wrote." See the *Washington Post*, November 24, 1976, Sec. A, p. 7.

105. J. Anthony Lukas, "The White House Press 'Club,' " *New York Times Magazine*, May 15, 1977, p. 68; John Osborne, "Carter's Bad Boys," *New Republic*, March 11, 1978, p. 8.

106. *New York Times*, May 14, 1978, p. 1.

107. *Wall Street Journal*, February 25, 1977, p. 1.

108. Ibid., August 12, 1977, p. 1.

109. Periscope, "Who's to Blame?" *Newsweek*, October 10, 1977, p. 27.

110. Jack Anderson, "Cabinet News Leaks Baffle Carter," *Washington Post*, April 13, 1978, Sec. E, p. 23; Joseph A. Califano, Jr., *Governing America: An Insider's Report from the White House and the Cabinet* (New York: Simon and Schuster, 1981), p. 417.

111. Minutes of the cabinet meeting, Monday, August 7, 1978.

112. "Tough Talk from the Boss," *Newsweek*, May 1, 1978, p. 21.

113. AP dispatch, *Washington Star*, May 4, 1981.

114. James Keogh, *President Nixon and the Press* (New York: Funk & Wagnalls, 1972), p. 25.

115. "Nofziger on Reagan," p. 27.

116. C. T. Hanson, "Gunsmoke and Sleeping Dogs: The Prez's Press at Midterm," *Columbia Journalism Review* 21:1 (May–June 1983): 27.

117. *Washington Post*, September 4, 1980, Sec. A, p. 2.

118. Ibid., March 16, 1982, Sec. A, p. 16.

119. Ibid., March 18, 1982, Sec. A, pp. 1, 7.

120. "President vs. the Press," *Newsweek*, March 29, 1982, p. 77.

121. DeFrank, "Fine-Tuning," p. 28.

122. *Washington Post*, January 29, 1983, Sec. A, p. 8.

123. *New York Times*, April 23, 1982, Sec. A, pp. 1, 23; *Washington Post*, April 23, 1982, Sec. A, pp. 1, 6.

124. "CBS, Reagan and the Poor," *Newsweek*, May 3, 1982, p. 22; See also *Washington Post*, April 22, 1982, Sec. C, pp. 1, 16.

125. *New York Times*, April 23, 1982, Sec. A, pp. 1, 23; "CBS, Reagan and the Poor," p. 22; *Washington Post*, April 24, 1982, Sec. A, p. 2; Lou Cannon, "Reagan & Co.," *Washington Post*, May 10, 1982, Sec. A, p. 3.

126. Lou Cannon, "Reagan & Co.," *Washington Post*, March 21, 1983, Sec. A, p. 3.

127. *Washington Star*, February 4, 1981, Sec. A, p. 10.

128. Lou Cannon, "Reagan & Co.," *Washington Post*, January 17, 1983, Sec. A, p. 3.

129. *New York Times*, January 11, 1983, Sec. A, p. 1, Sec. B, p. 10; *Washington Post*, January 11, 1983, Sec. A, pp. 1, 5.

130. *Washington Post*, January 11, 1983, Sec. A, p. 5.

131. Lou Cannon, "Reagan & Co.," *Washington Post*, March 21, 1983, Sec. A, p. 3.

132. *Washington Times*, May 12, 1983, Sec. A, pp. 1, 12.

133. *New York Times*, April 3, 1982, Sec. A, pp. 1, 9; *Washington Post*, April 3, 1982, Sec. A, pp. 1, 5.

134. *New York Times*, December 10, 1982, Sec. A, p. 1, Sec. D, p. 20.

135. *Washington Post*, March 12, 1983, Sec. A, pp. 1, 9. See also "Keeping the Cats in the Bag," *Newsweek*, April 18, 1983, pp. 92, 92D.

136. Ibid. See also Anthony Lewis, "Reagan vs. Madison," *New York Times*, March 17, 1983, Sec. A, p. 23.

137. *New York Times*, November 15, 1982, Sec. B, pp. 1, 5; *Washington Post*, April 8, 1982, Sec. B, pp. 1, 13; Jack Landau, "A Pattern of Censorship," *Washington Post*, Sec. A, p. 23.

138. *Washington Post*, April 21, 1983, Sec. A, p. 6.

Chapter 2

1. For a comprehensive history of the evolution of the free press in England, see Frederick Seaton Siebert, *Freedom of the Press in England, 1476–1776* (Urbana: University of Illinois Press, 1965).

2. Stephen Decatur, Jr., *The Private Affairs of George Washington* (Boston: Houghton Mifflin Co., 1933), pp. 45–46.

3. Paul Leichester Ford, ed., *The Writings of Thomas Jefferson* (New York: G. P. Putnam's Sons, 1892), 1: 254. Philip Freneau was the publisher of the Republican *National Gazette*.

4. David Halberstam, *The Powers That Be* (New York: Alfred A. Knopf, 1979), p. 490.

5. James E. Pollard, *The Presidents and the Press* (New York: Macmillan, 1947), pp. 41–43.

6. Ibid., pp. 52, 73–83.

7. Ford, *Jefferson*, 9: 637–639.

8. *National Journal*, August 18, 1829. Italics in original.

9. Emanuel Hertz, *Lincoln Talks* (New York: Viking, 1939), p. 273.

10. Pollard, *Presidents*, pp. 397–399.

11. Ibid., pp. 434–497.

12. *A Record of the Commemmoration, November Fifth to Eighth, 1886, on the Two Hundred and Fiftieth Anniversary of the Founding of Harvard College*, 2d ed. (Cambridge: John Wilson and Son, University Press, 1887), p. 269.

13. Allan Nevins, *Letters of Grover Cleveland* (Boston: Houghton Mifflin, 1933), pp. 94–95.

14. James Keogh, *President Nixon and the Press* (New York: Funk & Wagnalls, 1972), p. 25. Charles Willis Thompson, *Presidents I've Known* (Indianapolis: Bobbs-Merrill, 1929), p. 295. Jack Anderson with James Boyd, *Confessions of a Muckracker* (New York: Random House, 1979), pp. 222–223.

15. David S. Barry, *Forty Years in Washington* (Boston: Little, Brown, 1924), pp. 267–269.

16. Elmer E. Cornwell, Jr., *Presidential Leadership of Public Opinion* (Bloomington: Indiana University Press, 1965), pp. 17–18.

17. Ray Stannard Baker, *Life and Letters of Woodrow Wilson* (Garden City, N.Y. Doubleday, 1927–1939), 4:230.

18. Samuel I. Rosenman, comp., *Public Papers and Addresses of Franklin D. Roosevelt* (New York: Random House, 1938–1950), 2:30. Volumes 6 through 9 of the Roosevelt

papers were published by the Macmillan Company; volumes 10 through 13 were published by Harper & Row.

19. Rosenman, *Roosevelt Papers*, 2:30; Graham J. White, *FDR and the Press* (Chicago: University of Chicago Press, 1979), p. 22.

20. Halberstam, *Powers That Be*, pp. 15–16.

21. Theodore H. White, *The Making of the President 1972* (New York: Atheneum, 1973), pp. 266–267.

22. Henry Fairlie, "The Rise of the Press Secretary," *New Republic*, March 18, 1978, p. 22.

23. James E. Pollard, *The Presidents and the Press, Truman to Johnson* (Washington, D.C.: Public Affairs Press, 1964), p. 101.

24. Fairlie, "Rise of the Press Secretary," p. 23.

25. Pollard, *Truman to Johnson*, pp. 100–105.

26. Richard M. Nixon, *RN: The Memoirs of Richard Nixon* (New York: Grosset & Dunlap, 1978), p. 409.

27. Ibid., p. 411.

28. William Safire, *Before the Fall* (Garden City, N.Y.: Doubleday, 1975), p. 352.

29. Ibid., p. 342.

30. "The Press in the President's Transcripts," *Quill* 62:6 (June 1974): 16.

31. David Frost, *"I Gave Them a Sword": Behind the Scenes of the Nixon Interviews* (New York: Morrow, 1978), p. 171.

32. Ibid., p. 267.

33. Allen Drury, *Courage and Hesitation* (Garden City, N.Y.: Doubleday, 1971), p. 395.

34. Nixon, *Memoirs*, pp. 329–330. For contrasting views of Efron's book, see Sam Kuczun, Review of Edith Efron, The News Twisters, *Journalism Quarterly* 49:1 (Spring 1972): 192; Lawrence Laurent, "Television: 2. Primarily a Liberal Mouthpiece?" Review of Edith Efron, The News Twisters, *Columbia Journalism Review* 10:4 (November–December 1971): 55–56.

35. Nixon, *Memoirs*, pp. 354–355.

36. Safire, *Before the Fall*, p. 345.

37. Arthur Schlesinger, Jr., "Freedom of the Press: Who Cares?" *Wall Street Journal*, January 5, 1973, p. 6.

38. Jules Witcover, *The Resurrection of Richard Nixon* (New York: G. P. Putnam's Sons, 1970), p. 151.

39. Safire, *Before the Fall*, p. 312.

40. White, *Making of the President 1972*, p. 278.

41. White House memorandum, October 17, 1969.

42. David Wise, "The President and the Press," *Atlantic* (April 1973): 55.

43. Frost, *"I Gave Them a Sword,"* p. 134. See also Raymond Price, *With Nixon* (New York: Viking Press, 1977), p. 111.

44. Nixon, *Memoirs*, p. 664. See also James J. Kilpatrick, *Washington Star-News*, May 22, 1974, Sec. A, p. 14.

45. Arthur Woodstone, *Nixon's Head* (New York: St. Martin's Press, 1972), p. 40.

46. Nixon, *Memoirs*, pp. 934–935.

47. *Washington Post*, October 27, 1973, Sec. A, p. 1.

48. Marvin Barrett, ed., *The Alfred I. duPont–Columbia University Survey of Broadcast Journalism 1969–1970* (New York: Grosset & Dunlap, 1970), p. 47.

49. Ibid., p. 9.

50. James R. Dickenson, "Nixon and the Press," *National Observer*, October 28, 1972, p. 24.

Chapter 3

1. Henry D. Spalding, *The Nixon Nobody Knows* (Middle Village, N.Y.: Jonathan David Publishers, 1972), pp. 58–59.

2. Ibid., pp. 151–152. For sympathetic treatments of Nixon's life and career, see Richard M. Nixon, *RN: The Memoirs of Richard Nixon* (New York: Grosset & Dunlap, 1978); Earl Mazo, *Richard Nixon, A Political and Personal Portrait* (New York: Harper & Brothers, 1959); and Spalding, *Nixon Nobody Knows*. For more critical views, see Leonard Lurie, *The Running of Richard Nixon* (New York: Coward, McCann & Geoghegan, 1972), and Frank Mankiewicz, *Perfectly Clear: Nixon from Whittier to Watergate* (New York: Quadrangle, New York Times Book Company, 1973).

3. Spalding, *Nixon Nobody Knows*, pp. 154–159. See also "Chotiner's Comeback," *Newsweek*, June 22, 1970, p. 21.

4. Spalding, *Nixon Nobody Knows*, p. 172.

5. Ibid., p. 177.

6. Theodore H. White, *Breach of Faith: The Fall of Richard Nixon* (New York: Atheneum Publishers, 1975), pp. 67–68.

7. Thomas Whiteside, "Annals of Television," *New Yorker*, March 17, 1975, p. 41.

8. David Halberstam, *The Powers That Be* (New York: Alfred A. Knopf, 1979), pp. 259–261.

9. Spalding, *Nixon Nobody Knows*, p. 258.

10. Richard M. Nixon, *Six Crises* (Garden City, N.Y.: Doubleday, 1962), p. 69.

11. Jules Whitcover, *The Resurrection of Richard Nixon* (New York: G. P. Putnam's Sons, 1970), pp. 20–21.

12. Dan Rather and Gary Paul Gates, *The Palace Guard* (New York: Harper & Row, 1974), p. 114. See also, "Chotiner's Comeback," p. 21.

13. "Fighting Quaker," *Time*, August 25, 1952, p. 13.

14. Jack Anderson with James Boyd, *Confessions of a Muckraker* (New York: Random House, 1979), pp. 325–326.

15. Raymond Price, *With Nixon* (New York: Viking Press, 1977), pp. 53–54.

16. Anderson, *Confessions*, p. 326.

17. Nixon, *Six Crises*, p. 81.

18. Stewart Alsop, "The Mystery of Richard Nixon," *Saturday Evening Post*, July 12, 1958, p. 60.

19. Nixon, *Six Crises*, p. 95.

20. Ibid., pp. 96–108.

21. David Wise, "The President and the Press," *Atlantic* (April 1973): 56.

22. Garry Wills, *Nixon Agonistes* (New York: Signet, 1971), p. 109.

23. Nixon, *Six Crises*, p. 119.

24. H. R. Haldeman with Joseph DiMona, *The Ends of Power* (New York: New York Times Books, 1978), p. 49. According to Frank Mankiewicz, Haldeman's father was a contributor to the Nixon fund. See *Perfectly Clear*, p. 62.

25. Alsop, "Mystery of Richard Nixon," p. 66. Three years later, according to Arthur Woodstone, Nixon addressed a Radio and Television Executives Society luncheon and claimed he had staged the Checkers speech. He had meant every word of it, he said, but "let's be realistic: A dog is a natural." See Arthur Woodstone, *Nixon's Head* (New York: St. Martin's Press, 1972), pp. 26–31.

26. James Keogh, *President Nixon and the Press* (New York: Funk & Wagnalls, 1972), p. 5.

27. Jean Begeman, "Nixon: How the Press Suppressed the News," *New Republic*, October 6, 1952, pp. 11–13.

28. William Safire, *Before the Fall* (Garden City, N.Y.: Doubleday, 1975), pp. 3–6.

29. Halberstam, *Powers That Be*, pp. 328–329.

30. Stephen Hess, "Only the Style Was Important," *Washington Post*, September 1, 1972, Sec. A, p. 24.

31. Theodore H. White, *The Making of the President 1960* (New York: Atheneum Publishers, 1961), pp. 313–318.

32. Ibid., pp. 318–323. In the third debate Nixon—whose White House transcripts later would be replete with "expletives deleted"—censured Harry Truman's earthy language and lauded Eisenhower for restoring "dignity and decency and, frankly, good language to the conduct of the presidency." See *Washington Post* staff, *The Fall of a President* (New York: Delacorte Press, 1974), pp. 46–47.

33. Nixon, *Six Crises*, pp. 422–423.

34. Keogh, *Nixon and the Press*, pp. 5–6.

35. David Halberstam, "Press and Prejudice," *Esquire* (April 1974): 228.

36. Nixon, *Six Crises*, p. 396.

37. Mankiewicz, *Perfectly Clear*, pp. 65–75.

38. Walter Gieber, "California Campaign Reporting," *Columbia Journalism Review* 1:4 (Winter 1963): 19.

39. Eleven years later, Vice-President Spiro Agnew was under investigation for accepting bribes from Maryland contractors while governor of the state, and he defended his actions to Nixon as being a "common practice" in many states. Said Nixon, "Thank God I was never elected governor of California." See Nixon, *Memoirs*, p. 823.

40. Witcover, *Resurrection of Nixon*, pp. 14–22.

41. *New York Times*, November 8, 1962, Sec. A, p. 18.

42. "California: Career's End," *Time*, November 16, 1962, p. 28.

43. Haldeman, *Ends of Power*, p. 76.

44. Alsop, "Mystery of Richard Nixon," pp. 60–62. See also Nixon, *Memoirs*, pp. 246–247.

45. Nixon, *Memoirs*, pp. 256–271. See also *Washington Post*, September 26, 1973, Sec. A, p. 9.

46. Witcover, *Resurrection of Nixon*, pp. 238–239.

47. Nixon, *Memoirs*, pp. 303–304.

48. Joe McGinniss, *The Selling of the President 1968* (New York: Trident Press, 1969), pp. 42–44.

49. Witcover, *Resurrection of Nixon*, p. 238.

50. McGinniss, *Selling of the President*, p. 177.

51. Ibid., pp. 187–188.

52. Ibid., pp. 192–193. Italics in the original.

53. Witcover, *Resurrection of Nixon*, p. 237.

54. White, *Breach of Faith*, pp. 96–97. See also Rather, *Palace Guard*, pp. 145–146, and Halberstam, *Powers That Be*, pp. 589–590.

55. "The President's Palace Guard," *Newsweek*, March 19, 1973, p. 28.

56. Haldeman, *Ends of Power*, p. 183.

57. Paul Hoffman, *The New Nixon* (New York: Tower Publications, 1970), pp. 27–28.

58. Safire, *Before the Fall*, p. 55.

59. Witcover, *Resurrection of Nixon*, p. 374.

60. Rather, *Palace Guard*, pp. 142–147.

61. Witcover, *Resurrection of Nixon*, p. 375.

62. Safire, *Before the Fall*, pp. 59–61.

63. McGinniss, *Selling of the President*, pp. 64–66.

64. Ibid., pp. 10, 124–125.

65. Safire, *Before the Fall*, pp. 62–74.

66. Witcover, *Resurrection of Nixon*, pp. 445–447. See also Safire, *Before the Fall*, p. 92.

67. McGinniss, *Selling of the President*, p. 58.

68. Ibid., pp. 222–225.

69. Witcover, *Resurrection of Nixon*, pp. 375–379. See also Halberstam, *Powers That Be*, p. 594, and Woodstone, *Nixon's Head*, p. 106.

70. Safire, *Before the Fall*, p. 74.

71. Witcover, *Resurrection of Nixon*, p. 379.

72. Safire, *Before the Fall*, p. 92.

73 McGinniss, *Selling of the President*, p. 137.

74. Safire, *Before the Fall*, p. 80.

75. Nixon, *Memoirs*, pp. 354–355.

76. Witcover, *Resurrection of Nixon*, p. 456.

Chapter 4

1. "Will the Press Be Out to 'Get' Nixon?" *U.S. News & World Report*, December 2, 1968, p. 40.

2. William Safire, *Before the Fall* (Garden City, N.Y.: Doubleday, 1975), p. 75.

3. Ibid., pp. 284–285.

4. Jules Witcover, "Washington: Focusing on Nixon," *Columbia Journalism Review* 7:4 (Winter 1968–1969): 11.

5. "The President's Airborne Privacy," *Newsweek*, June 16, 1969, p. 20.

6. Safire, *Before the Fall*, p. 98.

7. Dan Rather and Gary Paul Gates, *The Palace Guard* (New York: Harper & Row, 1974), pp. 29–30.

8. "How Nixon's White House Works," *Time*, June 8, 1970, pp. 15–17.

9. Associated Press dispatch, *Washington Evening Star and Daily News*, November 13, 1972.

10. *Washington Post*, May 17, 1970, Sec. F, pp. 1, 3.

11. "How Nixon's White House Works," p. 16.

12. Rather, *Palace Guard*, p. 239.

13. Theodore H. White, *The Making of the President 1972* (New York: Atheneum Publishers, 1973), pp. 279–280. See also Jack Anderson, "Press Corps Smooths Way for Nixon," *Washington Post*, June 3, 1970, Sec. B. p. 11.

14. Jack Anderson, "President Gets News in Capsule Form," *Washington Post*, April 7, 1971, Sec. B, p. 15.

15. *Washington Post*, January 7, 1973, Sec. A, p. 3.

16. Richard Tanner Johnson, *Managing the White House: An Intimate Study of the Presidency* (New York: Harper & Row, 1974), p. 221.

17. Ben H. Bagdikian, "Mr. Nixon and the Press: A 27-Year Conflict," *New York Times*, November 1, 1973, p. 43.

18. Frank Mankiewicz, *Perfectly Clear: Nixon from Whittier to Watergate* (New York: Quadrangle, 1973), p. 185.

19. *Washington Post*, January 7, 1973, Sec. A, p. 3.

20. Safire, *Before the Fall*, pp. 342–343.

21. Henry Scarupa, "Camp David, Maryland White House," *Baltimore Sun Magazine*, March 11, 1973, p. 19.

22. Raymond Price, *With Nixon* (New York: Viking Press, 1977), pp. 69–70. See also Safire, *Before the Fall*, p. 617.

23. *Washington Post*, December 8, 1972, Sec. A, p. 2. See also "Nixon's Movable White House, *Newsweek*, August 24, 1970, pp. 16–19; Scarupa, "Camp David," pp. 19–25; Rather, *Palace Guard*, p. 27; Safire, *Before the Fall*, p. 618.

24. *Washington Post*, December 8, 1972, Sec. A, p. 2. See also Scarupa, "Camp David," pp. 19–25.

25. *Washington Post*, March 6, 1969, Sec. C, pp. 1, 3. See also Jules Witcover, "How Well Does the White House Press Perform?" *Columbia Journalism Review* 11:4 (November–December 1973): 41.

26. Rather, *Palace Guard*, pp. 115–133. The information on Haldeman's anticommunist background came from Frank Mankiewicz, who was at UCLA when Haldeman was there. Haldeman has claimed, on the other hand, that he was an "apolitical" student. "I was a rah-rah college type, a Homecoming chairman, no less, and a campus leader." See H. R. Haldeman with Joseph DiMona, *The Ends of Power* (New York: New York Times Books, 1978), p. 46.

27. "The President's Palace Guard," *Newsweek*, March 19, 1973, p. 24.

28. Rather, *Palace Guard*, pp. 234–236.

29. Safire, *Before the Fall*, p. 112.

30. James Keogh, *President Nixon and the Press* (New York: Funk & Wagnalls, 1972), p. 43.

31. *Washington Post*, October 27, 1972, Sec. B, p. 1. See also Rather, *Palace Guard*, p. 151, and Clark R. Mollenhoff, *Game Plan For Disaster* (New York: W. W. Norton, 1970), p. 34.

32. Helen Thomas, *Dateline: White House* (New York: Macmillan, 1975), p. 155.

33. Richard M. Nixon, *RN: The Memoirs of Richard Nixon* (New York: Grosset & Dunlap, 1978), pp. 337–338.

34. Safire, *Before the Fall*, pp. 116–117.

35. John Dean, *Blind Ambition* (New York: Simon and Schuster, 1976), p. 35.

36. Rather, *Palace Guard*, p. 238.

37. Mollenhoff, *Game Plan*, p. 140.

38. Ibid., p. 36.

39. Thomas, *Dateline*, p. 168.

40. Rather, *Palace Guard*, pp. 134–144.

41. White House memorandum, June 16, 1969.

42. *Washington Post*, October 27, 1972, Sec. B, p. 1.

43. Mollenhoff, *Game Plan*, pp. 183–185. See also Rather, *Palace Guard*, pp. 180–187.

44. *Washington Post*, February 2, 1971, Sec. B, p. 2.

45. *Washington Post*, May 17, 1970, Sec. F, pp. 1, 3.

46. Keogh, *Nixon and the Press*, p. 126.

47. *Washington Post*, October 27, 1972, Sec. B, p. 3.

48. "Writing Block," *Time*, March 27, 1972, p. 20.

49. Martin Nolan, "Ron among the Plastic Alligators," *[More]* 2:9 (September 1972): 11–13.

50. Ibid., p. 12.

51. Rather, *Palace Guard*, p. 152.

52. Ibid., pp. 151–152.

53. Nolan, "Ron," p. 11.

54. "His Master's Voice," *Newsweek*, May 14, 1973, p. 75. See also, David Wise, "Are You Worried about Your Image, Mr. President?" *Esquire* (May 1973): 120, and Haldeman, *Ends of Power*, p. 4.

55. Bob Woodward and Carl Bernstein, *The Final Days* (New York: Simon and Schuster, 1976), pp. 263–264.

56. Thomas, *Dateline*, p. 129, and Dean, *Blind Ambition*, p. 126.

57. David Wise, "The President and the Press," *Atlantic* (April 1973): 57.

58. *Wall Street Journal*, December 29, 1969, pp. 1, 14; Thomas, *Dateline*, p. 130; Timothy Crouse, *The Boys on the Bus: Riding with the Campaign Press Corps* (New York: Random House, 1973), p. 204.

59. Statement by a White House correspondent, personal interview, March 23, 1971.

60. James M. Naughton, "How the 2d Best-Informed Man in the White House Briefs the Worst-Informed Group in Washington," *New York Times Magazine*, May 30, 1971, p. 25.

61. Mollenhoff, *Game Plan*, p. 240.

62. Ibid., pp. 24–25.

63. Crouse, *Boys on the Bus*, p. 200.

64. *Washington Post*, January 12, 1973, Sec. B, p. 1.

65. Jack Anderson, "Press Corps Smooths Way for Nixon," *Washington Post*, June 3, 1970, Sec. B, p. 11.

66. John Osborne, *The Fourth Year of the Nixon Watch* (New York: Liveright, 1973), p. 114.

67. Price, *With Nixon*, p. 293.

68. Witcover, "How Well Does the White House Press Perform?" p. 41. See also Trudi Osborne, "The White House Press: Let AP Cover the Assassinations," *Washington Monthly* (February 1977): 17–19.

69. Witcover, "How Well Does the White House Press Perform?" pp. 41–42, and Thomas, *Dateline*, p. 126.

70. *Washington Evening Star*, April 3, 1970, Sec. C, p. 1. See also Luther A. Houston, "Nixon Puts Newsmen in Lap of Luxury," *Editor & Publisher*, April 18, 1970, pp. 1, 44.

71. Thomas, *Dateline*, p. 137.

72. "The Roughriders," *Newsweek*, June 18, 1973, p. 74.

73. George W. Johnson, ed., *The Nixon Presidential Press Conferences* (New York: Earl M. Coleman Enterprises, 1978), p. i; Arthur Schlesinger, Jr., "The Complete Presidential Press Conferences of Franklin Delano Roosevelt," review of Jonathan Daniels, introduction to *The Complete Press Conferences of Franklin Delano Roosevelt, Book World*, January 28, 1973, p. 3.

74. Associated Press dispatch, *Washington Evening Star*, February 4, 1972.

75. Jules Witcover, *The Resurrection of Richard Nixon* (New York: G. P. Putnam's Sons, 1970), p. 150.

76. " 'Presidential News Conference Not the Ideal Format'—Klein," *Quill*, 59:2 (February 1971): 11.

77. "More Presidential News Conferences? SDX Pursues the Issue," *Quill*, 59:2 (February 1971): 10.

78. Safire, *Before the Fall*, p. 351.

79. "How the President Gets Ready for a News Conference," *U.S. News & World Report*, December 22, 1969, p. 47.

80. "The Making of the Newest Nixon," *Time*, January 18, 1971, p. 12.

81. *Washington Sunday Star*, November 29, 1970, Sec. A, p. 6.

82. Julius Duscha, "The President and the Press," *Progressive* (May 1969): 26.

83. Hedrich Smith, "When the President Meets the Press," *Atlantic* (August 1970): 65.

84. Tom Wicker, *On Press* (New York: Viking, 1978), p. 94.

85. Ibid., p. 98.

86. *Washington Post*, September 27, 1973, Sec. A, p. 12.

87. Johnson, *Presidential Press Conferences*, pp. 184–186.

88. *Washington Evening Star*, June 29, 1972, Sec. A, p. 1.

89. Newsmakers, *Newsweek*, June 26, 1972, p. 49.

Chapter 5

1. Richard Nixon, *RN: The Memoirs of Richard Nixon* (New York: Grosset & Dunlap, 1978), p. 354.

2. William Safire, *Before the Fall* (Garden City, N.Y.: Doubleday, 1975), p. 108.

3. James Keogh, *President Nixon and the Press* (New York: Funk & Wagnalls, 1972), p. 38.

4. Dan Rather and Gary Paul Gates, *The Palace Guard* (New York: Harper & Row, 1974), p. 47.

5. Marvin Barrett, ed., *The Alfred I. DuPont-Columbia University Survey of Broadcast Journalism 1969–1970* (New York: Grosset & Dunlap, 1970), pp. 53–54.

6. "A Fair Share of Air," *Newsweek*, July 6, 1970, p. 59.

7. Herbert Block, *Herblock's State of the Union* (New York: Simon and Schuster, 1972), p. 66.

8. Barrett, *Survey*, pp. 47–48.

9. "And the War Goes On," *Newsweek*, May 8, 1972, p. 19, and Block, *State of the Union*, p. 66.

10. Safire, *Before the Fall*, p. 177.

11. Keogh, *Nixon and the Press*, p. 39.

12. David Wise, "The President and the Press," *Atlantic* (April 1973): 59.

13. John J. O'Connor, "When Does a Presidential Address Become a Public Relations Ploy?" *New York Times*, August 4, 1974, Part II, p. 14.

14. Safire, *Before the Fall*, p. 521. Henry Kissinger would receive instructions to take a three-page draft and "cut it to two pages," says Safire; the national security adviser would then hand it to a secretary with the command, "Type this on two pages."

15. Barrett, *Survey*, p. 19.

16. Robert A. Diamond, ed., *Watergate: Chronology of a Crisis* (Washington, DC: Congressional Quarterly, 1974), Vol. II, p. 159.

17. *Washington Post*, February 12, 1973, Sec. A, pp. 1, 16.

18. "TV Politics: Too High a Price," *Life*, October 11, 1970, p. 2. See also Barrett, *Survey*, p. 46.

19. Barrett, *Survey*, p. 46.

20. "Advantage: Mr. President," *Time*, January 18, 1971, p. 36.

21. "Again the Credibility Gap?" *Time*, April 5, 1971, p. 13.

22. "Media Report/ Nixon's Suprise Freeze Announcement Leaves Washington Press Ruffled, Not Furious," *National Journal*, October 30, 1971, p. 2164.

23. Ibid., pp. 2166–2168.

24. James R. Dickenson, "Nixon: He Denies He's 'Preening,' Wants U.S. to Look Again," *National Observer*, March 22, 1971, p. 14.

25. "The Making of the Newest Nixon," *Time*, January 18, 1971, p. 12; "The Nixon Watcher," *Newsweek*, June 22, 1970, p. 60.

26. Helen Thomas, *Dateline: White House* (New York: Macmillan, 1975), pp. 182, 145; David Frost, *"I Gave Them a Sword": Behind the Scenes of the Nixon Interviews* (New York: William Morrow, 1978), p. 93.

27. Nixon, *Memoirs*, p. 1010. See also, Safire, *Before the Fall*, p. 443, and Charles W. Colson, *Born Again* (Old Tappan, New Jersey: Chosen Books, 1976), p. 78.

28. Rather, *Palace Guard*, p. 221.

29. "Patton's Defection," *Time*, August 24, 1970, p. 8.

30. Peter Bogdanovich, "Hollywood," *Esquire* (December 1972): 31.

31. *Washington Post*, October 3, 1970, Sec. A, p. 3.

32. Ibid., May 6, 1972, Sec. A, p. 1.

33. United Press International dispatch, *Washington Post*, January 26, 1970.

34. Newsmakers, *Newsweek*, February 14, 1972, p. 30.

35. "White House All-Stars," *Time*, July 17, 1972, p. 10.

36. "Reports: Washington," *Atlantic* (May 1970): 4.

37. Jeff Greenfield, "Mr. Nixon's Sense of History," *Harper's Magazine* (November 1970): 66–67.

38. *Washington Post*, February 4, 1970, Sec. B, p. 3.

39. "The Palace Guard," *Time*, February 9, 1970, p. 7.

40. Safire, *Before the Fall*, p. 288.

41. H. R. Haldeman, with Joseph DiMona, *The Ends of Power* (New York: Times Books, 1978), p. 207.

42. Paul Hoffman, *The New Nixon* (New York: Tower Publications, 1970), p. 77.

43. Theodore H. White, *Breach of Faith: The Fall of Richard Nixon* (New York: Atheneum, 1975), p. 118.

44. Rather, *Palace Guard*, pp. 130–131.

45. Haldeman, *Ends of Power*, p. 52.

46. Safire, *Before the Fall*, p. 284.

47. Thomas E. Cronin, "The Swelling of the Presidency," *Saturday Review* (February 1973): 30.

48. *Washington Post*, June 1, 1971, Sec. A, p. 1; Rather, *Palace Guard*, pp. 235–236, and Frank Mankiewicz, *Perfectly Clear: Nixon from Whittier to Watergate* (New York: Quadrangle, 1973), p. 4.

49. Rather, *Palace Guard*, p. 132.

50. Richard Gorman, "Cambodia Move 'Major Success,' Klein Tells New Jersey Chapter," *Quill* 57:7 (July 1970): 39.

51. Hugh Sidey, "Loose Talk From an Old Lawyer," *Life*, August 14, 1970, p. 4. In 1977, Raymond Price wrote (*With Nixon*, New York: Viking Press, 1977, p. 134): "In a slip of the tongue, Nixon inadvertently referred to mass murderer Charles Manson as 'guilty' before Manson's trial was completed. Despite a quick correction, his critics made it a *cause celebre*, and continued ever after to harp on it as an example of Nixon's supposed disdain for due process." Some people never give up.

52. Henry Kissinger, *White House Years* (Boston: Little, Brown, 1979), p. 1399, and Rather, *Place Guard*, p. 174.

53. Rather, *Palace Guard*, pp. 212–243, and Safire, *Before the Fall*, p. 646.

54. Safire, *Before the Fall*, pp. 464–465.

55. Allen Drury, *Courage and Hesitation* (Garden City, N.Y.: Doubleday, 1971), pp. 210–214.

56. Nolan, "The Re-selling of the President," *Atlantic* (November 1972): 80.

57. Dickenson, "Nixon: He Denies He's 'Preening,' " p. 1.

58. *New York Times*, March 22, 1971, p. 24.

59. Jack Anderson, "Nixon Gambled on Moon Publicity," *Washington Post* July 29, 1969, Sec. B., p. 11. See also, Nixon, *Memoirs*, pp. 428–430 and Thomas, *Dateline*, pp. 127–128.

60. Hoffman, *New Nixon*, pp. 183–184. See also Nixon, *Memoirs*, pp. 466–467, and Charles Colson, *Born Again* (Old Tappan, N.J.: Chosen Books, 1976), p. 40.

61. The Word From Washington, *Progressive* (July 1970):13.

62. Haldeman, *Ends of Power*, p. 70.

63. Rather, *Palace Guard*, pp. 243–245.

64. Nixon, *Memoirs*, p. 493, and "Selling the President, 1970," *Newsweek*, November 16, 1970, p. 77.

65. Safire, *Before the Fall*, pp. 327–340, and Rather, *Palace Guard*, pp. 260–262.

66. Rather, *Palace Guard*, p. 246.

67. Don Oberdorfer, "The China Press Scenario," *Nation*, March 27, 1972, pp. 394–397.

68. "Peking Protest," *Time*, February 21, 1972, p. 64.

69. "A Guide to Nixon's China Journey," *Time*, February 21, 1972, p. 28.

70. Kissinger, *White House Years*, pp.1054–1055.

71. "TV: An Eyeful of China, a Thimbleful of Insight," *Newsweek*, March 6, 1972, p. 27.

72. "The President's Odyssey Day by Day," *Time*, March 6, 1972, p. 13, and "China Coverage: Sweet and Sour," *Time*, March 6, 1972, p. 50.

73. "China Meets the Press," *Newsweek*, March 6, 1972, p. 26. See also John Osborne, *The Fourth Year of the Nixon Watch* (New York: Liveright, 1973), p. 22, and Thomas, *Dateline*, p. 140.

74. Rather, *Palace Guard*, p. 246, and Osborne, *Fourth Year*, p. 20.

75. Stanley Karnow, "The Chinese Sayings of President Nixon," *Washington Post*, February 29, 1972, Sec. A, p. 18. See also, Thomas, *Dateline*, pp. 140–142.

76. "The China Trip and How It Was Covered," *Quill* 60:5 (April 1972):11.

77. Nolan, "The Re-Selling of the President," p. 180.

78. Dom Bonafede, "Commissar of Credibility," *The Nation*, April 6, 1970, p. 392, and Bob Wilson, "Klein and Ziegler: Nixon's PR Men," *Freedom of Information Center Report No. 244* (published at Columbia, Missouri, by the University of Missouri School of Journalism), June, 1970, p. 2.

79. "Has the Press Done a Job on Nixon?" *Columbia Journalism Review* 12:5 (January–February 1974):52.

80. Safire, *Before the Fall*, pp. 290–291, and Rather, *Palace Guard*, pp. 151–152. Haldeman, in *Ends of Power*, claimed he was "a good friend" of Klein's. See p. 74.

81. White House memorandum, February 4, 1970.

82. Ibid., December 11, 1970. Lyn Nofziger, another hard-sell artist and hard-line conservative, was originally on the White House staff and later moved to the Republican National Committee. Victor Lasky and James J. Kilpatrick are conservative columnists. The late David Lawrence was editor and columnist for the *U.S. News & World Report*. Harrison Salisbury was, at the time, an assistant managing editor of the *New York Times*.

83. Price, *With Nixon*, p. 336; Hugh Sidey, "So Long to Old Herb Klein," *Time*, June 18, 1973, p. 17.

84. *Washington Post*, January 9, 1973, Sec. A., pp. 1,7.

85. Luther A. Huston, "Clawson Purveys Nixon Policy to Opinion Writers," *Editor & Publisher*, April 6, 1974, p. 29.

86. Erwin Knoll, "The President and the Press: Eliminating the Middleman," *Progressive* (March 1970):15, and Jules Witcover, "The Two Hats of Herbert Klein," *Columbia Journalism Review* 8:1 (Spring 1970):26–28.

87. Wilson, "Klein and Ziegler," p. 2.

88. Witcover, "Two Hats," p. 27; *Wall Street Journal*, March 29, 1971, p. 1.

89. *Washington Post*, January 30, 1969, Sec. A, p. 6.

90. Ibid., January 18, 1973, Sec. A, p. 24.

91. Samuel J. Archibald, "Who's Running Government PR?" *Public Relations Journal* 26:7 (July, 1970):8.

92. *Washington Post*, January 18, 1973, Sec. A, p. 24.

93. Wilson, "Klein and Ziegler," p. 3, and Archibald, "Government PR," p. 6

94. *Wall Street Journal*, March 21, 1969, p. 23.

95. Ibid., p. 1.

96. Luther A. Huston, "How Herb Klein Assists the President," *Editor & Publisher*, February 15, 1969, p. 10.

97. Witcover, "Two Hats," p. 27.

98. Wilson, "Klein and Ziegler," p. 2.

99. Nixon, *Memoirs*, p. 355.

100. *Wall Street Journal*, March 21, 1969, p. 23.

101. Statement by Kenneth Clawson, personal interview, August 8, 1972; Knoll, "The President and the Press," p. 16; *Wall Street Journal*, February 9, 1971, p. 16; Bonafede, "Commissar of Credibility," p. 394.

102. *Washington Post*, June 8, 1969, Sec. A, p. 11; *Wall Street Journal*, February 9, 1971, p. 16.

103. Hugh Sidey, "Kingdom Come on Pennsylvania Avenue," *Life*, February 26, 1971, p. 2B.

104. *Wall Street Journal*, February 9, 1971, p. 16.

105. *New York Times*, August 24, 1970, p. 18.

106. James M. Naughton, "How the 2d Best-Informed Man in the White House Briefs the 2d Worst-Informed Group in Washington," *New York Times Magazine*, May 30, 1971, p. 27.

107. *New York Times*, August 24, 1970, p. 18; "The Press Covers Government: The Nixon Years from 1969 to Watergate," A Study by the Department of Communication, American University, Washington, D.C., for the National Press Club, July 1973, p. 26.

108. "Direct Communications," *Newsweek*, September 7, 1970, p. 57.

109. *New York Times*, August 24, 1970, p. 18.

110. *Wall Street Journal*, February 9, 1971, p. 16; *Washington Post*, December 26, 1973, Sec. A, p. 5.

111. Statement by Herb Klein, personal interview, March 16, 1971.

112. *Wall Street Journal*, February 9, 1971, p. 16.

113. Statement by Kenneth Clawson, personal interview, August 8, 1972.

114. Witcover, "Two Hats," p. 29.

115. Office of Communication fact kit; cover letter on White House letterhead, June 16, 1971.

116. *Wall Street Journal*, February 9, 1971, p. 16; *Washington Daily News*, February 10, 1972, p. 9.

117. Keogh, *Nixon and the Press*, p. 60.

118. All of the details about the Creel committee are from Elmer E. Cornwell, Jr., *Presidential Leadership of Public Opinion* (Bloomington: Indiana University Press, 1965), pp. 48–57.

Chapter 6

1. Richard M. Nixon, *RN: The Memoirs of Richard Nixon* (New York: Grosset & Dunlap, 1978), p. 355.

2. Patrick Buchanan to George White, telegram, October 29, 1968.

3. Jack Anderson, "Did Times Editorial Light Spiro's Fire?" *Miami Herald*, September 14, 1972, p. 23.

4. William Safire, *Before the Fall* (Garden City, N.Y.: Doubleday, 1975), p. 466.

5. David Halberstam, *The Powers That Be* (New York: Knopf, 1979), p. 606.

6. Safire, *Before the Fall*, p. 353.

7. Elmer C. Lower, "Fairness and Balance in Television Reporting," *Quill* 58:2 (February 1970):12.

8. White House memorandum, October 17, 1969.

9. Ibid.

10. Thomas Whiteside, "Annals of Television," *New Yorker*, March 17, 1975, p. 42.

11. Nixon, *Memoirs*, pp. 401–409.

12. James Keogh, *President Nixon and the Press* (New York: Funk & Wagnalls, 1972), pp. 171–185.

13. Nixon, *Memoirs*, p. 411. See also Safire, *Before the Fall*, p. 352.

14. Keogh, *Nixon and the Press*, p. 136.

15. Nixon, *Memoirs*, p. 411. See also Safire, *Before the Fall*, p. 352.

16. Whiteside, "Annals of Television," p. 43. Herbert Thompson was actually a member of Herb Klein's staff who acted also as Agnew's spokesman. Before long, however, Agnew's notoriety was such that he rated a full-time professional public relations expert, and Victor Gold was hired.

17. Keogh, *Nixon and the Press*, pp. 191–192. The Keogh book contains a complete transcript of the Des Moines speech on pp. 191–198.

18. Ibid., pp. 192–195.

19. Alfred Balk and James Boylan, eds., *Our Troubled Press, Ten Years of the Columbia Journalism Review* (Boston: Little, Brown, 1971), pp. 179–181.

20. Marvin Barrett, ed., *The Alfred I. duPont-Columbia University Survey of Broadcast Journalism 1969–1970* (New York: Grosset & Dunlap, 1970), p. 37.

21. Arthur Woodstone, *Nixon's Head* (New York: St. Martin's Press, 1972), p. 141n

22. Bill Gill, "Richard Nixon as News Editor," *Quill* 61:3 (March 1973): 8–9.

23. Jules Witcover, "The Two Hats of Herb Klein," *Columbia Journalism Review* 9:1 (Spring 1970):30. Klein said such calls were a routine way of obtaining a "private sampling" of opinion. See Herbert G. Klein, *Making it Perfectly Clear* (Garden City, N.Y.: Doubleday, 1980), p. 170.

24. Barrett, *Survey*, pp. 36–37.

25. Dom Bonafede, "Commissar of Credibility," *Nation*, April 6, 1970, p. 395. For Klein's version of his comment, see *Making It Perfectly Clear*, pp. 172–174.

26. Safire, *Before the Fall*, p. 353.

27. Keogh, *Nixon and the Press*, pp. 200–201.

28. William Rivers, *The Adversaries* (Boston: Beacon Press, 1970), p. 253.

29. "Sulzberger Notes Agnew Inaccuracy," *Editor & Publisher*, November 29, 1969, p. 11.

30. Rivers, *Adversaries*, p. 258.

31. "Agnew's Pungent Quotient," *Time*, January 29, 1970, p. 12.

32. Robert Lewis Shayon, "Propaganda Deflation," *Saturday Review*, March 20, 1971, p. 40.

33. "TV v. the Pentagon," *Time*, April 5, 1971, p. 46.

34. *Washington Post*, March 19, 1971, Sec. A, p. 2.

35. Associated Press dispatch, *Washington Evening Star*, March 19, 1971.

36. *Washington Post*, March 28, 1971, Sec. B, p. 4.

37. "An Arrow in the Air," *Newsweek*, March 29, 1971, p. 111.

38. *Washington Post*, March 25, 1971, Sec. A, p. 3. In early April 1971, the Special Investigations Subcommittee of the House Interstate and Foreign Commerce Committee waded into the fray with a formal subpoena against CBS that demanded "all film, workprints, outtakes, soundtape recordings, written scripts and/or transcripts" used in making "The Selling of the Pentagon." The network refused to respond, and the drama dragged on until July 13 when, under the incessant urging of subcommittee chairman Harley O. Staggers, Democrat of West Virginia, the full House voted on a contempt citation against CBS. The members decided, by a margin of 226 to 181, to "recommit" the matter to the Commerce Committee—a bit of legislative legerdemain that is often used to kill a bill or resolution. That settled the affair. An excellent, detailed account of the episode may be found in William E. Porter, *Assault on the Media: The Nixon Years* (Ann Arbor: University of Michigan Press, 1976), pp. 113–126

39. "Agnew: Managing the News," *Columbia Journalism Review* 10:6, (March–April 1972):38.

40. "Judging the Fourth Estate, A Time-Louis Harris Poll," *Time*, September 5, 1969, pp. 38–39.

41. Barrett, *Survey*, p. 33.

42. Ibid.

43. Ibid., p. 38.

44. "Are the Rules Changing?" *Columbia Journalism Review* 10:5 (January–February 1972):9.

45. Safire, *Before the Fall*, p. 341.

46. Julius Duscha, "The White House Watch over TV and the Press," *New York Times Magazine*, August 20, 1972, p. 9.

47. *Washington Star-News*, August 2, 1973, Sec. A, p. 6.

48. *Washington Post*, June 8, 1969, Sec. A, p. 11.

49. *Washington Post*, December 3, 1973, Sec. A, p. 17.

50. White House memorandum, July 16, 1970.

51. "Cavett's Complaint," *Newsweek*, April 5, 1971, p. 59.

52. Statement by Alvin Snyder, personal interview, March 9, 1971.

53. Clark R. Mollenhoff, *Game Plan For Disaster* (New York: W.W. Norton, 1976), p. 129.

54. The Record, "Mitchell Tightens Press Guidelines," *Quill* 61:1 (January 1972):6.

55. "The Press Covers Government: The Nixon Years from 1969 to Watergate," A Study by the Department of Communication, American University, Washington, D.C. for the National Press Club, July 1973, p. 17.

56. Mike Causey, "Clam-Up Order Affects Some 800,000," *Washington Post*, March 20, 1971, Sec. B, p. 5.

57. *Washington Post*, March 20, 1971, Sec. A, p. 8.

58. *Washington Star-News*, August 2, 1973, Sec. A, p. 6.

59. Nixon, *Memoirs*, pp. 387–388.

60. H. R. Haldeman, with Joseph DiMona, *The Ends of Power* (New York: Times Books, 1978), p. 101.

61. Tad Szulc, *The Illusion of Peace: Foreign Policy in the Nixon Years* (New York: Viking Press, 1978), pp. 181–189.

62. Haldeman, *Ends of Power*, p. 103.

63. Nixon *Memoirs*, p. 508.

64. Haldeman, *Ends of Power*, p. 110–111.

65. Nixon, *Memoirs*, pp. 509–513.

66. Haldeman, *Ends of Power*, p. 111.

67. *New York Times*, June 27, 1973, p. 48.

68. Haldeman, *Ends of Power*, p. 112.

69. Safire, *Before the Fall*, p. 358.

70. Theodore H. White, *Breach of Faith: The Fall of Richard Nixon* (New York: Atheneum Publishers, 1975), pp. 148–150.

71. Haldeman, *Ends of Power*, p. 113.

72. Nixon, *Memoirs*, p. 514.

73. *New York Times*, May 4, 1974, p. 23, January 15, 1974, p. 16.

74. Nixon, *Memoirs*, p. 543.

75. Carl Bernstein and Bob Woodward, *All the President's Men* (New York: Simon and Schuster, 1974), pp. 133–134. Deep Throat was referring to Senator Thomas Eagleton of Missouri, nominated as George McGovern's vice-presidential running mate in 1972. But on July 25 Eagleton admitted in a press conference that he had been hospitalized three times in the past for emotional problems. Two days later columnist Jack Anderson reported over the Mutual Broadcasting System that the state of Missouri was rife with rumors that Eagleton had previously been arrested for drunken driving. Anderson also said he had "located" photostats of the arrest citations. The Anderson report was only slightly overstated. He had, in fact, been told about the arrests by True Davis, a native Missourian, wealthy businessman, former ambassador to Switzerland, former assistant secretary of the Treasury and then the president of the National Bank of Washington. Davis had run in the Democratic primary for the Senate in Missouri in 1968, and he claimed that copies of the Eagleton arrest citations had been delivered to him by a state trooper. He

had never made use of them and, while purging his files, had destroyed them. No copies were ever made. When Anderson could not produce them, he was subjected to a barrage of criticism from—as he put it—"a host of newspaper tub-thumpers, not known previously for journalistic enterprise or purity." See Jack Anderson with George Clifford, *The Anderson Papers* (New York: Random House, 1973), pp. 135-162.

76. Szulc, *Illusion of Peace*, p. 19.

77. Helen Thomas, *Dateline: White House* (New York: Macmillan, 1975), p. 251.

78. Ibid., p. 252. See also, Szulc, *Illusion of Peace*, p. 179.

79. Roger Morris, "Henry Kissinger and the Media: A Separate Peace," *Columbia Journalism Review* 13:1 (May–June 1974):14-25. The response of *New York Times* managing editor, A. M. Rosenthal, to the charge that the *Times* killed stories at Kissinger's request may be found in the *Columbia Journalism Review* 13:2 (July–August 1974):53-55.

80. "The Press in the President's Transcripts," *Quill* 63:6 (June 1974):14.

81. "Dean's List of White House 'Political Enemies,' " *Quill* 62:8 (August 1973):11.

82. White House memorandum, July 17, 1970.

83. White House memorandum, October 17, 1969.

84. David Halberstam, *Powers That Be*, pp. 665-666.

85. *New York Times*, May 4, 1974, p. 23.

86. Porter, *Assault on the Media*, p. 131.

87. Ibid., pp. 126-127.

88. *Washington Post*, April 14, 1974, Sec. B, p. 6.

89. Safire, *Before the Fall*, p. 614.

90. *New York Times*, June 27, 1973, p. 49. See also, "Auditing a Newsman," *Quill*, 63:6 (June 1974):9

91. Timothy Crouse, *The Boys on the Bus: Riding with the Campaign Press Corps* (New York: Random House, 1973), pp. 220-225.

92. *Washington Post*, December 3, 1973, Sec. A, p. 17. See also, *Washington Star-News*, November 5, 1973, Sec. A, p. 4.

93. "The Post's Peril of '71," *Quill* 62:9 (September 1973):9.

94. Mollenhoff, *Game Plan*, pp. 245-246.

95. Bernstein and Woodward, *All the President's Men*, pp. 181-182.

96. Ibid., pp. 184-185.

97. *Washington Post*, December 18, 1972, Sec. B, pp. 1,2.

98. Ibid., December 19, 1972, Sec. B, pp. 1,2.

99. *Washington Evening Star and Daily News*, January 6, 1973, Sec. A, p. 1.

100. Bernstein and Woodward, *All the President's Men*, pp. 220-221.

101. Whiteside, "Annals of Television," p. 61.

102. *Washington Post*, January 9, 1973, Sec. A, p. 6.

103. Ibid., January 4, 1973, Sec. A, p. 4.

104. Haldeman, *Ends of Power*, pp. 103-104.

105. Nixon, *Memoirs*, p. 389.

106. Haldeman, *Ends of Power*, p. 104.

107. Nixon, *Memoirs*, p. 389.

108. *New York Times*, January 15, 1974, p. 16.

109. Charles W. Colson, *Born Again* (Old Tappan, N.J.: Chosen Books, 1976, p. 242.

110. Anderson, *The Anderson Papers*, pp. v-vi.

111. Ibid., p. vii.

112. Jack Anderson, "FBI's Investigators Strike Again . . . " *Washington Post*, February 12, 1974, Sec. B, p. 13.

113. *Washington Post*, September 21, 1975, Sec. A, p. 20.

114. Ibid., October 22, 1975, Sec. A, p. 22.

115. Anderson, *The Anderson Papers*, p. 227.

116. Nixon, *Memoirs*, pp. 531–532.

117. Ibid., pp. 580–582.

118. Haldeman, *Ends of Power*, p. 152.

119. John Dean, *Blind Ambition* (New York: Pocket Books, 1977), pp. 46–50.

120. CIA Director Richard Helms later stated under oath that he personally ordered the surveillance of Anderson and his staff and did not inform the White House of it. Considering the context—an on-going press-suppression campaign by the White House—I find Helms's statement difficult to believe. Readers may draw their own conclusions. Information about Helms's statement came from Anderson's attorney, William Dobrovir, in an interview on January 14, 1980. Dobrovir deposed Helms in connection with a lawsuit filed by Anderson.

121. All of the subsequent details about PROJECT MUDHEN are outlined in CIA documents in my possession. An impartial observer, incidentally, would have to conclude that CHAMPAGNE is clearly the class of the lot.

122. United Press International dispatch, *Palm Beach Post*, June 9, 1976.

123. Statement by Leslie Whitten, personal interview, February 1, 1973.

124. *Washington Post*, February 16, 1973, Sec. A, pp. 1,10.

125. Jack Anderson, "FBI Used Arrest to Probe Anderson," *Washington Post*, February 23, 1973, Sec. D, p. 17.

126. White House memorandum, July 17, 1970.

127. Stephen R. Barnett, "The Fairness Doctrine: How Fair?" *Nation*, August 7, 1972, pp. 78–80. The court decision, rendered in November 1971, upheld CBS and strongly chastized the FCC. In the interim, however, CBS became involved in the controversy surrounding "The Selling of the Pentagon," and decided to drop "The Loyal Opposition."

128. White House memorandum, August 26, 1970.

129. White House memorandum, September 25, 1970. When this memo surfaced during the Senate Watergate investigation, William Paley stated that the administration's overtures had never affected CBS news coverage. Goodman of NBC said that if the memo was "a correct representation of [Colson's] characterization of the meeting, his recollection and mine are completely different." Hagerty of ABC said that Colson "must be out of his ever loving mind." See the *New York Times*, November 2, 1973, p. 24.

130. Whiteside, "Annals of Television," p. 67. In his memoirs, Klein devotes several pages to an explanation of the antitrust suits and his visit with the network executives. The suits, he maintained, were strictly the product of Justice Department professionals—"a triumph for the bureaucracy not connected to the White House war with the press." See *Making It Perfectly Clear*, pp. 214–222.

131. "Justice vs. the Networks," *Newsweek*, April 24, 1972, p. 55.

132. Joe McGinniss, *The Selling of the President 1968* (New York: Trident Press, Book Club Edition, 1969), p. 60.

133. Whiteside, "Annals of Television," p. 45.

134. White House memorandum, July 16, 1970.

135. White House memorandum, July 17, 1970.

136. Crouse, *Boys on the Bus*, pp. 265–267.

137. Newsmakers, *Newsweek*, October 16, 1972, p. 59.

138. Statement by Cassie Mackin, personal interview, August 9, 1979. Mackin eventually moved on to ABC as a national correspondent.

139. Erwin Knoll, "Shaping Up CBS: A Case Study in Intimidation," *Progressive* (July 1970):18.

140. Ibid., pp. 18–19.

141. "Clark Mollenhoff Named Nixon Aide," *Quill* 57:10 (October 1969):43.

142. Knoll, "Shaping Up CBS," pp. 18–21. Dan Rather later wrote (with Mickey Herskowitz, *The Camera Never Blinks* [New York: Morrow, 1977], pp. 275–276) that "one syndicated columnist"—an obvious reference to Anderson—bought the White House line and published the story because he believed "that television is the root evil of society" and little more than "show biz, pretty faces and animated cartoons." I was there at the time and can state that, as an investigative reporter, Anderson obtained an internal White House memorandum, believed it to be a sound, exclusive story, and published it in good faith.

143. Statement by Clark Mollenhoff, personal interview, September 27, 1979.

144. David Wise, "The President and the Press," *Atlantic* (April 1973):64.

145. Associated Press dispatch, *Washington Post*, April 8, 1971. See also Fred Powledge, *The Engineering of Restraint, The Nixon Administration and the Press* (Washington D.C.: Public Affairs Press, 1971), p. 19.

146. Powledge, pp. 25–26.

147. Daniel Schorr, "A Chilling Experience," *Harper's* (March 1973):92–97. See also, Daniel Schorr, *Clearing the Air* (New York: Berkley Publishing, 1978), pp. 69–74.

148. Haldeman, *Ends of Power*, pp. 184–185; Schorr, *Clearing the Air*, pp. 80–86; *New York Times*, December 30, 1973, p. 19.

149. Schorr, *Clearing the Air*, p. 86.

150. Gary Paul Gates, *Air Time: The Inside Story of CBS News* (New York: Harper & Row, 1978), pp. 303–307.

151. Rowland Evans and Robert Novak, "The White House vs. CBS," *Washington Post*, November 26, 1972, Sec. B, p. 7.

152. There are a number of published accounts of the administration's displeasure with CBS over the Watergate stories of October 1972. Among the best are Gates, *Air Time*, pp. 303–307; Halberstam, *Powers That Be*, pp. 654–663; and Schorr, *Clearing the Air* pp. 53–57. Stanton took notes when Colson called him and recounted the threats in a sworn statement that was filed with the court during the Justice Department's antitrust suit. On May 26, 1974, however, Colson appeared on "60 Minutes" and declared, "I think it's fair to say that I never had a conversation like that with Frank Stanton. I read that in the newspaper and I was really surprised." See Whitehead, "Annals of Television," p. 60.

153. "Restrained 'Freedom,'" *Time*, January 1, 1973, p. 63.

154. Porter, *Assault on the Media*, p. 173.

155. *Washington Post*, December 22, 1972, Sec. A, p. 22.

156. "Restrained 'Freedom,'" p. 63.

157. "Mr. Nixon Jawbones the Media," *Newsweek*, January 1, 1973, p. 13.

158. The Presidency, "Nixon's Proposed 1973 Budget Reflects Record Growth of Executive Office," *National Journal*, February 26, 1972, p. 370.

159. *Washington Evening Star and Daily News*, December 20, 1972, Sec. A, p. 11.

160. Julius Duscha, "Whitehead? Who's Whitehead?" *Progressive* (April 1973):41.

161. *Washington Evening Star and Daily News*, December 20, 1972, Sec. A, p. 11.

162. Duscha, "Whitehead?" p. 42.

163. James J. Kilpatrick, "Whitehead Off Base in Attack on TV Industry," *Washington Evening Star and Daily News*, December 26, 1972, Sec. A, p. 11.

164. Powledge, *Engineering of Restraint*, p. 34.

165. *Washington Post*, July 18, 1972, Sec. B, p. 2, December 27, 1972, Sec. E, p. 1.

166. John Friedman, "Nixon's the One," *Washington Journalism Review* 1:6 (April–May 1979):38.

167. Fred W. Friendly, "The Campaign to Politicize Broadcasting," *Columbia Journalism Review* 11:6 (March–April 1973):13.

168. Powledge, *Engineering of Restraint*, p. 38.

169. Newsmakers, *Newsweek*, February 2, 1972, p. 46. "Hanging by the Thumbs," *Columbia Journalism Review* 10:5 (January–February 1972):3. In 1973 a group of interested parties filed suit against Whitehead, Buchanan, the CPB, and PBS charging that the defendants had manipulated and censored programming. It was finally dismissed in early 1979 for a number of reasons, including that fact that the Nixon administration was no longer around. See *Broadcasting*, February 19, 1979, pp. 60–62.

170. *Washington Post*, July 18, 1972, Sec. B, p. 2.

171. Ibid., February 24, 1979, Sec. A, p. 12.

172. Ibid.

173. Friedman, "Nixon's the One," p. 39.

174. Ibid., p. 38.

175. Bruce E. Thorp, "Media Report/White House Static over Structure, Funds Keeps Public Broadcasting Picture Fuzzy," *National Journal*, April 29, 1972, p. 735.

176. *Washington Post*, February 24, 1979, Sec. A, p. 12.

177. Thorp, "Media Report," p. 736.

178. *Washington Post*, February 3, 1972, Sec. B, p. 12.

179. Ibid.

180. Julius Duscha, "The White House Watch over TV and the Press," *New York Times Magazine*, August 20, 1972, pp. 9, 96.

181. "The Czar of the Airwaves," *Newsweek*, February 7, 1972, p. 44.

182. *Washington Post*, January 27, 1973, Sec. E, p. 4.

183. "Talk Show," *Newsweek*, January 18, 1971, p. 16.

184. *Washington Evening Star and Daily News*, August 24, 1972, Sec. A, p. 18.

185. "A Novice for Public TV," *Time*, October 16, 1972, p. 94.

186. *Washington Post*, November 2, 1972, Sec. C, p. 1.

187. Friedman, "Nixon's the One," p. 38.

188. Ibid.

189. *Washington Post*, December 15, 1972, Sec. E, pp. 1,2.

190. Friedman, "Nixon's the One," p. 38. See also "Public TV: A Glimmer," *Columbia Journalism Review* 11:2 (July–August 1973):3–4.

191. Friedman, "Nixon's the One," p. 38.

192. Porter, *Assault on the Media*, p. 153. See also "A Final Good Turn from Nixon," *Columbia Journalism Review* 12:3 (September–October 1974):2–3.

193. "The Press in the President's Transcripts," *Quill* 63:6 (June 1974):14.

194. *Wall Street Journal*, August 13, 1971, p. 1.

195. *Washington Post*, June 28, 1973, Sec. A, p. 14.

196. Mollenhoff, *Game Plan*, pp. 29, 110–113.

197. Dean, *Blind Ambition*, pp. 22–25.

198. Raymond Price, *With Nixon* (New York: Viking Press, 1977), pp. 231–233.

199. Statement by former ACLU attorney Douglas Lea, personal interview, January 25, 1980. Lea was the director of the project.

200. Crouse, *Boys on the Bus*, p. 225; *Washington Post*, January 5, 1978, Sec. A, p. 1; *New York Times*, June 27, 1973, p. 49, May 28, 1974, p. 25.

201. Whiteside, "Annals of Television," p. 42.

202. *New York Times*, November 2, 1973, p. 24.

203. Charles Long, "The CBS Summer of '71," *Quill* 60:8 (August 1971):15.

204. All statements in this paragraph were previously documented.

205. *Washington Post*, April 20, 1972, Sec. B, p. 1.

206. Roger Simon, "S.1, A Menace to the Press," *Quill* 64:7 (July–August 1975):19–21. See also "New Criminal Code Threatens Reporters, Sources," *Quill* 63:5 (May 1973):34, and *New York Times*, April 22, 1973, p. 18.

207. Jules Witcover, "Two Weeks That Shook the Press," *Columbia Journalism Review*, 10:3 (September–October 1971):7–15. An exhaustive account may be found in Sanford J. Unger, *The Papers & the Papers* (New York: E.P. Dutton, 1972).

208. Trudy Rubin, "Stalking Beacon Press," *[More]* 2:9 (September 1972):5–7.

209. Balk and Boylan, *Troubled Press*, pp. 185–186.

210. Powledge, *Engineering of Restraint*, p. 45.

211. Jules Witcover, "A Reporters' Committee That Works," *Columbia Journalism Review* 11:1 (May–June 1973):29.

212. Balk and Boylan, *Troubled Press*, p. 186.

213. "Mitchell's Guidelines," *Quill*, 63:7 (July–August 1973):18.

214. *New York Times*, November 21, 1973, p. 22.

215. "Mitchell's Guidelines," p. 18. See also Robert Walters, "Sharing the News with Justice," *Columbia Journalism Review* 13:3 (September–October 1975):21.

216. Nixon, *Memoirs*, p. 424.

217. Earl Caldwell, " 'Ask Me. I Know. I Was the Test Case,' " *Saturday Review*, August 5, 1972, pp. 406.

218. Powledge, *Engineering of Restraint*, p. 45.

219. *New York Times*, June 30, 1972, p. 15.

220. Norman E. Isaacs, "Beyond 'Caldwell'—2: 'The Decision is Tentative,' " *Columbia Journalism Review* 11:3 (September–October 1972):20.

221. *New York Times*, June 30, 1972, p. 15.

222. Hodding Carter III, "The Deteriorating First Amendment," *Grassroots Editor* (January–February 1973):16.

223. "Fight over Freedom and Privilege," *Time*, March 5, 1973, p. 64. See also Porter, *Assault on the Media*, p. 225.

224. *Washington Evening Star and Daily News*, October 9, 1972, Sec. A, p. 3.

225. Associated Press dispatch, *Washington Post*, October 25, 1972.

226. *Washington Post*, November 17, 1972, Sec. A, p. 5.

227. Ibid., February 5, 1973, Sec. A, p. 4.

228. *New York Times*, November 17, 1972, p. 24.

229. *Washington Post*, December 14, 1972, Sec. A, p. 30.

230. "Five-Plus Years on Trial," *Quill* 67:5 (May 1979):10. See also, "Farr Case Finis," *Quill*, 65:1 (January 1977):6, and "Summary: The Farr Case," *Quill* 62:11 (November 1974):8.

231. *Washington Post*, October 26, 1972, Sec. A, p. 8.

232. Ibid., February 6, 1973, Sec. A, p. 5.

233. Ibid., February 5, 1973, Sec. A, p. 4.

234. "Fight over Freedom and Privilege," *Time*, March 5, 1973, p. 64.

235. Associated Press dispatch, *Washington Post*, November 10, 1972.

236. Mark R. Arnold, "Pressure on the Press Alarms Newsmen," *National Observer*, December 30, 1972, p. 20.

237. Rep. Philip Crane, R-Ill., for example, introduced shield legislation after a *New York Times* reporter went to jail in 1978. See "The Press after Farber," *Quill* 67:3 (March 1979):22.

238. United Press International dispatch, *Washington Evening Star and Daily News*, December 15, 1972.

239. *Washington Post*, May 23, 1970, Sec. A, p. 2.

240. "The Press Covers Government," A Study by the Department of Communication, American University, p. 8.

241. David Wise, "The President and the Press," *Atlantic* (April 1973):64.

242. Ben H. Bagdikian, "The Fruits of Agnewism," *Columbia Journalism Review* 11:5 (January–February 1973):10.

243. Wes Gallagher, "Someone Must Search for the Facts," *Columbia Journalism Review* 11:5 (January–February 1973):70.

244. Peter Bridge, "Is the Press 'All Too Willing to be Neutralized?' " *National Observer*, December 9, 1972, p. 15.

245. "Nixon and the Media," *Newsweek*, January 15, 1973, p. 47.

246. Charles Long, "Are News Sources Drying Up?" *Quill* 61:3 (March 1973):10–12.

247. "Fight Over Freedom and Privilege," *Time*, March 5, 1973, p. 65.

248. Statement by Leslie Whitten, personal interview, March 2, 1973.

249. *Washington Post*, March 28, 1971, Sec. B, p. 4.

250. Barrett, *Survey*, p. 41.

251. *New York Times*, January 7, 1973, p. 60.

252. "The Cavett Cancellation: Violating the Will of the FCC?" *Quill* 62:3 (March 1974):12.

253. Barrett, *Survey*, p. 41.

254. Halberstam, *Powers That Be*, pp. 662–663.

255. Barrett, *Survey*, pp. 41–42.

256. Frank Getlein, "CBS at Feet of Clay," *Washington Evening Star and Daily News*, March 8, 1973, Sec. C, p. 1.

257. *Washington Post*, March 9, 1973, Sec. A, p. 17.

258. Barrett, *Survey*, pp. 42–44.

259. "Newspapers Should Help in Broadcasters' Fight," *Quill* 60:5 (May 1972):22.

260. Steven Knoll, "When TV Was Offered the Pentagon Papers," *Columbia Journalism Review* 10:6 (March–April 1972):46–48.

261. Barrett, *Survey*, p. 42.

262. Safire, *Before the Fall*, p. 178.

263. Duscha, "White House Watch," p. 9.

Chapter 7

1. Richard M. Nixon, *RN: The Memoirs of Richard Nixon* (New York: Grosset & Dunlap, 1978), pp. 665, 669.

2. *Washington Evening Star and Daily News*, August 22, 1972, Sec. A, p. 11.

3. *Washington Post*, August 19, 1972, Sec. A, p. 15.

4. "The President's Palace Guard," *Newsweek*, March 19, 1973, p. 28.

5. David Halberstam, *The Powers That Be* (New York: Alfred A. Knopf, 1979), p. 694.

6. Timothy Crouse, *The Boys On the Bus: Riding with the Campaign Press Corps* (New York: Random House, 1973), pp. 272–273.

7. *New York Times*, October 16, 1972, p. 39.

8. Crouse, *Boys on the Bus*, p. 252.

9. James R. Dickenson, "Nixon and the Press," *National Observer*, October 28, 1972, p. 32.

10. *New York Times*, October 3, 1972, p. 32.

11. *Washington Post*, August 26, 1972, Sec. A, p. 4.

12. Dickenson, "Nixon and the Press," p. 24.

13. "How to Rehearse for Deception," *Time*, July 9, 1973, p. 39.

14. "Travels with Nixon and McGovern," *Time*, October 9, 1972, p. 21.

15. *Washington Evening Star and Daily News*, November 4, 1972, Sec. A, p. 5. See also Crouse, *Boys on the Bus*, pp. 268–271.

16. John Osborne, *The Fourth Year of the Nixon Watch* (New York: Liveright, 1973), pp. 136–140.

17. George W. Johnson, ed., *The Nixon Presidential Press Conferences* (New York: Earl M. Coleman Enterprises, 1978), pp. 291–297.

18. Nixon, *Memoirs*, p. 653.

19. Associated Press dispatch, *Washington Evening Star and Daily News*, August 21, 1972.

20. *Washington Evening Star and Daily News*, August 22, 1972, Sec. A, p. 7.

21. *New York Times*, August 23, 1972, p. 26; August 24, 1972, p. 46.

22. *Washington Evening Star and Daily News*, August 23, 1972, Sec. A, p. 1; *New York Times*, August 24, 1972, p. 46.

23. "The Clockwork Convention," *Newsweek*, September 4, 1972, p. 36.

24. White House memorandum, March 14, 1972. See also Martin F. Nolan, "The Re-Selling of the President," *Atlantic* (November 1972):81.

25. *Washington Post*, November 11, 1972, Sec. A, p. 18.

26. *Miami Herald*, September 14, 1972, Sec. A, p. 9.

27. *Washington Evening Star and Daily News*, November 3, 1972, Sec. A, p. 4; *New York Times*, November 1, 1972, pp. 1,26.

28. *Washington Post*, November 11, 1972, Sec. A, p. 2.

29. Dickenson, "Nixon and the Press," p. 24.

30. Theodore H. White, *The Making of the President 1972* (New York: Atheneum, 1973), p. 283.

31. United Press International Dispatch, *Washington Post*, September 10, 1972.

32. Hugh Sidey, "Tying up the Lasagna Network," *Life*, September 29, 1972, p. 12.

33. Barry Sussman, *The Great Cover-Up: Nixon and the Scandal of Watergate* (New York: Signet, 1974), pp. 201–202. See also Carl Bernstein and Bob Woodward, *All the President's Men* (New York: Simon and Schuster, 1974), pp. 265–267.

34. "The Multiple Agent," *Time*, September 24, 1973, pp. 62–64.

35. *New York Times*, July 9, 1973, pp. 1,22.

36. Nixon, *Memoirs*, p. 774. See also H. R. Haldeman with Joseph DiMona, *The Ends of Power* (New York: Times Books, 1978), pp. 235–237; *New York Times*, July 9, 1973, p. 22.

37. *Washington Post*, October 4, 1973, Sec. A, p. 14.

38. "Watergate: Very Offensive Security," *Newsweek*, October 23, 1972, p. 36.

39. "Counterattack and Counterpoint," *Time*, August 13, 1973, pp. 15–16; United Press International dispatch, *Washington Evening Star and Daily News*, November 3, 1972; *Washington Post*, October 23, 1972, Sec. A, p. 7;*Washington Evening Star and Daily News*, October 11, 1972, Sec. B, p. 3.

40. *Washington Post*, August 19, 1972, Sec. A, p. 11.

41. *Washington Post*, August 21, 1972, Sec. A, p. 1; William Safire, *Before the Fall* (Garden City, N.Y.: Doubleday, 1975), p. 651; *Washington Post*, September 14, 1972, Sec. A, p. 2, October 16, 1972, Sec. A, p. 6, September 1, 1972, Sec. A, p. 1, August 27, 1972, Sec. A, p. 17.

42. "The Hard-to-Cover Campaign," *Newsweek*, October 23, 1972, p. 118.

43. "The White House vs. the Media," *Newsweek*, June 5, 1972, p. 23.

44. White House memorandum, March 14, 1972.

45. Safire, *Before the Fall*, p. 359–360.

46. "Nixon and the Media," *Newsweek*, January 15, 1973, p. 44.

47. Safire, *Before the Fall*, p. 631.

48. "The Agnew Peace Offering," *Quill* 60:9 (September 1972):8.

49. Julius Duscha, "The White House Watch over TV and the Press," *New York Times Magazine*, August 20, 1972, p. 93.

50. *New York Times*, June 20, 1973, p. 1.

51. Ben H. Bagdikian, "The Fruits of Agnewism," *Columbia Journalism Review* 11:5 (January–February 1973):9–20.

52. Ibid.

53. *Washington Post*, October 12, 1972, Sec. A, p. 18.

54. Reeves, "How Nixon Outwits the Press," p. 57.

55. Dickenson, "Nixon and the Press," p. 24.

56. Nixon, *Memoirs*, p. 762.

57. Henry Kissinger, *White House Years* (Boston: Little, Brown, 1979), pp. 1455–1456.

58. Nixon, *Memoirs*, p. 762.

59. Johnson, *Nixon Press Conferences*, p. 303.

60. Theodore H. White, *Breach of Faith: The Fall of Richard Nixon* (New York: Atheneum, 1975), p. 179.

61. *Washington Post*, February 10, 1973, Sec. A, p. 14.

62. Ibid., March 9, 1973, Sec. A, p. 10.

63. James McCartney, "The Washington 'Post' and Watergate: How Two Davids Slew Goliath," *Columbia Journalism Review* 11:2 (July–August 1973):21.

64. *New York Times*, February 27, 1973, p. 1. The subpoenas were later thrown out of court.

65. Safire, *Before the Fall*, p. 365.

66. *New York Times*, February 24, 1973, p. 71.

67. Ibid., February 9, 1973, p. 71.

68. Transcript of the Dick Cavett Show, prepared for Daphne Productions by Radio-TV Reports, Inc., March 22, 1973, p. 7.

69. Sussman, *Great Coverup*, p. 176–178.

70. Hugh Sidey, "Seeking a Magical Vista," *Time*, September 10, 1973, p. 22.

71. Charles W. Colson, *Born Again* (Old Tappan, New Jersey: Chosen Books, 1976), p. 74.

72. Trudi Osborne, "The White House Press: Let AP Cover the Assassinations," *Washington Monthly* (February 1977):18.

73. "Inside the White House," *Newsweek*, January 21, 1974, p. 21. See also, "From Candor to San Clemente," *Newsweek*, January 7, 1974, pp. 16–17.

74. United Press International dispatch, *Washington Star-News*, February 12, 1974.

75. *Washington Star-News*, August 22, 1973, Sec. A, p. 9. See also Editor's Notes, *Quill* 61:9 (September 1973): 4, and Dan Rather with Mickey Herskowitz, *The Camera Never Blinks* (New York: Morrow, 1977), pp. 243, 244. In his *Memoirs* (p. 962), Nixon scolded CBS for showing "the pushing episode twice in slow motion." He made no mention of the White House denials that prompted the network to run the film in such a manner.

76. Halberstam, *Powers That Be*, p. 718.

77. Associated Press dispatch, *New York Times*, November 10, 1973.

78. Helen Thomas, *Dateline: White House* (New York: Macmillan, 1975), pp. 218–223. See also "The White House Death Watch," *Newsweek*, August 19, 1974, p. 78.

79. McCartney, "The Washington 'Post' and Watergate," pp. 9–10.

80. "The Long Trail of Denials to Credibility Gap," *Newsweek*, April 30, 1973, p. 20.

81. "The Roughriders," *Newsweek*, June 18, 1973, p. 74.

82. Clark R. Mollenhoff, *Game Plan for Disaster* (New York: W. W. Norton, 1976), p. 293.

83. *Washington Post*, July 13, 1973, Sec. A, p. 15.

84. Mollenhoff, *Game Plan*, p. 293.

85. Carl Bernstein and Bob Woodward, *All the President's Men* (New York: Simon and Schuster, 1974), p. 311.

86. "The Roughriders," *Newsweek*, June 18, 1973, p. 74.

87. "Roughing Up Ron," *Time*, June 4, 1973, p. 62.

88. Charles Long, "His Master's Voice," *Quill* 61:7 (July 1973):20.

89. Nixon, *Memoirs*, p. 857.

90. John Osborne, *The Fifth Year of the Nixon Watch* (New York: Liveright, 1974), p. 123.

91. *Washington Post*, February 1, 1974, Sec. A, p. 12.

92. Ibid., February 2, 1974, Sec. A, pp. 1, 15.

93. Raymond Price, *With Nixon* (New York: Viking Press, 1977), p. 311.

94. Hugh Sidey, "A Watergate by the Sea?" *Time*, July 16, 1973, p. 17.

95. Transcript of White House press briefing, April 8, 1974. In an effort to restore his credibility, Nixon in December 1973 disclosed details of his personal finances. The "Joint Committee" reference was to the Congressional Joint Committee on Internal Revenue Taxation, from which Nixon had requested rulings on two tax deductions he had taken. See Robert A Diamond, ed., *Watergate: Chronology of a Crisis* (Washington, D.C.: Congressional Quarterly, 1974), 2:181.

96. Price, *With Nixon*, p. 349. See also *New York Times*, August 9, 1974, p. 2.

97. Osborne, *Fifth Year*, p. 48.

98. "The Roughriders," *Newsweek*, June 18, 1973, p. 74.

99. Johnson, *Nixon Press Conferences*, pp. 331–339. See also "On the Rebound?" *Newsweek*, September 3, 1973, pp. 22–26, and "A Savage Game of 20 Questions," *Time*, September 3, 1973, pp. 10–11.

100. "On the Rebound?" *Newsweek*, September 3, 1973, p. 23.

101. " 'Presidents Always Win,' " *Newsweek*, September 3, 1973, p. 66.

102. Johnson, *Nixon Press Conferences*, pp. 345–353.

103. Mark R. Arnold, "Nixon vs. Newsmen: A New War?" *National Observer*, September 15, 1973, p. 2

104. Johnson, *Nixon Press Conferences*, p. 359. One week late Agnew resigned and pleaded "no contest" to one count of tax evasion on unreported income he had received in 1967 when he was the governor of Maryland. In return for the plea and resignation, the Justice Department dropped numerous additional charges.

105. Bob Woodward and Carl Bernstein, *The Final Days* (New York: Simon and Schuster, 1976), p. 459. See also Sussman, *Great Coverup*, p. 278.

106. Thomas Whiteside, "Annals of Television," *New Yorker*, March 17, 1975, p. 68. See also, the *New York Times*, November 13, 1973, p. 91.

107. Johnson, *Nixon Press Conferences*, p. 368.

108. Ibid., p. 369.

109. Ibid., p. 373.

110. Ibid., pp. 373–374. See also, Mollenhoff, *Game Plan*, pp. 320–321.

111. "The President: 'I'm Not a Crook,' " *Newsweek*, November 26, 1973, p. 26. See also J. Anthony Lukas, "Watergate: The Story Continued," *New York Times Magazine*, January 13, 1974, p. 62.

112. United Press International dispatch, *Washington Post*, November 18, 1973.

113. "The President: 'I'm Not a Crook,' " *Newsweek*, November 26, 1973, p. 26. See also *Washington Post*, November 18, 1973, Sec. A, pp. 1, 14.

114. Nixon, *Memoirs*, p. 957.

115. Johnson, *Nixon Press Conferences*, pp. 375–381. See also *Washington Post*, February 26, 1974, Sec. A, p. 13, and *New York Times*, March 7, 1974, p. 1, 33.

116. Johnson, *Nixon Press Conferences*, p. 392.

117. *Washington Post*, February 26, 1974, Sec. A, p. 13.

118. Diamond, *Watergate*, 2:274. See also *New York Times*, March 20, 1974, p. 30.

119. Rather, *Camera Never Blinks*, pp. 12–13. See also Halberstam, *Powers That Be*, pp. 698–699.

120. Diamond, *Watergate*, pp. 282–288.

121. *New York Times*, March 20, 1974, p. 30.

122. Rather, *Camera Never Blinks*, pp. 17–18.

123. Ibid., p. 22.

124. "Adversary Relationship," *Newsweek*, April 1, 1974, p. 66.

125. Nixon, *Memoirs*, p. 1068.

126. Rather, *Camera Never Blinks*, pp. 257–258.

127. Thomas, *Dateline*, pp. 194–195.

128. Bernstein and Woodward, *All the President's Men*, pp. 310–311, and Sussman, *Great Coverup*, p. 227.

129. *New York Times*, May 1, 1973, pp. 1, 30, 31, and *Washington Post*, May 1, 1973, Sec. A, pp. 1, 11. See also Bernstein and Woodward, *President's Men*, p. 311.

130. Sussman, *Great Coverup*, p. 231.

131. Ibid., pp. 258–259.

132. "Now, It's Operation Candor," *Newsweek*, November 19, 1973, p. 35.

133. *Washington Post*, February 1, 1974, Sec. A, p. 30. See also "I'm Going to Fight Like Hell," *Newsweek*, February 4, 1974, p. 14.

134. Sussman, *Great Coverup*, pp. 291–296; *Washington Post*, May 5, 1974, Sec. C, p. 6.

135. *Washington Star-News*, May 6, 1974, Sec. A, pp. 1, 7.

136. Nixon, *Memoirs*, p. 1083, 1087.

137. Colson, *Born Again*, p. 94.

138. "Survival Strategy," *Time*, February 25, 1974, p. 13.

139. Hugh Sidey, "Trying to Get Right with Lincoln," *Time*, February 25, 1974, p. 14.

140. *Washington Post*, February 15, 1974, Sec. A, pp. 1, 10.

141. "Nixon Campaigns for His Presidency," *Time*, April 22, 1974, p. 13.

142. *New York Times*, April 25, 1974, p. 31; Thomas, *Dateline*, pp. 211–213; Nixon, *Memoirs*, pp. 1010–1018.

143. Price, *With Nixon*, pp. 296–297; Nixon, *Memoirs*, pp. 1026–1039.

144. Nixon, *Memoirs*, p. 1045.

145. "Now, It's Operation Candor," *Newsweek*, November 19, 1973, pp. 35–37. See also Lukas, "Watergate: The Story Continued," pp. 60–62, and "Nixon's All-Out Drive to Restore Confidence," *U.S. News & World Report*, November 26, 1973, pp. 27–28.

146. Lukas, "Watergate," p. 62; *New York Times*, November 28, 1973, p. 33.

147. Lukas, "Watergate," p. 63, and White, *Breach of Faith*, p. 294.

148. "Mr. Nixon Pays the Price," *Newsweek*, April 15, 1974, pp. 18–28.

149. "From Candor to San Clemente," *Newsweek*, January 7, 1974, p. 16, and Lukas, "Watergate," p. 63.

150. "I'm Going to Fight Like Hell," *Newsweek*, February 4, 1974, p. 14.

151. Ibid. See also *New York Times*, March 15, 1974, p. 14.

152. *New York Times*, February 19, 1974, pp. 1, 23.

153. "Operation Friendly Persuasion," *Newsweek*, March 25, 1974, pp. 22–27; *New York Times*, March 15, 1974, p. 14, March 20, 1974, p. 30.

154. John J. O'Connor, "Who Drew the Mustache on the Presidential Image? Not TV News," *New York Times*, May 12, 1974, Part II, p. 17.

155. Thomas, *Dateline*, p. 215; *New York Times*, June 15, 1974, p. 14.

156. *New York Times*, June 19, 1974, p. 34.

157. Ibid., June 20, 1974, p. 31.

158. Price, *With Nixon*, p. 311.

159. *New York Times*, July 18, 1974, p. 20.

160. *Washington Star-News*, May 28, 1974, Sec. A, pp. 1, 4. See also, "Cocktails with Clawson," *Newsweek*, July 1, 1974, pp. 25–26.

162. Luther A. Houston, "Clawson Purveys Nixon Policy to Opinion Writers," *Editor & Publisher*, April 6, 1974, p. 29.

162. "Cocktails with Clawson," pp. 25–26. See also *Washington Post*, June 2, 1974, Sec. G, pp. 1, 4.

163. "Serving Up the News—With a Twist," *Columbia Journalism Review* 12:2 (July–August 1974):48.

164. *Washington Post*, June 2, 1974, Sec. G, pp. 1, 4.

165. Mike Causey, "Political Appointees Get Press Jobs," *Washington Post*, April 19, 1973, Sec. G, p. 9.

166. *Washington Post*, May 11, 1973, Sec. A, p. 19.

167. *Washington Star-News*, May 28, 1974, Sec. A, p. 4.

168. Associated Press dispatch, *Washington Post*, January 30, 1974.

169. Associated Press dispatch, *Washington Star-News*, November 16, 1973; "That's the Way It Is," *Newsweek*, November 12, 1973, p. 87.

170. Rowland Evans and Robert Novak, "Serving America, the Presidency and Mr. Nixon," *Washington Post*, January 9, 1974, Sec. A, p. 25.

171. Thomas, *Dateline*, p. 208.

172. *New York Times*, July 19, 1974, p. 19.

173. "The Press in the President's Transcripts," *Quill* 63:6 (June 1974):18. Three days later Nixon accepted the resignations of Haldeman, Ehrlichman, and Kleindienst and fired John Dean. In his televised speech on that occasion the president praised "the system that has brought the facts to light and that will bring the guilty to justice—a system that in this case has included a determined grand jury, honest prosecutors, a courageous judge, John Sirica, and a vigorous free press." See the same *Quill* article.

174. Osborne, *Fifth Year*, p. 116.

175. *New York Times*, February 14, 1974, p. 8.

176. *Washington Post*, March 9, 1974, Sec. A, p. 1. See also Associated Press dispatch, *Washington Star-News*, March 7, 1974.

177. The Nixon interview was released to the press on July 16, 1974, when Rabbi Korff arrived at San Clemente to present the president with a copy of Korff's new book, *The Personal Nixon: Staying on the Summit*. It was published by Fairness Publishers, an off-shoot of Korff's organization, the National Citizen's Committee for Fairness to the Presidency. See the *New York Times*, July 17, 1974, pp. 1, 17; Price, *With Nixon*, p. 312; and Thomas, *Dateline*, p. 210.

178. *Washington Star-News*, May 3, 1973, Sec. A, p. 6; *Washington Post*, May 3, 1973, Sec. A, p. 11.

179. Associated Press dispatch, *New York Times*, May 9, 1973.

180. *New York Times*, August 22, 1973, pp. 1, 24. See also Nixon, *Memoirs*, p. 816, and William E. Porter, *Assault on the Media* (Ann Arbor: University of Michigan Press, 1976), pp. 227–228.

181. *New York Times*, August 22, 1973, pp. 1, 24.

182. *Washington Post*, August 23, 1973, Sec. A, pp. 1, 24; *Wall Street Journal*, August 23, 1973, p. 2.

183. *New York Times*, October 2, 1973, Sec. A, p. 8.

184. "Agnew Takes On the Justice Department," *Time*, October 8, 1973, p. 15.

185. *Washington Post*, October 3, 1973, Sec. A, p. 8, October 4, 1973, Sec. A, pp. 1, 22.

186. *New York Times*, October 6, 1973, pp. 1, 8; *Washington Post*, October 6, 1973, Sec. A, pp. 1, 4.

187. "Agnew: Condemned by Leak?" *Columbia Journalism Review* 11:4 (November–December 1973):3.

188. *Washington Post*, October 9, 1973, Sec. A, pp. 1, 6.

189. *New York Times*, October 11, 1973, pp. 1, 35, 38.

190. "Agnew: Condemned by Leak?" p. 2. Agnew's efforts to revise the record to reflect his own view of his resignation continued after he quit public office. In a May 6, 1975, interview with William Nault, editorial director of the World Book Encyclopedia, I learned that Agnew had returned his 1973 yearbook with the angry demand that his name be removed from the publication's mailing list. World Book's account of his resignation, he had said, was colored with the same leftist taint that

pervaded the daily media. World Book, according to Nault, did not change its treatment but did remove Agnew's name from its mailing list.

191. Halberstam, *Powers That Be*, p. 686.

192. *Washington Star-News*, October 30, 1973, Sec. A, p. 2; *New York Times*, October 31, 1973, p. 23.

193. *New York Times*, November 27, 1973, p. 1, and the *Washington Post*, November 27, 1973, Sec. A, p. 5.

194. *New York Times*, November 28, 1973, p. 44.

195. Patrick J. Buchanan, "Mr. Nixon as the Target," *New York Times*, August 2, 1973, p. 35.

196. "A Hard-Nosed Lesson in Politics," *Newsweek*, October 8, 1973, p. 36.

197. *New York Times*, November 1, 1973, p. 43.

198. Associated Press dispatch, *New York Times*, October 30, 1973.

199. "Buchanan Suggests Sponsors Lean On Networks to End Liberal Bias," *Broadcasting*, April 1, 1974, p. 36.

200. Aaron Latham, "The Reporter the President Hates," *New York*, January 21, 1974, pp. 38–40.

201. Robert C. Maynard, "The Press 'Firestorm' " *Washington Post*, November 8, 1973, Sec. A, p. 30.

202. Associated Press dispatch, *Washington Star-News*, March 18, 1974.

203. *Wall Street Journal*, February 14, 1974, pp. 1, 26.

204. *Washington Post*, November 25, 1973, Sec. A, p. 2.

205. United Press International dispatch, *Washington Post*, December 2, 1973.

206. *Wall Street Journal*, February 14, 1974, p. 1.

207. Associated Press dispatch, *New York Times*, June 2, 1973.

208. "That's the Way It Is," *Newsweek*, November 12, 1973, p. 87.

209. *Washington Post*, April 24, 1973, Sec. A, p. 6, October 5, 1973, Sec. A, p. 6.

210. Ibid., October 5, 1973, Sec. A, p. 6; *New York Times*, October 5, 1973, p. 13.

211. *Washington Post*, January 3, 1974, Sec. A, pp. 1, 20.

212. *Washington Post*, January 4, 1973, Sec. A, p. 2. See also, "Test Cases," *Newsweek*, January 14, 1974, p. 45.

213. *Washington Post*, January 20, 1974, Sec. A, pp. 1, 8.

214. Ibid., January 4, 1974, Sec. A, p. 2. In 1975, the FCC ruled that most of the nation's more than 140 newspaper-broadcasting combines could continue, but sixteen publishing companies that owned the only newspaper and the only broadcast property in their particular cities had to divest. The commission also barred all future transactions that would establish such media combinations in the same area. Parties on both sides of the issue filed suits, but the Supreme Court ruled on June 12, 1978, in favor of the FCC. "FCC Cross-Media Ban Backed," *Facts on File*, June 23, 1978, pp. 467–468.

215. *New York Times*, February 10, 1974, p. 44.

216. Ibid., February 12, 1974, p. 14, February 20, 1974, p. 19. AT&T, meanwhile, also announced a new policy: the company henceforth would notify anyone whose records were requested by the government and would not surrender the records

unless they were asked for in a formal subpoena or administrative summons. See the *New York Times*, February 16, 1974, p. 13.

217. *Washington Post*, June 7, 1973, Sec. A, p. 7. See also Associated Press dispatch, *New York Times*, June 8, 1973.

218. Washington Post staff, *The Fall of a President* (New York: Delacorte Press, 1974), p. ix.

219. Nixon, *Memoirs*, pp. 851, 945, 961.

220. Colson, *Born Again*, p. 105.

221. Price, *With Nixon*, p. 243.

222. *New York Times*, May 9, 1973, pp. 1, 28.

223. Ibid., February 19, 1974, p. 23.

224. Ibid., June 6, 1973, p. 36.

225. Thomas, *Dateline*, p. 199.

226. *New York Times*, June 14, 1973, p. 41.

227. White, *Breach of Faith*, p. 224.

228. "Has the Press Done a Job on Nixon?" *Columbia Journalism Review* 12:5 (January–February 1974):58.

229. Colson, *Born Again*, p. 99. See also Fred D. Thompson, *At That Point in Time* (New York: Quadrangle/New York Times Book Co., 1975), p. 238.

230. Thompson, *At That Point*, p. 238.

231. Finlay Lewis, "Some Errors and Puzzles in Watergate Coverage," *Columbia Journalism Review* 11:4 (November–December 1973):29.

232. *New York Times*, November 16, 1973, p. 26.

233. "Probing the 'Slap-Tap Flap,' " *Newsweek*, December 3, 1973, p. 69, and Osborne, *Fifth Year*, pp. 198–200.

234. Osborne, *Fifth Year*, pp. 199–200.

235. Nixon, *Memoirs*, pp. 934–936, and Price, *With Nixon*, pp. 249–260. These accounts, of course, are decidedly pro-Nixon. For other viewpoints, see Sussman, *Great Coverup*, pp. 261–277; Osborne, *Fifth Year*, pp. 173–179; White, *Breach of Faith*, pp. 253–271; Woodward and Bernstein, *Final Days*, pp. 60–71.

236. White, *Breach of Faith*, p. 268; Nixon, *Memoirs*, p. 935.

237. "New White House Blast," *Time*, November 12, 1973, p. 78.

238. Nixon, *Memoirs*, pp. 934–935.

239. "New White House Blast," *Time*, November 12, 1973, p. 78.

240. "Defending Nixon," *Time*, May 28, 1973, p. 61.

241. Ibid. See also, Murray Kempton, "Nixon's Nonsense," *Progressive* (June 1974):53, and Vermont Royster, "The Other Nixon," *Wall Street Journal*, March 27, 1974, p. 14.

242. Price, *With Nixon*, pp. 290–291.

243. James M. Perry, "Nixon vs. Cronkite, Rather & Schorr," *National Observer*, November 10, 1973, p. 9.

244. "Probing Nixon's Charges," *Quill* 61:12 (December 1973):10.

245. "Ziegler Still Mum on Specifics about 'Outrageous' Reporting," *Quill* 62:1 (January 1974):9; Associated Press dispatch, *New York Times*, December 9, 1973.

246. Perry, "Nixon vs. Cronkite," p. 9. CBS was the one network Nixon had mentioned by name.

247. Lawrence Lichty, "Getting Down to Specifics," [*More*] 4:2 (February 1974):6.

248. *New York Times*, March 26, 1974, p. 82.

249. *Washington Post*, January 29, 1974, Sec. A, p. 10. See also *New York Times*, January 29, 1974, p. 67.

250. "More on Nixon Charges," *Quill* 62:5 (May 1974):8. See also *Washington Star-News*, March 23, 1974, Sec. C, p. 8; *New York Times*, March 27, 1974, p. 86.

251. *New York Times*, June 2, 1974, p. 37. See also "News Council Says White House Failed to Back Charges," *Quill* 62:6 (June 1974):9.

252. Sussman, *Great Coverup*, pp. 322–323.

253. *Washington Post*, August 9, 1974, p. 13.

254. Thomas, *Dateline*, p. 222.

255. Rather, *Camera Never Blinks*, pp. 245–246.

256. *Washington Post*, August 9, 1974, p. 13.

257. "The White House Deathwatch," *Newsweek*, August 19, 1974, pp. 77–78. See also Halberstam, *Powers That Be*, p. 703.

258. Thomas, *Dateline*, pp. 225–226.

259. Frank Mankiewicz, *U.S. v. Richard Nixon* (New York: Quadrangle, 1975), p. 87.

Chapter 8

1. *Washington Post*, August 10, 1974, Sec. A, p. 1.

2. Gerald Ford, *A Time to Heal* (New York: Harper & Row and the Reader's Digest Association, Inc., 1979), p. 131.

3. Ibid., pp. 147, 186. See also, Ron Nessen, *It Sure Looks Different From the Inside* (Chicago: Playboy Press, 1978), p. 17.

4. Tom Wicker, *On Press* (New York: Viking Press, 1978), pp. 188–196; and Nessen, *It Sure Looks Different*, pp. 57–59.

5. *Washington Post*, May 10, 1975, Sec. D, p. 3, May 12, 1975, Sec. B, p. 4.

6. Helen Thomas, *Dateline: White House* (New York: Macmillan, 1975), pp. 271–272.

7. Benjamin Stein, "If You Liked Richard Nixon, You'll Love Jimmy Carter," *Penthouse* (November 1976):62–68, 98; Victor Lasky, *Jimmy Carter: The Man and the Myth* (New York: Richard Marek Publishers, 1979), pp. 75–97.

8. "Playboy Interview: Jimmy Carter," *Playboy* (November 1976):66.

9. "Carter Up Close: Absolutely Ruthless," *Newsweek*, July 19, 1976, p. 23.

10. "Playboy Interview" p. 66.

11. Lasky, *Jimmy Carter*, pp. 143–144. See also Peter Meyer, *James Earl Carter: The Man & the Myth* (Kansas City: Sheed Andrews and McMeel, 1978), pp. 126–127.

12. Statement by a White House correspondent, interview, August 18, 1979.

13. *Washington Post*, April 26, 1977, Sec. A, p. 3.

14. Wesley G. Pippert, "White House News Curbs Restrict Reporters," *Editor & Publisher*, April 7, 1979, p. 24.

15. *New York Times*, August 2, 1979, Sec. A, p. 14.

16. "Keeping 'Em Down on the Farm," *Time*, August 16, 1976, p. 73.

17. "The Prisoners of Thurmont," *Time*, September 18, 1978, p. 86. See also *Washington Post*, September 8, 1978, Sec. A, p. 19.

18. *Washington Post*, September 11, 1978, Sec. B, pp. 1, 19.

19. "President and Press: Honeymoon Lingers On," *U.S. News & World Report*, April 11, 1977, p. 44.

20. *New York Times*, July 7, 1977, p. 11; "Polishing the Carter Image," *U.S. News & World Report*, August 8, 1977, p. 15; And "Fancy Wrappings," *Nation*, September 17, 1977, p. 228; "Managing the News, White House Style," *U.S. News & World Report*, September 4, 1978, p. 17; *Washington Post*, July 29, 1978, Sec. A, p. 2; Hugh Sidey, "Savoring a Mellow Moment," *Time*, October 9, 1978, p. 31; *New York Times*, August 2, 1979, Sec. A, p. 14.

21. Statement by Curtis Wilkie, interview, August 9, 1979.

22. "Trapped in the Steel Cocoons," *Time*, November 8, 1976, p. 78.

23. Statement by Judy Woodruff, interview, August 3, 1979.

24. Andrew J. Glass, "The Invisible Candidate on Air Force One," *Washington Journalism Review* 2:8 (October 1980):36.

25. Statement by Lou Cannon, interview, June 14, 1983.

26. Bill Hogan, "Ronald Reagan's Close Encounters with the Fourth Estate," *Washington Journalism Review* 3:2 (March 1981):32.

27. *Washington Star*, April 27, 1981, Sec. D, pp. 1, 2.

28. Hogan, "Reagan's Close Encounters," p. 33.

29. "Oh, I'll Take the Low Road," *Newsweek*, September 29, 1980, p. 22; *Washington Post*, September 17, 1980, Sec. A, p. 3, August 19, 1980, Sec. A, p. 4.

30. Richard Reeves, " 'Batting Practice,' Dialogue," *Washington Star*, October 6, 1980, Sec. A, p. 15.

31. *Washington Post*, September 9, 1980, Sec. A, pp. 1, 6.

32. "Oh, I'll Take the Low Road," p. 23.

33. *Washington Post*, November 7, 1982, Sec. A, pp. 1, 5.

34. James Gerstenzang, "White House Press Relations Strained," *Editor & Publisher*, April 9, 1983, p. 5.

35. Sara Fritz, "Reagan's Honeymoon with the Press Is Over," *Washington Journalism Review* 4:3 (April 1982):38.

36. *USA Today*, October 20, 1982, Sec. A, p. 4; Fritz, "Reagan's Honeymoon," p. 38; and the *Washington Post*, October 19, 1982, Sec. A, pp. 1, 12.

37. *Washington Post*, November 7, 1982, Sec. A, pp. 1, 5.

38. Ibid., January 25, 1983, Sec. A, p. 2.

39. Statement by Terry Hunt, personal interview, June 22, 1981.

40. Andrew J. Glass, "The Secret Service vs. the Press," *Washington Journalism Review* 3:6 (July–August 1981):16.

41. *New York Times*, February 16, 1983, Sec. A, p. 20.

42. *Washington Post*, January 25, 1983, Sec. A, p. 2.

43. Dick Kirschten, "Reagan Seeks a New and Improved Image, But It May Not Play in South Succotash," *National Journal*, April 17, 1982, p. 685.

44. *Washington Post*, January 25, 1983, Sec. A, p. 2.

45. *New York Times*, February 16, 1983, Sec. A, p. 20.

46. Statement by Lou Gerig, personal interview, June 22, 1981; "A Talk with Dave Gergen," *Washington Journalism Review* 4:3 (April 1982):42; "A Day in the Life of the New President," *Time*, February 23, 1981, pp. 15–17; *Washington Post*, December 27, 1982, Sec. A, p. 3, March 26, 1983, Sec. A, p. 1, 7.

47. "Brady Meets the Press," *Newsweek*, February 23, 1981, p. 81.

48. *Washington Post*, May 8, 1983, Sec. A, p. 1, 13.

49. Lou Cannon, "Reagan & Co.," *Washington Post*, June 14, 1982, Sec. A, p. 3; "You Are Not Alone," *Time*, June 21, 1982, p. 30.

50. *New York Times*, April 12, 1982, Sec. A, p. 2.

51. *Washington Post*, April 10, 1982, Sec. A, p. 4.

52. *New York Times*, April 12, 1982, Sec. A, p. 2; *Washington Post*, April 11, 1982, Sec. A, pp. 1, 2.

53. Lloyd Shearer, "Intelligence Report: Reagan's Ranch," *Parade*, March 22, 1981, p. 14; Front Page, "Covering Reagan: No Sweat in the Sun," *Washington Post Magazine*, March 7, 1982, p. 2; Curtis Wilkie, "How I Spent Ronald Reagan's Summer Vacation," *Washington Journalism Review* 4:8 (October 1982) 32.

54. *Washington Post*, February 21, 1981, Sec. A, pp. 1, 6.

55. *Washington Post*, November 27, 1981, Sec. A, p. 11, May 24, 1981, Sec. A, pp. 1, 6.

56. *New York Times*, November 29, 1982, Sec. B, p. 6; *Washington Post*, August 8, 1981, Sec. A, p. 8.

57. *Washington Post*, August 17, 1981, Sec. A, pp. 1, 5; Lynn Olson, "The Reticence of Ronald Reagan," *Washington Journalism Review* 3:9 (November 1981):42.

58. *Washington Post*, March 8, 1982, Sec. B, pp. 1, 3.

59. Aaron Latham, "The Messenger's Messenger," *New York*, June 2, 1975, pp. 7–9. See also Charles A. Krause, "House News," [*More*] 3:12 (December 1973):3–4; *New York Times*, April 24, 1975, p. 9.

60. Hedley Donovan, "How the White House Reads the Press," *Fortune*, December 29, 1980, p. 45; John Osborne, "Images," *New Republic*, September 9, 1978, p. 10.

61. Statement by William Hart, personal interview, June 22, 1981.

62. *Chicago Tribune*, May 5, 1982, p. 6.

63. "An Interview with Jim Brady," *Washington Journalism Review* 3:2 (March 1981):38.

64. Jerald F. terHorst, *Gerald Ford and the Future of the Presidency* (New York: Third Press, 1974), pp. 225–240.

65. Nessen, *It Sure Looks Different*, p. 14.

66. "The Nessen Pledge," *Newsweek*, March 24, 1975, p. 66; *Washington Post*, June 27, 1975, Sec. A, pp. 1, 4. In late October 1974 Nixon was operated on for phlebitis, subsequently went into shock, and came close to dying. For a detailed account of Ford's visit with Nixon, see Ford, *A Time to Heal*, pp. 201–202.

67. Lou Cannon, "Nessen's Briefings: Missing Questions (and Answers,)" *Columbia Journalism Review* 13:1 (May–June 1975):12–16.

68. "Is Ron a Ziegler?" *Time*, December 9, 1974, p. 82.

69. *Wall Street Journal*, June 13, 1975, pp. 1, 25; *Washington Post*, June 7, 1975, Sec. A, p. 8, June 27, 1975, Sec. A, p. 4.

70. *Washington Post*, June 27, 1975, Sec. A, p. 4. See also *Wall Street Journal*, June 27, 1975, p. 20, and "Nessen's Complaint," *Newsweek*, July 7, 1975, p. 43.

71. *Wall Street Journal*, June 27, 1975, p. 20; "Nessen's Complaint," p. 43.

72. Statement by Ron Nessen, personal interview, August 14, 1979.

73. *New York Times*, February 28, 1977, Sec. A, p. 12. See also "The President's Boys," *Time*, June 6, 1977, pp. 17–24; *Washington Post*, April 13, 1978, Sec. B, pp. 1, 6.

74. "Jody Faces Life," *Newsweek*, September 19, 1972, p. 119; Curtis Wilkie, "What, Indeed, About Jody Powell?" *Quill* 65:1 (January 1977):15; John Osborne, "In Jody's Shop (II)," *New Republic*, March 25, 1978, p. 11.

75. "Turning the Bird Dogs Loose," *Time*, September 19, 1977, p. 117. In a telephone interview on April 22, 1982, Powell said this remark was "specifically aimed at investigative reporters."

76. *New York Times*, July 21, 1976, p. 24. See also "Carter's Mouth," *Time*, August 2, 1976, p. 51.

77. Statement by a White House wire service correspondent, interview, August 1, 1979.

78. Charles Peters, "Concerns about Carter and His Chief Courtier," *Washington Monthly*, (December 1976):4.

79. J. Anthony Lukas, "The White House Press 'Club' " *New York Times Magazine*, May 15, 1977, p. 22; Andrew J. Glass, "The Invisible Candidate on Air Force One," *Washington Journalism Review* 2:8 (October 1980):36.

80. Periscope, "Carter's New Itinerary," *Newsweek*, November 7, 1977, p. 25.

81. *New York Times*, November 24, 1976, p. 14.

82. *Washington Post*, August 5, 1979, Sec. A, p. 2.

83. Hedley Donovan, "How the White House Reads the Press," *Fortune*, December 29, 1980, p. 47.

84. *Washington Post*, January 28, 1979, Sec. F, p. 2.

85. *New York Times*, May 2, 1980, p. 10. See also *Washington Post*, May 12, 1980, Sec. D, pp. 1, 4, and "Some Closing Words from Jody," *Time*, December 8, 1980, p. 96.

86. "Inside the White House: Powell Planned to Resign After Iran Rescue Mission Failed," *Washingtonian* (July 1980):15.

87. Diane K. Shah, "The Capitol Letter: Shades of Ron Ziegler and Other White House Ghosts," *New York*, August 15, 1977, p. 9.

88. "Carter's Mouth," *Time*, August 2, 1976, p. 51.

89. *Washington Post*, April 13, 1978, Sec. B, pp. 1, 6.

90. J. Anthony Lukas, "The White House Press 'Club,' " *New York Times Magazine*, May 15, 1977, p. 64, and John Osborne, "Carter's Bad Boys," *New Republic*, March 11, 1978, p. 10.

91. *Washington Post*, January 28, 1979, Sec. F, p. 2.

92. Aaron Latham, "The Jody Watch: Powell Panned," [*More*] 7:4 (April 1977):41.

93. Sanford J. Ungar, "Reports & Comment: Washington," *Atlantic* (April 1977):14.

94. Curtis Wilkie, "What, Indeed, About Jody Powell?" *Quill* 65:1 (January 1977):14.

95. "Press Sours on Carter—and Vice Versa," *U.S. News & World Report*, August 7, 1978, p. 29; "Turning the Bird Dogs Loose," *Time*, September 19, 1977, p. 117;

John Osborne, "In Jody's Shop (I)," *New Republic*, March 18, 1978, pp. 17–19, and "In Jody's Shop (II)," pp. 10–12.

96. Statement by Chris Ogden, personal interview, April 24, 1981.

97. Ron Lovell, "Keepers of the Flame: Jody Powell," *Quill* 69:2 (February 1981):14.

98. Statement by Robert Timberg, interview, June 14, 1983.

99. Statement by Lou Cannon, interview, June 14, 1983.

100. "Trapped in the Imperial Presidency," *Time*, April 26, 1982, p. 20.

101. Jay Matthews, "All the President's Men," *Columbia Journalism Review* 20:4 (November–December 1981):5–7.

102. "Talk with Dave Gergen," 42; John Herbers, "The President and the Press Corps," *New York Times Magazine*, May 9, 1982, p. 75; *Washington Post*, June 6, 1981, Sec. C, pp. 1, 7.

103. *Washington Post*, August 15, 1982, Sec. A, p. 2, March 7, 1982, Sec. H, pp. 1, 12.

104. *Washington Post*, August 15, 1982, Sec. A, p. 2, September 1, 1981, Sec. A, p. 2. See also *New York Times*, February 16, 1983, Sec. A, p. 20.

105. *Washington Star*, July 30, 1981, Sec. A, p. 6.

106. *Washington Post*, August 15, 1982, Sec. A, p. 2.

107. Ibid.

108. Statement by Chris Wallace, interview, June 13, 1983.

109. Statement by Jim Gerstenzang, interview, June 9, 1983.

110. Statement by Lou Cannon, interview, June 14, 1983.

111. *Washington Post*, December 30, 1975, Sec. A, p. 3.

112. Ford, *Time to Heal*, pp. 156–158. See also "Ford: Plain Words before an Open Door," *Time*, September 9, 1974, pp. 11–12.

113. Clark Mollenhoff, *The Man Who Pardoned Nixon* (New York: St. Martin's Press, 1976), p. 99.

114. Nessen, *It Sure Looks Different*, pp. 349–350.

115. *Washington Post*, January 30, 1978, Sec. A, p. 2.

116. Ibid. See also John Osborne, "Number 41," *New Republic*, December 23, 30, 1978, p. 9, and "Carter and the Press As Jody Powell Sees It," *U.S. News & World Report*, October 10, 1977, p. 26.

117. "First Billy, Then Teddy," *Time*, August 18, 1980, p. 22. See also *Washington Post*, August 4, 1980, Sec. A, pp. 1, 7, August 5, 1980, Sec. A, pp. 1, 11.

118. *Washington Star*, August 6, 1980, Sec. A, p. 6.

119. *New York Times*, April 18, 1980, Sec. A, p. 1.

120. James J. Kilpatrick, "Of Presidents and Press: What Will Reagan Do?" *Washington Star*, December 27, 1981, Sec. A, p. 9.

121. *Washington Post*, November 7, 1982, Sec. A, p. 5.

122. *New York Times*, October 26, 1982, Sec. B, p. 6; *Washington Post*, November 7, 1982, Sec. A, p. 5.

123. *USA Today*, September 29, 1982, Sec. A, p. 8.

124. *New York Times*, July 30, 1982, Sec. B, p. 4.

125. *Washington Post*, February 19, 1982, Sec. A, p. 5, January 21, 1982, Sec. A, p. 2. See also *New York Times*, February 19, 1982, Sec. A, p. 21.

126. *USA Today*, June 28, 1983, Sec. A, p. 2.

127. *Washington Post*, January 6, 1983, Sec. A, p. 8.

128. Ibid., October 2, 1981, Sec. A, pp. 1, 11.

129. "Jordan and Powell: Literary Voices," *Newsweek*, August 17, 1981, p. 16B.

130. Thomas Griffith, "Newswatch: The Bite without the Sting," *Time*, August 16, 1982, p. 44.

131. "Ford's News Supply," *Quill* 62:10 (October 1974):8. Ford, *Time to Heal*, p. 376; Nessen, *It Sure Looks Different*, pp. 213–214; "Prepping Ford," *Newsweek*, September 27, 1976, p. 33.

132. Ford, *Time to Heal*, pp. 376–377.

133. Peter Meyer, *James Earl Carter*, p. 151.

134. David Halberstam, "The Coming of Carter," *Newsweek*, July 19, 1976, p. 11.

135. *Washington Post*, January 30, 1978, Sec. A, p. 2.

136. Frederick B. Hill, "Media Diplomacy: Crisis Management with an Eye on the TV Screen," *Washington Journalism Review* 3:4 (May 1981):24.

137. *Washington Post*, June 25, 1980, Sec. A, p. 24.

138. "Carter Up Close," *Newsweek*, May 2, 1977, p. 35.

139. *Wall Street Journal*, January 3, 1977, p. 2.

140. *Washington Post*, January 30, 1978, Sec. A, pp. 1, 2; "Carter Up Close," p. 35.

141. *Wall Street Journal*, January 31, 1977, p. 2, and March 18, 1977, p. 1; Meyer, *James Earl Carter*, p. 127.

142. "The President's Men," *Time*, December 14, 1981, p. 19; *Washington Star*, November 21, 1980, Sec. A, p. 3; *New York Times*, October 15, 1982, Sec. A, p. 24.

143. Lou Cannon, "Reagan & Co.," *Washington Post*, February 21, 1983, Sec. A, p. 3.

144. *Washington Post*, February 13, 1983, Sec. A, p. 18.

145. Tom Hamburger, "How the White House Cons the Press," *Washington Monthly* (January 1982):23. See also *New York Times*, December 10, 1982, Sec. A, p. 32.

146. *Washington Post*, February 13, 1983, Sec. A, p. 18.

147. Carl P. Leubsdorf, "Ups and Downs on a Campaign Roller Coaster," *Washington Journalism Review* 2:8 (October 1980):37.

148. Thomas M. DeFrank, "Fine-Tuning the White House Press Conference," *Washington Journalism Review* 4:8 (October 1982):28.

149. John Carmody, "The TV Column," *Washington Post*, October 8, 1982, Sec. B, p. 12.

150. *Washington Post*, October 8, 1982, Sec. A, p. 6.

151. *New York Times*, February 16, 1983, Sec. A, p. 20.

152. *Washington Post*, July 13, 1980, Sec. E, pp. 1, 5.

153. Ibid., October 22, 1980, Sec. A, pp. 1, 10; Bill Hogan, "Ronald Reagan's Close Encounters with the Fourth Estate," *Washington Journalism Review* 3:2 (March 1981):34.

154. James David Barber, "Reagan's Sheer Personal Likability Faces Its Sternest Test," *Washington Post*, January 20, 1981, p. 8.

155. *Washington Post*, March 19, 1982, Sec. F, p. 10.

156. Ford, *Time to Heal*, pp. 194–196. See also Richard Reeves, *A Ford, Not a Lincoln* (New York: Harcourt Brace Jovanovich, 1975), pp. 159–161.

157. Osborne, "Jody's Shop (II)," p. 12.

158. "Carter Takes Charge," *Time*, February 4, 1980, pp. 12–13.

159. *Washington Post*, January 25, 1983, Sec. C, p. 9. See also James Reston, "Like the Fireworks, Reagan Is Spectacular," *Washington Star*, January 21, 1981, Sec. A, p. 16, and William Safire, "Respectable Marks for Reagan's Two Speeches," *Washington Star*, January 22, 1981, Sec. A, p. 15.

160. *New York Times*, April 29, 1981, Sec. A, pp. 1, 23; "The Second Hundred Days," *Newsweek*, May 11, 1981, pp. 22–24; *Washington Post*, April 29, 1981, Sec. B, pp. 1, 3, Sec. A, pp. 1, 14, 15.

161. Ford, *Time to Heal*, pp. 230–231.

162. *Wall Street Journal*, January 14, 1975, p. 3; *Washington Post*, January 14, 1975, sec. A, p. 8; Nessen, *It Sure Looks Different*, pp. 80–83; Ford, *Time to Heal*, pp. 230–233.

163. "Our Far-Flung Correspondents: Settling In," *New Yorker*, February 28, 1977, p. 84; "President McLuhan," *Nation*, February 11, 1977, p. 132; "Fireside Manner," *Newsweek*, February 14, 1977, pp. 23–24.

164. Robert G. Kaiser, "Blowing Smoke and Calling It Reality," *Washington Post*, October 17, 1982, Sec. B, p. 1; *New York Times*, October 15, 1982, Sec. A, p. 24.

165. "A Prime-Time Coup," *Newsweek*, October 25, 1982, p. 28; *Washington Post*, October 12, 1982, Sec. A, p. 5.

166. *New York Times*, October 15, 1982, Sec. A, p. 24.

167. Kaiser, "Blowing Smoke," pp. 1, 3; *Washington Post*, October 14, 1982, Sec. A, pp. 1, 12, 13.

168. "Public President," *Time*, January 12, 1976, p. 34.

169. *Washington Post*, January 13, 1980, Sec. A, p. 3, and Mary McGrory, "Carter Makes Kennedy Sound Like an Echo," *Washington Star*, January 21, 1980, Sec. A, p. 4.

170. *Washington Post*, November 27, 1981, Sec. D, pp. 1, 11.

171. Nessen, *It Sure Looks Different*, pp. 194–195.

172. *Washington Post*, July 30, 1980, Sec. A, pp. 1, 6.

173. "Turbulence in the Tower," *Time*, August 17, 1981, pp. 14–20.

174. *Wall Street Journal*, March 28, 1978, pp. 1, 36.

175. *Washington Post*, December 1, 1981, Sec. B, p. 11.

176. Ibid., August 4, 1982, Sec. A, p. 2.

177. Ibid., February 5, 1983, Sec. A, pp. 1, 6; "President vs. Press," *Newsweek*, February 14, 1983, p. 21.

178. *New York Times*, August 2, 1979, Sec. A, p. 14.

179. Curtis Wilkie, "Carter's Televised Presidency," *Boston Globe Magazine*, November 2, 1980, p. 23; "Jody Powell on the Press and the Presidency," *Washington Journalism Review* 3:3 (April 1981):36.

180. Statement by Hugh Sidey, interview, August 1, 1979.

181. *Washington Post*, July 29, 1979, Sec. D, p. 8.

182. Charles B. Seib, "A Traveling President's Media Entourage," *Washington Post*, December 16, 1977, Sec. A, p. 19; *Washington Post*, December 30, 1977, Sec. A, pp. 1, 8.

183. John Osborne, "Carter on Show," *New Republic*, April 2, 1977, p. 17.

184. Richard Reeves, "The Make-Believe Memo," *Washington Star*, January 4, 1980, Sec. A, p. 9.

185. *Washington Post*, January 20, 1981, Sec. A, p. 3.

186. "A Disengaged Presidency," *Newsweek*, September 7, 1981, p. 21.

187. *Washington Post*, July 9, 1983, Sec. A, pp. 1, 7.

188. Ford, *Time to Heal*, pp. 126–127; "Happiness Is Filming the President Making Breakfast," *Columbia Journalism Review* 13:5 (January–February 1975):3; White House memorandums, September 24, November 1, 1975.

189. "Jes' Write, Wire—or Dial PEANUTS," *Time*, January 17, 1977, p. 12. See also *Wall Street Journal*, December 31, 1976, Sec. A, p. 7.

190. "Playboy Interview: Jimmy Carter," *Playboy* (November 1976):74.

191. "Around Two Worlds in Two Days," *Time*, March 28, 1977, p. 15; "Long-Distance Runner," *Newsweek*, March 28, 1979, p. 14.

192. *Washington Post*, November 29, 1981, Sec. A, p. 1.

193. *Washington Star*, June 28, 1980, Sec. A, p. 3; C. T. Hanson, "Gunsmoke and Sleeping Dogs: The Prez's Press at Midterm," *Columbia Journalism Review* 21:1 (May–June 1973):34.

194. *Washington Post*, May 4, 1982, Sec. A, pp. 1, 11.

195. *New York Times*, October 16, 1976, p. 7.

196. Associated Press dispatch, *New York Times*, October 27, 1976.

197. "Playing Catch-Up Ball," *Newsweek*, November 30, 1980, pp. 33–34; *Wall Street Journal*, August 14, 1980, pp. 1, 12.

198. "Now for the Hard Part," *Newsweek*, August 25, 1980, p. 19; "Drawing the Battle Lines," *Time*, August 25, 1980, p. 21; *Washington Star*, September 16, 1980, Sec. A, p. 3; David Halberstam, "How Television Failed the American Voter," *Parade*, January 11, 1981, p. 4; Jack W. Germond and Jules Witcover, "Carter Reverts to Low Blows in Desperation," *Washington Star*, October 7, 1980, Sec. A, p. 2.

199. Hugh Sidey, "More Than a Candidate," *Time*, September 29, 1980, p. 21.

200. "The Great Homestretch Debate," *Newsweek*, November 10, 1980, pp. 18–20.

201. *Washington Post*, July 19, 1980, Sec. A, pp. 1, 10; *Washington Star*, August 27, 1980, Sec. A, p. 3; *Washington Post*, October 1, 1980, Sec. A, p. 3.

202. *Washington Post*, October 21, 1980, Sec. A, pp. 1, 4.

203. *Washington Post*, September 9, 1980, Sec. A, p. 15.

204. Nessen, *It Sure Looks Different*, p. 171; Richard Reeves et al., "Notes from Our Boys in the Back of the Bus," *New York*, October 25, 1976, p. 35; Ford, *Time to Heal*, p. 289; "The Ridicule Problem," *Time*, January 5, 1976, p. 33.

205. Nessen, *It Sure Looks Different*, pp. 163–176. See also *Washington Post*, April 19, 1976, Sec. C, p. 6; "Ron and Chevy Yock It Up," *Newsweek*, May 3, 1976, p. 17.

206. Reeves et al., "Notes from Our Boys," p. 39.

207. *Washington Post*, July 7, 1979, Sec. A, p. 10.

208. Jack W. Germond and Jules Witcover, "Reagan's Joke Was a Fumble for Press, Too," *Washington Star*, February 22, 1980, Sec. A, p. 3; "How's That Again, Ronnie?" *Newsweek*, April 21, 1980, p. 47.

209. *Washington Post*, October 11, 1980, Sec. A, p. 9; "A Vow to Zip His Lip," *Time*, October 20, 1980, p. 17; *Washington Post*, October 11, 1980, Sec. A, p. 10, October 15, 1980, Sec. A, p. 4.

210. *Washington Post*, August 18, 1982, Sec. A, p. 16, December 6, 1982, Sec. A, pp. 1, 17; *USA Today*, October 18, 1982, Sec. A, p. 4.

211. "20 Months, 12 Vacations," *Newsweek*, September 6, 1982, p. 18; *USA Today*, September 24, 1982, Sec. A, p. 8; Periscope, "Playing the Holiday Gambit," *Newsweek*, April 19, 1982, p. 27.

212. *New York Times*, October 28, 1982, Sec. A, p. 1, Sec. B, p. 14; *Washington Post*, October 28, 1982, Sec. A, pp. 1, 4.

213. *Washington Post*, April 8, 1983, Sec. A, pp. 1, 8.

214. Herbert G. Klein, *Making It Perfectly Clear* (Garden City, N.Y.: Doubleday, 1980), p. 21.

215. *Washington Post*, January 20, 1977, Sec. E, p. 1.

216. "Talk with Dave Gergen," p. 41.

217. *Washington Post*, January 20, 1977, Sec. E, p. 1.

218. Sanford J. Ungar, "Reports & Comment: Washington," *Atlantic* (April 1977):12–13.

219. Michael Baruch Grossman and Martha Joynt Kumar, *Portraying the President* (Baltimore: Johns Hopkins University Press, 1981), p. 102.

220. "Talk with Dave Gergen," April, 1982, p. 41.

221. *Washington Post*, January 19, 1982, Sec. A, p. 3.

222. Ibid., January 14, 1982, Sec. A, p. 18.

223. Ford, *Time to Heal*, pp. 422–423.

224. Nessen, *It Sure Looks Different*, p. 276.

225. *Wall Street Journal*, September 17, 1976, p. 1.

226. Nessen, *It Sure Looks Different*, pp. 294–296.

227. Ibid., p. 133. See also "Palace Intrigue," *Newsweek*, April 28, 1975, p. 35; *Washington Post*, April 17, 1975, Sec. A, p. 9.

228. White House memorandum, September 10, 1976.

229. Joseph A. Califano, Jr., *Governing America* (New York: Simon and Schuster, 1981), p. 415.

230. Meyer, *James Earl Carter*, pp. 144–148.

231. *Washington Post*, June 4, 1979, Sec. A, p. 3. A Secret Service spokesman denied that such an order had been given.

232. Lasky, *Jimmy Carter*, pp. 207, 234–235.

233. "Playboy Interview: Jimmy Carter," *Playboy*, November, 1976, p. 66.

234. Meyer, *James Earl Carter*, p. 134.

235. *Washington Post*, October 25, 1980, Sec. A, pp. 1, 14.

236. Jimmy Carter, *Keeping Faith* (New York: Bantam Books, 1982), pp. 131–132.

237. Statement by Fred Barnes, interview, August 3, 1979. According to Barnes, Powell had attempted and failed to reach him a day or two after the story was published.

238. *Washington Post*, August 26, 1979, Sec. A, p. 2.

239. Curtis Wilkie, "Carter's Televised Presidency," *Boston Globe Magazine*, November 2, 1980, p. 9.

240. *Washington Post*, September 18, 1977, Sec. B, p. 6.

241. Statement by Jack McWethy, interview, August 3, 1979.

242. *New York Times*, May 14, 1978, pp. 1, 24.

243. Jack Anderson, "Carter and Nixon Are Far Too Similar," *Baltimore News American*, June 8, 1978, p. 15.

244. *New York Times*, July 12, 1978, p. 9; *Washington Post*, July 12, 1978, Sec. A, p. 2.

245. *Washington Post*, July 16, 1980, Sec. A, p. 4. See also Hodding Carter III, "Life inside the Carter State Department," *Playboy* (February 1981):212; John Osborne, "Under Pressure," *New Republic*, March 3, 1979, p. 11; *Washington Star*, July 21, 1980, Sec. A, pp. 1, 10; *New York Times*, February 9, 1979, Sec. A, p. 32; "Operation Stifle," *Newsweek*, February 19, 1979, p. 34; "Button Your Lip," *Time*, July 28, 1980, p. 35. The Bakhtiar government fell a few days after Carter's tirade.

246. *Washington Post*, July 16, 1980, Sec. A, pp. 1, 4. See also "Button Your Lip," p. 35.

247. Kirschten, "Reagan Seeks a New and Improved Image," p. 683.

248. John Herbers, "The President and the Press Corps," *New York Times Magazine*, May 9, 1982, p. 75.

249. Gary Schuster, "An Interview with James Brady," *Washington Journalism Review* 3:2 (March 1981):36.

250. Hogan, "Ronald Reagan's Close Encounters," p. 33.

251. *Time*, May 30, 1983, p. 19.

252. Statement by Lou Cannon, interview, June 14, 1983.

253. United Press International dispatch, *Washington Post*, October 30, 1981.

254. John Carmody, "The TV Column: Dan Rather Gets Call From 'Upset' Reagan," *Washington Post*, August 18, 1982, Sec. B, pp. 1, 4.

255. Thomas Griffith, "Newswatch: 'Drumbeat of Criticism,'" *Time*, April 19, 1982, p. 51.

256. Statement by Chris Wallace, interview, June 13, 1983.

257. "President vs. the Press," p. 77.

258. *New York Times*, February 16, 1983, Sec. A, p. 20.

259. Ibid., November 4, 1982, Sec. A, p. 18.

260. *Washington Post*, March 19, 1982, Sec. A, p. 6.

261. Ibid., February 13, 1983, Sec. A, p. 8.

262. Lou Cannon, "Reagan & Co.," *Washington Post*, January 17, 1983, Sec. A, p. 3.

263. Judy Woodruff, "Diary of a Reporter," *Washington Post Magazine*, April 26, 1981, p. 13. See also "Just Bray It Again, Sam," *Time*, April 11, 1983, p. 79.

264. *Washington Post*, June 8, 1981, Sec. A, p. 3.

265. Sara Fritz, "Reagan's Honeymoon with the Press Is Over," *Washington Journalism Review* 4:3 (April 1982):37.

266. *Washington Post*, August 28, 1981, Sec. A, p. 2.

267. United Press International dispatch, *New York Times*, March 15, 1982.

268. *New York Times*, March 16, 1982, Sec. A, p. 6.

269. "Lyn Nofziger on Ronald Reagan & the Press," *Washington Journalism Review* 4:2 (March 1982) 24.

270. *New York Times*, February 23, 1982, Sec. A, p. 18.

271. United Press International dispatch, *Washington Post*, February 26, 1982.

272. Jay Peterzell, "The Government Shuts Up," *Columbia Journalism Review* 20:2 (July–August 1982):35.

273. *Washington Post*, March 26, 1981, Sec. A, p. 35; *New York Times*, May 9, 1981, Sec. A, p. 8, May 28, 1981, Sec. A, p. 13; "The CIA's 'Inverse PR' Man," *Newsweek*, July 13, 1981, p. 19. See also *Washington Post*, June 30, 1981, Sec. A, p. 3.

274. United Press International dispatch, *Washington Post*, May 28, 1981.

Index

DATE DUE